C000132350

PART 1

Paper 1.1

Preparing Financial Statements

ACCA Study Text

Official Publisher

FTC Foulks Lynch
A **Kaplan Professional** Company

ii

British Library Cataloguing-in-Publication Data

A catalogue record for this book is available from the British Library.

Published by:
FTC Foulks Lynch
Swift House
Market place
Wokingham
Berkshire
RG40 1AP

ISBN 1 84390 349 0

© The Financial Training Company Ltd, 2004

Printed and bound in Great Britain.

Acknowledgements

We are grateful to the Association of Chartered Certified Accountants and the Chartered Institute of Management Accountants for permission to reproduce past examination questions. The answers have been prepared by FTC Foulks Lynch.

Contents

iv

Introduction

This Study Text is the ACCA's official text for Paper 1.1 *Preparing Financial Statements*, and is part of the ACCA's official series produced for students taking the ACCA examinations.

This new 2004 edition has been produced with direct guidance from the examiner. It covers the syllabus and study guide in great detail, giving appropriate weighting to the various topics. Targeted very closely on the examination, this study text is written in a way that will help you assimilate the information easily. Numerous practice questions and exam type questions at the end of each chapter reinforce your knowledge.

DEFINITION

KEY POINT

ACTIVITY 1

SELF-TEST
QUESTIONS

EXAM-TYPE
QUESTIONS

- **Definitions.** The text defines key words and concepts, placing them in the margin, with a clear heading, as on the left. The purpose of including these definitions is to focus your attention on the point being covered.

- **Key points**. In the margin you will see key points at regular intervals. The purpose of these is to summarise concisely the key material being covered.

- **Activities**. The text involves you in the learning process with a series of activities designed to catch your attention and make you concentrate and respond. The feedback to activities is at the end of each chapter.

- **Self-test questions**. At the end of each chapter there is a series of self-test questions. The purpose of these is to help you revise some of the key elements of the chapter. All the answers to these questions can be found in the text.

- **End of chapter questions**. At the end of each chapter we include examination-type questions. These will give you a very good idea of the sort of thing the examiner will ask and will test your understanding of what has been covered.

Syllabus and study guide

Objectives of the study guide

This study guide is designed to help you plan your studies and to provide a more detailed interpretation of the syllabus for Paper 1.1 *Preparing Financial Statements*. It contains both the syllabus and the study guide, which you can follow when preparing for the examination.

The syllabus outlines the content of the paper. The study guide takes the syllabus content and expands it into study sessions of similar length. These sessions indicate what the examiner expects of candidates for each part of the syllabus, and therefore gives you guidance in the skills you are expected to demonstrate in the examinations.

Syllabus content

1   GENERAL FRAMEWORK

a   Types of business entity – limited companies, partnerships and sole traders.

b   Forms of capital and capital structures in limited companies.

c   The role of the Financial Reporting Council, the Financial Reporting Review Panel, Accounting Standards Board (ASB) and the Urgent Issues Task Force.

d   Application of Financial Reporting Standards (FRSs) and Statements of Standard Accounting Practice (SSAPs) to the preparation and presentation of financial statements.

e   The ASB's Statement of Principles for Financial Reporting (chapters 1, 2 and 3 only).

2   ACCOUNTING CONCEPTS AND PRINCIPLES

a   Basic accounting concepts and principles as stated in the ASB's Statement of Principles for Financial Reporting.

b   Other accounting concepts
  i   historical cost
  ii   money measurement
  iii   entity
  iv   dual aspect
  v   time interval.

3   DOUBLE-ENTRY BOOKKEEPING AND ACCOUNTING SYSTEMS

a   Double entry bookkeeping and accounting systems
  i   form and content of accounting records (manual and computerised)
  ii   books of original entry, including journals
  iii   sales and purchase ledgers
  iv   cash book
  v   general ledger

  vi   trial balance
  vii   accruals, prepayments and adjustments
  viii   asset registers
  ix   petty cash.

b   Confirming and correcting mechanisms
  i   control accounts
  ii   bank reconciliations
  iii   suspense accounts and the correction of errors.

c   General principles of the operation of a value added tax.

d   Computerised accounting systems.

4   ACCOUNTING TREATMENTS

a   Fixed assets, tangible and intangible
  i   distinction between capital and revenue expenditure
  ii   accounting for acquisitions and disposals
  iii   depreciation – definition, reasons for and methods, including straight line, reducing balance and sum of digits
  iv   research and development
  v   elementary treatment of goodwill.

b   Current assets
  i   stock (excluding long-term contracts)
  ii   debtors, including accounting for bad and doubtful debts
  iii   cash.

c   Current liabilities and accruals.

d   Shareholders' equity.

e   Post balance sheet events.

f   Contingencies.

5   FINANCIAL STATEMENTS

a   Objectives of financial statements.

b   Users and their information needs.

c   Key features of financial statements

    i   balance sheet

    ii   profit and loss account

    iii cash flow statement

    iv notes to the financial statements (examined to a limited extent – see d (iii) below).

d   Preparation of financial statements for:

    i   sole traders, including incomplete records techniques

    ii   partnerships

    iii limited companies, including profit and loss accounts and balance sheets for internal purposes and for external purposes in accordance with Companies Act 1985 formats and preparation of basic cash flow statements for limited liability companies (excluding group cash flow statements). The following notes to the financial statements will be examinable and no others:

       – Statement of movements in reserves

       – Fixed assets

       – Exceptional and extraordinary items

       – Post balance sheet events

       – Contingent liabilities and contingent assets

       – Research and development expenditure

    iv groups of companies – preparation of a basic consolidated balance sheet for a company with one subsidiary.

6   INTERPRETATION

a   Ratio analysis of accounting information and basic interpretation.

Excluded topics

The syllabus content outlines the area for assessment. No questions will be asked on: clubs and societies, partnerships other than preparation of financial statements for partnerships.

Key areas of the syllabus

The objective of Paper 1.1, *Preparing Financial Statements*, is to ensure that candidates have the necessary basic accounting knowledge and skill to progress to the more advanced work of Paper 2.5 *Financial Reporting*. The two main skills required are:

- the ability to prepare basic financial statements and the underlying accounting records on which they are based

- an understanding of the principles on which accounting is based.

The key topic areas are as follows:

- preparation of financial statements for limited companies for internal purposes or for publication

- preparation of financial statements for partnerships and sole traders (including incomplete records)

- basic group accounts – consolidated balance sheet for a company with one subsidiary

- basic bookkeeping and accounting procedures

- accounting conventions and concepts

- interpretation of financial statements

- cash flow statements

- accounting standards – SSAPs 9, 13 and 17 plus FRSs 1, 3, 18 and the relevant sections of FRSs 12 and 15.

Additional information

Candidates need to be aware that questions involving knowledge of new examinable regulations will not be set until at least six months after the last day of the month in which the regulation was issued.

The study guide provides more detailed guidance on the syllabus. Examinable documents are listed in the 'Exam Notes' section of the *Student Accountant*.

Study guide

1   INTRODUCTION TO ACCOUNTING

Syllabus reference 1a, b, c, d, e, 5a and b

- Define accounting – recording, analysing and summarising transaction data.   1

- Explain types of business entity   1
    - sole trader
    - partnership
    - limited company.

- Explain users of financial statements and accounting information.   1

- Explain the main elements of financial statements:
    - balance sheet
    - profit and loss account.

- Explain the purpose of each of the main statements.   1

- Explain the nature, principles and scope of accounting.   1

- Identify the desirable qualities of accounting information and the usefulness of each (see also Session 14).   1

- Explain the regulatory system: 1
    - Financial Reporting Council, Financial Reporting Review Panel, Accounting Standards Board, Urgent Issues Task Force, Companies legislation.

- Explain the difference between capital and revenue items.   1

Examinable documents

Prior to each sitting of the examination, the ACCA issues Exam Notes setting out which official documents are examinable.

The documents examinable for Paper 1.1 are set out below. We recommend that students read the *Student Accountant* to keep up-to-date.

Accounting Standards

Statements of Standard Accounting Practice (SSAPs)

No	Title	Issue date
9	Stocks and long-term contracts (revised) (excluding long-term contracts)	Sept 1988
13	Accounting for research and development (revised)	Jan 1989
17	Accounting for post balance sheet events	Sept 1980

Financial Reporting Standards (FRSs)

No	Title	Issue date
FRS 1	Cash flow statements (excluding group cash flow statements) (revised)	Oct 1996
FRS 2	Accounting for subsidiary undertakings	July 1992
FRS 3	Reporting financial performance (excluding group aspects)	Oct 1992
FRS 12	Provisions, contingent liabilities and contingent assets	Sept 1998
FRS 15	Tangible fixed assets	Feb 1999
FRS 18	Accounting policies	Dec 2000

Note:

The following paragraphs of FRS 12 are examinable in so far as they relate to contingent liabilities and contingent assets: 2, 3, 27–33, 91, 94, 96, 97 Appendix 2. The measurement rules in paragraphs 36-55 are not examinable.

The following paragraphs of FRS 15 are examinable in so far as they relate to tangible fixed assets: 1–7, 34–36, 42–46, 61, 63, 72, 77–82 and 93.

In relation to paragraph 2, only the following definitions are examinable: current value, depreciable amount, depreciation, recoverable amount, residual value, tangible fixed assets and useful economic life.

Other statements

Title	Issue date
Statement of Principles for Financial Reporting	Dec 1999

For students sitting Paper 1.1, Chapters 1, 2 and 3 of the *Statement of Principles* are examinable in detail. A detailed knowledge of the remainder of the Statement of Principles is not examinable.

The examination

Format of the examination

Paper-based examination

	Number of marks
Section A: 25 compulsory multiple choice questions (2 marks each)	50
Section B: 5 compulsory short form questions (8 – 12 marks each)	50
	——
	100
Total time allowed: 3 hours	——

Computer-based examination

	Number of marks
Objective test questions (approximately 50)	100
Total time allowed: 3 hours	

The overall balance in the examination will be approximately 60% computational and 40% non-computational.

Computer-based examination (CBE)

If you are sitting a CBE make sure that you are fully familiar with the software before you start the exam. If in doubt, ask the assessment centre staff to explain it to you.

With CBEs the questions are displayed on the screen and answers are entered using the keyboard and mouse. All the questions are of multiple choice and objective testing type. Answer every question - if you do not know the answer, you do not lose anything by guessing. Don't panic if you realise you answered a question incorrectly you can always go back and change the answer. At the end of the examination you will be given a certificate showing the result you have achieved.

You can take a CBE at any time during the year - you do not need to wait for June and December exam sessions. However, do not attempt a CBE until you have completed all the study material relating to it. Do not skip parts of the syllabus. For a CBE demo and the list of assessment centres that offer CBEs see ACCA website at www.accaglobal.com.

Examination tips: paper-based exam

- Spend the first few minutes of the examination **reading the paper**.

- Where you have a **choice of questions**, decide which ones you will do.

- **Divide the time** you spend on questions in proportion to the marks on offer. One suggestion is to allocate 1½ minutes to each mark available, so a 10 mark question should be completed in 15 minutes.

- Unless you know exactly how to answer the question, spend some time **planning** your answer. Stick to the question and **tailor your answer** to what you are asked.

- **Fully explain** all your points but be **concise**. Set out all workings **clearly and neatly**, and state briefly what you are doing. Don't write out the question.

- If you do not understand what a question is asking, **state your assumptions**. Even if you do not answer precisely in the way the examiner hoped, you should be given some credit, if your assumptions are reasonable.

- If you **get completely stuck** with a question, leave space in your answer book and **return to it later.**

- Towards the end of the examination spend the last **five minutes** reading through your answers and **making any additions or corrections**.

- Before you finish, you must fill in the required information on the front of your answer booklet.

Answering the questions

- **Multiple-choice questions**: Read the questions carefully and work through any calculations required. If you don't know the answer, eliminate those options you know are incorrect and see if the answer becomes more obvious. Remember that only one answer to a multiple choice question can be right!

- **Objective test questions:** These might ask for numerical answers, but could also involve paragraphs of text which require you to fill in a number of missing blanks, or for you to write a definition of a word or phrase, or to enter a formula. Others may give a definition followed by a list of possible key words relating to that description.

- **Essay questions**: Make a quick plan in your answer book and under each main point list all the relevant facts you can think of. Then write out your answer developing each point fully. Your essay should have a clear structure; it should contain a brief introduction, a main section and a conclusion. Be concise. It is better to write a little about a lot of different points than a great deal about one or two points.

- **Case studies**: To write a good case study, first identify the area in which there is a problem, outline the main principles/theories you are going to use to answer the question, and then apply the principles/theories to the case. Include relevant points only and then reach a conclusion and, if asked for, recommendations. If you can, compare the facts to real-life examples – this may gain you additional marks in the exam.

- **Computations**: It is essential to include all your workings in your answers. Many computational questions require the use of a standard format: company profit and loss account, balance sheet and cash flow statement for example. Be sure you know these formats thoroughly before the examination and use the layouts that you see in the answers given in this book and in model answers. If you are asked to comment or make recommendations on a computation, you must do so. There are important marks to be gained here. Even if your computation contains mistakes, you may still gain marks if your reasoning is correct.

- **Reports, memos and other documents**: Some questions ask you to present your answer in the form of a report or a memo or other document. Use the correct format - there could be easy marks to gain here.

Study skills and revision guidance

This section aims to give guidance on how to study for your ACCA exams and to give ideas on how to improve your existing study techniques.

Preparing to study

Set your objectives

Before starting to study decide what you want to achieve – the type of pass you wish to obtain. This will decide the level of commitment and time you need to dedicate to your studies.

Devise a study plan

• Determine which times of the week you will study.

• Split these times into sessions of at least one hour for study of new material. Any shorter periods could be used for revision or practice.

• Put the times you plan to study onto a study plan for the weeks from now until the exam and set yourself targets for each period of study – in your sessions make sure you cover the course, course assignments and revision.

• If you are studying for more than one paper at a time, try to vary your subjects, this can help you to keep interested and see subjects as part of wider knowledge.

• When working through your course, compare your progress with your plan and, if necessary, re-plan your work (perhaps including extra sessions) or, if you are ahead, do some extra revision/practice questions.

Effective studying

Active reading

You are not expected to learn the text by rote, rather, you must understand what you are reading and be able to use it to pass the exam and develop good practice. A good technique to use is SQ3Rs – Survey, Question, Read, Recall, Review:

1 **Survey** the chapter – look at the headings and read the introduction, summary and objectives, so as to get an overview of what the chapter deals with.

2 **Question** – whilst undertaking the survey, ask yourself the questions that you hope the chapter will answer for you.

3 **Read** through the chapter thoroughly, answering the questions and making sure you can meet the objectives. Attempt the exercises and activities in the text, and work through all the examples.

4 **Recall** – at the end of each section and at the end of the chapter, try to recall the main ideas of the section/chapter without referring to the text. This is best done after a short break of a couple of minutes after the reading stage.

5 **Review** – check that your recall notes are correct.

You may also find it helpful to reread the chapter and try to see the topic(s) it deals with as a whole.

Note-taking

Taking notes is a useful way of learning, but do not simply copy out the text. The notes must:

- be in your own words
- be concise
- cover the key points
- be well-organised
- be modified as you study further chapters in this text or in related ones.

Trying to summarise a chapter without referring to the text can be a useful way of determining which areas you know and which you don't.

Three ways of taking notes:

- **summarise the key points** of a chapter.

- **make linear notes** – a list of headings, divided up with subheadings listing the key points. If you use linear notes, you can use different colours to highlight key points and keep topic areas together. Use plenty of space to make your notes easy to use.

- **try a diagrammatic form** – the most common of which is a mind-map. To make a mind-map, put the main heading in the centre of the paper and put a circle around it. Then draw short lines radiating from this to the main sub-headings, which again have circles around them. Then continue the process from the sub-headings to sub-sub-headings, advantages, disadvantages, etc.

Highlighting and underlining

You may find it useful to underline or highlight key points in your study text – but do be selective. You may also wish to make notes in the margins.

Revision

The best approach to revision is to revise the course as you work through it. Also try to leave four to six weeks before the exam for final revision. Make sure you cover the whole syllabus and pay special attention to those areas where your knowledge is weak. Here are some recommendations:

- **Read through the text and your notes again** and condense your notes into key phrases. It may help to put key revision points onto index cards to look at when you have a few minutes to spare.

- **Review any assignments** you have completed and look at where you lost marks – put more work into those areas where you were weak.

- **Practise exam standard questions** under timed conditions. If you are short of time, list the points that you would cover in your answer and then read the model answer, but do try and complete at least a few questions under exam conditions.

- Also **practise producing answer plans** and comparing them to the model answer.

- If you are stuck on a topic find somebody (a tutor) to explain it to you.

- **Read good newspapers and professional journals**, especially ACCA's *Student Accountant* – this can give you an advantage in the exam.

- Ensure you **know the structure of the exam** – how many questions and of what type you will be expected to answer. During your revision attempt all the different styles of questions you may be asked.

Chapter 1
INTRODUCTION TO ACCOUNTING

This chapter introduces some of the principles underlying the preparation of financial statements and emphasises the reasons why accounting information is prepared. You will find it useful to return to this chapter later in your studies.

Objectives

By the time you have finished this chapter you should be able to:

- define what is meant by accounting and understand the kind of information provided by accounting systems
- identify the users of financial accounting information
- understand the different types of accounting which exist
- identify the desirable qualities of accounting information
- identify the principal features of the regulatory framework of financial reporting
- explain the difference between capital and revenue items.

1   What is accounting?

1.1   Recording and summarising transactions

Accounting has two elements:

- **recording** the transactions of a business to provide information for day-to-day management.

  For example, sales to customers on credit must be recorded so that statements of account can be sent to the customers and the money due collected.

- **summarising** the transactions of a period to provide interested parties with information about the performance and position of a business.

Two important summary statements produced are as follows:

- a statement showing the profit or loss made by the business in a year – this is usually called the **profit and loss account** or **income statement.**

- a statement showing the position of the business at the end of the year covered by the profit and loss account – this is called the **balance sheet**. It shows all the assets and liabilities of the business and enables users to judge, for example, whether the business is in a sound financial position and able to pay its debts as they fall due.

> **KEY POINT**
>
> Accounting consists of two elements:
> - **recording** transactions
> - **summarising** transactions.

> **KEY POINT**
>
> Two important summary statements are:
> - profit and loss account or income statement
> - balance sheet.

1.2   Business entities

Businesses can be organised in several ways. At its simplest, a business is owned and operated by one person with or without employees – a **sole trader.** The next level of complexity is the **partnership** – several people jointly owning and running the business.

A third type of entity is the **company**. A company is formed using contributions from what may be thousands of people, each of whom puts in a share of the total money needed to operate the business. These contributors are called the **shareholders** or **members** of the company. They own it, but they do not necessarily participate in the management. The shareholders appoint **directors** to run the company on their behalf. In small companies the role of directors and that of shareholders may be fulfilled by the same people: such companies are often referred to as **owner-managed companies**, because the owners (shareholders) and managers (directors) are the same people.

> **KEY POINT**
>
> Types of business entity include:
> - sole trader
> - partnership
> - company.

Companies are almost always **limited** companies. A limited company is a legal entity in its own, separate from its owners, the shareholders. This limited liability is achieved by counting the company as a completely separate legal entity. The creditors of the company can lay claim to the assets of the company but cannot, except in rare circumstances, get at the personal assets of the shareholders. In contrast, if a sole trader becomes insolvent, there is no such separation, and all the trader's assets, business and personal, may be sold to raise money to pay creditors.

For all three types of entity the money put up by the individual, the partners or the shareholders is referred to as the business **capital**. In the case of a company this capital is divided into **shares** with a face value which varies from company to company. For example, one company may have a share capital of £1,000, divided into 1,000 shares of £1 each; another company may have a share capital of £5,000, divided into 10,000 shares of 50p each.

1.3   Types of company

Most companies are small, with only a few shareholders, some or all of whom may also be directors. These are **private** companies.

Larger companies that wish to raise finance from the general public by inviting them to buy shares are **public** companies. Only a small proportion of companies are **public** companies, and of these less than 2,000 are **listed** or **quoted** on the London Stock Exchange. A Stock Exchange listing means that a company's shares may be bought and sold easily and cheaply using the market created by the Stock Exchange.

Private companies must have the word **'limited'** as the last word of their name, and public companies must have the words **'public limited company'**, or its abbreviation **'plc'**, at the end of their names. This makes it quite clear to those dealing with them that they have a separate legal identity from their members and that consequently the potential assets available to pay creditors are limited to those of the company.

1.4   Availability of accounting information

The financial statements (profit and loss account and balance sheet) of sole traders and partnerships are completely private and are not seen by anyone other than the trader or partners concerned unless they choose to show them to third parties. A trader might, for example, show his financial statements to a bank manager in support of an application for a loan or overdraft. Tax authorities will also need to see the accounts of sole traders and partnerships to assess liability to tax.

By contrast, the financial statements of all companies, public and private, are made available for inspection by members of the public. A copy of a company's annual financial statements must be lodged with the **Registrar of Companies**. The Registrar of Companies maintains a file for each company which is open to public inspection, so the financial statements are available to all.

2   Users and uses of financial accounts and statements

One of the purposes of accounting is to provide information to users of financial statements. It is therefore appropriate to consider the needs of the users and the uses to which they put the information.

2.1   Users of financial information

The users of financial information are as follows:

Management

Management will be interested in an analysis of revenues and expenses which will provide information that is useful when plans are formulated and decisions made.

Shareholders and potential shareholders

This group includes the investing public at large, as well as the stockbrokers and commentators who advise them. The shareholders should be informed of the manner in which management has used their funds which have been invested in the business.

Employees and their trade union representatives

These use accounting information to assess the potential performance of the business. Employees need to make sure the company can offer them safe employment and promotion through growth over a period of years.

Lenders

This group includes some who have financed the business over a long period by lending money which is to be repaid, as well as short-term creditors such as bank, and suppliers of raw materials, which permit a company to buy goods from them and pay in, say, four to twelve weeks' time.

Government agencies

These use accounting information, either when collecting statistical information to reveal trends within the economy as a whole or, in the case of the Inland Revenue, to check the company's calculation of its tax liability.

The business contact group

Customers of a business may use accounting data to assess the viability of a company if a long-term contract is soon to be placed. Competitors will also use the accounts for purposes of comparison.

The public

From time to time the public may have an interest in the company, e.g. members of a local community where the company operates or environmental pressure groups.

2.2   The main financial statements available to users

DEFINITIONS

An **asset** is any tangible or intangible item which has value, e.g. an office building, an item of computer equipment, an item of stock held for resale, a favourable bank balance.
Liabilities are the financial obligations of a business, e.g. to creditors, debenture-holders and, in the case of a bank loan or overdraft, to a bank.

There are two main financial accounting statements.

- **the balance sheet** – a statement of assets and liabilities at a point in time (the balance sheet date). Each asset and liability is valued according to certain accounting conventions.

- **the profit and loss account** – this summarises income and expenditure over a period of time. If income exceeds expenditure there is a profit; if vice versa, there is a loss. Note that again income and expenditure are measured using accounting conventions.

Note that the balance sheet is a 'position' statement, i.e. it shows the financial position at a point in time. On the other hand, the profit and loss account is a 'period statement', explaining changes over time.

There are other financial statements too. One of these is a cash flow statement. Cash flow statements are described in a later chapter.

2.3 The purpose of each of the main financial statements

A balance sheet shows the assets owned by the business and the liabilities owed by the business at a particular point in time. It satisfies the stewardship needs of users rather than their decision-making needs. For example, if they are creditors, the balance sheet shows the assets which are available to pay off their debts.

The primary purpose of a profit and loss account is to show the amount of profit or loss made in an accounting period, i.e. a period of time. Generally a business exists in order to make profits for its owners. They will make decisions about the future direction of the business based on its current ability to make profits.

A cash flow statement provides information about cash receipts and cash payments during the period.

2.4 Non-financial statements

In general, the need for historical financial information has been met by company law and accounting standards requiring disclosures in the profit and loss account, balance sheet and other financial statements, plus supporting notes giving more detail. Some non-financial information is contained in other documents which accompany financial statements in a company's corporate report.

- A **directors' report** is required by company law to be included within the annual report and accounts.

- An auditors' report is also required by law.

- Many public companies include a chairman's statement in their annual reports and accounts describing aspects of the company and its operations during the years.

3 Nature, principles and scope of accounting

3.1 Financial and management accounting

The financial accounts are used to record transactions between the business and its customers, suppliers, employees and owners. The managers of the business must account for the way in which funds entrusted to them have been used and, therefore, records of assets and liabilities are required, as well as a statement of any increase in the total wealth of the business. This is done by presenting a balance sheet and profit and loss account, at least once every year. The law requires that accounts for certain businesses shall be presented in a specific way and particular details of transactions may be required by the Inland Revenue in checking the business tax liability.

However, in performing their job, managers will need to know a great deal about the detailed workings of the business. This knowledge must embrace production methods and the cost of processes, products, etc. It is not the function of financial accounting to provide such detail and therefore the managers require additional accounting information geared to their own needs.

Management accounting is an integral part of management; such accounting is concerned with identifying, presenting and interpreting information used for:

- formulation of strategy
- planning and controlling the activities
- decision-making
- optimising the use of resources.

Financial and management accounts can be contrasted as shown in the following table.

Financial accounts	Management accounts
• In many instances (e.g. companies) are required by law.	• Records are not mandatory.
• Accordingly, the cost of record-keeping is a necessity.	• Accordingly, the cost of record-keeping needs to be justified.
• Objectives and uses of financial accounts are not defined by management.	• Objectives and uses of management accounts can be laid down by management.
• Are mainly concerned with profits.	• Are mainly concerned with cash flow, profits and business management generally.
• Are mainly a historical record.	• Are regularly concerned with predictions.
• Information should be computed prudently, and in accordance with legal and accounting requirements.	• Information should be computed as management requires, the key criterion being relevance.

3.2   Auditing

An **external** audit can be defined as an 'independent examination of, and expression of opinion on, the financial statements of an enterprise'.

An internal audit is 'a review of operations and records, sometimes continuous, undertaken within a business by specially assigned staff'.

3.3   The role of the accountancy profession within society

There are a number of professional accounting bodies in the UK including the **ACCA**. Their aims are to set standards for their members to follow so that outsiders dealing with members have a clear idea of the standard of competence of members.

The main auditing body is the **Institute of Chartered Accountants in England and Wales (ICAEW)** along with the Scottish and Irish Institutes in their respective countries. The ACCA is also an auditing body but many of its members train in industry rather than in auditing practices.

Members of the **Chartered Institute of Management Accountants (CIMA)** predominantly train in industry or in the public sector; they are not qualified to perform audits of limited companies.

Members of the **Chartered Institute of Public Finance and Accountancy (CIPFA)** train in the public sector, e.g. local authorities.

All the professional accounting bodies acted together in pioneering the establishment of an accounting standard setting system and ethical guidelines. Accounting standards are the responsibility of an independent body, the Accounting Standards Board (see later in this chapter).

4   Desirable qualities of accounting information

Having defined the uses of financial statements, the problem arises as to what information is useful. Some criteria are listed briefly here, together with problems in meeting them. These criteria are considered in more detail later in this text.

Relevance

The information should be relevant to the needs of the users, so that it helps them to evaluate the financial performance of the business and to draw conclusions from it.

• **Problem** – A difficulty lies in identifying these needs, given the variety of users.

Reliability

The information should be of a standard that can be relied upon by external users, so that it is free from error and can be depended upon by users in their decisions.

- **Problem** – The complexities of modern business makes reliability difficult to achieve in all cases.

Comparability

Accounts should be comparable with those of other similar enterprises, and from one period to the next.

- **Problem** – The main problem has been the use of different accounting policies by different enterprises. Accounting standards have reduced this problem but have not eliminated it.

Understandability

The information should be in a form which is understandable by user groups.

- **Problems** – Users have very different levels of financial sophistication. Also the very complexity of business transactions makes it difficult to provide adequate disclosure whilst maintaining simplicity.

Completeness

Accounting statements should show all aspects of the business.

- **Problem** – The only problem this leads to is the resultant volume of the information.

Neutrality

Accounting statements should be free from systematic or deliberate bias towards the needs of one user; they should be objective.

- **Problem** – Accounts are prepared by one user group, namely management. The external audit should address any management bias, but some authorities question the effectiveness of the audit in this respect.

Timeliness

Accounting statements should be published as soon as possible after the year end.

- **Problem** – There is a conflict between this criterion and that of reliability, in that quicker accounts mean more estimates, and hence reduce reliability.

5　The regulatory framework

The regulatory framework of accounting in the UK is affected by:

- Company law
- Accounting standards issued by the Accounting Standards Board (ASB)
- European Union Directives
- The Stock Exchange
- UK Listing Rules.

The first three are briefly considered as follows. The impact of the UK Listing Rules on financial reporting by listed companies is covered in the later chapters on company accounts.

KEY POINT

The regulatory framework of accounting in the UK is affected by:
- Company law
- Accounting standards issued by the Accounting Standards Board (ASB)
- European Union Directives
- The Stock Exchange
- The UK Listing Rules.

5.1 Company law

The regulatory framework of accounting is affected by company law in a number of areas.

1 Financial statements of companies must show a 'true and fair view'.

2 Accounting standards issued by the Accounting Standards Board are given legal authority as recognised accounting standards.

3 Prescribed formats for the profit and loss account and balance sheet must be used.

4 Detailed disclosures of information are required.

5 A company is limited in the amount of profit it can distribute to its shareholders.

6 Various provisions have to be satisfied if a company wishes to increase or reduce its share capital.

Items 3 to 6 are covered in the chapters on limited company accounts to the extent that knowledge is required at this level of accounting. Items 1 and 2 are dealt with below.

5.2 The true and fair view

With regard to accounts of companies prepared under the Companies Act, there is an overriding requirement that those accounts show a **true and fair view**. However, there is no universal definition of 'true and fair view'.

5.3 Accounting standards

The Companies Act is mainly designed to deal with the problem of companies producing inadequate information. Accounting standards set out to tackle a different problem: that of the diversity of treatment of certain items in published accounts. Accounting standards are used to apply a consistent set of accounting principles to the preparation of financial statements.

Because types of businesses often vary so much, what is suitable as an accounting policy for one business may be unsuitable for another. It is, however, important for a given business to follow its accounting policies from one year to the next, so that valid comparisons of performance may be made.

The following are examples of the areas where variations in accounting practices exist:

- depreciation of fixed assets
- research and development expenditure
- hire purchase or instalment transactions
- stock and work-in-progress.

These areas will be discussed in more detail in later chapters.

5.4 Standard-setting bodies

The **Accounting Standards Committee** was set up as a result of criticism of the scope allowed for manipulation of published accounts by the variety of acceptable bases. The ASC attempted to build up a definitive body of rules to govern the presentation of published accounts.

Before a standard was introduced, it was first published by the ASC in the form of an **Exposure Draft (ED)**. This was purely a discussion document. Once the discussion (or exposure) period elapsed, the document, amended in the light of the results of that discussion, was issued in the form of a **Statement of Standard Accounting Practice (SSAP)**.

Some SSAPs are still in force today. However a new standard setting process came into effect in August 1990. There are now four main bodies:

KEY POINT

With regard to accounts of companies prepared under the Companies Act, there is an overriding requirement that those accounts show a **true and fair view**

KEY POINT

There are many areas of accounting where there is more than one generally accepted method of dealing with particular transactions. **Accounting standards** set out to deal with this potential problem.

KEY POINT

Statements of Standard Accounting Practice (SSAPs) were issued by the Accounting Standards Committee (ASC).

1   The Financial Reporting Council (FRC)

The FRC comprises around 25 members drawn from the users and preparers of accounts and auditors. It has two operating companies – the **Accounting Standards Board (ASB)** and the **Financial Reporting Review Panel (FRRP)**.

The FRC is responsible for guiding the ASB on its planned work programme.

2   The Accounting Standards Board (ASB)

The ASB has both a full-time chairman and a full-time technical director plus part-time members.

The ASB issues accounting standards, now known as **Financial Reporting Standards (FRSs)**.

Prior to the issue of an FRS a discussion draft (DD) may be issued to a restricted number of interested parties setting out a planned approach to an FRS. Later a Financial Reporting Exposure Draft (FRED) is issued for general circulation. The issue of the FRED allows for a further consultation process before the FRS is issued.

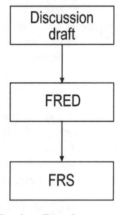

3   The Financial Reporting Review Panel

The Review Panel is concerned with the examination, investigation and departures from accounting standards by large companies.

4   The Urgent Issues Task Force (UITF)

This is an offshoot of the ASB. Its function is to tackle urgent matters not covered by existing standards and for which, given the urgency, the normal standard-setting process would not be practicable.

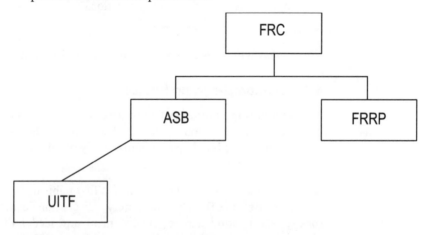

Significant aspects of standard-setting structure are as follows.

1   The ASB can issue standards on its own authority.

2   Under the Companies Act the accounting standards issued by the ASB are recognised as 'accounting standards' for the purposes of the Act. Directors of

public companies are under a statutory duty to disclose whether there has been a material departure from accounting standards.

3   The Review Panel can apply to the court following a material departure by a public company from an accounting standard. The court may, as a result, order the company concerned to prepare revised accounts.

5.5   SSAPs, FRSs, IASs and SORPs

In order to avoid the confusion that might result from accounting standards having different sources of authority because they were/are issued by the ASC or the ASB, the ASB formally adopted the SSAPs issued by the ASC as its own SSAPs. They are therefore 'accounting standards' under the Companies Act 1985.

Most SSAPs and FRSs have to be complied with by all companies, but some apply only to larger or listed companies.

International Accounting Standards (IASs)

The International Accounting Standards Committee (IASC) came into existence in 1973 as a result of an agreement by the leading accountancy bodies of several countries. The IASC has now been replaced by **International Accounting Standards Board (IASB)** which issues International Accounting Standards.

Since 1973 the influence and authority of International Accounting Standards (IAS) have gradually increased. In 2000 the International Organisation of Securities Commissions (IOSCO), the representative body of securities regulators, endorsed a set of 30 'core' IASs. The 'core' standards are binding upon IOSCO members in respect of cross-border listings. In 2001 the European Commission (EC) decided to require all European listed companies to use IASs in their group accounts by 2005. Some listed companies in the EU (for example, in Germany) are already permitted the option of reporting under IAS and many choose to do so. The EC decision is made in the interests of eliminating barriers to cross-border listing of securities. This decision will have major impact on larger companies in the UK. International Accounting Standards will in future be called **International Financial Reporting Standards (IFRSs)**.

IFRS 1 First time adoption of International Financial Reporting Standards

From 2005, International Financial Reporting Standards dominate UK financial reporting. EU regulations require UK quoted companies to apply international standards for periods beginning on or after January 2005. These companies and their subsidiaries will therefore be first time adopters that year. Non quoted companies have the option to adopt IFRSs but do not have to.

IFRS 1 sets out the procedures for making the transition from national accounting standards to international standards, and applies to all first time adopters for accounting periods beginning on or after 1st January 2004. This means that for companies that have to make the transition, the task has to be started sooner.

Statements of Recommended Practice (SORPs)

Statements of Recommended Practice (SORPs) were issued on subjects on which it was not considered appropriate to issue an accounting standard at the time.

The ASB has stated that well prepared SORPs have a useful part to play in the development of good financial reporting, but that it must not allow its own limited time and resources to be diverted from its central task – the development of accounting standards with a broad scope. It has therefore decided to limit its involvement in the development of SORPs.

5.6   European Union Directives

It is the aim of the European Union (formerly known as the European Community or EC) that its member states will eventually become parts of a single economic entity. To achieve this goal, businesses throughout the EU must operate under the same legal and accounting requirements. The Fourth Company Law Directive resulted in accounts formats and detailed disclosure requirements being contained in the 4th Schedule to the Companies Act 1985. The Seventh Directive on group accounts was passed in June 1983. The provisions are contained in the Companies Act 1989.

5.7 The elements of generally accepted accounting practice (GAAP)

In the UK, published accounts of companies should be 'true and fair'. In the US the equivalent requirement is 'fair presentation in conformity with GAAP'.

As a consequence references to GAAP are rarely found in the UK literature and, where it is used, the term is loosely defined.

Broadly, GAAP is accounting practice which has substantial authoritative support amongst users of financial information. Accounting standards will generally represent GAAP, but there may be a GAAP which is not reflected in an accounting standard.

Accordingly, the boundaries of UK GAAP extend beyond the principles contained in accounting standards. It includes the requirements of the Companies Act and those of the Financial Services Authority (FSA), as well as other acceptable accounting treatments not incorporated in legislation or quasi-legislation.

The elements of GAAP are thus:

- accounting standards
- company law
- stock exchange requirements (controlled by the FSA)
- other acceptable accounting treatments.

Ideally, GAAP should be the practical application of a conceptual framework. The elements of a conceptual framework are discussed in a later chapter. Examples of how this relationship would work are the following.

- **Assets** – A conceptual framework would have general principles for recognising assets and for determining the value to be placed on assets. GAAP would be the policy to follow for a certain type of asset, tangible fixed assets for example.

- **Profit** – A conceptual framework would have general principles for the determination of profit including the expenses and quantification of expenses. GAAP would include the accounting standard on the appropriate methods of depreciation, for example.

6 Ethics and the independence of the accounting profession

6.1 The role of the financial accountant

The role of the financial accountant varies from organisation to organisation, but his or her primary function is to assist in the communication process of producing financial information on behalf of the directors of a company which is shown to a wide range of users, i.e. the production of annual financial statements. In such a role, the financial accountant must be aware of relevant ethical issues such as the need to produce information which is fair and not distorted.

6.2   The ethical guidelines for accounting

Each professional body issues **ethical guidelines** which it expects its members to observe.

Examples of ethical principles are as follows.

- Members should behave with integrity in all professional and business relationships. Integrity implies not merely honesty but fair dealing and truthfulness.

- Members should strive for objectivity in all professional and business judgements. Objectivity is the state of mind which has regard to all considerations relevant to the task in hand but no other.

- Members should not accept or perform work which they are not competent to undertake unless they obtain such advice and assistance as will enable them competently to carry out the work.

- Members should carry out their professional work with due skill, care, diligence and expedition and with proper regard for the technical and professional standards expected of them as members.

- Members should conduct themselves with courtesy and consideration towards all with whom they come into contact during the course of performing their work.

7   The difference between capital and revenue items

Receipts and expenditure can be classified as **capital** or as **revenue**.

This distinction is of more importance to expenditure and thus we concentrate on the distinction from that point of view.

7.1   Distinction between capital and revenue expenditure

The life of a business extends over a long period of time. The problem is that reports on the profitability of the business are needed at fairly regular intervals, usually of twelve months. This requirement gives rise to certain problems. For example, how should one treat £5,000 expenditure on an item of equipment which is expected to be useful to the business for the next ten years? This expenditure is referred to as capital expenditure because of the long-term nature of the benefits which are expected to be received.

The distinction between capital expenditure and revenue expenditure derives from the fact that, by convention, financial statements are produced on an annual basis. Examples of each category are shown in the table below.

Example of capital expenditure and revenue expenditure

Category	Types of expenditure included
Capital expenditure	(a) Expenditure on the acquisition of new fixed assets required for use in the business and not for resale.
	(b) Expenditure on existing fixed assets aimed at increasing their earning capacity.
Revenue expenditure	(a) Expenditure on current assets (stock).
	(b) Expenditure relating to running the business (administration, selling expenses).
	(c) Expenditure on maintaining the earning capacity of fixed assets (repairs and renewals).

7.2   Capital and revenue receipts

A **capital receipt** is one which relates to an item that would be regarded as capital on the balance sheet.

A capital receipt, or part of it, may be accounted for through the profit and loss account, but not necessarily so. If the receipt represents a profit or loss on the disposal of a fixed asset, it represents a gain or loss to the owners of the business and thus should be shown in the profit and loss account (after matching the receipt with the cost of the asset).

A capital receipt will also include additional cash invested in the business by the owner(s) and the raising of a loan from a bank. As these receipts represent sums which need to be paid back at some stage, they are not reported through the profit and loss account.

Conclusion

This chapter has introduced some of the principles underlying the preparation of financial statements and emphasising the reasons why accounting information is prepared.

You should now appreciate some of the problems of preparing financial statements. There is a wide variety of users each of whom has differing needs and requirements from those financial statements. Financial statements are a method of communicating information about a business entity to those who are interested in it. As such the financial statements should satisfy the generally accepted criteria for useful information.

SELF-TEST
QUESTIONS

Users and uses of financial statements

1   Which are the main categories of users of financial statements? (2.1)

Nature, principles and scope of accounting

2   What types of accounting are there? (3.1)

The regulatory framework

3   What is the regulatory framework in the UK affected by? (5)

4   What does UITF stand for? (5.4)

5   Who issues FRSs? (5.4)

6   What is a SORP? (5.5)

7   What is GAAP? (5.7)

The difference between capital and revenue items

8   State two examples of capital expenditure and revenue expenditure. (7.1)

EXAM-TYPE
QUESTION

Financial statements

(a)   To whom should information contained in a company's financial statements be communicated?   **(4 marks)**

(b)   What are the desirable characteristics of information, which will satisfy the needs of users?   **(4 marks)**

(c)   Describe briefly the kind of information needed by two of the groups of people you mentioned in your answer to part (a).   **(2 marks)**

(Total: 10 marks)

For the answer to this question, see the 'Answers' section at the end of the book.

Chapter 2
BALANCE SHEET AND PROFIT AND LOSS ACCOUNT

We consider the two main financial statements in this chapter and the relationship between individual accounting transactions and the financial statements. Understanding the relationship is essential in order to understand double entry bookkeeping. The use of the accounting equation or balance sheet equation demonstrates the link. This is a short chapter but one which needs to be thoroughly understood before you proceed.

Objectives

By the time you have finished this chapter you should be able to:

- understand the typical components of a profit and loss account and balance sheet

- have an awareness of the some of the concepts and principles underlying the preparation of financial statements

- understand the accounting equation and be able to recognise the two effects of a transaction

- prepare a simple profit and loss account and balance sheet.

1 The balance sheet and the balance sheet equation

1.1 Formats for the balance sheet

There are two possible ways of setting out the balance sheet.

- **horizontal** (or double-sided) format

- **vertical** format.

1.2 Horizontal format

The vertical format is today the more popular form of presentation in the UK, but for illustration both formats will be shown here. As an example, the balance sheet of a sole trader using the horizontal format might appear as shown below.

Mr B Ashton
Balance sheet as at 31 December 20X6

	£	£		£	£
Fixed assets:			Capital account:		
Motor van		2,400	Balance at 1 Jan 20X6		5,200
			Net profit	3,450	
			Less drawings	2,960	
Current assets:					
Stock	2,390		Retained profit		490
Debtors	1,840				
Cash at bank	1,704		Balance at 31 Dec 20X6		5,690
Cash in hand	56		Current liabilities:		
		5,990	Creditors		2,700
		8,390			8,390

DEFINITION

The **capital** of a business entity is
the amount that the business owes
back to the owner of the business.

1.3   Definitions of assets, liabilities and capital

In the horizontal format, the assets of the business are shown on the left-hand side; the capital and liabilities of the business are shown on the right-hand side. The **capital** of a business entity is the amount the business owes back to the owner of the business. Assets and liabilities have already been defined in the previous chapter.

1.4   The balance sheet equation

The most important point is that the balance sheet shows the position of Mr Ashton's business at one point in time – in this case at close of business on 31 December 20X6. A balance sheet must always satisfy the basic equation:

Assets = Proprietor's capital + Liabilities

This is known as the **balance sheet equation** or the **accounting equation**.

The balance sheet equation underlies the balance sheet in that every transaction of the business affects the balance sheet twice. By recording the dual effect of each transaction we ensure that the equation always remains in balance. We will see later in the chapter how this is achieved.

1.5   The business entity concept

DEFINITION

The **business entity concept**
states that financial accounting
information relates only to the
activities of the business entity
and not to the activities of its
owner.

The **business entity concept** states that financial accounting information relates only to the activities of the business entity and not to the activities of its owner.

Under this concept accounting is seen as relating to an independent unit, the entity. The entity is treated as being separate from its owners, whatever its legal status. Thus, a company is both legally and for accounting purposes a separate entity distinct from its owners, the shareholders. On the other hand, the business of a sole trader is not a legal entity distinct from its proprietor; however, for accounting purposes, the business is regarded as being a separate entity and accounts are drawn up for the business separately from the trader's own personal financial dealings.

The entity concept is essential in order to be able to account for the business as a separate economic unit. Flows of money between the business and the proprietors may be separately identified from other money flows:

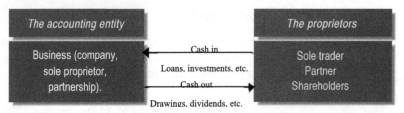

The correct terms for these cash movements are:

Cash movement from/to proprietors	Sole trader, partnership	Company
IN	Either 'loans from proprietors' or 'capital introduced'	Proceeds of issuing shares
OUT	Either 'drawings' or 'reduction in capital'	Dividends

The key link between the owner and the business is the amount stated as capital. In B Ashton's balance sheet, at the beginning of the year, the amount owing to the proprietor was £5,200. During the year the overall profit of the business of £3,450 increased the amount owing to the proprietor, whereas the drawings reduced the amount owing to him.

It may not seem clear why the balance sheet shows the movements in capital account. The reason is one of convention: although its key figure is £5,690 (balance at 31 December 20X6), it is useful to show Mr Ashton why his balance has increased from £5,200 to £5,690. Briefly, the balance has increased because the business has earned profit of £3,450 which it 'owes' to the proprietor, Mr Ashton; but Mr Ashton has withdrawn £2,960 of this amount, leaving the business owing him just £490 of the profit earned in the period. This amount of £490 (called the 'profit retained in the business' or simply 'retained profit') is the increase in the amount owed by the business to the proprietor.

It is important to appreciate that the **balance**, i.e. the amount that is added to the other balances on the balance sheet, is £5,690. The balance sheet could be presented without the disclosure of information as to the movements in capital during the year as follows.

Mr B Ashton
Balance sheet as at 31 December 20X6

	£	£		£	£
Fixed assets:			Capital account:		5,690
Motor van		2,400	Current liabilities:		
Current assets:			Creditors		2,700
Stock	2,390				
Debtors	1,840				
Cash at bank	1,704				
Cash in hand	56				
	———				
		5,990			
		———			———
		8,390			8,390

1.6   Disclosure of assets and liabilities in the balance sheet

The assets used in the business amount to £8,390. The individual amounts making up the £8,390 are usually referred to as the **book values**. It cannot be assumed that these assets could be sold in the open market for £8,390 – in fact this is very unlikely. The valuation is on a 'historical' not a 'market value' basis. In other words, the historical cost balance sheet reflects what was paid to acquire the various assets, not what it might be possible to realise by selling them.

Note: Current accounting practice in the UK allows for some assets and liabilities to be disclosed at current values. Revaluation of fixed assets is dealt with in Chapter 7.

As regards the listing of assets in the balance sheet, the least liquid assets are dealt with first, followed by the more liquid assets. The term **liquid assets** refers to cash and those assets which are close to cash. Looking at assets and starting with the least liquid assets:

- The motor van is classified as a **fixed asset**. A **fixed asset** is any asset, tangible or intangible, acquired for retention by an entity for the purpose of providing a service to the business, and not held for resale in the normal course of trading.

- The remaining assets are classified as **current assets**:

  - stock, i.e. goods held for resale. When the goods are eventually sold, the business will receive in exchange cash or a claim to cash (usually referred to as a debtor).

  - debtors, i.e. amounts owing from customers which will eventually result in the receipt of cash.

  - cash at bank, i.e. cash on current account at the bank.

  - cash in hand, i.e. notes and coins.

Liabilities are claims on the business by outsiders. Current liabilities are those liabilities which are payable within twelve months of the balance sheet date. Creditors are amounts owing in respect of goods and services previously received.

1.7 The vertical format

The balance sheet of the same sole trader using the vertical format would appear as follows:

Mr B Ashton
Balance sheet as at 31 December 20X6

	£	£
Fixed assets:		
Motor van		2,400
Current assets:		
Stock	2,390	
Debtors	1,840	
Cash at bank	1,704	
Cash in hand	56	
	5,990	
Current liabilities:		
Creditors	2,700	
Net current assets		3,290
		5,690
Capital account:		
Balance at 1 January 20X6		5,200
Net profit	3,450	
Less drawings	2,960	
Retained profit		490
Balance at 31 December 20X6		5,690

There are three points to note.

- Unless instructed otherwise, always use this vertical layout for the balance sheet.

- The fact that the totals on the horizontal layout are £8,390, and on the vertical are £5,690 is of no significance. The different totals are explained by the way the current liabilities are dealt with. Both balance sheets satisfy the fundamental accounting equation referred to earlier. This time:

  Assets – Liabilities = Proprietor's capital

- Net current assets are simply current assets less current liabilities.

1.8 A comparison of the layouts

The two balance sheets may be illustrated diagrammatically.

Horizontal balance sheet

Vertical balance sheet

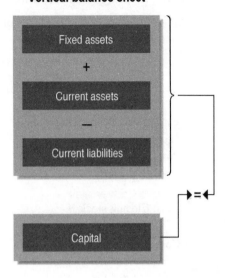

ACTIVITY 1

List the following items showing the least liquid item first and the most liquid last:

- cash in hand
- stocks of finished goods
- cash at bank
- debtors
- stocks of raw materials.

Feedback to this activity is at the end of the chapter.

2   The trading and profit and loss account

2.1   The matching convention

DEFINITION

The comparison of sale proceeds with the costs associated with making a sale is known as the **matching convention**.

Assume that Mr Ashton is a retailer and makes his profit from selling goods. In principle there are two steps in calculating his profit:

- deciding what his sales are for the year

- deducting from this figure:
    - the cost of buying goods from his suppliers;
    - various expenses such as wages, rent and insurance.

2.2   Layout of profit and loss account: vertical format

Mr Ashton's profit and loss account would appear as follows:

Mr B Ashton
Profit and loss account for the year ended 31 December 20X6

	£	£
Sales		33,700
Opening stock	3,200	
Purchases	24,490	
	27,690	
Less: Closing stock	2,390	
Cost of sales		25,300
Gross profit		8,400
Wages	3,385	
Rent and rates	1,200	
Sundry expenses	365	
		4,950
Net profit		3,450

2.3   Disclosure of revenue and expenses in the profit and loss account

The detailed preparation of balance sheets and profit and loss accounts will be considered later, but it is useful at this stage to obtain an overall view.

- The first point, in direct contrast with the balance sheet, is that the profit and loss account summarises the trading activities of a business **over a period of time**, usually twelve months. It relates to a *period* of time, not to a *moment* in time.

- Secondly, the figure of £33,700 for sales relates to goods sold during the year, whether or not the cash was actually received during the year. For example, if sales are made on credit to certain customers, some of those customers might still owe money for goods sold during the year. In such cases we do not wait until the cash is received before recording the sale; instead, we record the sale when it is made, even though the customer will not pay until later.

- Having arrived at a figure for sales, one must deduct the cost of buying the goods sold. It is quite likely that some of the goods sold at the beginning of the year were goods which were in stock at the previous year-end. One must therefore add these onto goods which were actually purchased during the year. However, some of this year's purchases were unsold at 31 December 20X6. These must be deducted from purchases as they will be set off against next year's sales.

Sales less cost of sales gives **gross profit**. **Net profit** is arrived at by deducting expenses from gross profit.

- Note that for convenience, the profit and loss account is divided into two parts. The part dealing with sales and cost of sales may be referred to as the **trading account**, the remainder as the **profit and loss account**. The overall account is referred to as the trading and profit and loss account or simply as the profit and loss account.

- Finally, one must be very careful to distinguish between **wages** and **drawings**. Wages relate to payments to third parties (employees) and represent a deduction or charge in arriving at net profit. Amounts paid to the proprietor (even if he calls them 'salary'!) must be treated as drawings. It would be wrong to treat drawings as a business expense, because the amounts drawn are not used to further a sale. They represent an **appropriation** (or withdrawal) of profit earned by the business and are eventually deducted from the proprietor's capital account.

2.4   Relationship between the profit and loss account and the balance sheet

Balance sheets are pictures of the business at particular points in time, while the profit and loss accounts show the activities of the business in between those balance sheet dates. Therefore the linkage between the accounting statements can be represented as follows.

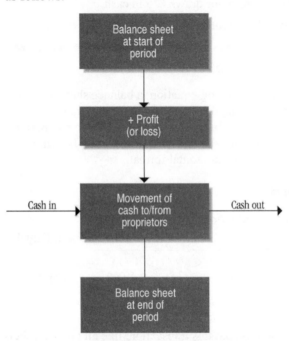

Thus, the balance sheets are not merely isolated statements; they are linked over time by the profit (or loss) as analysed in the profit and loss account, plus or minus movements of cash with the proprietors.

3   The balance sheet equation in action

3.1   Introduction

The accounting equation states that at any point in time the assets of the business will be equal to its liabilities plus the capital of the business.

$$\text{Assets} = \text{Proprietor's capital} + \text{Liabilities}$$
$$\text{Assets} - \text{Liabilities} = \text{Proprietor's capital}$$

Each and every transaction that the business makes or enters into has two aspects to it and has a double effect on the business and the accounting equation. This is known as the **dual aspect of transactions**.

So if a business buys some goods for cash the two aspects of the transaction are that it now has some goods but it has less cash. Equally if it sells some goods for cash the effect is that cash has increased and a sale has been made.

Example

This example involves a series of transactions using the accounting equation to build up a set of financial statements.

Day 1   Avon commences in business introducing £1,000 cash.

Day 2   Buys a motor car for £400 cash.

Day 3   Buys stock for £200 cash.

Day 4   Sells all the goods bought on Day 3 for £300 cash.

Day 5   Buys stock for £400 on credit.

Day 6   Sells half of the goods bought on Day 5 on credit for £250.

Day 7   Pays £200 to his trade creditor.

Day 8   Receives £100 from a debtor.

Day 9   Proprietor draws £75 in cash.

Day 10   Pays rent of £40 in cash.

Day 11   Receives a loan of £600 repayable in two years.

Day 12   Pays cash of £30 for insurance.

Using the accounting equation, a balance sheet will be drawn up for the end of each day (representing the cumulative effect of transactions to date) and later a profit and loss account will be drawn up for the twelve day period. For simplicity, the distinction between cash at bank and cash in hand will be ignored. Each day's balance sheet is shown using the horizontal format.

Solution

Day 1: introduction of cash as capital

Balance sheet Day 1

	£		£
Cash	1,000	Capital	1,000

Note carefully that this transaction, like all others, affects two aspects of the balance sheet. The business has £1,000 of cash but also owes £1,000 back to Avon; this is the capital of the business.

Day 2: purchase of fixed asset for cash

This is merely a change of the form in which the assets are held.

Balance sheet Day 2

	£		£
Motor car	400	Capital	1,000
Cash (£1,000 – £400)	600		
	1,000		1,000

The acquiring of an asset must lead to one of the following.

- reducing another asset by a corresponding amount (as above)

- incurring a corresponding liability (Day 5)

- increasing the capital contributed by the proprietor (Day 1).

Day 3: purchase of stock for cash

Again this is merely a change in the form in which the assets are held. £200 is withdrawn from cash and invested in stock.

Balance sheet Day 3

	£		£
Motor car	400	Capital	1,000
Stock	200		
Cash (£600 – £200)	400		
	1,000		1,000

Day 4: sale of stock at a profit

This is an important new development. It is true that one asset (stock) is being replaced by another (cash), but the amounts do not correspond.

	£
Cash acquired (sale proceeds)	300
Asset relinquished (stock)	200
Difference (= profit)	100

Thus total assets have increased by £100. Since there are no liabilities involved, if the fundamental equation is to remain valid the capital must increase by £100.

Profit is the difference between purchase price and sale proceeds and it belongs to the proprietor(s) of the business. It is an increase in the capital of the business.

Balance sheet Day 4

	£		£
Motor car	400	Capital introduced	1,000
Cash (£400 + £300)	700	Add: Profit	100
	1,100		1,100

Day 5: purchase of stock on credit

Assets can be increased by a corresponding increase in liabilities as follows:

Balance sheet Day 5

	£		£
Motor car	400	Capital introduced	1,000
Stock	400	Add: Profit	100
Cash	700		
			1,100
		Creditors	400
	1,500		1,500

Note that the creditors are acting in effect as a source of finance for the business.

Day 6: sale of part of stock on credit terms

This transaction introduces two new concepts:

- sale on credit – Essentially this is the same as a sale for cash, except that the asset increased is not cash, but debtors.

- sale of *part* of the stock – In practice this is the normal situation. The important accounting requirement is to separate:

  - stock still held as an asset, from

  - cost of stock sold.

This is best viewed diagrammatically (see diagram below).

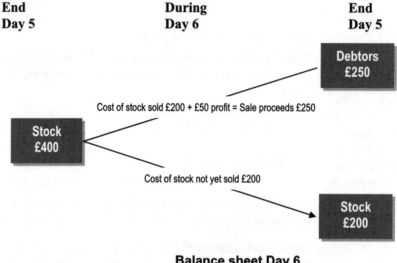

Balance sheet Day 6

	£		£
Motor car	400	Capital introduced	1,000
Stock	200	Add: Profit to date	
Debtors	250	(£100 + £50)	150
Cash	700		——
			1,150
		Creditors	400
	——		——
	1,550		1,550
	——		——

Note that profit is recorded when the sale is made, not when the cash is received. Thus the payment of the creditors (Day 7) or the receipt of cash from debtors (Day 8) will not alter the total profit.

It would be useful at this stage to draw up a summary of the profit to date:

Statement of profit for first six days of trading

		£	£
Sales:	Cash		300
	Credit		250
			——
			550
Purchases:	Cash	200	
	Credit	400	
		——	
Goods available for sale		600	
Less: Goods not sold (closing stock)		200	
		——	
Cost of goods sold			400
			——
Gross profit			150
			——

Notice that in this trading account the goods not sold, i.e. the closing stock, are stated at their original purchase price. This is part of the traditional historical cost convention of accounting.

The cost of goods sold is also known as the cost of sales.

Day 7: payment to trade creditor

This is simply the reduction of one liability (creditors) and one asset (cash) by a corresponding amount (£200).

Balance sheet Day 7

	£		£
Motor car	400	Capital introduced	1,000
Stock	200	Add: Profit to date	150
Debtors	250		
Cash (£700 – £200)	500		1,150
		Creditors (£400 – £200)	200
	1,350		1,350

Day 8: receipt of cash from debtor

This is a change in the form in which assets are held.

Balance sheet Day 8

	£		£
Motor car	400	Capital introduced	1,000
Stock	200	Add: Profit to date	150
Debtors (£250 – £100)	150		
Cash (£500 + £100)	600		1,150
		Creditors	200
	1,350		1,350

Day 9: cash withdrawal by the proprietor

This arises where the proprietor wishes to withdraw some of his interest in the business, i.e. his original capital as increased by profits earned. This shows on the balance sheet as a reduction of capital, and as a reduction of cash.

Withdrawals of cash or of other assets from the business by the owner are called drawings.

Balance sheet Day 9

	£			£
Motor car	400	Capital introduced		1,000
Stock	200	Profit to date	150	
Debtor	150	Less drawings	75	
Cash (£600 – £75)	525	Retained profit		75
				1,075
		Creditors		200
	1,275			1,275

Day 10: payment of rent

This is an example of a business expense. The payment of the expense reduces the profit and reduces the cash.

Balance sheet Day 10

	£		£	£
Motor car	400	Capital introduced		1,000
Stock	200	Profit to date		
Debtor	150	(£150 – £40)	110	
Cash (£525 – £40)	485	Less drawings	75	
		Retained profit		35
				1,035
		Creditors		200
	1,235			1,235

Day 11: medium-term loan received of £600

This increases an asset (cash) and increases a liability (loan).

Balance sheet Day 11

	£		£	£
Motor car	400	Capital introduced		1,000
Stock	200	Profit to date	110	
Debtors	150	Less drawings	75	
Cash (£485 + £600)	1,085			
		Retained profit		35
				1,035
		Creditors		200
		Loan		600
	1,835			1,835

Day 12: payment of insurance

This is a further example of a business expense. The payment reduces both profit and cash.

Balance sheet Day 12

	£		£	£
Motor car	400	Capital introduced		1,000
Stock	200	Profit to date		
Debtors	150	(£110 – £30)	80	
Cash (£1,085 – £30)	1,055	Less drawings	75	
		Retained profit		5
				1,005
		Creditors		200
		Loan		600
	1,805			1,805

After each transaction the accounting equation will always be equal:

Assets = Capital + Liabilities

This marks the end of the transactions. The financial statements for the twelve-day period can now be considered.

3.2 The financial statements

The trading and profit and loss account can be prepared by summarising all the sales, purchases and expenses that have taken place in the 12 day period, not forgetting the closing stock at the end of the period.

Both the trading and profit and loss account and the balance sheet are to be presented in vertical form as follows:

Trading and profit and loss account for the twelve days ended ... 20..

		£	£
Sales:	Cash		300
	Credit		250
			550
Purchases:	Cash	200	
	Credit	400	
		600	
Less: Closing stock		200	
Cost of goods sold			400
Gross profit			150
Rent		40	
Insurance		30	
			70
Net profit			80

Balance sheet as at end of Day 12

		£	£
Fixed asset:	Motor car (at cost)		400
Current assets:	Stock	200	
	Debtors	150	
	Cash	1,055	
		1,405	
Less: Current liabilities: Creditors		200	
			1,205
			1,605
Less: Long-term liability: Loan			600
			1,005
Capital account of Avon: Capital introduced			1,000
	Net profit	80	
	Less: drawings	75	
Retained profit			5
			1,005

Notes:

1   Gross profit is an important indicator of performance. Gross profit percentage expresses the relationship between sales and gross profit. In this example it is

$$^{150}\!\!/_{\!550} \times 100 = 27\%.$$

2   Although the alternative (horizontal) form of balance sheet is acceptable, the above vertical presentation is generally regarded as preferable.

3   Current liabilities are payable within twelve months of the balance sheet date and cannot therefore include a loan of £600 repayable in two years. Note the presentation of this loan as a long-term liability in the vertical form balance sheet.

4   The motor car is stated in the balance sheet at its original cost of £400. The important subject of depreciation will be considered at a later stage.

Summary of the effect of each transaction

Transaction	Assets	Capital and liabilities	Reference
Introduction of cash as capital	+ Cash	+ Capital	Day 1
Purchase of asset for cash	+ Asset − Cash	No effect	Days 2 + 3
Purchase of asset on credit	+ Asset	+ Liabilities	Day 5
Sale of stock at a profit – for cash	− Stock + Cash	+ Capital	Day 4
Sale of stock at a profit – on credit	− Stock + Debtor	+ Capital	Day 6
Payment of creditor	− Cash	− Liabilities	Day 7
Receipt from debtor	+ Cash − Debtor	No effect	Day 8
Drawings by proprietor	− Cash	− Capital	Day 9
Payment of expense in cash	− Cash	− Capital	Days 10 + 12
Cash received as a loan	+ Cash	+ Liabilities	Day 11

As the above table shows:

*   Every business transaction affects at least two items in the accounting equation.

*   The accounting equation must always balance (Assets = Capital + Liabilities, or Assets − Liabilities = Capital.

*   The net profit for the period is made up of the gross profit less business expenses.

*   The gross profit is recorded in the trading account and is calculated as sales proceeds less the original cost of the goods sold.

ACTIVITY **2**

Summarise the effects of each of these transactions on the accounting equation.

1   Payment of £200 to a creditor.

2   Payment of £1,000 by cheque for office furniture.

3   A sale on credit of £350 (goods sold originally cost £250).

4   Receipt of £140 from a debtor.

5   Taking out of a bank loan of £4,000.

6   Drawings by the owner of £100.

7   Payment of £40 casual wages.

8   Purchase of a computer for the office on credit for £1,500.

9   Sale for cash of £800 (goods sold originally cost £600).

Conclusion

The two main financial statements have been examined in this chapter and we have looked at how individual transactions are represented in these financial statements using the balance sheet equation. The accounting equation holds true no matter how complex a business seems to be. Every transaction or event of a business has two equal and opposite effects on the business.

We will be reinforcing your knowledge of these areas in later chapters.

SELF-TEST QUESTIONS

The balance sheet and balance sheet equation

1   What is meant by the capital of a business? (1.3)

2   What is the definition of a fixed asset? (1.6)

3   What are current liabilities? (1.6)

The trading and profit and loss account

4   What is the difference between gross profit and net profit? (2.3)

5   How are the balance sheet and the profit and loss account inter-related? (2.4)

The balance sheet equation in action

6   Who does the profit of a business belong to? (3.1)

7   What are drawings? (3.1)

PRACTICE QUESTION

The Frog Shop

1   Kermit starts a business and introduces £2,000 in cash.

2   He buys a motor van for £1,000 and some shop fittings for £800.

3   He buys some stock from Fozzie costing £500 on credit.

4   He sells one half of the goods to Scooter for £650 cash.

5   He pays £500 to Fozzie.

6   He draws £50 of cash from the business for his own use.

7   He buys goods costing £1,000 on credit terms from Fozzie.

8   He sells goods which cost him £900 to Miss Piggy on credit terms for £1,200.

9   He receives £500 from Miss Piggy.

10   He pays wages of £100 to Rolf, his employee.

(a)   Prepare the balance sheet of Kermit's business (known as 'The Frog Shop') at the end of each day.   **(20 marks)**

(b)   Prepare a trading and profit and loss account for The Frog Shop for the ten days ended above.   **(6 marks)**

(Total: 26 marks)

For the answer to this question, see the 'Answers' section at the end of the book.

FEEDBACK TO ACTIVITY 1	The correct order is:

1   stocks of raw materials

2   stocks of finished goods

3   debtors

4   cash at bank

5   cash in hand.

FEEDBACK TO ACTIVITY 2	

1   Decrease in cash £200

Decrease in creditor £200

2   Increase in fixed asset (office furniture) £1,000

Decrease in cash £1,000

3   Increase in debtor £350

Decrease in stock £250

Profit (increase in capital) £100

4   Increase in cash £140

Decrease in debtor £140

5   Increase in cash £4,000

Increase in creditors (loan) £4,000

6   Decrease in cash £100

Decrease in capital £100

7   Decrease in cash £40

Decrease in profit (expense) (decrease in capital) £40

8   Increase in fixed assets (computer) £1,500

Increase in creditors £1,500

9   Increase in cash £800

Decrease in stock £600

Profit (increase in capital) £200.

Chapter 3
BOOKKEEPING PRINCIPLES

In the previous chapter we recorded each transaction immediately into the financial statements. In practice such an approach is neither sensible nor desirable. What is needed is a set of accounting records which can provide information for the day-to-day running of the business and for the periodic preparation of financial statements showing the profit or loss the business has made (trading and profit and loss account) and the position of the business at the end of the period covered by the trading and profit and loss account (balance sheet).

The purpose of this chapter is to explain the main elements of the bookkeeping system which provides this information.

In this chapter ledger accounts will be introduced and the rules of double entry bookkeeping examined. The process of balancing the ledger accounts and producing a trial balance will be examined, but the actual preparation of financial statements will be dealt with in a later chapter.

Objectives

By the time you have finished this chapter you should be able to:

- understand the principles of double entry bookkeeping
- write up simple transactions in the ledger accounts
- balance off ledger accounts and prepare a trial balance
- deal with opening balances in ledger accounts
- understand the operation of a value added tax.

1   The main data sources and their function

1.1   Introduction

Whenever a business transaction takes place there is a need to record the transaction in a document. In the previous chapter we recorded each transaction immediately into the financial statements. Clearly, in practice, with a large number of transactions such an approach is neither sensible nor desirable. Financial statements only need to be prepared at set intervals; not every day. The first stage therefore is to have a sensible system of source documents which can be used as the raw material for recording transactions.

A **source document** is an individual record of a business transaction – for example, a sales invoice is a formal record of a sale having occurred.

In this section we will examine the types of source documents which exist. Most business transactions revolve around the purchase and sale of goods and services and thus most source documents relate to one or other of these items.

1.2   Sales and purchase orders

A **purchase order** is an agreement to purchase goods/services from a business. It is prepared by the purchaser.

A **sales order** is an agreement to sell goods/services to a business. It is prepared by the seller.

A sales or purchase order is normally the first occasion when an intended transaction is put in writing. It does however record an *intended* rather than an *actual* transaction, and for this reason is not used to record the transaction in the books of account. (This avoids the inconvenience of recording transactions which for one reason or another are frustrated and never actually happen.) A more important document is the **invoice**, which records the formal occurrence of the transaction.

1.3 Sales and purchase invoices

When a business sells goods or services to a customer it sends a sales invoice to the customer. A **sales invoice** is a formal record of the amount of money due from the customer as a result of the sale transaction. To the customer, the invoice represents a purchase and thus he will refer to it as a purchase invoice.

The invoice may contain a lot of detailed information about the transaction:

- name and address of seller and purchaser
- date of sale
- reference to order
- description of goods
- amount due
- terms of payment.

It is an essential document which provides the information which will be entered into the accounting records of a business.

1.4 Credit notes and debit notes

A **credit note** records goods returned by a customer or the reduction of monies owed by a customer.

The credit note is issued subsequent to a sales invoice and will refer to that invoice. There are many reasons why the original sale may have been incorrect. Faulty goods may have been supplied or the price charged on the invoice may have been incorrect.

A **debit note** is sometimes raised by a purchaser of goods and is a formal request for a credit note to be issued by the supplier.

2 Accounting records

2.1 Summary of stages of accounting

Accounting records are any listing or book which records the transactions of a business in a logical manner.

The source documents above are part of the accounting records of a business, but the information contained in them needs to be recorded and summarised clearly. This is achieved by the use of **books of prime entry**.

The chart below shows the route by which transactions are recorded in the final output of the accounting system: the financial statements.

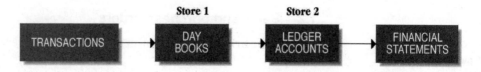

DEFINITIONS

Day books record the transactions of each day, and are used as an initial 'store' of information of the business transactions prior to storing the information in the ledger accounts.
A **ledger account** or **'T' account** is a less detailed (more summary) record of transactions.

Day books record the transactions of each day, and are used as an initial 'store' of information of the business transactions prior to storing the information in the ledger accounts.

A **ledger account** or **'T' account** is a less detailed (more summary) record of transactions.

There is a different day book for each type of transaction: for example, sales invoices are recorded in a sales day book, purchase invoices are recorded in a purchases day book, and so on.

— registradas

Ledger accounts are pages in a book (the ledger) with a separate page reserved for transactions of the same type. For example, the ledger will contain an account for 'sales'. While individual sales invoices are logged separately in the sales day book, the sales ledger account will contain just the total value of sales from the day book.

The form of day books will be considered in a later chapter. Their prime function is to list transactions of a like nature and these listings will be used to make further entries in the accounting system.

For example, a sales day book will list all the sales invoices raised by the business, and will contain sufficient information about each sale so that further entries can be made at a convenient later date without having to refer back to the sales invoices. By logging the sales invoices in a day book, and entering only the *total* value of sales in the sales account, we ensure that the sales account does not become crowded with too much detail.

This system is essential in a real business because of the volume of transactions. However, the intermediate stage of recording transactions in a day book before entering them in the accounting system (the ledger accounts) may obscure your understanding at this early stage. To avoid this, we will proceed by entering all transactions directly into the ledger accounts; this will give you a clearer understanding of how the accounting system works. In a later chapter we will return to the subject of day books.

2.2   Ledger accounts and double entry

In the previous chapter, we looked at the effect on the balance sheet, day by day, of a series of transactions.

KEY POINT

All transactions affect the accounting equation and all transactions could, if we wished, be recorded directly by drawing up a balance sheet.

All transactions affect the accounting equation and all transactions could, if we wished, be recorded directly by drawing up a balance sheet.

The problem with this approach is that it becomes impractical in a real-life situation involving a large number of transactions. In practice, therefore, it is necessary to summarise all categories of transactions so that the balance sheet need only be produced at intervals of, say, twelve months. The approach used is called the **double entry** system of bookkeeping. This involves the use of day books and ledger accounts.

2.3   The theory of double entry

Every transaction affects two items in the balance sheet. To follow the rules of double entry, every time a transaction is recorded, both aspects must be taken into account.

Traditionally, one aspect is referred to as the debit side of the entry (abbreviated to Dr) and the other as the credit side of the entry (abbreviated to Cr).

2.4   Ledger accounts

Each aspect is recorded in the relevant ledger account. Any business of reasonable size will have a large number of ledger accounts. Each account has two sides – the **debit** side and the **credit** side.

Ledger account

Debit side (Dr)	£	Credit side (Cr)	£

For each transaction it is now not only necessary to identify the two effects of the transaction and therefore the two ledger accounts to be used but also to decide which ledger account has the debit entry and which has the credit entry.

2.5 Debit and credit and the format of ledger accounts

In bookkeeping, the terms 'debit' and 'credit' have meanings different from those attached to them in ordinary speech. You will soon get used to their technical meaning in bookkeeping. Here is a table to explain.

Entries on the DEBIT side	Entries on the CREDIT side
Assets	Liabilities
Expenses	Income
Losses	Profits

One fundamental ledger account in a bookkeeping system is the **cash account,** recording cash received and paid by the business. If we spend some of this cash, this could be for three reasons:

1 to buy an asset

2 to pay an expense

3 to repay a debt or liability.

The bookkeeping entry to record a payment of cash is on the *credit* side of the cash account (reducing the cash balance) and on the *debit* side of the account recording the other aspect of the transaction:

For (1): Debit the asset account to record the fact that we have more of the asset concerned.

For (2): Debit the expense account to record the fact that we have paid the expense.

For (3): Debit the liability account to record the fact that we owe less as a result of the payment.

The example which follows shows the procedure in action. Note the format of the ledger account, with columns for the date and the details of the transaction.

2.6 Drawing up ledger accounts

In practising the following examples, provide plenty of space between the ledger accounts so that the entries can be made. It is *essential* that you practise the examples by opening ledger accounts and writing down the entries. In this way you will understand the practice and theory of double entry more quickly.

Also allow a full page width for each ledger account. This will enable narrative and figures to be clearly written and also emphasise the 'left-hand' and 'right-hand' nature of the entries.

Example

To illustrate the rules of double entry, we will use the example in the previous chapter again. Twelve separate transactions were considered. For convenience, these are summarised again below:

Day 1	Avon commences in business introducing £1,000 cash.
Day 2	Buys a motor car for £400 cash.
Day 3	Buys stock for £200 cash.
Day 4	Sells all the goods bought on Day 3 for £300 cash.
Day 5	Buys stock for £400 on credit.
Day 6	Sells half of the goods bought on Day 5 on credit for £250.
Day 7	Pays £200 to his trade creditor.
Day 8	Receives £100 from a debtor.
Day 9	Proprietor draws £75 in cash.
Day 10	Pays rent of £40 in cash.
Day 11	Receives a loan of £600 repayable in two years.
Day 12	Pays cash of £30 for insurance.

Solution

Day 1

Avon introduced cash of £1,000 into the business. What are the two aspects of this transaction? Quite clearly cash (an asset) is increased and so are the claims of the proprietor (his capital). As this is a new business we must open up ledger accounts for cash and capital.

The cash account has the debit entry and the capital account has the credit entry.

Cash account

Date	Details	£	Date	Details	£
(1)	Capital	1,000			

Capital account

Date	Details	£	Date	Details	£
			(1)	Cash	1,000

Note that the figure (1) refers to the date of the transaction (Day 1). The details refer to the other account that is being debited or credited.

On the cash account, the receipt of £1,000 is entered on the left-hand side (the debit side) and its description 'capital' indicates where the other side of the double entry may be found. In the capital account, £1,000 appears on the right-hand side (the credit side) and the description 'cash' shows where the other side of the double entry may be found.

Day 2

On this day the business purchases a motor car (which is a fixed asset) for cash. The payment of cash is a credit in the cash account and the other side of the double entry is a debit in the motor car account.

Using the cash account already opened, the transaction appears as follows:

Cash account

Date	Details	£	Date	Details	£
(1)	Capital	1,000	(2)	Motor car	400

Motor car account

Date	Details	£	Date	Details	£
(2)	Cash	400			

An asset (or an increase in an asset) is always a debit entry.

Day 3

The purchase of goods on Day 3 is a cash purchase and so the cash account is credited.

So which account is debited? The temptation may well be to answer 'stock, of course', but this would be wrong. Stock is a special case as will be explained later. For the moment the thing to remember is that it is the purchases account which is debited.

Cash account

Date	Details	£	Date	Details	£
(1)	Capital	1,000	(2)	Motor car	400
			(3)	Purchases	200

Purchases account

Date	Details	£	Date	Details	£
(3)	Cash	200			

The purchases account contains items which are held for resale by the business or are raw materials which will be used to manufacture goods.

Day 4

The sale of goods for cash involves a receipt of cash and thus a debit to the cash account. What then is credited? Again the answer is not stock but sales account.

Cash account

Date	Details	£	Date	Details	£
(1)	Capital	1,000	(2)	Motor car	400
(4)	Sales	300	(3)	Purchases	200

Sales account

Date	Details	£	Date	Details	£
			(4)	Cash	300

The sales account collects the sales that have been made by the business during the period. Income to the business is always a credit entry.

The effect of having separate sales and purchases accounts is that profit is not computed when each sale is made as it was in the previous example. As many sales are being made each day, it is not practical to compute profit on each transaction. Profit is instead calculated at the end of the period.

Day 5

This transaction produces a minor problem: cash is not involved!

The transaction involves a purchase of goods (as did the Day 3 transaction). Purchases account is therefore debited.

But what is credited? The answer is a creditor account for the supplier of the goods. The credit on his account represents a liability to him. A liability (or an increase in a liability) is always a credit entry.

Purchases account

Date	Details	£	Date	Details	£
(3)	Cash	200			
(5)	Creditors	400			

Creditor account

Date	Details	£	Date	Details	£
			(5)	Purchases	400

Day 6

A similar problem now arises. The transaction is a sale (like Day 4), so the sales account, representing all the sales taking place in the period, is credited.

The debit side of the double entry goes to a debtors account. Debtors are assets – they represent amounts owing to the business, i.e. promises to pay cash at some future date.

Sales account

Date	Details	£	Date	Details	£
			(4)	Cash	300
			(6)	Debtors	250

Debtor account

Date	Details	£	Date	Details	£
(6)	Sales	250			

The information about only half of the goods being sold does not concern us at this stage. At the end of the period when the final accounts (financial statements) are drawn up, account will be taken of any closing stock (representing unsold goods).

Day 7

The payment of £200 to the trade creditor firstly, reduces the asset cash (a credit) and, secondly, reduces liabilities or amounts owing (debit to creditor's account).

Cash account

Date	Details	£	Date	Details	£
(1)	Capital	1,000	(2)	Motor car	400
(4)	Sales	300	(3)	Purchases	200
			(7)	Creditor	200

Creditor account

Date	Details	£	Date	Details	£
(7)	Cash	200	(5)	Purchases	400

Day 8

The receipt of £100 from a debtor increases the asset cash (debit cash) and reduces the amount owed (credit debtor). This reflects the fact that the debtor now owes us less than previously.

Cash account

Date	Details	£	Date	Details	£
(1)	Capital	1,000	(2)	Motor car	400
(4)	Sales	300	(3)	Purchases	200
(8)	Debtor	100	(7)	Creditor	200

Debtor account

Date	Details	£	Date	Details	£
(6)	Sales	250	(8)	Cash	100

Day 9

Drawings of cash must clearly be credited to cash. The debit side of the double entry should be taken to a drawings account.

Cash account

Date	Details	£	Date	Details	£
(1)	Capital	1,000	(2)	Motor car	400
(4)	Sales	300	(3)	Purchases	200
(8)	Debtor	100	(7)	Creditor	200
			(9)	Drawings	75

Drawings account

Date	Details	£	Date	Details	£
(9)	Cash	75			

Day 11

The loan represents a receipt of cash (debit cash). But the business now owes £600 to a third party (i.e. a liability). A loan account must be credited. Note that a separate account should be opened for each liability (i.e. each third party).

Cash account

Date	Details	£	Date	Details	£
(1)	Capital	1,000	(2)	Motor car	400
(4)	Sales	300	(3)	Purchases	200
(8)	Debtor	100	(7)	Creditor	200
(11)	Loan	600	(9)	Drawings	75

Loan account

Date	Details	£	Date	Details	£
			(11)	Cash	600

Days 10 and 12

The payments of rent and insurance represents expenditure. Cash is credited and the respective expense accounts debited.

Cash account

Date	Details	£	Date	Details	£
(1)	Capital	1,000	(2)	Motor car	400
(4)	Sales	300	(3)	Purchases	200
(8)	Debtor	100	(7)	Creditor	200
(11)	Loan	600	(9)	Drawings	75
			(10)	Rent	40
			(12)	Insurance	30

Rent account

Date	Details	£	Date	Details	£
(10)	Cash	40			

Insurance account

Date	Details	£	Date	Details	£
(12)	Cash	30			

KEY POINT

Expenses of the business are always a debit entry.

An expense account collects the costs of the various expenses of running the business. The total of these expenses is included periodically in the profit and loss account.

2.7 Final ledger accounts

The final ledger accounts would appear as follows.

(*Note*: the totals in brackets are there merely for convenience later in the chapter. They form no part of the double entry.)

Capital account

Date	Details	£	Date	Details	£
			(1)	Cash	1,000

Cash account

Date	Details	£	Date	Details	£
(1)	Capital	1,000	(2)	Motor car	400
(4)	Sales	300	(3)	Purchases	200
(8)	Debtor	100	(7)	Creditor	200
(11)	Loan	600	(9)	Drawings	75
		(Total £2,000)	(10)	Rent	40
			(12)	Insurance	30
					(Total £945)

Motor car account

Date	Details	£	Date	Details	£
(1)	Cash	400			

Purchases account

Date	Details	£	Date	Details	£
(3)	Cash	200			
(5)	Creditors	400			
		(Total £600)			

Sales account

Date	Details	£	Date	Details	£
			(4)	Cash	300
			(6)	Debtors	250
					(Total £550)

Creditor account (for each supplier)

Date	Details	£	Date	Details	£
(7)	Cash	200	(5)	Purchases	400

Debtor account (for each customer)

Date	Details	£	Date	Details	£
(6)	Sales	250	(8)	Cash	100

Drawings account

Date	Details	£	Date	Details	£
(9)	Cash	75			

Rent account

Date	Details	£	Date	Details	£
(10)	Cash	40			

Loan account

Date	Details	£	Date	Details	£
			(11)	Cash	600

Insurance account

Date	Details	£	Date	Details	£
(12)	Cash	30			

ACTIVITY 1

Summarise the debit and the credit entries for each of the transactions that Avon made.

Can you draw any general conclusions regarding the entries to be made for assets, liabilities, income and expenses?

Feedback to this activity is at the end of the chapter.

2.8 Asset, liability, revenue and expense accounts

The above activity should provide some clues as to the distinction between asset, liability, revenue and expense accounts.

- An **asset account** collects information about particular assets of a business.

- A **liability account** collects information about particular liabilities of a business.

Asset and liability accounts appear on the balance sheet at the end of the accounting period.

- An **expense account** collects information about costs of a business.

- A **revenue account** collects information about income of a business.

Revenue and expenses are transferred to the profit and loss account in order to compute profit for a period. The only revenue account we have come across so far is the sales account.

We will see later that some revenue/expense accounts will also record assets and liabilities – known as accruals and prepayments.

utilidad / valor / provecho

2.9 Usefulness of cash

Only a combination of experience and thought will provide familiarity with double entry techniques. Even experienced accountants occasionally have to ask which account is credited!

It was clear in the previous illustration how useful cash was in establishing one side of the double entry. If cash was received, then cash account was debited and it was a question of deciding what had to be credited. Conversely, a payment of cash involved a credit to cash account and it was then a question of deciding in which ledger account the debit was to appear.

a la inversa

ACTIVITY 2

Harold commenced business on 1 July 20X4. The following transactions took place during the month of July.

1 July	Introduced cash of £4,000 and a car valued at £1,750.
2 July	Bought goods for cash at a cost of £1,130.
8 July	Paid wages of £13 and sundry expenses of £2.
9 July	Sold goods on credit to Victor for £190.
14 July	Sold goods on credit to Susan for £240.
18 July	Bought goods on credit from Williams for £85.
22 July	Bought fixtures and fittings for cash at a cost of £350.
25 July	Paid wages of £38.
26 July	Paid drawings to himself of £80.
31 July	Victor paid the full amount owing.
31 July	Paid rent of £500.

gastos varios

Write up the ledger accounts for the month of July 20X4.

Feedback to this activity is at the end of the chapter.

3   The trial balance

3.1   The nature and purpose of a trial balance

The large number of transactions recorded in ledger accounts means that there is the possibility of errors occurring. Periodically, some assurance is required as to the accuracy of the procedures. This can be done by taking out a **trial balance**. In the case of a moderate-sized business, although final accounts will usually be prepared annually, a trial balance will be extracted at more frequent intervals (say, monthly).

A **trial balance** is a memorandum listing of all the ledger account balances. In an accounting context **memorandum** means that the listing is not a part of the double entry.

If the double entry procedures have been carefully followed, then the trial balance should show that the total of the debit balances agrees with the total of the credit balances, because every transaction has been recorded by means of a debit entry and a credit entry.

3.2   Balancing the ledger accounts

Before a trial balance can be drawn up, the ledger accounts must be balanced.

Where there are several entries in a ledger account, the computation of the balance of the ledger account to go onto the trial balance can be shown in the ledger account by carrying down and bringing down a balance. The procedure is as follows:

Step 1 Add up the total debits and credits in the account and make a (memorandum) note of the totals.

Step 2 Insert the **higher** total at the bottom of **both** the debits and credits, leaving one line for the inclusion of a **balance c/d** (carried down).

The totals should be in level with each other and underlined.

Step 3 Insert on the side which has the lower arithmetical total, the narrative 'balance c/d' and an amount which brings the arithmetical total to the total that has been inserted under step 2 above.

Step 4 The same figure is shown on the other side of the ledger account but **underneath** the totals. This is the **balance b/d** (brought down).

The balance c/d is known as the **closing balance** (at the end of the period just completed). The balance b/d is known as the **opening balance** (at the beginning of the period just about to begin).

debajo
por debajo
superficie interior

Example

The cash account from the example of Avon is reproduced below:

Cash account

Date	Details	£	Date	Details	£
(1)	Capital	1,000	(2)	Motor car	400
(4)	Sales	300	(3)	Purchases	200
(8)	Debtor	100	(7)	Creditor	200
(11)	Loan	600	(9)	Drawings	75
		(Total £2,000)	(10)	Rent	40
			(12)	Insurance	30
					(Total £945)

Step 1 The arithmetic totals have already been computed.

Step 2 The higher total is inserted, £2,000.

Cash account

Date	Details	£	Date	Details	£
(1)	Capital	1,000	(2)	Motor car	400
(4)	Sales	300	(3)	Purchases	200
(8)	Debtor	100	(7)	Creditor	200
(11)	Loan	600	(9)	Drawings	75
			(10)	Rent	40
			(12)	Insurance	30
		2,000			2,000

Note that the credit entries do not yet add up to £2,000.

Steps 3 & 4 Insert the balances b/d and c/d. The balance can be found from the arithmetical totals £2,000 – £945 = £1,055.

Cash account

Date	Details	£	Date	Details	£
(1)	Capital	1,000	(2)	Motor car	400
(4)	Sales	300	(3)	Purchases	200
(8)	Debtors	100	(7)	Creditors	200
(11)	Loan	600	(9)	Drawings	75
			(10)	Rent	40
			(12)	Insurance	30
				Balance c/d	1,055
		2,000			2,000
	Balance b/d	1,055			

The £1,055 is known as a debit balance because the b/d figure is on the debit side of the account, i.e. the debit entries in the account before it was totalled must have exceeded the credit entries by that amount.

This balance means that there is £1,055 cash left within the business at the end of the period just completed and also at the beginning of the next period.

The carrying down of balances causes problems to some students. However, if you practise the procedure, it soon becomes second nature. It is helpful to have a clear mental picture of the form of a ledger account when practising examples.

ACTIVITY 3

Balance off the remaining ledger accounts in the example Avon. (Note that where there is only one entry in an account there is no necessity to carry out the balancing procedure as this one entry is the balance c/d and the balance b/d.)

Feedback to this activity is at the end of the chapter.

3.3 Drawing up the trial balance

Once the ledger accounts have all been balanced the trial balance can be drawn up. This is done by listing each of the ledger account names in the business's books showing against each name the balance on that account and whether that balance is a debit or a credit balance brought down. Note that it is the balance **brought down** which determines whether the account is said to have a debit or a credit balance.

Example

Continuing the example of Avon the trial balance at the end of Day 12 would appear as shown on the next page.

Trial balance at the end of Day 12

Account	Debit	Credit
	£	£
Capital		1,000
Cash	1,055	
Motor car	400	
Purchases	600	
Sales		550
Creditor		200
Debtor	150	
Drawings	75	
Rent	40	
Loan		600
Insurance	30	
	2,350	2,350

ACTIVITY 4

The debit and the credit totals of the trial balance are equal. Consider why this should be the case.

Feedback to this activity is at the end of the chapter.

3.4   Errors not revealed by trial balance

The fact that the two totals agree may be reassuring, but it is not final proof that the accounts are correct! It is possible for certain types of error to occur and yet the overall effect is that the trial balance still appears to balance.

Such errors include:

1   **errors of omission** – where no entry of a transaction has been made at all.

DEFINITION

To **post** amounts to a ledger account means to write the amount up in the ledger accounts.

2   **errors of commission** – where an amount has been correctly posted but to the wrong account, although it is the right type of account, e.g. B Smith, a customer, pays £50 by cheque which is debited to the cash book and then in error posted to the credit of the account of R Smith, another customer.

Although there will have been a debit and a credit, nevertheless the account of R Smith shows a credit balance of £50 higher than it should be, while the account of B Smith is also £50 out.

3   **errors of principle** – where an item is incorrectly classified by the bookkeeper and posted to the wrong type of account, e.g. the sale of surplus office equipment has been classified as sales of goods.

4   **errors of entry** – where an incorrect amount is posted to both the accounts in question, e.g. £2.00 is misread as £200 and so entered on both debit and credit sides of the correct accounts.

Some accountants refer to this error as an **error of original entry** as it often arises due to the entry originally being recorded in a **day book** (see later) at the wrong amount.

5   **compensating errors** – where two or more errors cancel out each other. They are difficult to locate and fortunately tend not to occur frequently.

A trial balance is a memorandum listing of all the ledger account balances. It is *not* part of the double entry, e.g. cash is not being credited with £1,055 and the trial balance debited with £1,055. It merely summarises the net result of all the debits and credits that have been made during the period.

4 Ledger accounts – further complications

4.1 Introduction

If a business has been in operation for a number of years, then at the beginning of any accounting period, it will have assets and liabilities such as cash, debtors, fixed assets and creditors left over from the previous period. Such opening amounts are shown in the ledger accounts as opening balances.

Remember that assets are always debits and therefore the opening balance on an asset account will be a debit entry and, as liabilities are credits, the opening balance on liability accounts will be credit entries.

ACTIVITY 5

Draw up the opening position on the ledger accounts for the following items:

	£
Cash opening balance	1,000
Creditors opening balance	2,000
Debtors opening balance	2,500
Overdraft opening balance	800
Fixtures and fittings opening balance	3,000

Feedback to this activity is at the end of the chapter.

Example

Elton makes up his accounts to 31 December each year. His balance sheet at 31 December 20X8 showed the following position:

Balance sheet at 31 December 20X8

	£	£
Fixed assets:		
Freehold shop		17,600
Current assets:		
Stock	5,343	
Debtors	4,504	
Cash	2,801	
	12,648	
Less: Current liabilities:		
Creditors	5,430	
		7,218
Net current assets		24,818
Less: Long-term liability:		
Loan account		8,000
		16,818
Capital account:		
Balance at 1 January 20X8		16,730
Net profit for 20X8	4,708	
Less drawings	4,620	
Retained profit for 20X8		88
Balance at 31 December 20X8		16,818

Notes:

1 Debtors consist of:

	£
E	2,600
F	987
G	536
H	381
	4,504

2 Creditors consist of:

	£
M	2,840
N	1,990
O	600
	5,430

The following transactions took place during January 20X9.

3 January	G settled his account in full.
5 January	Paid £847 to N.
8 January	F returned as faulty, goods with an invoice value of £264 and paid off the balance owing on his account.
12 January	Sold goods to G, invoice value £706.
18 January	Purchased goods on credit from P, invoice value £746.
19 January	E paid his account subject to a discount of 2% for prompt payment.
24 January	Paid O subject to 1.5% discount for early settlement.
28 January	Bought goods on credit from O with invoice value £203.
31 January	Returned goods to P, invoice value £76.

You are required to prepare:

1 ledger accounts relating to all the above matters;

2 a trial balance at 31 January 20X9.

Solution

Step 1 Open up all of the ledger accounts that have opening balances on them. These are all of the accounts shown in the balance sheet at 31 December 20X8.

Capital account

	£	20X9		£
		1 Jan	Balance b/d	16,818

Note that balance b/d is short for balance brought down from the previous period. (Last year's ledger account would have shown all the figures, including drawings of £4,620, leading up to the final balance of £16,818.) Thus the b/d figure records the fact that at the beginning of the accounting period the credits on the capital account exceed the debits by £16,818.

Loan account

	£	20X9		£
		1 Jan	Balance b/d	8,000

Freehold shop account

20X9		£		£
1 Jan	Balance b/d	17,600		

Stock account

20X9		£			£
1 Jan	Balance b/d	5,343			

Cash account

20X9		£			£
1 Jan	Balance b/d	2,801			

Debtor account – E

20X9		£			£
1 Jan	Balance b/d	2,600			

Debtor account – F

20X9		£			£
1 Jan	Balance b/d	987			

Debtor account – G

20X9		£			£
1 Jan	Balance b/d	536			

Debtor account – H

20X9		£			£
1 Jan	Balance b/d	381			

Creditor account – M

		£	20X9		£
			1 Jan	Balance b/d	2,840

Creditor account – N

		£	20X9		£
			1 Jan	Balance b/d	1,990

Creditor account – O

		£	20X9		£
			1 Jan	Balance b/d	600

Step 2 Record the transactions for the period in the ledger accounts.

Note: you should look carefully at the following items in particular.

(a) 8 January

Some of the goods sold to F were faulty so he returned them. When the sale was originally made the double entry was to credit sales and debit F's debtor account.

When goods are returned the debtor's account must be credited with the invoice amount of the goods as the debtor is obviously not going to pay for the goods. The corresponding debit entry is not to sales but instead to a sales returns account (or returns inwards account).

Sales returns are goods returned by a customer because they are unsatisfactory.

(b) 19 January

When the goods were originally sold to E the terms of the sale were that if he paid his account by a certain date then he would be entitled to a 2% discount for prompt payment. This is known as a cash discount or settlement discount. E owes £2,600 but the cash that Elton will receive will be £2,548 (98% of £2,600).

DEFINITION

Sales returns are goods returned by a customer because they are unsatisfactory.

This payment satisfies his liability in full and therefore his debtor account must be cleared. This is done by crediting it with £52, the amount of the discount, and debiting a discount allowed account. The discount allowed is an expense of the business that will appear in the profit and loss account – as the business is sacrificing £52 in order to receive the money earlier.

(c) 24 January

This is an example of a discount received from a supplier. A **cash discount received** is a discount received from a supplier if the business pays its invoices by a certain date. Elton owes O £600 but as he is evidently paying the invoice early Elton needs only pay £591 (98.5% of £600).

In order to clear the creditor account for O it must be debited with the £9 of the discount as well as with the cash payment and the £9 is then credited to a discount received account. This £9 will appear as income beneath gross profit in the profit and loss account for the period.

(d)   31 January

This is an example of a purchase return. **Purchases returns** are goods returned to a supplier because they are unsatisfactory. Goods purchased from P are being returned and therefore P's creditor account will be debited as the goods will not be paid for. The credit entry is to a purchases returns account (or returns outwards account).

Cash account

20X9		£	20X9		£
1 Jan	Balance b/d	2,801	5 Jan	N	847
3 Jan	G	536	24 Jan	O	591
8 Jan	F	723	31 Jan	Balance c/d	5,170
19 Jan	E	2,548			
		6,608			6,608
	Balance b/d	5,170			

Sales account

		£	20X9		£
			12 Jan	G	706

Sales returns account

20X9		£		£
8 Jan	F	264		

Purchases account

20X9		£	20X9	£
16 Jan	P	746	Balance c/d	949
28 Jan	O	203		
		949		949
	Balance b/d	949		

Purchases returns account

	£	20X9		£
		31 Jan	P	76

Discount allowed account

20X9		£		£
19 Jan	E	52		

Discount received account

		£	20X9		£
			24 Jan	O	9

E's account

20X9		£	20X9		£
1 Jan	Balance b/d	2,600	19 Jan	Cash (98% × £2,600)	2,548
				Discount allowed	52
		2,600			2,600

F's account

20X9		£	20X9		£
1 Jan	Balance b/d	987	8 Jan	Sales returns	264
				Cash	723
		987			987

G's account

20X9		£	20X9		£
1 Jan	Balance b/d	536	3 Jan	Cash	536
12 Jan	Sales	706	31 Jan	Balance c/d	706
		1,242			1,242
	Balance b/d	706			

H's account

20X9		£			£
1 Jan	Balance b/d	381			

M's account

		£	20X9		£
			1 Jan	Balance b/d	2,840

N's account

20X9		£	20X9		£
5 Jan	Cash	847	1 Jan	Balance b/d	1,990
31 Jan	Balance c/d	1,143			
		1,990			1,990
				Balance b/d	1,143

O's account

20X9		£	20X9		£
24 Jan	Cash (98.5% × £600)	591	1 Jan	Balance b/d	600
	Discount received	9	28 Jan	Purchases	203
31 Jan	Balance c/d	203			
		803			803
				Balance b/d	203

P's account

20X9		£	20X9		£
31 Jan	Purchase returns	76	18 Jan	Purchases	746
31 Jan	Balance c/d	670			
		——			——
		746			746
		——			
				Balance b/d	670

Step 3 Balance off all of the accounts where necessary (see above).

Step 4 Prepare the trial balance.

Trial balance at 31 January 20X9

		Dr £	Cr £
1	Capital		16,818
2	Loan		8,000
3	Freehold shop	17,600	
4	Stock	5,343	
5	Cash	5,170	
6	Sales		706
7	Sales returns	264	
8	Purchases	949	
9	Purchases returns		76
10	Discount allowed	52	
11	Discount received		9
12	E	-	
13	F	-	
14	G	706	
15	H	381	
16	M		2,840
17	N		1,143
18	O		203
19	P		670
		———	———
		30,465	30,465
		———	———

ACTIVITY 6

Continue with the example of Elton above and prepare his trading and profit and loss account in vertical form and the balance sheet at the end of January. Assume that the stock remaining at 31 January 20X9 totalled £6,100.

Note: the treatment of sales returns and purchases returns is to net them off against sales and purchases respectively in the trading and profit and loss account.

Feedback to this activity is at the end of the chapter.

ACTIVITY 7

Ian Wright owes ABC & Co £2,000 and is owed £3,400 by Templeman Associates. Ian offers a cash discount to his customers of 2.5% if they pay within 14 days and ABC & Co have offered Ian a cash discount of 3% for payment within ten days.

Ian decides to pay ABC & Co within ten days and Templeman Associates take advantage of the cash discount offered to them.

Write up the ledger account for ABC and Co, Templeman Associates, discounts received and discounts allowed in Ian Wright's books.

Feedback to this activity is at the end of the chapter.

5　The operation of a value added tax

5.1　Introduction

Value Added Tax (VAT) is the UK sales tax. A **value added tax** is a tax levied at the point of sale of goods or services, usually by way of a percentage add-on to the pre-tax (net) selling price.

- Some sales have VAT at 17.5% added onto the net amount (business selling price or list price). The VAT element is owed *by* the business to **Her Majesty's Customs and Excise (HMCE)**, which is the tax authority responsible for collecting VAT.

- Some purchases also have VAT at 17.5% of the net amount added on to them. The VAT element is owed *to* the business by HMCE.

- The business merely collects VAT on behalf of HMCE. At no time does the VAT belong to the business.

- At regular intervals in the year, the business either pays VAT to, or has VAT repaid by, HMCE.

5.2　Working out VAT

In practice and in exams, there is often a need to work out VAT from either the VAT inclusive figure (gross), or the VAT exclusive figure (net).

Net to gross

The net figure is given and VAT is added to this. The VAT is calculated at 17.5% of the net amount, or $(\text{Net} \times \frac{17.5}{100})$. Therefore, the gross amount is built up as follows:

		%
	Net amount	100
Add	VAT (Net $\times \frac{17.5}{100}$)	17.5
		———
	Gross amount	117.5
		———

The gross amount can be calculated directly from the net amount as it represents 117.5% of the net amount as shown above. Therefore an alternative calculation of the gross figure is:

Net amount	$\times$	$\frac{117.5}{100}$	= Gross amount
100	$\times$	$\frac{117.5}{100}$	= 117.5

ACTIVITY 8

Given a net sale of £200, calculate the VAT at 17.5% and the gross amount.

Feedback to this activity is at the end of the chapter.

Gross to net

This time the gross figure, which already includes VAT, is given. Therefore, to find the net amount, VAT will have to be deducted. We can see how this works using a rearranged version of the net/gross build up:

		%
	Gross amount	117.5
Less	VAT	(17.5)
		———
	Net amount	100
		———

This time the VAT represents $\frac{17.5}{117.5}$ of the gross amount, so the VAT to be deducted will be (Gross $\times \frac{17.5}{117.5}$). The net amount can also be obtained directly by taking

Gross amount $\times$ $\frac{100}{117.5}$ = Net amount

117.5 $\times$ $\frac{100}{117.5}$ = 100

Note that $\frac{17.5}{117.5}$ and $\frac{100}{117.5}$ cancel to $\frac{7}{47}$ and $\frac{40}{47}$ respectively.

ACTIVITY 9

Given a gross sale of £470, calculate the VAT at 17.5% and the net amount.

Feedback to this activity is at the end of the chapter.

To summarise:

- At a 17.5% rate of VAT, the gross price will be 117.5% ($\frac{117.5}{100}$) of the net price.

- If the gross price is given, the net price will be the gross price multiplied by $\frac{100}{117.5}$.

5.3 Credit sales and VAT

This section looks at the accounting for VAT where there is a credit sale.

The double entry required for a credit sale with VAT is:

Debit	Debtors (gross amount)	X	
Credit	Sales (net amount)		X
	VAT (tax amount)		X

If a business is registered for VAT, it must add VAT to the value of sales invoices at the current VAT rate. For example:

	£	
Net sale	6,000	what the business will ultimately have left from the sale in its bank account
VAT	1,050	17.5% of net sales – what the business will pay to HMCE
Total	7,050	what the customer (debtor) will pay to the business

The steps in accounting for VAT on this transaction are as follows:

Step 1   The net sale is credited to the sales account as normal, but because the VAT is owed to HMCE, the VAT is credited to a VAT account (a liability account) and finally the total is debited to the debtor.

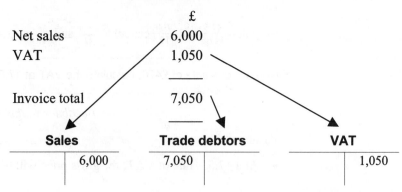

Recording of a credit sale

VAT is not accounted for when the money is received from the customer. The VAT has already been accounted for when the sale was made.

Step 2   When the customer pays the debt, the total invoice amount goes into the bank account and the amount showing as owed in debtors is eliminated.

Sales		Trade debtors		VAT		Cash at bank	
6,000		7,050	7,050		1,050	7,050	
(1)		(1)	(2)		(1)	(2)	

Step 3   Finally, when the business is due to pay HMCE for the VAT that the business owes (£1,050 in this example), then the money comes out of the bank account and the amount owing to HMCE is eliminated.

Sales		Trade debtors		VAT		Cash at bank	
6,000		7,050	7,050	1,050	1,050	7,050	1,050
(1)		(1)	(2)	(3)	(1)	(2)	(3)

5.4   Credit purchases and VAT

This section looks at the accounting for VAT where there is a credit purchase.

The double entry required for a credit purchase with VAT is

Debit	Purchases/expense (net amount)	X
	VAT (tax amount)	X
Credit	Creditors (gross amount)	X

If a business is registered for VAT, it can reclaim the VAT that its suppliers have added to purchase invoices. For example:

Net purchase	4,000	what the business will ultimately have paid from its bank account
VAT	700	17.5% of net purchases – what the business will receive from HMCE
Total	4,700	what will be paid to the supplier (creditor) by the business

The steps in accounting for VAT on this transaction are as follows:

Step 1   The net purchase is debited to the purchases of stock account as normal. VAT in this instance is reclaimable from HMCE, thus the VAT amount is debited to the VAT account. Finally the total is credited to the trade creditors account.

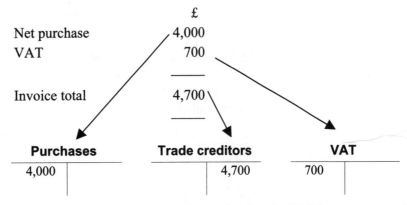

	£
Net purchase	4,000
VAT	700
Invoice total	4,700

Purchases	Trade creditors	VAT
4,000	4,700	700

As with the sales invoice receipt, notice that the VAT is not accounted for again when the payment to trade creditors is made.

Step 2   When the business pays the debt to the supplier the total invoice amount is paid from the bank account and the amount showing as owing in creditors is eliminated.

Purchases of stock	VAT	Trade creditors		Cash at bank
4,000	700	4,700	4,700	4,700
(1)	(1)	(2)	(1)	(2)

Step 3   Finally, the business can reclaim VAT from HMCE (£700 in this example). A cheque would then be received from HMCE that would be paid into the bank account. In accounting terms, this would be reflected by increasing the amount in the cash at bank account and reducing the amount showing as owed by HMCE to the business in the VAT account.

Purchases of stock	Trade creditors		VAT		Bank	
4,000	4,700	4,700	700	700	700	4,700
(1)	(2)	(1)	(1)	(3)	(3)	(2)

5.5   The VAT account

In reality the business will be buying and selling goods all the time. The VAT account therefore will have amounts of VAT from sales transactions recorded on the credit side (the business owes HMCE the VAT), and also amounts of VAT from purchase transactions recorded on the debit side (the business is owed the VAT by HMCE).

When a payment date to HMCE falls due, the business will calculate the net balance on the VAT account and this will be the amount paid to, or reclaimed from, HMCE.

So, if the above two transactions were combined, the VAT account would look like this:

VAT account

	£		£
VAT on purchases	700	VAT on sales	1,050
Net payment to HMCE	350		
	1,050		1,050

Finally, look at the effects of the sales and purchase transactions on the bank account.

	£
Received from debtor	7,050
Paid to creditor	(4,700)
Net amount	2,350
Paid to HMCE	(350)
Net amount in bank	2,000

KEY POINT

The profit of a business is always based on the figures net of VAT.

It is no coincidence that the final figure is the same amount that can be worked out by comparing the net sale (£6,000) with the net purchase (£4,000). Whilst VAT is an integral part of business accounting, ultimately it has nothing to do with business profitability. The profit of a business is always based on the figures (net of VAT).

Where net sales in a period exceed net purchases, more VAT will have been collected than suffered; the VAT account will thus have a **credit** balance on it, representing the amount **owed to** HMCE.

It net purchases exceed net sales, the VAT account will have a **debit** balance, representing the amount **owed by** HMCE.

ACTIVITY 10

Credit purchases are made for £9,400. This figure includes VAT.

Half those goods are sold on credit for £6,400 **exclusive** of VAT.

Record the above transactions in the following T accounts: purchases, trade creditors, VAT, sales and trade debtors.

Feedback to this activity is at the end of the chapter.

Conclusion

This has been a long chapter in which you should have grasped the basics of double entry bookkeeping. It is essential material on which many later chapters are based. Do make sure you understand it fully before proceeding. As always, work through the questions that follow before moving to the next chapter.

The previous chapter began with the accounting equation which states that:

Assets = Liabilities + Proprietor's capital

In double entry bookkeeping the key point is that every transaction or event has two effects on the accounting of the business. One of these effects is recorded as a *debit* entry in a ledger account and the other is recorded as a *credit* entry in a ledger account.

There are a number of helpful rules that can be learnt in order to assist in finding the correct accounts to debit and credit for each transaction but the key to double entry bookkeeping is practice at writing up ledger accounts.

Accounting records

1   If cash is received by the business is that a debit or a credit entry in the cash account? (2.5)

2   Are liabilities debit or credit entries in the liability accounts? (2.8)

The trial balance

3   What is a trial balance? (3.1)

4   What is meant by the balance b/d on a ledger account? (3.2)

5   What is the double entry for a sales return? (4.1)

6   What is a return outwards? (4.1)

Ledger accounts – further complications

7   What is a discount allowed? (4.1)

8   What is the double entry for a discount received? (4.1)

The operation of a value added tax

9   On whose behalf does a business collect VAT? (5.1)

10 What is the double entry to record a credit sale with VAT? (5.3)

11 What does a credit balance on the VAT account represent? (5.5)

Grace

Grace commenced business on 1 June 20X9 with cash of £5,000 and she introduced a car valued at £4,500. The following transactions took place:

1 June	Purchased goods for £1,000 cash
2 June	Purchased fixtures and fittings £900
3 June	Purchased goods on credit from Eileen £1,500
4 June	Sold goods for £1,200 cash
5 June	Sold goods on credit to Tom for £900
8 June	Paid wages £100 in cash
9 June	Bought goods from Eric for £850 on credit
10 June	Sold goods to Trevor £800 on credit
11 June	Sold goods on credit to Tom for £1,000
12 June	Paid Eileen all that was owed to her
15 June	Tom paid in full
16 June	Purchased £700 goods for cash
17 June	Sold £500 goods for cash
18 June	Trevor paid £500 on account
19 June	Paid wages £150
22 June	Paid Eric in full
24 June	Loan received from Guy £1,000
25 June	Purchased leasehold premises £4,000
26 June	Paid wages £150.

Write up the ledger accounts for the month of June and extract a trial balance.

(Ignore dates in the ledger accounts.)   **(15 marks)**

For the answer to this question, see the 'Answers' section at the end of the book.

FEEDBACK TO ACTIVITY 1

Ledger account

Day	Transaction	Debit	Credit
1	Introduction of cash as capital	Cash	Capital
2	Purchase of fixed asset for cash	Fixed asset	Cash
3	Purchase of stock for cash	Purchases	Cash
4	Sale of stock for cash	Cash	Sales
5	Purchase of stock on credit	Purchases	Creditor
6	Sale of stock on credit	Debtor	Sales
7	Payment of cash to creditor	Creditor	Cash
8	Receipt of cash from debtor	Cash	Debtor
9	Cash withdrawn by proprietor	Drawings	Cash
10 & 12	Payment of expense in cash	Expense	Cash
11	Receipt of cash as loan	Cash	Loan

This can be summarised as follows:

	Debits	Credits
Balance sheet items	**Assets**	**Liabilities**
Profit and loss account items	**Expenses**	**Income**

FEEDBACK TO ACTIVITY 2

The ledger accounts for Harold's business for the month of July are shown below.

Cash account

20X4 Jul	Details	£	20X4 Jul	Details	£
1	Capital	4,000	2	Purchases	1,130
31	Victor	190	8	Wages	13
			8	Sundry expenses	2
			22	Fixtures and fittings	350
			25	Wages	38
			26	Drawings	80
			31	Rent	500

Capital account

20X4 Jul	Details	£	20X4 Jul	Details	£
			1	Cash	4,000
			1	Motor car	1,750

Motor car account

20X4 Jul	Details	£	20X4 Jul	Details	£
1	Capital	1,750			

(Note: the introduction of capital in a form other than cash has the same double entry as if it were cash, i.e. debit the asset account and credit the capital account.)

Purchases account

20X4 Jul	Details	£	20X4 Jul	Details	£
2	Cash	1,130			
18	Williams	85			

Wages account

20X4 Jul	Details	£	20X4 Jul	Details	£
8	Cash	13			
25	Cash	38			

Sundry expenses account

20X4 Jul	Details	£	20X4 Jul	Details	£
8	Cash	2			

Sales account

20X4 Jul	Details	£	20X4 Jul	Details	£
			9	Victor	190
			14	Susan	240

Debtor account – Victor

20X4 Jul	Details	£	20X4 Jul	Details	£
9	Sales	190	31	Cash	190

Debtor account – Susan

20X4 Jul	Details	£	20X4 Jul	Details	£
14	Sales	240			

Rent account

20X4 Jul	Details	£	20X4 Jul	Details	£
31	Cash	500			

Creditor account – Williams

20X4 Jul	Details	£	20X4 Jul	Details	£
			18	Purchases	85

Fixtures and fittings account

20X4 Jul	Details	£	20X4 Jul	Details	£
22	Cash	350			

Drawings account

20X4 Jul	Details	£	20X4 Jul	Details	£
26	Cash	80			

FEEDBACK TO ACTIVITY 3

The balanced off accounts for Avon are shown below.

Capital account

Date	Details	£	Date	Details	£
			(1)	Cash	1,000

Motor car account

Date	Details	£	Date	Details	£
(2)	Cash	400			

Purchases account

Date	Details	£	Date	Details	£
(3)	Cash	200		Balance c/d	600
(5)	Creditors	400			
		600			600
	Balance b/d	600			

Sales account

Date	Details	£	Date	Details	£
	Balance c/d	550	(4)	Cash	300
			(6)	Debtors	250
		550			550
				Balance b/d	550

Creditors account

Date	Details	£	Date	Details	£
(7)	Cash	200	(5)	Purchases	400
	Balance c/d	200			
		400			400
				Balance b/d	200

Debtors account

Date	Details	£	Date	Details	£
(6)	Sales	250	(8)	Cash	100
				Balance c/d	150
		250			250
	Balance b/d	150			

Drawings account

Date	Details	£	Date	Details	£
(9)	Cash	75			

Rent account

Date	Details	£	Date	Details	£
(10)	Cash	40			

Loan account

Date	Details	£	Date	Details	£
			(11)	Cash	600

Insurance account

Date	Details	£	Date	Details	£
(12)	Cash	30			

FEEDBACK TO
ACTIVITY 4

The trial balance balances because, for every debit entry in the ledger accounts, there has been an equal and opposite credit entry.

FEEDBACK TO ACTIVITY 5

The opening position of the ledger accounts is as follows:

Cash

Balance b/d	£ 1,000		£

Creditors

	£	Balance b/d	£ 2,000

Debtors

Balance b/d	£ 2,500		£

Overdraft

	£	Balance b/d	£ 800

Fixtures and fittings

Balance b/d	£ 3,000		£

FEEDBACK TO ACTIVITY 6

The trading and profit and loss account, and balance sheet are shown below.

Trading and profit and loss account for the month of January 20X9

	£	£	£
Sales			706
Less: Sales returns			264
			——
			442
Cost of goods sold			
Opening stock		5,343	
Purchases	949		
Less: Purchases returns	76		
	——		
		873	
		——	
		6,216	
Less: Closing stock		6,100	
		——	
			116
			——
Gross profit			326
Discount received (income)			9
			——
			335
Less: Expenses			
Discount allowed			52
			——
Net profit			283
			——

Balance sheet as at 31 January 20X9

	£	£
Fixed assets		
Freehold shop		17,600
Current assets		
Stock	6,100	
Debtors (706 + 381)	1,087	
Cash	5,170	
	12,357	
Current liabilities		
Creditors (2,840 + 1,143 + 203 + 670)	4,856	
		7,501
		25,101
Long-term liability		
Loan		8,000
		17,101
Capital at 1 January		16,818
Profit for the month		283
		17,101

The ledger accounts are shown below.

ABC & Co

	£		£
Cash (97% × 2,000)	1,940	Balance b/d	2,000
Discount received	60		
	2,000		2,000

Templeman Associates

	£		£
Balance b/d	3,400	Cash (97.5% × 3,400)	3,315
		Discount allowed	85
	3,400		3,400

Discount received

	£		£
		ABC & Co	60

Discount allowed

	£		£
Templeman Associates	85		

FEEDBACK TO ACTIVITY 8		£
	Net amount	200
Add	VAT ($200 \times \frac{17.5}{100}$)	35
	Gross amount ($200 \times \frac{117.5}{100}$)	235

FEEDBACK TO ACTIVITY 9		£
	Gross amount	470
Less	VAT ($470 \times \frac{17.5}{117.5}$)	70
	Net amount ($470 \times \frac{100}{117.5}$)	400

FEEDBACK TO ACTIVITY 10

Step 1   Work out the VAT elements

On purchases:

		£
	Gross amount	9,400
Less	VAT ($9,400 \times \frac{17.5}{117.5}$)	1,400
	Net amount	8,000

On sales:

		£
	Net amount	6,400
Add	VAT ($6,400 \times \frac{17.5}{100}$)	1,120
	Gross amount ($6,400 \times \frac{117.5}{100}$)	7,520

Step 2   Record the transactions in the T accounts.

Purchases account

	£		£
Creditors (1)	8,000		

Trade creditors account

	£		£
		Purchases including VAT (1)	9,400

VAT account

	£		£
Purchases (1)	1,400	Sales (2)	1,120

Sales account

	£		£
		Debtors (2)	6,400

Trade debtors account

	£		£
Sales including VAT (2)	7,520		

Chapter 4
STOCK AND THE PREPARATION OF FINANCIAL STATEMENTS

Having learnt how to write up the transactions of a business in its ledger accounts, and how to balance off those ledger accounts and prepare a trial balance, it is now necessary to consider how the profit and loss account and balance sheet of the business are prepared.

In order to do this one further piece of double entry bookkeeping must be considered: how to treat closing stock. Once the treatment of closing stock in the ledger accounts is understood, then the preparation of the profit and loss account and balance sheet from the ledger accounts and the trial balance can be tackled.

Objectives

By the time you have finished this chapter you should be able to:

- deal with opening and closing stock in the ledger accounts of a business

- prepare a simple set of financial statements from the ledger account balances or a trial balance

- explain alternative stock valuation methods.

1   Closing stock

1.1   Introduction

D E F I N I T I O N

Gross profit is sales revenue minus cost of goods sold.

To calculate gross profit, we match sales revenue with the cost of goods sold, the difference being the gross profit. It is not sufficient to match sales revenue with the cost of purchases, because the goods purchased in the period may not coincide exactly with the goods sold in the period:

- Some of the goods purchased may not have been sold by the period end. In other words, we have **closing stock** at the end of the period.

- Equally, some of the goods sold may not have been purchased in the period, but in an earlier period. In other words, there may have been **opening stock** at the beginning of the period.

We therefore need to adjust the purchases figure in respect of both closing stock and opening stock.

Example

A trader starts in business and by the end of his first year, he has purchased goods costing £21,000 and has made sales totalling £25,000. Goods which cost him £3,000 have not been sold by the end of the year.

What profit has he made in the year?

Solution

The unsold goods are referred to as closing stock. This stock is deducted from purchases in the trading account section of the profit and loss account.

Gross profit is thus:

	£	£
Sales		25,000
Purchases	21,000	
Less: Closing stock	3,000	
Cost of goods sold		18,000
Gross profit		7,000

Closing stock appears on the balance sheet as an asset. Note that the term 'cost of goods sold' is usually replaced by the term 'cost of sales'.

The situation becomes slightly more complicated when the business has been in existence for more than one year as we shall now see.

Example

A wholesaler buys goods from a manufacturer at £2 per unit and sells them on credit terms to various retailers at £3 per unit. He has summarised his transactions for 20X7 as follows:

	Units	
Opening stock (1 January 20X7)	500	
Purchases	6,200	(Cost at £2 = £12,400)
	6,700	
Sales	5,900	(Proceeds at £3 = £17,700)
Closing stock (31 December 20X7)	800	

How is the gross profit to be calculated?

Solution

Gross profit is sales less cost of sales. We must apply the principle of **accruals** or **matching**. Against the revenue from the 5,900 units sold, we must 'match' what it cost to buy those goods in the first place. The purchases figure does not give the answer, since clearly some of the goods sold during the year come from the goods the wholesaler started off with at the beginning of the year (last year's closing stock, or this year's opening stock) and some from the goods bought during the year (purchases). When comparing sales and cost of sales, it is important to make sure that you are comparing like with like.

In the example assume that both opening and closing stock are valued for accounts purposes at £2 per unit, giving stock figures of £1,000 and £1,600 respectively.

Gross profit can be calculated as follows:

	£	£
Sales		17,700
Opening stock (at cost)	1,000	
Purchases (at cost)	12,400	
	13,400	
Less: Closing stock (at cost)	1,600	
Cost of sales		11,800
Gross profit		5,900

1.2 Trading and profit and loss account

The first crucial point to remember is that the trading and profit and loss account is part of the double entry bookkeeping system, whereas the balance sheet is not.

Do not be put off by the fact that the trading and profit and loss account is usually set out in vertical form whereas other ledger accounts are set out in 'T' account form.

1.3 Balance sheet

The balance sheet is an ordered list of the balances on the ledger accounts after double-entry has been completed. The balance sheet is not itself part of the double entry system.

Example

From the previous example we arrived at a gross profit of £5,900. Let us examine the relevant ledger accounts. We will consider the accounts at two separate points in time:

1 immediately before extracting a trial balance at 31 December 20X7

2 immediately after the financial statements have been prepared and the various accounts ruled off.

Solution

1 Ledger accounts before extracting a trial balance:

Stock account

		£		£
20X7				
1 Jan	Balance b/d	1,000		

The stock is an asset and therefore is a debit entry in the stock account.

Purchases account

		£		£
20X7				
	Various creditors	12,400		

Sales account

	£	20X7		£
			Various debtors	17,700

Points to note:

- The balance of £1,000 in stock account originated from last year's balance sheet when it appeared as closing stock. Remember that last year's closing stock is this year's opening stock. This figure remains unchanged in the stock account until the very end of the year when closing stock at 31 December 20X7 is considered.

- The closing stock figure (which is known to be £1,600) is not usually provided to us until after we have extracted the trial balance at 31 December 20X7.

- The purchases and sales figures have been built up over the year and represent the year's accumulated transactions.

2 Ledger accounts reflecting the closing stock:

Assume that we are now told that closing stock for accounts purposes has been valued at £1,600. What adjustments are required?

Step 1: The trading and profit and loss account forms part of the double entry. At the year end the accumulated totals from the sales and purchases accounts must be transferred to it.

Ref	Debit	Credit	With
1	Trading and P&L a/c	Purchases	£12,400
2	Sales	Trading and P&L a/c	£17,700

These transfers are shown in the ledger accounts below.

Step 2 The opening stock figure (£1,000) must be transferred to the trading and profit and loss account in order to arrive at cost of sales:

3	Trading and P&L a/c	Stock	£1,000

Step 3 The trading and profit and loss account cannot be completed (and hence gross profit cannot be calculated) until the closing stock is included.

4	Stock	Trading and P&L a/c	£1,600

After summarising and balancing off, the ledger accounts (cross-referenced to the above summaries) then become as follows.

Stock account

20X7		£	20X7		£
1 Jan	Balance b/d	1,000	31 Dec (3)	Trading and P&L a/c	1,000
31 Dec (4)	Trading and P&L a/c	1,600	31 Dec	Balance c/d	1,600
		2,600			2,600
20X8					
1 Jan	Balance b/d	1,600			

Purchases account

20X7		£	20X7		£
Various dates	Creditors	12,400	31 Dec (1)	Trading and P&L a/c	12,400

Sales account

20X7		£	20X7		£
31 Dec (2)	Trading and P&L a/c	17,700	Various dates	Debtors	17,700

Trading account ('T' form)

20X7		£	20X7		£
31 Dec (1)	Purchases	12,400	31 Dec (2)	Sales	17,700
(2)	Stock	1,000	(4)	Stock	1,600
	Gross profit c/d	5,900			
		19,300			19,300
				Gross profit b/d	5,900

The key points regarding ledger accounts reflecting the closing stock are shown below.

- The sales and the purchases accounts are cleared out to, and summarised in, the trading and profit and loss account.

- Opening stock is cleared out to the trading and profit and loss account and closing stock is entered into the stock account and the trading and profit and loss account.

- The balance on the stock account remains at the end of the period and is listed in the balance sheet under current assets as stock.

- The trading account can be balanced at this stage to show the gross profit figure carried down and brought down.

The above layout of the trading account is not particularly useful, but it assists the appreciation of the actual double entry processes and demonstrates that the trading and profit and loss account is part of the double entry.

A more useful (and by now familiar) layout of the trading and profit and loss account is as follows:

	£	£
Sales		17,700
Opening stock	1,000	
Add: Purchases	12,400	
	13,400	
Less: Closing stock	1,600	
Cost of sales		11,800
Gross profit		5,900

1.4   Stock account

After the financial statements have been completed, it is usual to balance the various ledger accounts. Note particularly the treatment of the stock account. The balance carried down (c/d) is a balance at the end of the year which will be entered on the balance sheet representing closing stock. This is brought down (b/d) at the beginning of the following year, representing the opening stock for the next accounting period. This illustrates two key features in bookkeeping:

- Any balance carried down at the end of an accounting period should be included on the balance sheet.

- Any balance carried down at the end of an accounting period, on an account, will become the opening balance at the beginning of the next accounting period.

Entries are only ever made to the **stock account** at the end of the accounting period, when the opening stock is transferred to the trading and profit and loss account and the closing stock is entered into the stock account.

ACTIVITY 1

The trading position of a simple cash based business for its first week of trading was as follows:

	£
Capital introduced by the owner	1,000
Purchases for cash	800
Sales for cash	900

At the end of the week there were goods left in stock which had cost £300.

Write up the ledger accounts for this first week of trading, including a trading and profit and loss account, and then prepare a vertical trading and profit and loss account as well as a balance sheet.

Feedback to this activity is at the end of the chapter.

ACTIVITY 2

The business described in the previous activity now continues into its second week. Its transactions are as follows:

	£
Sales for cash	1,000
Purchases for cash	1,100

The goods left at the end of this second week originally cost £500.

Write up the ledger accounts for this second week, including the trading and profit and loss account, and then prepare a vertical trading and profit and loss account together with a balance sheet at the end of the second week.

Feedback to this activity is at the end of the chapter.

2   Preparation of financial statements

2.1   Approach

The ledger accounts which you drew up in Activities 1 and 2 may appear complex and bewildering. For examination purposes however, it is not necessary to write up the ledger accounts if the question asks only for the presentation of final accounts.

For example, the information contained in the first example in this chapter would often be given in the form of a trial balance.

Trial balance as at 31 December 20X7

	£	£
Sales		17,700
Stock	1,000	
Purchases	12,400	
Other balances	X	X
	XX	XX

Additional information would be given as follows:

• Stock has been valued at 31 December 20X7 as £1,600.

Remember that the stock shown on the trial balance is *last year's* stock as profit has not yet been computed by transferring sales and purchases to the profit and loss account. This fact should be reinforced by the additional information given concerning closing stock (which is *not* on the trial balance).

Final accounts can be prepared straight from the information given:

Trading and profit and loss account for the year ended 31 December 20X7 (extract)

	£	£
Sales (from TB)		17,700
Opening stock (from TB)	1,000	
Purchases (from TB)	12,400	
	13,400	
Closing stock (from additional information)	1,600	
Cost of sales		11,800
Gross profit		5,900

Balance sheet as at 31 December 20X7 (extract)

	£	£
Current assets		
Stock (from additional information)	1,600	

Example

The trial balance of Elmdale at 31 December 20X8 is as follows:

	Dr	Cr
	£	£
Capital account		8,602
Stock	2,700	
Sales		21,417
Purchases	9,856	
Rates	1,490	
Drawings	4,206	
Electricity	379	
Freehold shop	7,605	
Debtors	2,742	
Creditors		3,617
Cash at bank		1,212
Cash in hand	66	
Sundry expenses	2,100	
Wages and salaries	3,704	
Other balances	34,848	34,848

In addition, Elmdale calculates that closing stock should be valued for accounts purposes at £3,060.

You are required to prepare a trading and profit and loss account for the year ended 31 December 20X8 and a balance sheet at that date.

Solution

Step 1: Remember that the stock in the trial balance is opening stock and goes to the trading account. Stock not on the trial balance is closing stock which goes to the trading account *and* the balance sheet.

Step 2: Deal with the other items on the trial balance.

In the case of trading and profit and loss account items, this entails debiting the relevant accounts and crediting trading and profit and loss account (in the case of income) and debiting trading and profit and loss account and crediting the relevant accounts (in the case of expenses). However as the ledger accounts are not required in a question like this the items will simply be put into the vertical trading and profit and loss account.

Step 2: Deal with the other items on the trial balance.

In the case of trading and profit and loss account items, this entails debiting the relevant accounts and crediting trading and profit and loss account (in the case of income) and debiting trading and profit and loss account and crediting the relevant accounts (in the case of expenses). However as the ledger accounts are not required in a question like this the items will simply be put into the vertical trading and profit and loss account.

The remaining balances are arranged in the vertical balance sheet format.

Step 3:   Prepare the trading and profit and loss account.

Trading and profit and loss account for the year ended 31 December 20X8

	£	£
Sales		21,417
Opening stock	2,700	
Purchases	9,856	
	12,556	
Closing stock	3,060	
Cost of sales		9,496
Gross profit		11,921
Rates	1,490	
Electricity	379	
Wages and salaries	3,704	
Sundry expenses	2,100	
		7,673
Net profit		4,248

Step 4:   Prepare the balance sheet.

Balance sheet as at 31 December 20X8

	£	£
Fixed assets:		
Freehold shop		7,605
Current assets:		
Stock	3,060	
Debtors	2,742	
Cash in hand	66	
	5,868	
Less: Current liabilities:		
Creditors	3,617	
Bank overdraft	1,212	
	4,829	
Net current assets		1,039
		8,644
Capital account:		
Balance at 1 January 20X8		8,602
Net profit	4,248	
Less drawings	4,206	
Retained profit for the year		42
Balance at 31 December 20X8		8,644

Note: remember that the closing stock in the balance sheet must agree with the closing stock in the trading account.

Note that the balance on the trial balance for cash at bank is a credit balance (a liability), and therefore an overdraft.

ACTIVITY 3

H Hillman extracted the following trial balance from his ledger on 31 March 20X6.

	Dr £	Cr £
Light and heat	100	
Sales		6,000
Debtors	2,000	
Wages	600	
Drawings	2,100	
Rent and rates	400	
Postage and stationery	200	
Capital at 1 April 20X5		5,500
Purchases	2,800	
Stock	400	
Creditors		800
Fixtures and fittings	3,500	
Cash	200	
	12,300	12,300

Stock at 31 March 20X6 is valued at £300.

You are required to prepare the accounts of H Hillman, using the vertical format.

Feedback to this activity is at the end of the chapter.

---

3   Stock valuation

3.1   Introduction

So far in examples, we have been given the valuations of stock, normally the opening stock being found on the trial balance, and the closing stock being given in readiness for the final adjustments to that trial balance.

However, in practice it is anything but a simple procedure to arrive at the valuation placed on closing stock, because:

- initially the existence and quantities of stock, have to be ascertained by means of a stocktaking, and

- following on from this, a valuation has to be placed on the stock which, as will be seen, may differ according to which accounting policy a company adopts.

The valuation of stock is governed by accounting standard SSAP 9, *Stocks and Long-Term Contracts*. For this examination you are required to know the provisions relating to stock, but *not* those relating to long-term contracts.

3.2   Definition of stock and work-in-progress

At any point in time most manufacturing and retailing enterprises will hold several categories of stock including:

- goods purchased for resale

- consumable stores (such as oil)

- raw materials and components (used in the production process)

- partly finished goods (usually called **work-in-progress**)

- finished goods (which have been manufactured by the enterprise).

3.3 The matching and prudence concepts

We considered the concept of matching earlier in the chapter to justify the carrying forward of purchases not sold by the end of the accounting period to leave the remaining purchases to be 'matched' with sales.

When it comes to placing a value on the stock carried forward we have a further concept to consider: the **prudence concept**.

The prudence concept requires the exercise of caution in valuing items for inclusion in the accounts.

In the context of the value of stock, the application of the prudence concept means that if goods are expected to be sold below cost after the balance sheet date (for example, because they are damaged or obsolete), account must be taken of the loss in preparing the balance sheet. The stock should therefore be stated in the balance sheet at the lower of cost and net realisable value.

3.4 What is cost?

Cost includes all the expenditure incurred in bringing the product or service to its present location and condition.

Cost includes:

- cost of **purchase** – material costs, import duties, freight;
- cost of **conversion** – this includes **direct costs** and **production overheads**. These terms are explained in the example below.

Example

Gordano Ltd is a small furniture manufacturing company. All of its timber is imported from Scandinavia and there are only three basic products – a dining table, a cupboard and a bookcase. At the end of the year the company has 200 completed bookcases in stock. For final accounts purposes, these will be stated at the lower of cost and net realisable value. How is 'cost' arrived at?

Solution

'Cost' will include several elements:

- **Cost of purchase** – First of all we must identify the timber used in the manufacture of bookcases (as opposed to dining tables and cupboards). The relevant costs will include the £ sterling cost of the timber, the import duty and all the insurance and freight expenses associated with transporting the timber from Scandinavia to the factory.

- **Cost of conversion** – This will include costs which can be directly linked to the bookcases produced during the year. This includes labour costs 'booked' and sundry material costs (e.g. hinges and screws). **Production overheads** present particular problems. Costs such as factory heat and light, salaries of supervisors and depreciation of equipment (explained in detail in Chapter 7) are likely to relate to the three product ranges. These costs must be allocated to these product ranges on a reasonable basis. In particular, any percentage additions to cover overheads must be based on the normal level of production. If this proviso was not made, the stock could be overvalued at the end of a period of low production, because there would be a smaller number of items over which to spread the overhead cost.

These groups of cost must relate to either:

- bookcases sold during the year, or
- bookcases in stock at the year-end (i.e. 200 bookcases).

3.5   What is net realisable value (NRV)?

Net realisable value (NRV) is the revenue (sales proceeds) expected to be earned in the future when the goods are sold, less any costs that will be incurred in selling them. Each individual item or each group of similar items of stock should be stated in financial statements at the lower of cost and net realisable value. At the balance sheet date, it is necessary to make a reasonable estimate of NRV.

In what circumstances do you think that the net realisable value of stocks might be lower than their cost?

Feedback to this activity is at the end of the chapter.

3.6   Methods of arriving at cost

A problem arises when a business makes frequent purchases of the same stock item. Different batches will be purchased at different costs. At the year end some of the items will remain in stock and require to be valued. Without very detailed record keeping, it will not be clear which batches the remaining stock items belong to, and therefore it will not be clear what cost to attribute to them.

If the stock item in question is a very valuable one, it may be sensible to keep very detailed records so that we can track individual units and ascertain their cost one by one. This is the unit cost method referred to below. However, in most cases the value of the stock item will not justify such a complicated exercise. In these cases, we resort to one of a number of 'rules of thumb', described below. The idea is to arrive at an approximation to the actual cost of stock on hand.

1   *Unit cost*

Unit cost: The actual cost of purchasing identifiable units of stock.

This method is only likely to be used in situations where stock items are of high value and individually distinguishable. Examples would include jewellery retailers and art dealers, where in each case the proprietors would need to value each item individually.

2   *FIFO: first-in-first-out*

FIFO: The assumption is made for costing purposes that the first items of stock received are the first items to be sold.

Every time a sale is made the cost of goods sold is identified as representing the cost of the oldest goods remaining in stock. Closing stock at the end of the period therefore consists of the units purchased most recently.

3   *LIFO: last-in-first-out*

This method is the reverse of FIFO. **LIFO:** The assumption for costing purposes is that the last items of stock received are the first items to be sold.

Every time a sale is made, the cost of goods sold is identified as representing the cost of the newest goods remaining in stock.

Contrasting LIFO and FIFO:

- In a period of inflation the newest goods are likely to have cost more than the oldest goods. Hence, by matching the cost of the oldest goods with the sales revenues, FIFO will give a lower cost of goods sold figure, a higher closing stock valuation and a higher reported profit than LIFO.

- LIFO is not generally permitted by accounting standards. This is because LIFO usually does not give a sufficiently close approximation to the actual cost of the stock.

- In theory the matching of cost and revenues should be carried out each time a sale is made. In practice some modifications to this are likely.

DEFINITION

Average cost: Stock is valued at the average price of stock on hand, calculated by dividing the total cost of units by the total number of such units.

4   *Average cost*

Average cost: Stock is valued at the average price of stock on hand, calculated by dividing the total cost of units by the total number of such units.

This calculation can be carried out periodically, or continuously after every purchase. It is a compromise between the extremes of FIFO and LIFO, but it involves much arithmetic.

DEFINITION

Base stock: A fixed unit value is ascribed to a predetermined number of units of stock. Any excess over this number is valued on the basis of some other method (such as FIFO).

5   *Base stock*

Base stock: A fixed unit value is ascribed to a predetermined number of units of stock. Any excess over this number is valued on the basis of some other method (such as FIFO).

This method views the base level of stock as being more in the nature of a fixed asset rather than stock to be sold or consumed. The reasoning behind this is that some stock must always be held in any ongoing business.

To comply with SSAP 9, the method of arriving at cost should give a close approximation to actual cost. This means that methods **1**, **2** and **4** are generally acceptable, but **3** and **5** are not, because they tend to produce a value for stock below its cost if prices are rising.

3.7   Calculation of stock and cost of sales under these methods

Example

A business is commenced on 1 January and purchases are made as follows:

Month	No of units	Unit price £	Value £
Jan	380	2.00	760
Feb	400	2.50	1,000
Mar	350	2.50	875
Apr	420	2.75	1,155
May	430	3.00	1,290
Jun	440	3.25	1,430
	2,420		6,510

During this period, 1,420 articles were sold for £7,000.

1   Compute the cost of stock on hand at 30 June using the following methods:

(a)· FIFO

(b)   LIFO

(c)   average cost.

2   Show the effect of each method on the trading results for the six months.

Solution

1　Stock valuation (stock in hand 2,420 – 1,420 = 1,000 units):

(a)　**FIFO – stock valued at latest purchase prices**

	£
440 articles at £3.25	1,430
430 articles at £3.00	1,290
130 articles at £2.75	357
1,000	3,077

(b)　**LIFO – stock valued at earliest purchase prices**

	£
380 articles at £2.00	760
620 articles at £2.50	1,550
1,000	2,310

(c)　**Average cost – stock valued at average purchase price**

$$\frac{\text{Total value}}{\text{Total number of articles}} = \frac{£6,510}{2,420} = £2.69 \text{ per unit}$$

∴ 1,000 articles at £2.69 = £2,690.

2　Effect of different methods of computing cost of stock in hand on trading results

	No of units	(a) FIFO £	£	(b) LIFO £	£	(c) Average £	£
Sales	1,420		7,000		7,000		7,000
Purchases	2,420	6,510		6,510		6,510	
Less: Closing stock	1,000	3,077		2,310		2,690	
Cost of goods sold	1,420		3,433		4,200		3,820
Gross profit			3,567		2,800		3,180

KEY POINT

It is vital to adhere to the same method of stock valuation from one period to the next.

Each of the above is a means of determining the cost of closing stock. As can be seen they each give rise to different gross profits. It is therefore vital to adhere to the same method of stock valuation from one period to the next, so as to give a meaningful trend of trading results (i.e. the consistency concept).

4　Other matters

4.1　Disclosure of stocks and WIP in the financial statements

SSAP 9 *Stocks and Long-Term Contracts* stipulates a number of requirements relating to stock:

- definition of cost and NRV (covered above)
- use of cost flow assumptions (FIFO, LIFO, as above)

- accounting for long-term contracts (not examined at this level)
- disclosure of information in the financial statements.

The disclosures relate to the balance sheet and not the profit and loss account. The disclosures provide information regarding the degree to which stock consists of raw materials, which may take some time to be converted into finished goods and then sold, and other stages of the manufacturing process.

There are three main headings:

- raw materials
- work-in-progress
- finished goods and goods for resale.

4.2   Continuous and period end stock records

In preparing the financial statements, the calculation of the closing stock figure can be a major exercise for a business. The business may need to count its stock at the balance sheet date and prepare **period end stock records** which record the results of the stock count.

An alternative would be to have records which show the amount of stock at any date, i.e. **continuous** stock records. These records may take a variety of forms but in essence, a record of each line of stock would be maintained showing all the receipts and issues for that stock line.

The merits of continuous stock records are as follows:

- There is better information for stock control.
- It avoids excessive build up of certain lines of stock and having insufficient stock of other lines.
- There is less work to be done to calculate stock at the end of the accounting period.

The merits of period end stock records are as follows.

- It is cheaper in most situations than the costs of maintaining continuous stock records.
- Even if there is a continuous stock record, there will still be a need to check the accuracy of the information on record by having a physical check of some of the stock lines.

Conclusion

In this chapter we have considered the preparation of financial statements – the trading and profit and loss account and balance sheet. The trading and profit and loss account is in fact a ledger account and it is important to understand the accounting entries that are necessary for stock at the end of each accounting period.

Stock is a major adjustment required to the information stored in the ledger accounts and summarised in the trial balance in order to prepare the profit and loss account and balance sheet.

SELF-TEST
QUESTIONS

Closing stock

1　Which accounting concept influences the calculation of gross profit? (1.1)

2　Is it the trading and profit and loss account or the balance sheet that is an account in the double entry accounting system? (1.2)

3　Is opening stock a debit or a credit balance on the stock account? (1.3)

4　What is the double entry for closing stock? (1.3)

Preparation of financial statements

5　Is an overdraft an asset or a liability? (2.1)

Stock valuation

6　What is the general definition for the cost of stock? (3.4)

7　What are production overheads? (3.4)

8　Will FIFO or LIFO give a higher cost of sales figure when prices are rising? (3.6)

Other matters

9　What three headings need to be disclosed in the balance sheet in order to comply with SSAP 9? (4.1)

MULTIPLE-
CHOICE
QUESTIONS

Question 1

SSAP 9 *Stocks and Long-term Contracts* defines the items that may be included in computing the value of a stock of finished goods manufactured by a business.

Which one of the following lists consists only of items which may be included in the balance sheet value of such stock according to SSAP 9?

A　Foreman's wages, carriage inwards, carriage outwards, raw materials

B　Raw materials, carriage inwards, costs of storage of finished goods, plant depreciation

C　Plant depreciation, carriage inwards, raw materials, foreman's wages

D　Carriage outwards, raw materials, foreman's wages, plant depreciation.

Question 2

The closing stock of X Limited amounted to £116,400 *excluding* the following two stock lines:

1　400 items which had cost £4 each. All were sold after the balance sheet date for £3 each, with selling expenses of £200 for the batch.

2　200 different items which had cost £30 each. These items were found to be defective at the balance sheet date. Rectification work after the balance sheet amounted to £1,200, after which they were sold for £35 each, with selling expenses totalling £300.

Which of the following total figures should appear in the balance sheet for X Ltd's stock?

A　£122,300

B　£121,900

C　£122,900

D　£122,300

For the answers to these questions, see the 'Answers' section at the end of the book.

Blabbermouth

Blabbermouth extracted the following trial balance from his ledger on 31 March 20X7:

	Dr £	Cr £
Light and heat	100	
Debtors	8,250	
Sales		25,375
Wages	8,237	
Drawings	3,500	
Rent and rates	500	
Postage and stationery	727	
Capital at 1 April 20X6		18,250
Purchases	17,280	
Stock	4,100	
Creditors		7,247
Fixtures and fittings	2,100	
Cash	6,078	
	50,872	50,872

Stock at 31 March 20X7 is valued at £5,200.

Prepare the final accounts of Blabbermouth, using the vertical format.   **(14 marks)**

Alpha

From the following list of balances taken from the books of Alpha and the additional information given, you are required to prepare the trading and profit and loss account for the year ended 31 December and a balance sheet as at that date:

	£
Sales	39,468
Insurance	580
Plant repairs	110
Rent and rates	1,782
Motor van	980
Plant	2,380
Purchases	27,321
Stock at 1 Jan (opening)	3,655
Wages	3,563
Discount allowed to customers	437
Motor van expenses	1,019
Shop fittings	1,020
General expenses	522
Capital account – balance 1 Jan (opening)	2,463
Sundry debtors	3,324
Sundry creditors	4,370
Cash on hand	212
Personal drawings	2,820

Additional information:

(1)   The difference in the trial balance is the bank balance at 31 December.

(2)   Stock at 31 December amounted to £3,123.

(3)   Adjust for cost of goods taken by Alpha for personal use amounting to £220.

(25 marks)

For the answers to these questions, see the 'Answers' section at the end of the book.

Step 1   Record the transactions for the week in the ledger accounts.

Cash

	£		£
Capital	1,000	Purchases	800
Sales	900		

Capital

	£		£
		Cash	1,000

Purchases

	£		£
Cash	800		

Sales

	£		£
		Cash	900

Step 2   Balance off the accounts. Note that as only the cash account has more than one transaction this is the only one that needs to be balanced. The total on the remaining accounts is simply the value of the single transaction.

Cash

	£		£
Capital	1,000	Purchases	800
Sales	900	Balance c/d	1,100
	1,900		1,900
Balance b/d	1,100		

Step 3   The sales and purchases should be transferred to the trading and P&L a/c.

Sales

	£		£
Trading and P&L a/c	900	Cash	900

Purchases

	£		£
Cash	800	Trading and P&L a/c	800

Trading and P&L a/c

	£		£
Purchases	800	Sales	900

Step 4   As this is the first week of trading for this business there is no opening stock but the closing stock must be accounted for by debiting the stock account (an asset) and crediting the trading and profit and loss account.
The trading and P&L a/c can then be balanced off to give the figure for gross profit.

Stock

	£		£
Trading and P&L a/c	300		

Trading and P&L a/c

	£		£
Purchases	800	Sales	900
Gross profit c/d	400	Closing stock	300
	1,200		1,200
		Gross profit b/d	400

Step 5 The trading and P&L a/c can be prepared in vertical form simply by rearranging the ledger account.

Trading and profit and loss account for week 1

	£	£
Sales		900
Cost of goods sold:		
Purchases	800	
Less: Closing stock	300	
		500
Gross profit		400

Step 6 The balance sheet can then be prepared by listing all of the remaining balances from the ledger accounts.

Balance sheet at the end of week 1

	£
Stock	300
Cash	1,100
	1,400
Capital	1,000
Profit for the week	400
	1,400

FEEDBACK TO ACTIVITY 2

Step 1 Write up the ledger accounts for the second week. Remember that at the end of week 1 there was £1,100 of cash remaining and this will be shown as the opening balance on the cash account. (Opening balances will be dealt with in more detail later in this chapter.)

There are no opening balances on the sales or purchases accounts as these were cleared out to the trading and profit and loss account at the end of week 1.

Once the ledger entries have been written up the cash account can be balanced off.

Cash

	£		£
Balance b/d	1,100	Purchases	1,100
Sales	1,000	Balance c/d	1,000
	2,100		2,100
Balance b/d	1,000		

Sales

	£		£
		Cash	1,000

Purchases

	£		£
Cash	1,100		

Step 2 Transfer the balances on the sales and purchases account to the trading and profit and loss account.

Sales

	£		£
Trading and P&L a/c	1,000	Cash	1,000

Purchases

	£		£
Cash	1,100	Trading and P&L a/c	1,100

Trading and P&L a/c

	£		£
Purchases	1,100	Sales	1,000

Step 3 Remember that this time as well as there being some closing stock there is also some opening stock, i.e. the closing stock at the end of week 1. This will still be a balance on the stock account at the end of week 2 and must be transferred to the trading and profit and loss account.

Stock

	£		£
Balance b/d	300	Trading and P&L a/c	300

Trading and P&L a/c

	£		£
Purchases	1,100	Sales	1,000
Opening stock	300		

Step 4 The closing stock at the end of week 2 must then be accounted for by debiting the stock account and crediting the trading and profit and loss account.

Stock

	£		£
Balance b/d	300	Trading and P&L a/c	300
Trading and P&L a/c	500		

Trading and P&L a/c

	£		£
Purchases	1,100	Sales	1,000
Opening stock	300	Closing stock	500
Gross profit c/d	100		
			1,500
	1,500		
		Gross profit b/d	100

Step 5 Prepare a vertical trading and profit and loss account.

Trading and profit and loss account for week 2

	£	£
Sales		1,000
Cost of goods sold:		
Opening stock	300	
Purchases	1,100	
	1,400	
Less: Closing stock	500	
		900
Gross profit		100

Step 6 List the remaining balances in the balance sheet.

Balance sheet at the end of week 2

	£
Stock	500
Cash	1,000
	1,500
Capital at start of week 2	1,400
Profit for week 2	100
	1,500

Note: the capital at the beginning of week 2 is the total capital from the end of week 1, that is the opening capital of £1,000 plus the £400 of profit made in week 1.

The trading and profit and loss account and balance sheet are shown below.

Trading and profit and loss account for the year ended 31 March 20X6

	£	£
Sales		6,000
Opening stock	400	
Purchases	2,800	
	3,200	
Less: Closing stock	300	
Cost of sales		2,900
Gross profit		3,100
Wages	600	
Rent and rates	400	
Postage and stationery	200	
Light and heat	100	
		1,300
Net profit		1,800

Balance sheet as at 31 March 20X6

	£	£
Fixed assets:		
Fixtures and fittings		3,500
Current assets:		
Stock	300	
Debtors	2,000	
Cash	200	
	2,500	
Less: Current liabilities:		
Creditors	800	
		1,700
		5,200
Capital employed:		
Capital at 1 April 20X5		5,500
Net profit for the year	1,800	
Less drawings	2,100	
Retained loss for the year		(300)
Capital at 31 March 20X6		5,200

Notice that the amount of Hillman's drawings (£2,100) exceeds the amount of profit earned by the business (£1,800). Instead of the usual retained profit (increasing the amount of opening capital) we have a retained loss, which reduces the opening capital. Hillman's capital account has therefore fallen from £5,500 at the start of the year to £5,200 at the end.

FEEDBACK TO ACTIVITY 4

NRV may be relevant in special cases, such as where goods are slow-moving, damaged or obsolete. However, most items of stock will be stated at cost.

Chapter 5
ACCRUALS, PREPAYMENTS, CASH AND LIABILITIES

In this chapter, we examine the expenses and miscellaneous income of a business. The main point we are concerned with is that the expenses incurred by a business during an accounting period, and the income it earns, may not correspond exactly to the sums of money paid and received during the period. For example, suppose that a business pays £3,000 office rent on 1 May 20X1, covering the quarter to 31 July. If the business has a year end of 30 June only part of the rent payment relates to the year ended 30 June 20X1, even though the whole amount has been paid in that year.

The profit and loss account must reflect the income earned and expenditure incurred in the period, not the cash received and paid out. This chapter explains the accounting adjustments required to achieve this objective.

Such year end adjustments to expense items can take the form of an entire examination question themselves or (more likely) may form part of a larger question on some other topic such as the accounts of a sole trader.

Objectives

By the time you have finished this chapter you should be able to:

- explain the meaning of the accruals or matching concept
- understand the practical implications of the accruals concept for items of expense and miscellaneous income
- calculate the amounts that should appear in the profit and loss account and balance sheet where there are accruals or prepayments of expenses and income
- carry out the double entry required to account for accrued and prepaid expenses and miscellaneous income
- explain the meaning of liabilities and understand where liabilities and cash appear in the balance sheet.

1   The accruals concept

1.1   A fundamental accounting concept

The accruals or matching concept is identified as a pervasive accounting concept by Financial Reporting Standard (FRS) 18 *Accounting policies*. The accruals concept demands that all of the expenses involved in making the sales for a period should be matched with the sales income and dealt with in the period in which the sales themselves are accounted for.

Why should cash received and paid differ from income earned and expenditure incurred? This is best understood by means of some examples.

- Sales revenue is earned when a sale is made to a customer. However, if the sale is on credit terms it may be some time before the customer pays the amount owing.
- Similarly, expenditure on stationery, say, is incurred when the supplier delivers the goods. The goods may not be paid for until some time later.
- Some items of expenditure and income relate to periods that exceed the boundaries of an accounting year end. An example has already been given of an office rent payment covering the period 1 May to 31 July 20X1. If the business has a year end of 30 June, the payment must be accounted for partly in year ended 30 June 20X1,

and partly in year ended 30 June 20X2, even though the whole payment is made on 1 May 20X1.

Below we look in more detail at some examples of this problem.

Sales

The sales for an accounting period are included in the profit and loss account when they are made. This means that when a sale is made on credit, it is recognised in the profit and loss account when the goods are delivered or the service is rendered to the customer, rather than waiting until the cash for the sale is received. This is done by setting up a debtor in the balance sheet for the amount of cash that is due from the sale (debit debtor and credit sales).

Purchases

Similarly, purchases are matched to the period in which they are made by accounting for all credit purchases when they take place and setting up a creditor in the balance sheet for the amount due (debit purchases and credit creditor).

Cost of sales

The major cost involved in making sales in a period is the actual cost of the goods sold. As well as including purchases in the cost of goods sold, the cost of any closing items of stock at the end of an accounting period must be carried forward to the following period, to be matched with the actual sales of those items. Equally, any items of stock that were not sold in the previous period are brought forward as opening stock in the trading account to be matched against their sale in the current period by adding their cost to the cost of the purchases for the period.

Expenses

The expenses of the period that the business has incurred in making its sales, such as rent, electricity and telephone, must also be matched with the sales for the period. This means that the actual expense incurred in the period should be included in the profit and loss account, rather than the amount of the expense that has been paid for in cash.

- If the rental due on a factory is £5,000 every quarter, then the annual rental expense will be £20,000 whatever the pattern of cash payments for the rental.

- If a business has an accounting year to 31 December 20X1 and during that year has paid £1,000 of electricity bills and has outstanding a bill for the quarter from 1 October to 31 December 20X1 of £300, then the electricity expense incurred by the business is £1,300 for the year to 31 December 20X1.

- If, in the previous example, the outstanding bill was for the period from 1 November 20X1 to 31 January 20X2, then an estimate of the electricity expense for the period to 31 December 20X1 would be

$$£1,000 + \left(\tfrac{2}{3} \times £300\right) = £1,200$$

- If a business with an accounting year end of 31 December 20X1 pays for 18 months of insurance on its buildings on 1 January 20X1 at a total cost of £3,000 then the insurance expense for the year to 31 December 20X1 would be

$$\tfrac{12}{18} \times £3,000 = £2,000$$

ACTIVITY 1

Calculate the appropriate expense for the accounting period in the following examples:

1   For the year to 30 September 20X5 a business paid heating bills of £2,700. At 30 September 20X5, the year end, there was an unpaid bill outstanding of £600 for the three months to 30 November 20X5.

2   A business paid its rates for the six months to 31 March 20X3 £1,200, for the six months to 30 September 20X3 £1,800 and for the six months to 31 March 20X4 £1,800. If the business's year end is 31 December 20X3 what is the rates expense for that accounting year?

Feedback to this activity is at the end of the chapter.

2   Accrued expenses

2.1   The nature and purpose of an accrual

DEFINITION

An **accrued expense** is an item of expense that has been incurred during the accounting period, but for which no payment has been made.

An **accrued expense** is an item of expense that has been incurred during the accounting period, but for which no payment has been made.

In order to ensure that the full expenses of the period have been included in the profit and loss account, the accountant must ensure that the expense accounts include not only those items that have been invoiced and paid for during the period, but any outstanding amounts due. In some instances, a bill or invoice will have been received for any outstanding amounts. In other instances, any additional expense items will need to be estimated from previous years and earlier bills or invoices.

Example with no opening accrual

John Simnel's business has an accounting year end of 31 December 20X1. He rents factory space at a rental cost of £5,000 per quarter payable in arrears. During the year to 31 December 20X1 his cash payments of rent have been as follows:

	£
31 March (for quarter to 31 March 20X1)	5,000
29 June (for quarter to 30 June 20X1)	5,000
2 October (for quarter to 30 September 20X1)	5,000

The final payment due on 31 December 20X1 for the quarter to that date was not paid until 4 January 20X2.

It should be quite clear that the rental expense for John Simnel's business for the year to 31 December 20X1 is £20,000 (4 × £5,000), even though the final payment for the year was not made until after the year end. It should also be noted that at 31 December 20X1 John Simnel's business owes the landlord £5,000 of rental for the period from 1 October to 31 December 20X1.

Solution

Step 1   In order to account for this situation the cash payments would first be entered into the factory rent account.

Factory rent			
20X1	£	*20X1*	£
31 Mar Cash	5,000		
29 June Cash	5,000		
2 Oct Cash	5,000		

Step 2 The charge to the profit and loss account that is required at 31 December 20X1 is £20,000 and this is entered into the account on the credit side (the debit is the expense in the profit and loss account).

Factory rent

20X1		£	20X1		£
31 Mar	Cash	5,000	31 Dec	P&L a/c	20,000
29 June	Cash	5,000			
2 Oct	Cash	5,000			

Step 3 In order for the account to balance, a further debit entry of £5,000 is required.

- This is in fact the balance carried down on the account.
- The double entry is to debit the account above the total with £5,000 and show a credit in the account below the total.
- This gives a brought down credit balance representing the amount owed to the landlord for the final quarter's rent.

Step 3 In order for the account to balance, a further debit entry of £5,000 is required.

- This is in fact the balance carried down on the account.
- The double entry is to debit the account above the total with £5,000 and show a credit in the account below the total.
- This gives a brought down credit balance representing the amount owed to the landlord for the final quarter's rent.

Factory rent

20X1		£	20X1		£
31 Mar	Cash	5,000	31 Dec	P&L a/c	20,000
29 June	Cash	5,000			
2 Oct	Cash	5,000			
31 Dec	Bal c/d	5,000			
		20,000			20,000
			20X2		
			1 Jan	Bal b/d	5,000

- By this method the correct expense, £20,000 has been charged to the profit and loss account under the accruals concept, and the amount of £5,000 owed to the landlord has been recognised as a credit balance on the account (i.e. a liability).
- This credit balance would be listed in the balance sheet under the heading of current liabilities and described as an accrued expense.

Example with an opening accrual

During the year to 31 December 20X2, John Simnel's rental charge remained the same and his payments were as follows:

	£
4 January (for quarter to 31 December 20X1)	5,000
28 March (for quarter to 31 March 20X2)	5,000
28 June (for quarter to 30 June 20X2)	5,000
4 October (for quarter to 30 September 20X2)	5,000
23 December (for quarter to 31 December 20X2)	5,000

The first step in accounting for these transactions is to enter the cash payments in the factory rent account. Note that there is already a brought down balance on the account at 1 January 20X2 being the accrued expense of £5,000, a creditor and therefore a credit balance, at 31 December 20X1.

Factory rent

20X2	£	20X2	£
4 Jan Cash	5,000	1 Jan Bal b/d	5,000
28 Mar Cash	5,000		
28 June Cash	5,000		
4 Oct Cash	5,000		
23 Dec Cash	5,000		

Even though £25,000 has been paid in cash during the year the profit and loss account expense is still only £20,000 (4 × £5,000). When this transfer to the profit and loss account is made the account will balance at 31 December 20X2. There is no accrued expense to be carried forward this year since the amount due for the final quarter of the year was paid before the year end.

Factory rent

20X2	£	20X2	£
4 Jan Cash	5,000	1 Jan Bal b/d	5,000
28 Mar Cash	5,000		
28 June Cash	5,000		
4 Oct Cash	5,000		
23 Dec Cash	5,000	31 Dec P&L a/c (bal fig)	20,000
	25,000		25,000

ACTIVITY 2

A business has paid the following electricity bills during the year to 31 December 20X6.

	£
28 Feb: For the three months to 28 February 20X6	300
31 May: For the three months to 31 May 20X6	540
31 Aug: For the three months to 31 August 20X6	220
30 Nov: For the three months to 30 November 20X6	360

It is estimated that the electricity used in December 20X6 totalled £120.

Write up the electricity account for the year ended 31 December 20X6.

Feedback to this activity is at the end of the chapter.

3   Prepaid expenses

KEY POINT

A **prepaid expense** is an item of expense that has been paid during the current accounting period, but which relates to the next accounting period.

3.1   The nature and purpose of a prepayment

A **prepaid expense** is an item of expense that has been paid during the current accounting period, but which relates to the next accounting period.

The accountant must *exclude* any items of expense that relate to future periods, even if they have been paid in the current period.

Example with no opening prepayment

John Simnel also pays insurance on the factory that he rents and this is paid in advance. His payments during 20X1 for this insurance were as follows:

	£
1 January (for three months to 31 March 20X1)	800
28 March (for six months to 30 September 20X1)	1,800
2 October (for six months to 31 March 20X2)	1,800

The insurance expense for the year to 31 December 20X1 can be calculated as follows:

	£
1 January to 31 March 20X1	800
1 April to 30 September 20X1	1,800
1 October to 31 December 20X1 ($\frac{3}{6} \times 1{,}800$)	900
	3,500

The remaining £900 that was paid on 2 October is a prepaid expense. It will not be charged to the profit and loss account for the year to 31 December 20X1. It has the characteristics of a debtor, the insurance company effectively owing £900 of insurance services to John Simnel at 31 December 20X1.

Solution

Step 1 In order to account for the insurance expense, the cash payments should be entered first into the factory insurance account.

Factory insurance

20X1		£	20X1		£
1 Jan	Cash	800			
28 Mar	Cash	1,800			
2 Oct	Cash	1,800			

Step 2
- The charge to the profit and loss account calculated above as £3,500 is then entered in the account and in order for the account to balance a further credit entry of £900 is required.

- The double entry is to credit the account above the total with £900 and put the debit entry in below the total at 1 Jan 20X2.

- This is the prepayment that is to be carried down and will appear as a brought down debit balance or debtor.

Factory insurance

20X1		£	20X1		£
1 Jan	Cash	800			
28 Mar	Cash	1,800	31 Dec	P&L a/c	3,500
2 Oct	Cash	1,800	31 Dec	Bal c/d	900
		4,400			4,400
20X2					
1 Jan	Bal b/d	900			

- This has given the correct charge to the profit and loss account of £3,500 for the year to 31 December 20X1 and has recognised that there is a prepayment of £900 at 31 December 20X1.

- The £900 balance will appear in the balance sheet under the heading of prepayments or prepaid expenses.

Example with opening prepayment

In writing up expense accounts, care must be taken to include any opening balances on the account which were accruals or prepayments at the end of the previous year. For example, John Simnel pays his annual rates bill of £4,000 in two equal instalments of £2,000 each on 1 April and 1 October each year. His rates account for the year to 31 December 20X1 would therefore look like this.

Rates

20X1		£	20X1		£
1 Jan	Bal b/d ($\frac{3}{6} \times$ £2,000)	1,000			
			31 Dec	P&L a/c (bal fig)	4,000
1 April	Cash	2,000	31 Dec	Bal c/d ($\frac{3}{6} \times$ £2,000)	1,000
1 Oct	Cash	2,000			
		─────			─────
		5,000			5,000
		─────			─────

Note that at 1 January there is an opening debit balance on the account of £1,000. This is the three months' rates from 1 January 20X1 to 31 March 20X1 that had been paid for on 1 October 20X0. You were not specifically told this opening balance but would be expected to work it out from the information given.

The treatment of a prepaid expense is to credit the expense account with the amount of the prepayment, thereby reducing the expense to be charged to the profit and loss account, and to carry the balance forward as a prepayment in the balance sheet.

4   Examination-style problems

Exam questions can be more complicated than the examples given above, with both brought down and carried down accruals and prepayments. An example might use a telephone expense because the telephone bill will usually be made up of two elements. There is a charge for the rental of the lines, which will normally be paid in advance, and a further charge for the actual calls, paid in arrears.

Example

The details of John Simnel's telephone bills for 20X1 are as follows:

	£
Quarterly rental payable in advance on 1 February, 1 May, 1 August and 1 November each year	60
Calls paid in arrears for previous three months	
1 February 20X1	120
1 May 20X1	99
1 August 20X1	144
1 November 20X1	122
1 February 20X2	132

His telephone account for the year to 31 December 20X1 is to be written up.

Solution

Step 1   Any opening balances for accruals or prepayments at the beginning of the year should be calculated and then entered into the account.

- The opening debit balance represents the prepayment of the rental at 31 December 20X0. On 1 November 20X0 a payment of £60 would have been made to cover the period from 1 November 20X0 to 31 January

20X1. The amount of the 20X1 expense paid in 20X0 is therefore $\frac{1}{3} \times £60 = £20$.

- The opening credit balance represents the calls made in November and December 20X0 that were not paid for until 1 February 20X1. This can be estimated as $\frac{2}{3} \times £120 = £80$.

Telephone

20X1		£	20X1		£
1 Jan	Bal b/d	20	1 Jan	Bal b/d	80

Step 2 The cash payments made during the year should be entered into the account.

Telephone

20X1		£	20X1		£
1 Jan	Bal b/d	20	1 Jan	Bal b/d	80
1 Feb	Cash – rental	60			
1 Feb	Cash – calls	120			
1 May	Cash – rental	60			
1 May	Cash – calls	99			
1 Aug	Cash – rental	60			
1 Aug	Cash – calls	144			
1 Nov	Cash – rental	60			
1 Nov	Cash – calls	122			

Step 3 Any closing accruals and prepayments should be calculated and entered into the account.

- There is a closing prepayment of telephone rental. £60 was paid on 1 November 20X1 for the following three months rental. This covers November and December 20X1 as well as January 20X2. The prepayment is the amount that relates to January 20X2 $\frac{1}{3} \times £60 = £20$.

- The accrued expense at 31 December 20X1 is for November and December's calls that will not be paid for until 1 February 20X2. These can be estimated as $\frac{2}{3} \times £132 = £88$.

- Finally the profit and loss account charge can be entered as the balancing figure in the account.

Telephone

20X1		£	20X1		£
1 Jan	Bal b/d	20	1 Jan	Bal b/d	80
1 Feb	Cash – rental	60			
1 Feb	Cash – calls	120			
1 May	Cash – rental	60			
1 May	Cash – calls	99			
1 Aug	Cash – rental	60			
1 Aug	Cash – calls	144			
1 Nov	Cash – rental	60			
1 Nov	Cash – calls	122	31 Dec	P&L a/c (bal fig)	733
31 Dec	Bal c/d (accrual)	88	31 Dec	Bal c/d (prepayment)	20
		833			833
20X2			20X2		
1 Jan	Bal b/d	20	1 Jan	Bal b/d	88

Step 4 The profit and loss account expense that was included in the account as a balancing figure could be proved although this is not generally necessary in actual questions.

	£
Rental charge for 1 January to 31 December 20X1 (4 × 60)	240
Calls:	
1 January to 31 January 20X1 ($\frac{1}{3} \times 120$)	40
1 February to 30 April 20X1	99
1 May to 31 July 20X1	144
1 August to 31 October 20X1	122
1 November to 31 December 20X1 ($\frac{2}{3} \times 132$)	88
	733

5   Miscellaneous income

So far all of the examples have concerned expenses of the business as these are the most common areas for accruals and prepayments to occur. However some organisations also have sources of miscellaneous income which may also be prepaid or accrued.

Example

John Simnel sublets part of his factory space for a quarterly rental in advance of £900.

The payments are due on 1 March, 1 June, 1 September and 1 December each year and are always paid on time. The rental receivable account for the year to 31 December 20X1 will show both an opening and a closing prepayment of rental of ($\frac{2}{3} \times £900$) = £600. However, the account is showing income (rather than an expense) and therefore income received in advance is effectively a creditor. The opening prepayment will therefore be a credit balance brought down and the closing prepayment a debit balance carried down and credit balance brought down on 1 January 20X2.

The cash entries are also cash receipts and therefore will be credit entries in the rental income account (debit in the cash account).

The income which will be credited to the profit and loss account (debit the rental income account) will be £3,600 (4 × £900).

KEY POINT

Income received in advance is effectively a creditor on the balance sheet.

Rental income

20X1		£	20X1			£
			1 Jan	Bal b/d		600
			1 Mar	Cash		900
			1 June	Cash		900
31 Dec	P&L a/c	3,600	1 Sept	Cash		900
31 Dec	Bal c/d	600	1 Dec	Cash		900
		4,200				4,200
			20X2			
			1 Jan	Bal b/d		600

The £600 credit balance brought down at 31 December 20X1 would be shown in the balance sheet as a creditor and described as **income received in advance** or **deferred income** or **deferred revenue**.

A business receives rental income in cash of £2,000 on 30 June 20X4 and at its year end of 30 September 20X4 there is another £1,500 of rental income due which has not yet been received. Write up the ledger account for rental income for the year ended 30 September 20X4.

Feedback to this activity is at the end of the chapter.

6   Liabilities and cash

6.1   Definition and examples of liabilities

Liabilities are financial obligations of a business arising from transactions or events which have taken place by the balance sheet date. Examples of liabilities are trade creditors, loans from a bank, and accruals made at the year end before an invoice has been received.

6.2   Distinction between current and long-term liabilities

It is conventional to distinguish between current and long-term liabilities when preparing a balance sheet. The distinction is useful information to a user of the accounts as he can better determine the ability of the business to pay the liabilities when they become due for payment.

A **current liability** is a liability which is payable within 12 months of the balance sheet date. A long-term liability is any other liability.

This rule about defining liabilities is precisely applied. If a liability is due for payment after 12 months and one day, it is shown as a long-term liability.

6.3   Disclosure of liabilities on the balance sheet

Liabilities are disclosed under the two headings: current and long-term. Other terms may be used for long-term such as 'non-current'.

It is mainly loans which are shown under the heading 'long-term'. Most other liabilities are due for payment quite quickly, e.g. trade creditors typically have a 30-day settlement, and bank overdrafts are technically repayable on demand (i.e. when the bank asks for the money back).

The two groups of liabilities appear in different places in the balance sheet. Current liabilities are deducted from the total of current assets to show net current assets. Long-term liabilities are usually shown as a deduction to arrive at net assets or may be shown as additions to capital employed in the business. The latter presentation is rarely adopted in the UK.

6.4   Bank and cash balances in a balance sheet

Bank and cash balances are the most liquid item that a business possesses. It is conventional to show them as the last item under current assets. Cash at the bank and cash in hand (i.e. actually in the form of cash at the balance sheet date) are often shown as one item in the balance sheet under the heading 'cash at bank and in hand'.

A business may have more than one type of bank account, even with the same bank. A current account for example will deal with all the trading transactions, and a deposit account may be used to store temporary surpluses of money so that interest can be earned. When some of the cash is required to pay for trading transactions it will be transferred back from the deposit account to the current account. It can happen that such transfers are not made in time with the consequence that the current account becomes overdrawn. If this happens at the balance sheet date, it is important to show the overdraft as a current liability and the deposit account as a current asset, i.e. the two amounts should not be netted off.

7   Liabilities and provisions

A liability should be distinguished from a provision. The term 'provision' applies in two situations:

- Where an amount is written off to provide for the diminution in value of an asset (for example, a depreciation provision or a doubtful debts provision), or

- Where an amount is retained to provide for a known liability whose amount cannot be determined with accuracy (for example, a provision for a contingent liability).

Provisions are treated as an expense in arriving at the net profit for a period.

Conclusion

This chapter has examined the accruals (or matching) concept applied to the expenses and miscellaneous income of a business.

SELF-TEST
QUESTIONS

The accruals concept

[handwritten: all the expenses involved in making the sales for a period should matched with the sales income and dealt with in the correspondent accounting period.]

1   What is meant by the accruals or matching concept? (1.1)

[handwritten: 18 accounting policies]

2   Which Financial Reporting Standard (FRS) introduces the matching concept? (1.1)

[handwritten: Debtors]

3   When a sale is made on credit what is the other side of the double entry? (1.1)

4   How is the cost of sales expense matched to the sales for the period? (1.1)

Accrued expenses

5   What is the definition of an accrued expense? (2.1) *[handwritten: it is an item of expense that has been incurred during the accounting period but for which no payment has been made.]*

Prepaid expenses

6   What is the definition of a prepaid expense? (3.1) *[handwritten: has been paid during the current accounting period but relates to the next accounting period]*

Miscellaneous income

7   If income is received in advance will this be shown as a debtor or a creditor in the balance sheet? (5)

EXAM-TYPE
QUESTIONS

Question 1: Dundee Engineering

Dundee Engineering has a number of motor vehicles that are used within the business. The expenses of running these vehicles are recorded in the motor expenses and insurance account. At 1 May 20X7 there were garage bills accrued of £478 and insurance that had been prepaid of £290. During the year to 30 April 20X8 the following transactions took place.

	£
30 June 20X7 paid garage bills	698
1 September 20X7 paid insurance for half of the motor vehicles for the year to 31 August 20X8	3,480
1 December 20X7 paid insurance for remaining motor vehicles for the year to 30 November	3,900
At 30 April 20X8 there were garage bills unpaid totalling £356.	

You are required to write up the motor expenses and insurance account for the year ended 30 April 20X8.   **(12 marks)**

Question 2: Heilbronn Properties

Heilbronn Properties has purchased a number of different properties over the years that it has been in business, financed by a variety of loans. Some of the interest on the loans is paid in arrears and some in advance.

Several of these properties are rented out to tenants some of whom pay their rent in advance and some in arrears.

Interest payable and prepaid and rental due and received in advance at the beginning and end of Heilbronn Properties' accounting year are as follows:

	31 July 20X4	31 July 20X5
	£	£
Interest payable	12,000	14,500
Interest prepaid	8,000	6,400
Rental due from tenants	15,000	19,000
Rental received in advance from tenants	3,000	2,500

During the year to 31 July 20X5 the amount of interest payable charged to the profit and loss account was £56,000 and the cash collected from rental tenants was £116,000.

Required:

Write up the interest payable account and the rental income account for the year ended 31 July 20X5.   **(13 marks)**

For the answers to these questions, see the 'Answers' section at the end of the book.

FEEDBACK TO ACTIVITY 1

The solutions to the examples given are as follows:

1   £2,700 + ($\frac{1}{3}$ × £600) = £2,900

2

	£
Rates for 1 January to 31 March 20X3 ($\frac{3}{6}$ × £1,200)	600
Rates for 1 April to 30 September 20X3	1,800
Rates for 1 October to 31 December 20X3 ($\frac{3}{6}$ × 1,800)	900
Rates expense for the year to 31 December 20X3	3,300

FEEDBACK TO ACTIVITY 2

Step 1   Calculate the opening accrual as at 31 December 20X5. If the bill for the three months to 28 February 20X6 is £300 then the amount that relates to December 20X5 (the opening accrual) is $\frac{1}{3}$ × £300 = £100.

Enter the opening accrual in the ledger account.

Electricity

20X6	£	20X6		£
		1 Jan	Bal b/d	100

Step 2   Enter the cash payments in the ledger account.

Electricity

20X6		£	20X6		£
28 Feb	Cash	300	1 Jan	Bal b/d	100
31 May	Cash	540			
31 Aug	Cash	220			
30 Nov	Cash	360			

Step 3   Calculate and enter the closing accrual (in this instance the amount for December 20X6 is given as £120).

Enter the profit and loss account transfer as a balancing figure.

Electricity

20X6		£	20X6		£
28 Feb	Cash	300	1 Jan	Bal b/d	100
31 May	Cash	540			
31 Aug	Cash	220			
30 Nov	Cash	360			
31 Dec	Bal c/d	120	31 Dec	P&L a/c (bal fig)	1,440
		1,540			1,540
			1 Jan	Bal b/d	120

FEEDBACK TO
ACTIVITY 3

The income transferred to the profit and loss account is increased by crediting the rental income account with the £1,500 due but not yet received. The £1,500 is also carried down as a debit balance, a debtor for rental due which would be shown under current assets in the balance sheet.

Rental income

20X4		£	20X4		£
30 Sept	P&L a/c	3,500	30 June	Cash	2,000
			30 Sept	Bal c/d	1,500
		3,500			3,500
1 Oct	Bal b/d	1,500			

Chapter 6
DEBTORS AND BAD DEBTS

In this chapter we look at two situations that can arise when sales are made on credit terms (i.e. the customer does not have to pay until some time after he receives the goods). The first situation is where we judge that the money owing will definitely not be collectable from the customer, perhaps because he is in financial difficulties. The second is where we suspect, but are not certain, that some of the money included in debtors will not be collectable. We look at the ledger entries required to reflect both of these situations, and we also examine how they are reflected in the financial statements.

Objectives

By the time you have finished this chapter you should be able to:

- understand the meaning of the terms bad debt and doubtful debt

- explain the accounting treatment of a bad debt written off

- explain the ledger entries for setting up a provision for doubtful debts and for both increasing and decreasing that provision

- explain the ledger entries for a bad debt recovered

- understand the financial statement presentation for bad debts and doubtful debt provisions.

1   Sales and accounting concepts

1.1   Introduction

If a sale is for cash, the customer pays for the goods immediately the sale is made and will probably take the goods away with him or arrange for them to be delivered. If the sale is on credit terms, the customer will not pay for the goods at that time. Instead he will be given or sent an invoice detailing the goods and their price and the normal payment terms. This will tell him when he is expected to pay for the goods.

1.2   Accruals or matching concept

Under the accruals or matching concept a sale is included in the ledger accounts at the time that it is made. For a cash sale this will be when the cash or cheque is paid by the customer and the double entry will be as follows.

> Dr   Cash account
>
> Cr   Sales account

For a sale on credit, the sale is made at the time that goods are delivered or a service is rendered to the customer. Accounting entries are made at that time as follows.

> Dr   Debtor account
>
> Cr   Sales account

When the customer eventually settles the invoice the double entry will be as follows.

> Dr   Cash account
>
> Cr   Debtor account

This clears out the balance on the debtor's account, reflecting the fact that the customer no longer owes us any money.

1.3   Realisation concept

The **realisation concept** requires that gains or profits, such as those made on sales, should be recognised and accounted for at the time that the transaction is made and the receipt of cash is reasonably certain.

Under the realisation concept there is no necessity to wait until the cash from a credit sale is received before the sale is recognised. That is why, in the double entry shown above, it is appropriate to record a sale and related debtor.

1.4   Collectability of debts

Credit customers do not always pay the amounts they owe. If a customer is fraudulent and disappears without trace before payment of the amount due, then it is unlikely that the debt will ever be recovered. If a customer is declared bankrupt, then again it is unlikely that he will be able to pay the amount due. If a customer is having financial difficulties or is in liquidation, then there is likely to be some doubt as to his eventual ability to pay.

If it is highly unlikely that the amount owing by a debtor will be received, then this debt is known as a bad debt. As it will probably never be received, it is written off by writing it out of the ledger accounts completely. This is in line with the prudence concept, which requires that assets are not overstated, and losses are not understated.

In other cases, we may have some doubt about whether a customer can or will pay his debt, but without being quite certain that the debt is bad. This is described by the term **doubtful debt**. It is still hoped that the debt will be received and therefore it will remain in the ledger accounts. However, in order to be prudent, a provision will be made. This means that the possible loss from not receiving the cash will be accounted for immediately, whilst the amount of the original debt will still remain in the ledger account just in case the debtor does eventually pay.

2   Bad debts

2.1   Introduction

If a debt is considered to be uncollectable, then it is prudent to remove it from the accounts and to charge the amount as an expense to the profit and loss account. The original sale remains in the accounts as this did actually take place. The debtor, however, is removed as it is now considered that the debt will never be paid and an expense is charged to the profit and loss account for bad debts.

The double entry required to achieve these effects is as follows.

Dr   Bad debts expense account

Cr   Debtors account

Example

Abacus & Co have total debtors at the end of their accounting period of £45,000. It is discovered that one of them, Mr James Scott, who owes £790, has been declared bankrupt and another who gave his name as Peter Campbell has totally disappeared owing Abacus & Co £1,240. Show the entries required in the ledger accounts of Abacus & Co.

Solution

Step 1   Enter the opening balance in the debtors account. As debtors are an asset then this will be on the debit side of the ledger account.

Debtors

20XX		£	20XX		£
Opening balance		45,000			

Step 2   As the two debts are considered to be irrecoverable then they must be removed from debtors by a credit entry to the debtors account and a corresponding debit entry to a bad debts expense account.

Debtors

20XX		£	20XX		£
Opening balance		45,000	Bad debts expense – J Scott		790
			Bad debts expense – P Campbell		1,240

Bad debts expense

20XX		£	20XX		£
Debtors – J Scott		790			
Debtors – P Campbell		1,240			

Step 3   The debtors account must now be balanced and the closing balance would appear in the balance sheet as the debtors figure at the end of the period.

Debtors

20XX		£	20XX		£
Opening balance		45,000	Bad debts expense – J Scott		790
			Bad debts expense – P Campbell		1,240
			Balance c/d		42,970
		———			———
		45,000			45,000
		———			———
Balance b/d		42,970			

£42,970 would appear in the balance sheet as the figure for debtors under current assets at the end of the accounting period.

Step 4   Finally, the bad debts expense account should be balanced and the balance written off to the profit and loss account as an expense of the period.

Bad debts expense

20XX		£	20XX		£
Debtors – J Scott		790	P&L a/c		2,030
Debtors – P Campbell		1,240			
		———			———
		2,030			2,030
		———			———

Note that the sales account has not been altered and the original sales of £790 to James Scott and £1,240 to Peter Campbell remain. This is because these sales actually took place and it is only after the sale that the expense of not being able to collect these debts has occurred.

3   Doubtful debts

3.1   Introduction

A doubtful debt is one about which there is some cause for concern but which is not yet definitely irrecoverable. Therefore although it is prudent immediately to recognise the possible expense of not collecting the debt in the profit and loss account it would also be wise to keep the original debt in the accounts in case the debtor does in fact pay up.

This is achieved by the following double entry:

> Dr   Bad debts expense account
>
> Cr   Provision for doubtful debts account

3.2   The difference between a bad debt written off and a doubtful debt provision

Although the expense is written off in the bad debts expense account, the debt is not removed from debtors. Instead, a provision is set up which is a credit balance. This is netted off against debtors in the balance sheet to give a net figure for debtors that are probably recoverable.

3.3   Types of doubtful debt

There are two types of amount that are likely to be considered as doubtful debts in an organisation's accounts.

- There will be some specific debts where the debtor is known to be in financial difficulties and therefore the amount owing from that debtor may not be recoverable. The provision to be made against such a debtor is known as a **specific provision**.

- The past experience and history of a business will indicate that not all of its debts will be recoverable in full. It may not be possible to indicate the precise debtors that will not pay, but an estimate may be made that a certain percentage of debtors is likely not to pay. The provision made against this percentage of debtors is known as a **general provision**.

Example – general provision for doubtful debts

On 31 December 20X1 Jake Williams had debtors of £10,000. From past experience Jake estimated that 3% of these debtors were likely never to pay their debts and he therefore wished to make a general doubtful debt provision against this amount.

During 20X2 Jake made sales on credit totalling £100,000 and received cash from his debtors of £94,000. He still considered that 3% of the closing debtors were doubtful and should be provided against.

During 20X3 Jake made sales of £95,000 and collected £96,000 from his debtors. At 31 December 20X3 Jake still considered that 3% of his debtors were doubtful and should be provided against.

Solution

Step 1   Enter the balance on the debtors account at 31 December 20X1.

Debtors				
20X1		£	*20X1*	£
31 Dec		10,000		

Step 2 Set up a provision against 3% of £10,000, £300, by debiting the bad debts expense account and crediting the provision for doubtful debts account.

Bad debts expense

20X1	£	*20X1*	£
31 Dec Provision for doubtful debts	300		

Provision for doubtful debts

20X1	£	*20X1*	£
		31 Dec Bad debts expense	300

Step 3 Balance off the three accounts.

Debtors

20X1	£	*20X1*	£
31 Dec	10,000	31 Dec Bal c/d	10,000
	10,000		10,000
20X2			
1 Jan Bal b/d	10,000		

This balance of £10,000 will appear as debtors in the balance sheet under current assets at 31 December 20X1.

Bad debts expense

20X1	£	*20X1*	£
31 Dec Provision for doubtful debts	300	P&L a/c	300
	300		300

This is the expense for the period to be included in the profit and loss account.

Provision for doubtful debts

20X1	£	*20X1*	£
31 Dec Bal c/d	300	31 Dec Bad debts expense	300
	300		300
		20X2	
		1 Jan Bal b/d	300

This credit balance of £300 is included in the balance sheet under current assets and netted off against the debtors at the end of 20X1 in order to indicate the amount of debtors that are doubtful.

An extract from the balance sheet would be as follows

	£	£
Current assets		
Debtors	10,000	
Less: Provision for doubtful debts	300	
		9,700

Step 4 Write up the debtors account for 20X2 and balance it off to find the debtors figure at 31 December 20X2.

Debtors

20X2		£	20X2		£
1 Jan	Bal b/d	10,000	31 Dec	Cash	94,000
31 Dec	Sales	100,000	31 Dec	Bal c/d	16,000
		110,000			110,000
20X3					
1 Jan	Bal b/d	16,000			

Step 5 Set up the provision required of 3% of £16,000, £480. Remember that there is already an opening balance on the provision account of £300. Therefore in order to end 20X2 with a total balance on the provision account of £480 only a further £180 will need to be charged to the bad debts expense account for the period and thus to the profit and loss account.

Bad debts expense

20X2		£	20X2		£
31 Dec	Provision for doubtful		31 Dec	P&L a/c	180
	debts	180			
		180			180

Provision for doubtful debts

20X2		£	20X2		£
31 Dec	Bal c/d	480	1 Jan	Bal b/d	300
			31 Dec	Bad debts expense	180
		480			480
			20X3		
			1 Jan	Bal b/d	480

Step 6 The extract from the balance sheet at 31 December 20X2 would be as follows:

	£	£
Current assets		
Debtors	16,000	
Less: Provision for doubtful debts	480	
		15,520

Step 7 Write up the debtors account for 20X3. Balance off the account to find the debtors at 31 December 20X3.

Debtors

20X3		£	20X3		£
1 Jan	Bal b/d	16,000	31 Dec	Cash	96,000
31 Dec	Sales	95,000	31 Dec	Bal c/d	15,000
		111,000			111,000
20X4					
1 Jan	Bal b/d	15,000			

Step 8 Set up the provision required at 31 December 20X3 of 3% of £15,000, £450. This time there is already an opening balance on the provision for doubtful debts account of £480.

The provision is to be reduced and this is done by debiting the provision account with the amount of the decrease required (£480 – £450 = £30) and crediting the bad debts expense account.

The credit on the bad debts expense account is transferred to the profit and loss account for the period as an item of sundry income or a negative expense and is described as 'decrease in doubtful debts provision'.

Provision for doubtful debts

20X3		£	20X3		£
31 Dec	Bad debts expense	30	1 Jan	Bal b/d	480
31 Dec	Bal c/d	450			
		480			480
			20X4		
			1 Jan	Bal b/d	450

Bad debts expense

20X3		£	20X3		£
31 Dec	P&L a/c	30	31 Dec	Provision for doubtful debts	30
		30			30

The extract from the balance sheet at 31 December 20X3 would be as follows.

	£	£
Current assets		
Debtors	15,000	
Less: Provision for doubtful debts	450	
		14,550

If the provision for doubtful debts is to be decreased from one period end to another then the provision for doubtful debts account will be debited with the amount of the decrease and the bad debts expense account will be credited.

ACTIVITY 1

John Stamp has opening balances at 1 January 20X6 on his debtors account and provision for doubtful debts account of £68,000 and £3,400 respectively. During the year to 31 December 20X6 John Stamp makes credit sales of £354,000 and receives cash from his debtors of £340,000.

At 31 December 20X6 John Stamp reviews his debtors listing and acknowledges that he is unlikely ever to receive debts totalling £2,000. These are to be written off as bad. John also wishes to provide against 5% of his remaining debtors after writing off the bad debts.

You are required to write up the debtors account, provision for doubtful debts account and the bad debts expense account for the year to 31 December 20X6.

Feedback to this activity is at the end of the chapter.

Example – specific provision for doubtful debts

Steven Saunders has debtors of £11,200 at his year end of 31 May 20X4. Of these he decides that there is some doubt as to whether or not he will receive a sum of £500 from Peter Foster and he also wishes to provide against the possibility of not receiving 2% of his remaining debtors.

At 1 June 20X3 Steven Saunders had a balance on his provision for doubtful debts account of £230.

Calculate the provision for doubtful debts required at 31 May 20X4.

Solution

	£
Specific provision against Peter Foster's debt	500
General provision against remaining debtors ((£11,200 – 500) × 2%)	214
Total provision required	714

Write up the provision for doubtful debts account putting in the opening balance of £230 and the closing balance required of £714. The difference, the increase in provision required, is the expense to the bad debts expense account and subsequently to the profit and loss account.

Provision for doubtful debts

20X3–4	£	*20X3–4*	£
31 May Bal c/d	714	1 June Bal b/d	230
		31 May Bad debts expense	484
	714		
			714
		20X4–5	
		1 June Bal b/d	714

Bad debts expense

20X3–4	£	*20X3–4*	£
31 May Provision for doubtful debts	484	31 May P&L a/c	484
	484		484

4   Bad debts recovered

It is possible that a debt may be written off as bad in one accounting period, perhaps because the debtor has been declared bankrupt, and the money due, or part of it, is then unexpectedly received in a subsequent accounting period.

4.1   Double entry

When a debt is written off the double entry is as follows.

> Dr   Bad debts expense account (an expense in the profit and loss account)
>
> Cr   Debtor's account (removing the debtor from the accounts)

The full double entry for the cash being received from that debtor in a subsequent accounting period is as follows.

> Dr   Debtors account (to reinstate the debtor that had been cancelled when the debt was written off)
>
> Cr   Bad debts recovered account (unexpected sundry income credited to the profit and loss account)

and

> Dr   Cash account
>
> Cr   Debtors account

Note that this is the usual double entry for cash received from a debtor.

This double entry can be simplified as follows:

> Dr   Cash account
>
> Cr   Bad debts recovered account

This is because the debit and the credit to the debtors account cancel each other out. However, it may be useful to pass the transaction through the debtor's account so that the fact that the debt was eventually paid, or partly paid, is recorded there.

Note that it is not acceptable to credit bad debts recovered to the bad debts account. To do this would obscure the cost to the business of bad debts for the period, important control information.

ACTIVITY 2

Celia Jones had debtors of £3,655 at 31 December 20X7. At that date she wrote off a debt from Lenny Smith of £699. During the year to 31 December 20X8 Celia made credit sales of £17,832 and received cash from her debtors totalling £16,936. She also received the £699 from Lenny Smith that had already been written off in 20X7.

Write up these transactions in Celia Jones's ledger accounts for 20X7 and 20X8.

Feedback to activity is at the end of the chapter.

Conclusion

Having studied this chapter you should now understand the reason for examining the collectability of debts and the accounting concepts that are relevant to this area: accruals or matching, realisation and prudence.

SELF-TEST QUESTIONS

Sales and accounting concepts

1   What is the double entry for a sale on credit? (1.2)

2   How is the realisation concept relevant to accounting for credit sales? (1.3)

3   Which accounting concept would require a provision for doubtful debts to be set up? (1.4)

4   What is the definition of a bad debt? (1.4)

Bad debts

5   What is the double entry for writing off a bad debt? (2.1)

Doubtful debts

6   What is a provision for doubtful debts? (3.1)

7   What is the double entry required when a provision for doubtful debts is initially set up? (3.1)

8   What is a specific provision for doubtful debts? (3.3)

9   If there is to be a decrease in the provision for doubtful debts over a period will this result in a debit or a credit entry in the profit and loss account? (3.3)

Bad debts recovered

10   What is the full double entry required to account for cash received from a debt that had been written off in a previous accounting period? (4.1)

EXAM-TYPE
QUESTION

Harry Evans

Harry Evans set up in business on 1 January 20X0 as a violin maker. At the end of his first year of trading, 31 December 20X0, the amounts owing to him from customers totalled £6,570. After some consideration Harry decided that, of these debts, a total of £370 was unlikely ever to be received and should be written off as bad. Of the remaining debtors he decided to be prudent and provide against 4%.

By 31 December 20X1, Harry's debtors had increased to £8,400 and of these £1,500 were considered to be bad. Harry decided that his provision for doubtful debts could be reduced to 2% of the remaining debtors.

At 31 December 20X2, Harry's debtors totalled £6,250. There were no debts that were considered bad but a specific provision was to be made against one debt of £350 and a general provision of 2% was to be continued on the remaining debtors.

You are required to write up the provision for doubtful debts account and the bad debts expense account for the years ended 31 December 20X0, 20X1 and 20X2.

(12 marks)

For the answer to this question, see the 'Answers' section at the end of the book.

FEEDBACK TO
ACTIVITY 1

Step 1   Write up the debtors account showing the opening balance, the credit sales for the year and the cash received.

Debtors

20X6		£	20X6		£
1 Jan	Bal b/d	68,000	31 Dec	Cash	340,000
31 Dec	Sales	354,000			

Step 2   Write off the bad debts for the period:

Dr Bad debts expense account

Cr Debtors account

Bad debts expense

20X6		£	20X6		£
31 Dec	Debtors	2,000			

Debtors

20X6		£	20X6		£
1 Jan	Bal b/d	68,000	31 Dec	Cash	340,000
31 Dec	Sales	354,000	31 Dec	Bad debts expense	2,000

Step 3   Balance off the debtors account to find the closing balance against which the provision is required.

Debtors

20X6		£	20X6		£
1 Jan	Bal b/d	68,000	31 Dec	Cash	340,000
31 Dec	Sales	354,000	31 Dec	Bad debts expense	2,000
			31 Dec	Bal c/d	80,000
		422,000			
					422,000
20X7					
1 Jan	Bal b/d	80,000			

Step 4   Set up the provision required of 5% of £80,000, £4,000. Remember that there is already an opening balance on the provision for doubtful debts account of £3,400. Therefore, only the increase in provision required of £600 is credited to the provision account and debited to the bad debts expense account.

Bad debts expense

20X6		£	20X6		£
31 Dec	Debtors	2,000	31 Dec	P&L a/c	2,600
31 Dec	Provision for doubtful				
	debts	600			
		2,600			2,600

Provision for doubtful debts

20X6		£	20X6		£
31 Dec	Bal c/d	4,000	1 Jan	Bal b/d	3,400
			31 Dec	Bad debts expense	600
		4,000			
					4,000
			20X7		
			1 Jan	Bal b/d	4,000

Note that only the one bad debts expense account is used to both write off bad debts and to increase or decrease the provision for doubtful debts. There is no necessity to use separate accounts for each type of expense.

The relevant extract from the balance sheet at 31 December 20X6 would be as follows:

	£	£
Current assets		
Debtors	80,000	
Less: Provision for doubtful debts	4,000	
		76,000

Step 1   Write up the debtors account and bad debts expense account at
31 December 20X7.

Debtors

20X7	£		20X7	£
31 Dec Bal b/d	3,655		31 Dec Bad debts expense	699
			31 Dec Bal c/d	2,956
	———			———
	3,655			3,655
	———			———
20X8				
1 Jan Bal b/d	2,956			

Bad debts expense

20X7	£		20X7	£
31 Dec Debtors	699		31 Dec P&L a/c	699
	———			———
	699			699
	———			———

Step 2   Write up the debtors account for 20X8 showing the credit sales and cash
received from debtors.

Debtors

20X8	£		20X8	£
1 Jan Bal b/d	2,956		31 Dec Cash	16,936
31 Dec Sales	17,832			

Step 3   Continue with the debtors account and put through the entries for the bad
debt recovered.

Dr   Debtors account

Cr   Bad debts recovered account

and

Dr   Cash

Cr   Debtors account

Debtors

20X8	£		20X8	£
1 Jan Bal b/d	2,956		31 Dec Cash	16,936
31 Dec Sales	17,832		31 Dec Cash	699
31 Dec Bad debts recovered	699			

Bad debts recovered

20X8	£		20X8	£
			31 Dec Debtors	699

Step 4   Balance off the debtors account and transfer the balance on the bad debts
expense account to the profit and loss account. Note that the two entries of
£699 in the debtors account cancel each other out. The remaining entries are
a debit to the cash account for cash received and a credit in the bad debts
recovered account that is transferred to the profit and loss account as sundry
income.

Debtors

20X8		£	20X8		£
1 Jan	Bal b/d	2,956	31 Dec	Cash	16,936
31 Dec	Sales	17,832	31 Dec	Cash	699
31 Dec	Bad debts recovered	699	31 Dec	Bal c/d	3,852
		21,487			21,487
20X9					
1 Jan	Bal b/d	3,852			

Bad debts recovered

20X8		£	20X8		£
31 Dec	P&L a/c	699	31 Dec	Debtors	699
		699			699

It is best to show the bad debts recovered separately in the profit and loss account. If they are netted off against bad debts written off in the year the total cost of bad debts is obscured.

Chapter 7
FIXED ASSETS AND DEPRECIATION

When a fixed asset is purchased by a business, the double entry is to debit a fixed asset account and credit either cash or a creditor account. The balance on the fixed asset account (i.e. the original cost of the asset) will be reported in the balance sheet.

A fixed asset will remain in the business for several accounting periods. Some way must be found of allocating the cost of the asset to the accounting periods that will benefit from its use. This is necessary in order to comply with the matching concept: the cost of the asset must be matched with the revenue it helps to earn, and this revenue will arise over a number of accounting periods.

Depreciation is a method of charging a proportion of a fixed asset's original cost to the profit and loss account each year to match the revenues that the asset earns. The depreciation charge for each year accumulates in a provision account which is netted off against the original cost of the asset in the balance sheet.

Objectives

By the time you have finished this chapter you should be able to:

- define and explain the purposes of depreciation
- calculate the annual depreciation charge for a fixed asset under a variety of methods
- account for depreciation in the ledger accounts and financial statements
- account for the disposal of a fixed asset
- account for the revaluation of a fixed asset.

1   Fixed assets and depreciation

1.1   Introduction

A **fixed asset** is an asset intended for use on a continuing basis in the business.

Fixed assets include items such as an office building, an item of computer equipment, a delivery van, a machine used in the business's manufacturing operations, and so on.

The above are examples of **tangible fixed assets** (assets that have a physical existence, that can be touched). There are also **intangible fixed assets**, such as goodwill, patents, trademarks etc. Such assets also have a continuing value to the business, but do not have an actual physical existence. We look at intangible fixed assets in a later chapter. For now, all you need to know is that almost all fixed assets, whether tangible or intangible, are subject to depreciation.

1.2   What is depreciation?

Depreciation is the measure of the cost or revalued amount of a tangible fixed asset that has been consumed during an accounting period.

The definition suggests that a fixed asset is eventually 'consumed', i.e. it has no further value. This consumption may arise because of any of the following factors.

- **Use** – e.g. plant and machinery or motor vehicles are eventually used so much that they are not fit for further use.
- **Passing of time** – e.g. a ten year lease of property eventually expires when the ten years have passed.

- **Obsolescence** through technology and market changes – e.g. plant and machinery of a specialised nature can quickly become obsolete and will need to be replaced by more modern equivalents.
- **Depletion** – e.g. the extraction of material from a quarry.

1.3   Purpose of depreciation

Assume an item of plant cost £5,000 and that it has a nil scrap value at the end of ten years. Since expenditure on the asset will benefit the revenues of the next ten years, the accruals (or matching) concept requires us to match the £5,000 costs against all of those revenues. The simplest way is to use the straight line method (discussed below) and charge one-tenth (i.e. £500) against the revenue of each year.

Under historical cost accounting, the purpose of depreciation is to allocate the cost of £5,000 over the expected life of the asset (in this case ten years). The profit and loss account for each year is charged with part of the cost of the asset.

1.4   The relationship between depreciation and asset replacement

Note that the provision of depreciation is not intended to provide a fund for the replacement of the asset. It is simply a method of allocating the cost of the asset over the periods estimated to benefit from its use. In our example it is unlikely that an equivalent replacement asset will cost £5,000 in ten years' time, because of inflation, and in any event charging depreciation does not provide the funds to replace it.

2   Methods of calculating depreciation

2.1   Introduction

There are several possible methods of calculating depreciation. The methods below are included in the syllabus.

- Straight line method
- Reducing balance method
- Sum of the digits method.

Examiners will normally specify which method is to be used. If they do not, the straight line method should generally be adopted as it is the easiest to compute.

2.2   Straight line method

This is the simplest and most popular method of calculating depreciation. Under this method the depreciation charge is constant over the life of the asset. To calculate the depreciation charge, we require three pieces of information:

- the original (historical) cost of the asset
- an estimate of its useful life to the business
- an estimate of its residual value at the end of its useful life.

The depreciation charge is then calculated as follows.

$$\text{Annual depreciation charge} = \frac{\text{Original cost} - \text{Residual value}}{\text{Estimated useful life}}$$

Example – straight line method

Mead is a sole trader with a 31 December year-end. He purchased a car on 1 January at a cost of £12,000. He estimates that its useful life is four years, after which he will trade it in for £2,400. The annual depreciation charge is to be calculated using the straight line method.

Solution – Straight line method

$$\text{Depreciation charge} = \frac{(£12{,}000 - £2{,}400)}{4} = £2{,}400 \text{ p.a.}$$

Notes:

1   If the car had been purchased on 30 September 20X3, strictly speaking we should only charge three months' depreciation in 20X3. The depreciation charged each year would be:

	£
20X3	600
20X4	2,400
20X5	2,400
20X6	2,400
20X7	1,800

You should follow this strict approach unless the question specifies that a full year's depreciation should be charged in the year when the asset is acquired, irrespective of the date of purchase.

2   Frequently, residual value is not specified, in which case you should assume it to be zero and the whole original cost will be written off over the life of the asset. In such a case it is common to see the depreciation rate expressed as a percentage; straight line depreciation over four years would be expressed as 'straight line depreciation at 25% per annum on cost'.

2.3   Reducing balance method

Under this method the depreciation charge is higher in the earlier years of the life of the asset. If examiners require this method, they will usually give you a percentage to apply. In the first year the percentage is applied to cost but in subsequent years it is applied to the asset's **net book value** (alternatively known as **written down value**). The net book value (NBV) or written down value (WDV) of a fixed asset is its original cost less the accumulated depreciation on the asset to date.

Example – Reducing balance method

A trader purchased an item of plant for £1,000. The depreciation charge for each of the first five years is to be calculated, assuming the depreciation rate on the reducing balance to be 20% per annum.

Solution – Reducing balance method

Year	$\% \times NBV$ = Depreciation charge	Depreciation charge £	Cumulative depreciation £
1	20% × £1,000	200	200
2	20% × £(1,000 – 200)	160	360
3	20% × £(1,000 – 360)	128	488
4	20% × £(1,000 – 488)	102	590
5	20% × £(1,000 – 590)	82	672

Notice how this method results in higher depreciation charges in earlier years and also that a much higher annual rate is required than for the straight line method if the asset is to be written off over the same period.

What type of fixed asset might the reducing balance method of depreciation be most useful for?

Feedback to this activity is at the end of the chapter.

DEFINITION

The **sum of the digits** method is a variation on the reducing balancing method.

2.4 Sum of the digits method

This is a variation on the reducing balance method and, as with that method, the aim is to show a higher depreciation charge in the early years of the life of an asset.

Example – sum of the digits method

Cost of asset		£4,200
Scrap value		£200
Estimated useful life		Four years

Solution – sum of the digits method

Sum of digits: 4 years + 3 years + 2 years + 1 year = 10

Year		Depreciation charge £	Cumulative depreciation £
1	4/10 × £(4,200 – 200)	1,600	1,600
2	3/10 × £4,000	1,200	2,800
3	2/10 × £4,000	800	3,600
4	1/10 × £4,000	400	4,000

A fixed asset originally cost £12,000 and is estimated to have a scrap value of £2,000 after the eight years of its estimated useful life.

What is the depreciation charge in year two of the asset's life under:

(a)   the straight line method?

(b)   the reducing balance method using an annual rate of 20%?

Feedback to this activity is at the end of the chapter.

3 Accounting for depreciation

3.1 Ledger accounts

Whichever of the methods is used, the bookkeeping remains the same.

1   On acquisition of the fixed asset the following entries are made.

Debit	Credit	With
Fixed asset – cost	Cash or creditor	Cost of the asset

2   At the end of each year make the adjustment for depreciation.

Debit	Credit	With
Profit and loss – depreciation expense	Fixed asset - Provision for depreciation	Depreciation charge

This entry sets up the provision for depreciation on the asset.

Note that the depreciation is not recorded by an entry in the fixed asset account. The fixed asset account is retained at cost and the depreciation charge is credited to a separate account. This is in order to show the net book value in the balance sheet by disclosing the full original cost of the asset minus the **accumulated** depreciation over the years since the asset was acquired. We illustrate the balance sheet presentation later in this chapter.

Example

A trader buys a motor car on 1 January 20X3 for £12,000. It is to be depreciated on the straight line basis over 5 years, with an assumption of a NIL residual value. Show the ledger accounts for the first three years, together with the effect on the financial statements.

Solution

Step 1   Set up a motor car cost account and a motor car provision for depreciation account.

Step 2   Account for the purchase of the car by debiting the motor car cost account with £12,000 on 1 January 20X3.

Step 3   At 31 December 20X3 carry down the cost of the car on the motor car cost account.

Step 4   At 31 December 20X3 account for the first year's depreciation charge of £2,400 by debiting the profit and loss account and crediting the motor car provision for depreciation account. Carry down the balance on the motor car provision for depreciation account.

Step 5   Repeat steps 3 and 4 at 31 December 20X4 and 20X5. Note how the balance on the motor car provision for depreciation account increases each year as this is the total of the depreciation charged to date on that motor car.

Motor car – cost account

20X3		£	*20X3*		£
1 Jan	Cash	12,000	31 Dec	Balance c/d	12,000
20X4			*20X4*		
1 Jan	Balance b/d	12,000	31 Dec	Balance c/d	12,000
20X5			*20X5*		
1 Jan	Balance b/d	12,000	31 Dec	Balance c/d	12,000
20X6					
1 Jan	Balance b/d	12,000			

Motor car – provision for depreciation account

20X3		£	*20X3*		£
31 Dec	Balance c/d	2,400	31 Dec	Profit and loss	2,400
20X4			*20X4*		
			1 Jan	Balance b/d	2,400
31 Dec	Balance c/d	4,800	31 Dec	Profit and loss	2,400
		4,800			4,800
20X5			*20X5*		
			1 Jan	Balance b/d	4,800
31 Dec	Balance c/d	7,200	31 Dec	Profit and loss	2,400
		7,200			7,200
			20X6		
			1 Jan	Balance b/d	7,200

Alternative solution

An alternative approach, which is normally used in more complex situations, is to open an additional account for depreciation expense. The overall effect will be exactly the same, as can be shown if we consider the year 20X3 in the example above.

Motor car – cost account

20X3		£	20X3		£
1 Jan	Cash	12,000	31 Dec	Balance c/d	12,000
20X4					
1 Jan	Balance b/d	12,000			

Motor car – provision for depreciation account

20X3		£	20X3		£
31 Dec	Balance c/d	2,400	31 Dec	Depreciation	2,400
			20X4		
			1 Jan	Balance b/d	2,400

Depreciation expense account

20X3		£	20X3		£
31 Dec	Motor car provision for depreciation	2,400	31 Dec	Profit and loss	2,400

The annual charge for depreciation is made by debiting either a depreciation expense account or the profit and loss account directly, and crediting the provision for depreciation account.

3.2 Disclosure in the financial statements

The fixed asset will be shown in the financial statements as follows:

Profit and loss account

Year	Depreciation charge
	£
20X3	2,400
20X4	2,400
20X5	2,400

Balance sheet

	20X3	20X4	20X5
	£	£	£
Fixed asset:			
Motor car: Cost	12,000	12,000	12,000
Provision for depreciation	2,400	4,800	7,200
Net book value	9,600	7,200	4,800

The balance on the provision for depreciation account is netted off against the cost of the fixed asset in the balance sheet each year to give the net book value of the fixed asset.

3.3 Summary of the effect of depreciation

- Without depreciation the full cost of the asset would appear on the balance sheet each year.

- With depreciation the value of the asset on the balance sheet is reduced by the amount of the cumulative annual depreciation charges.

- The annual depreciation charge appears in the profit and loss account each year thereby charging the profit and loss account with a proportion of the cost of the fixed asset each year in accordance with the matching or accruals concept.

ACTIVITY 3

S Telford purchases a machine for £6,000. He estimates that the machine will last for eight years and its scrap value then will be £1,000.

Prepare the ledger accounts for the first three years of the machine's life and show the balance sheet extract at the end of each year, charging depreciation on the straight line method.

Feedback to this activity is at the end of the chapter.

4   Sale of fixed assets

4.1   Introduction

KEY POINT

When a fixed asset is sold, the cost of that asset together with the related accumulated depreciation should be transferred to a fixed asset disposals account.

When a fixed asset is sold, the cost of that asset together with the related accumulated depreciation should be transferred to a fixed asset disposals account. The profit or loss on disposal is calculated by comparing:

- the net book value of the asset at the date of sale (i.e. cost less depreciation provision), and

- the proceeds of sale.

4.2   Ledger account entries

Summary of the bookkeeping entries:

Ref	Debit	Credit	With
1	Disposals account	Fixed asset – cost account	Original cost of asset
2	Fixed asset – provision for depreciation	Disposals account	Accumulated depreciation up to the date of disposal
3	Cash	Disposals account	Proceeds of sale
4A	Disposals account *or*	Profit and loss	Profit on sale
4B	Profit and loss	Disposals account	Loss on sale

Example

The motor car used in the previous example was sold on 7 January 20X6 for proceeds of £5,100. Show the entries in the relevant ledger accounts.

Solution

Step 1   The profit on sale can be calculated arithmetically or derived from the use of the disposals account. The arithmetic computation is:

	£
Proceeds of sale	5,100
Less: Net book value at date of sale £(12,000 – 7,200)	4,800
Profit on sale	300

Step 2   Write up the ledger accounts.

Motor car – cost account

20X6		£	20X6		£
1 Jan	Balance b/d	12,000	7 Jan	(1) Disposals	12,000

Motor car – depreciation provision

20X6		£	20X6		£
7 Jan	(2) Disposals	7,200	1 Jan	Balance b/d	7,200

Motor car – disposals account

20X6		£	20X6		£
7 Jan	(1) Motor car – cost	12,000	7 Jan	(2) Depreciation	7,200
31 Dec(4A)	Profit and loss (bal fig)	300		(3) Cash	5,100
		12,300			12,300

(Numbers in brackets refer to the reference numbers in the summary chart above.)

4.3 Presentation

A final point – how should the £300 be presented in the profit and loss account? There are two possibilities:

1 Show the profit on sale of £300 as a separate item of miscellaneous income below gross profit.

2 Describe the £300 as depreciation over-provided and deduct it from the total depreciation charge for the year.

Both these presentations are acceptable, though the first is probably easier and clearer.

5 Revaluation of fixed assets

5.1 Reasons for revaluation

During a period of inflation, the current monetary value of fixed assets such as freehold land and buildings may be much in excess of their net book value (historical cost less depreciation). A business may wish to reflect the current worth of such assets on its balance sheet. This is particularly the case with large companies who wish to show to the users of their financial statements the current worth of significant assets in the company.

Where the revalued amount is greater than the net book value the surplus must be credited to an account separate from the profit and loss account as the gain is not realised (i.e. there is no intention of turning the asset into cash by selling it). The account is known as a **revaluation reserve**.

5.2 Depreciation of a revalued asset

When a fixed asset has been revalued, the charge for depreciation should be based on the revalued amount and the remaining useful economic life of the asset. Therefore, following an upward revaluation, the depreciation is higher than previously. This may appear strange: an upward revaluation has resulted in a higher depreciation charge to the profit and loss account. However, it should be remembered that the prime function of depreciation is to write off the 'cost' of an asset over its expected life. If the 'cost' is increased, therefore the depreciation to be charged increases.

The accounting treatment of fixed asset revaluations can be seen in the following example.

Example

A company revalues its buildings and decides to incorporate the revaluation into the books of account. The following information is relevant.

- Extract from the balance sheet at 31 December 20X7

	£
Buildings:	
Cost	1,500,000
Less accumulated depreciation	450,000
	1,050,000

- Depreciation has been provided at 2% per annum on the straight line basis.
- The building is revalued at 30 June 20X8 at £1,380,000. There is no change in its remaining estimated future life.

You are required to show the relevant extracts from the final accounts at 31 December 20X8.

Solution

At 31 December 20X7 it is clear that the asset has been in use for 15 years (because accumulated depreciation of £450,000 amounts to 30% of original cost). The annual depreciation charge at 2% on cost has been £30,000.

For the first six months of the year ended 31 December 20X8, we charge depreciation of £15,000, leaving the asset's net book value equal to (£1,050,000 – £15,000 =) £1,035,000. At this point the asset is revalued to £1,380,000, leading to a revaluation surplus of £345,000.

From this point on, depreciation is based on the revalued amount of £1,380,000 and a remaining useful life of 34 years and six months. This is an annual depreciation charge of £40,000. For the period 1 July 20X8 to 31 December 20X8 the charge is therefore £20,000. Over the whole year, this means that depreciation is (£15,000 + £20,000 =) £35,000, i.e. £5,000 higher than it would have been without the revaluation.

Profit and loss account – depreciation charge

	£
Based on original cost	30,000
Based on increase in valuation	5,000
Total	35,000

Balance sheet

	£
Buildings	
Valuation 30 June 20X8	1,380,000
Provision for depreciation	20,000
	1,360,000

Workings

Buildings account (NBV)

20X8		£	20X8		£
1 Jan	Balance b/d	1,050,000	30 Jun	Profit and loss depreciation first half year	15,000
30 Jun	Revaluation surplus (bal fig)	345,000	30 Jun	Balance c/d	1,380,000
		1,395,000			1,395,000
30 Jun	Balance b/d	1,380,000	31 Dec	Profit and loss depreciation second half year	20,000
			31 Dec	Balance c/d	1,360,000
		1,380,000			1,380,000

Note: there are two important points to appreciate:

- Depreciation must continue to be charged on original cost until the date of the revaluation.

- The accumulated depreciation on the old cost is effectively 'cleared out' when the gain is transferred to the revaluation reserve. Thus accumulated depreciation at the year end only consists of the depreciation charged on the revalued amount.

Depreciation calculations

	£
First half year $0.5 \times 2\% \times 1,500,000$	15,000
Second half year $0.5 \times \dfrac{1,380,000}{34.5*}$	20,000
	35,000

Had this building not been revalued, the charge for the year would have been £30,000.

* *This is arrived at as follows*

Years		
Total number of years before building fully depreciated		50.0
Less: Depreciation in years to 31 December 20X7 $\dfrac{450,000}{30,000}$	15.0	
Depreciation 1 January 20X8 to 30 June 20X8	0.5	
		15.5
Number of years for depreciation to run		34.5

6   FRS 15 *Tangible fixed assets* – main requirements

6.1   Introduction

FRS 15 provides a general definition of depreciation: it is the measure of the cost or revalued amount of the economic benefits of the tangible fixed asset that have been consumed during the period. FRS 15 does not state a preference for any particular method of depreciation but states that the business must decide which is the most appropriate.

FRS 15 also covers special situations including:

- revision of useful lives
- change of method of depreciation
- land and buildings
- depreciation on revalued assets.

The first three items in this list are covered below. Revaluations have already been covered.

6.2   Revision of useful lives

The useful economic lives of assets should be reviewed at each year end and, when necessary, revised. When, as a result of experience or of changed circumstances, it is considered that the original estimate of the useful economic life of an asset requires revision, the effect of the change in estimate on the profit and loss account needs to be considered. The net book amount is written off over the revised remaining useful economic life.

Example

An asset was purchased for £100,000 on 1 January 20X5 and straight line depreciation of £20,000 per annum was charged (five year life, no residual value). A general review of asset lives is undertaken and for this particular asset, the remaining useful life as at 31 December 20X7 is estimated at seven years.

The accounts for the year ended 31 December 20X7 are being prepared.

The calculations are as follows:

NBV as at 31 December 20X6 (60% × £100,000)	£60,000
Remaining years useful life	8 years
Annual depreciation charge	£7,500

Note that the estimated remaining life is seven years from 31 December 20X7, but this information is used to compute the current year's charge as well.

In the ledgers, cost remains at £100,000 and accumulated depreciation at 31 December 20X7 is £47,500 (40,000 + 7,500).

6.3   Change in method of depreciation

A change from one method of providing depreciation to another is permissible only on the grounds that the new method will give a fairer presentation. The net book amount should be written off over the remaining useful economic life, commencing with the period in which the change is made.

6.4   Land and buildings

FRS 15 makes two points regarding land and buildings:

- Freehold land does not normally require a provision for depreciation, unless it is subject to depletion by, for example, the extraction of minerals. However, the value of freehold land may be adversely affected by considerations such as changes in the desirability of its location and in these circumstances it should be written down.

- Buildings are no different from other fixed assets in that they have a limited useful economic life, although it is usually significantly longer than that of other types of assets. They should, therefore, be depreciated having regard to the same criteria.

Note, however, that a number of large companies do not depreciate their buildings, particularly in the hotel and public house industries.

The argument of these companies is that their buildings are maintained in such a condition that they do not have finite lives. For example, if a company owns a 500-year-old public house, expenditure is incurred on the building to ensure that it does not deteriorate.

FRS 15, however, is clear on this point: 'Subsequent expenditure on a tangible fixed asset that maintains or enhances … the asset does not negate the need to charge depreciation'.

6.5 The role of consistency

The consistency concept is important in the context of depreciation in two ways.

- Once a business has decided on a suitable method of depreciation for a fixed asset, it should not change the method in future periods. FRS 15 does state that a change in method may be permissible, however, if the new method gives a fairer presentation of profits and balance sheet assets.

- Similar items should be depreciated in the same way. This does not mean however that all the fixed assets of a business must be depreciated in the same way, but classes of assets should be similarly treated. Thus a business may conclude that it is appropriate to depreciate its plant using the reducing balance method and its buildings using the straight line method.

6.6 The role of subjectivity

Accounting for depreciation is an area where subjective judgements play a significant part. In order to compute depreciation an estimate must be made of the eventual residual value and the useful life. Both of these require subjective judgements. In addition the business may decide to revalue assets and the decision to revalue is also subjective.

As a consequence, it is difficult to make comparisons of profits and balance sheets between two businesses, even if they are in the same trade, as they may have validly come to different conclusions as to any of these subjective elements.

Conclusion

You should now be able to discuss the reasons for the depreciation of fixed assets and the various methods of calculating the annual depreciation charge that are available. You should be able to account for depreciation, disposals and revaluations of fixed assets.

Fixed assets and depreciation

1   What is the meaning of depreciation? (1.2)

Methods of calculating depreciation

2   What is the formula for calculating the annual depreciation charge using the straight line method of depreciation? (2.2)

Accounting for depreciation

3   How should fixed assets be shown in the balance sheet of an organisation? (3.2)

Sale of fixed assets

4   What is the double entry required to account for the disposal of a fixed asset? (4.2)

5   What are the two alternative presentations for a profit on sale of a fixed asset? (4.3)

Revaluation of fixed assets

6   How is depreciation calculated when an asset is revalued? (5.2)

FRS 15 – main requirements

7   Which method of depreciation does FRS 15 prefer? (6.1)

B acquired a lorry on 1 May 20X0 at a cost of £30,000. The lorry has an estimated useful life of four years, and an estimated resale value at the end of that time of £6,000. B charges depreciation on the straight line basis, with a proportionate charge in the period of acquisition.

What will the depreciation charge for the lorry be in B's accounting period to 30 September 20X0?

A   £3,000

B   £2,500

C   £2,000

D   £5,000

For the answer to this question, see the 'Answers' section at the end of the book

Question 1: Depreciation 1

Explain the purpose of providing for depreciation and give details of one method of computing the annual depreciation on an asset.   **(7 marks)**

Question 2: Depreciation 2

A firm has the following transactions in motor cars:

    20X4
    1 Jan   Purchased car for £800 (Car 'A')
    1 Jul   Purchased additional car for £1,200 (Car 'B')

    20X5
    1 Jul   Car 'A' sold for £600

The firm's accounting year ends on 31 December in each year, and the following amounts of depreciation have been calculated as being relevant to those years:

Accounting year ending 31 December 20X4	Car 'A'	£160
Accounting year ending 31 December 20X4	Car 'B'	£120
Accounting year ending 31 December 20X5	Car 'A'	£80
Accounting year ending 31 December 20X5	Car 'B'	£240
Accounting year ending 31 December 20X6	Car 'B'	£240

You are required to show the motor cars accounts for each of the three accounting years, together with the entry for motor cars in the balance sheet at 31 December 20X5.   **(12 marks)**

Question 3: Grasmere

Grasmere has been trading for many years, preparing his accounts to 31 December.

On 1 July 20X2 he purchased a van for £2,400. He estimates that its useful life is five years, with a £300 residual value. He provides depreciation on a straight line basis on all his fixed assets.

Grasmere sold the van on 1 April 20X4 for proceeds of £1,800.

You are required to enter the above transactions in the relevant ledger accounts and to show the effect on the financial statements for each year. **(13 marks)**

For the answers to these questions, see the 'Answers' section at the end of the book.

| **FEEDBACK TO ACTIVITY 1** | The type of fixed asset that loses a large proportion of its value in the early years of its life and a lesser proportion in later years, such as a new car. (However, FRS 15 *Tangible fixed assets* emphasises that depreciation is an allocation of cost, not an attempt to value the asset.) It is also sometimes argued that assets that require little maintenance in the early years of their life but much more as they get older should be depreciated using the reducing balance method as the total of depreciation and maintenance costs each year should then be evened out. |

FEEDBACK TO ACTIVITY 2

1   Straight line method

$$\frac{£12,000 - 2,000}{8} = £1,250$$

2   Reducing balance method

Year	NBV	Depreciation charge
	£	£
1	12,000	$(12,000 \times 20\%) = £2,400$
2	$(12,000 - 2,400) = 9,600$	$(9,600 \times 20\%) = £1,920$

FEEDBACK TO ACTIVITY 3

Straight line method

$$\text{Annual depreciation} = \frac{\text{Cost} - \text{Scrap value}}{\text{Estimated life}}$$

$$= \frac{£6,000 - £1,000}{8 \text{ years}}$$

$$= £625 \text{ pa}$$

Machine account

	£		£
Year 1:			
Cost	6,000		

Provision for depreciation

	£		£
Year 1:		Year 1:	
Balance c/d	625	Profit and loss account	625
Year 2:		Year 2:	
Balance c/d	1,250	Balance b/d	625
		Profit and loss account	625
	1,250		1,250
Year 3:		Year 3:	
Balance c/d	1,875	Balance b/d	1,250
		Profit and loss account	625
	1,875		1,875
		Year 4:	
		Balance b/d	1,875

Note: a **depreciation** account (i.e. an **expense** account) could have also been shown. The function of a depreciation account is to store the information regarding provisions for depreciation made for the **current** year until it is closed off to the profit and loss account.

FIXED ASSETS AND DEPRECIATION

Balance sheet extract:

		Cost £	Accumulated depreciation £	Net book value £
Fixed asset				
Year 1	Machine	6,000	625	5,375
Year 2	Machine	6,000	1,250	4,750
Year 3	Machine	6,000	1,875	4,125

Chapter 8

FROM TRIAL BALANCE TO FINANCIAL STATEMENTS

The main areas of double entry bookkeeping have now been covered. This chapter will introduce you to the type of question you might meet in an examination. You may be given a trial balance together with other information such as accruals and prepayments, depreciation, stock and bad and doubtful debts. All of the information must be assimilated and a full set of financial statements prepared.

The large example in this chapter will bring together the double entry covered in the previous chapters as well as introducing some new items into the accounts such as carriage inwards and outwards and customs duties.

It is important to take note of the points of presentation and approach that will be emphasised throughout the chapter.

Objectives

By the time you have finished this chapter you should be able to:

- draw up a set of financial statements from a trial balance plus additional information.

- understand the different accounting presentation of carriage inwards and carriage outwards.

- account for the disposal of a fixed asset that is traded in for a new fixed asset.

- handle the approach necessary for more complex examination type questions.

1   Trial balance type question

Example

The trial balance of Tyndall at 31 May 20X6 is shown on the following page.

You ascertain the following information:

1   Closing stock has been valued for accounts purposes at £8,490.

2   The motor van was sold on 31 August 20X5 and traded in against the cost of a new van. The trade-in price was £1,400 and the cost of the new van was £3,600.

3   Depreciation on the straight line basis is to be provided at the following annual rates:

    Motor vans   25%
    Furniture and equipment   10%

4   5% of the closing debtors total is estimated to be doubtful.

5   An accrual of £372 is required in respect of light and heat.

6   A quarter's rent to 30 June 20X6 amounting to £900 was paid on 2 April 20X6. Rates for the year to 31 March 20X7 amounting to £1,680 were paid on 16 April 20X6.

You are required to prepare a trading and profit and loss account for the year ended 31 May 20X6 and a balance sheet as at 31 May 20X6.

Trial balance of Tyndall at 31 May 20X6

	£	£
Capital account		15,258
Drawings	5,970	
Purchases	73,010	
Returns inwards (sales returns)	1,076	
Returns outwards (purchase returns)		3,720
Discounts	1,870	965
Credit sales		96,520
Cash sales		30,296
Customs duty	11,760	
Carriage inwards	2,930	
Carriage outwards	1,762	
Salesman's commission	711	
Salesman's salary	3,970	
Office salaries	7,207	
Bank charges	980	
Loan interest	450	
Light and heat	2,653	
Sundry expenses	2,100	
Rent and rates	7,315	
Printing and postage	2,103	
Advertising	1,044	
Bad debts	1,791	
Doubtful debts provision		437
Stock	7,650	
Debtors	10,760	
Creditors		7,411
Cash at bank	2,634	
Cash in hand	75	
New delivery van (less trade-in)	2,200	
Motor expenses	986	
Furniture and equipment:		
Cost	8,000	
Depreciation at 1 June 20X5		2,400
Old delivery van:		
Cost	2,000	
Depreciation at 1 June 20X5		1,000
Loan account at 9% (repayable in five years)		5,000
	163,007	163,007

Solution

Step 1   Stock

The closing stock figure of £8,490 is identified for the final accounts. No working is required.

Step 2   Fixed assets and depreciation

This is the most difficult part of the question. Considering the motor vehicles initially, the approach should be in three stages:

1   depreciation on the old vehicle up to the point of sale: $25\% \times 3/12 \times £2,000 = £125$

2   dealing with the trade-in: the way to approach this is to treat the sale and the purchase as two separate transactions. Effectively the old vehicle is treated as sold to the dealer for £1,400 and the new vehicle is treated as being purchased from him for £3,600.

3 depreciation on the new vehicle from the date of purchase to the year end:
$25\% \times 9/12 \times £3,600 = £675$.

'T' accounts should be used.

Old delivery van – accumulated depreciation

	£		£
Old delivery van – disposal	1,125	Per trial balance	1,000
		Depreciation expense	125
	1,125		1,125

Old delivery van – disposal

	£		£
Old delivery van – cost (per TB)	2,000	Old delivery van – accumulated depreciation	1,125
Profit and loss – profit on sale	525	New delivery van – cost (trade in value)	1,400
	2,525		2,525

Note: the trade in value of £1,400 is effectively the sales proceeds from the sale of the old van.

New delivery van – cost

	£		£
Per trial balance	2,200	Balance c/d	3,600
Old delivery van – disposal	1,400		
	3,600		3,600

Note: the disposal 'proceeds' on the old delivery van are treated as reducing the cost of the new delivery van in practice. To reflect this in the books the following entry is made.

Dr   New delivery van – cost   £1,400

Cr   Old delivery van – disposal   £1,400

This ensures that the disposal proceeds are correctly reflected in the disposal account and that the new van is shown at its full cost for accounting purposes.

New delivery van – accumulated depreciation

	£		£
Balance c/d	675	Depreciation expense	675

Depreciation expense – motor vans

	£		£
Old delivery van – accumulated depreciation account	125	Profit and loss – depreciation	800
New delivery van – accumulated depreciation account	675		
	800		800

In this case, depreciation has been provided on the old van up to the date of disposal, and on the new van from the date of acquisition. The assumption may be made to charge no depreciation on an asset in the year in which it is sold, and to charge depreciation for a whole year on a new asset regardless of the date in the year on which it was purchased.

However, for examination purposes, the clue is to check whether the dates of the purchase and sale are given. If they are, take proportional depreciation. If they are not, you have no alternative but to make the simplifying assumption stated above.

Depreciation on the furniture and equipment is much more straightforward.

Furniture and equipment – accumulated depreciation

	£		£
Balance c/d	3,200	Per trial balance	2,400
		Depreciation expense	
		(£8,000 × 10%)	800
	3,200		3,200

Step 3   Bad debts

Careful scrutiny of the trial balance will reveal two accounts of importance here:

- Bad debts – a debit balance of £1,791 representing bad debts already written off in the year

- Doubtful debts provision – a credit balance of £437 representing the current provision against doubtful debts

Bad debts

	£		£
Per trial balance	1,791	Profit and loss	1,892
Doubtful debts provision	101		
	1,892		1,892

Doubtful debts provision

	£		£
Balance c/d (5% × £10,760)	538	Per trial balance	437
		Bad debts (bal fig)	101
	538		538

The increase in the doubtful debts provision is charged to the profit and loss account through the bad debts account.

Step 4   Light and heat

A straightforward accrual.

Light and heat

	£		£
Per trial balance	2,653	Profit and loss (bal fig)	3,025
Balance c/d	372		
	3,025		3,025

The accrual increases the expense shown in the profit and loss account and will also appear in the balance sheet as a current liability.

Step 5   Rent and rates

		£
1	Rent prepaid ($\frac{1}{3}$ × £900)	300
2	Rates prepaid ($\frac{10}{12}$ × £1,680)	1,400
		1,700

Rent and rates

	£		£
Per trial balance	7,315	Profit and loss (bal fig)	5,615
		Balance c/d	1,700
	7,315		7,315

The prepayment of rent and rates reduces the expense to the profit and loss account and will appear in the balance sheet as a current asset.

Step 6

Prepare the trading and profit and loss account and balance sheet

Trading and profit and loss account for the year ended 31 May 20X6

	£	£	£
Sales:			
Credit			96,520
Cash			30,296
			126,816
Less: Sales returns			1,076
			125,740
Opening stock		7,650	
Purchases	73,010		
Less: Purchase returns	3,720		
	69,290		
Carriage inwards	2,930		
Customs duty	11,760		
		83,980	
		91,630	
Closing stock		8,490	
Cost of sales			83,140
Gross profit			42,600
Discount received			965
Profit on sale of van			525
			44,090

Less: Expenses:		
Depreciation:		
Van (Step 2)		800
Equipment (Step 2)		800
Bad debts (Step 3)		1,892
Light and heat (Step 4)		3,025
Rent and rates (Step 5)		5,615
Discount allowed		1,870
Carriage outwards		1,762
Salesman's commission		711
Salesman's salary		3,970
Office salary		7,207
Bank charges		980
Loan interest		450
Sundry expenses		2,100
Printing and postage		2,103
Advertising		1,044
Motor expenses		986
		35,315
Net profit		8,775

Balance sheet at 31 May 20X6

Fixed assets:	Cost £	Acc dep'n £	NBV £
Motor van	3,600	675	2,925
Furniture and equipment	8,000	3,200	4,800
	11,600	3,875	7,725
Current assets:			
Stock		8,490	
Debtors	10,760		
Less: Provision for			
doubtful debts	538		
		10,222	
Prepayments			
(rent and rates)		1,700	
Cash at bank		2,634	
Cash in hand		75	
		23,121	
Less: Current liabilities:			
Trade creditors	7,411		
Accrued expenses			
(light and heat)	372		
		7,783	
			15,338
			23,063
Less: Long-term liability:			
Loan account			5,000
			18,063

Capital account:

Balance at 1 June 20X5		15,258
Net profit	8,775	
Less drawings	5,970	
Retained profit		2,805
Balance at 31 May 20X6		18,063

Notes on presentation

1 The trading account includes all expenditure incurred in bringing the goods to their present location and condition. This includes:

- purchase cost including import duty
- carriage inwards and freight costs.

Carriage means transport costs.

Carriage inwards refers to the cost of bringing in raw materials from suppliers. **Carriage outwards** is thus delivery charges incurred in supplying goods to customers.

Carriage outwards is treated as an expense of selling and is included with all the other expenses. Note that both carriage inwards and carriage outwards are debits (i.e. expenses).

2 'Returns' often causes difficulties. Returns inwards are the same as sales returns. Since sales are credits, sales returns are debits. For presentation purposes, sales returns are deducted from sales. In the same way purchase returns are deducted from purchases.

In our work so far, the deduction of purchases and sales returns has been shown on the face of the profit and loss account. In more advanced examples it is customary to show the sales and purchases figures in the profit and loss account, with no deductions shown.

3 The discounts are shown as one line in the trial balance with both a debit and a credit balance. Remember that expenses are debit balances and income credit balances. Therefore the discount allowed is the debit balance and the discount received the credit balance.

4 In examinations the answers should precede the workings, which should clearly be labelled as such. The idea behind this is that the examiner only wishes to look at the workings if errors have been made – he will not need to do so if everything is correct.

If the workings are numbered then a reference to the working can be made in the final accounts.

Therefore, in an examination, the trading and P&L a/c and balance sheet should be shown before the workings in Step 1 and Step 5.

Conclusion

The purpose of this chapter was to illustrate the approach necessary with more complex examination type questions where a trial balance is given and a number of adjustments have to be made before the financial statements can be prepared. The illustration should have brought together all of the basic double entry that has been studied piecemeal in the earlier chapters of this text.

A number of new items were also introduced such as carriage inwards and outwards, customs duties and the trade in of an old fixed asset in part exchange for a new fixed asset.

Trial balance type question

1   Is opening stock a debit or a credit balance in the trial balance?

2   Where a fixed asset is part exchanged for another fixed asset should the cost of the new fixed asset be net of the trade in value or include the trade in value?

3   What is the double entry necessary to ensure that the trade in value of an old fixed asset is correctly reflected in the accounts?

4   If the provision for doubtful debts is increased is this a debit or a credit to the profit and loss account?

5   Does a prepayment increase or decrease the expense shown in the profit and loss account?

6   Are discounts allowed a debit or a credit balance?

7   What are returns inwards?

8   How are returns inwards presented in the financial statements?

9   What is the correct treatment for carriage inwards in the trading and profit and loss account?

10 What is carriage outwards?

Delta

Below is the trial balance extracted from the books of Delta at 31 December 20X9.

	£	£
Capital at 1 Jan 20X9		20,000
Loan account, Omega		2,000
Drawings	1,750	
Freehold premises	8,000	
Furniture and fittings	500	
Plant and machinery	5,500	
Stock at 1 Jan	8,000	
Cash at bank	650	
Provision for doubtful debts		740
Purchases	86,046	
Sales		124,450
Bad debts	256	
Bad debts recovered		45
Trade debtors	20,280	
Trade creditors		10,056
Bank charges	120	
Rent	2,000	
Returns inwards	186	
Returns outwards		135
Salaries	3,500	
Wages	8,250	
Travelling expenses	1,040	
Carriage inwards	156	
Discounts allowed	48	
Discounts received		138
General expenses	2,056	
Gas, electricity and water	2,560	
Carriage outwards	546	
Travellers' salaries and commission	5,480	
Printing and stationery	640	
	157,564	157,564

You are required to draw up the trading, profit and loss account for the year to 31 December 20X9 and the balance sheet at that date, after taking into account the following.

(a) Stock at 31 December 20X9 was valued at £7,550.

(b) Interest on the loan at 5% pa had not been paid at 31 December.

(c) Rent includes £250 for premises paid in advance to 31 March next year.

(d) Depreciate plant and machinery by 10% pa.

   Depreciate furniture and fittings by 5% pa.

(e) Adjust the provision for doubtful debts to 5% of trade debtors.

(f) Show wages as part of cost of sales.   **(25 marks)**

For the answer to this question, see the 'Answers' section at the end of the book.

Chapter 9
DAY BOOKS AND CONTROL ACCOUNTS

In this chapter we will take a step back to the process of the initial recording of transactions before they are entered into the ledger accounts.

This chapter will consider the main books of prime entry and explain the system of sales and purchases ledgers and control accounts. Finally, the areas of cash discounts and petty cash will be studied.

Objectives

By the time you have finished this chapter you should be able to:

- record most types of transactions in the relevant book of prime entry
- post the totals from the books of prime entry to the ledger accounts
- record cash discounts in the cash book.

1   Division of ledgers

1.1   The advantages of dividing the ledger

So far we have assumed that all transactions are directly entered into the double entry books of account. However, there are two major reasons why this is not likely to be the case in practice.

- The result would be a vast number of entries in the nominal ledger making it unwieldy, and making the discovery of errors extremely difficult.

- The nominal ledger is likely to be under the control of a senior accountant. He or she is not likely to have the time to enter a vast number of transactions every day. By making use of **books of prime entry** and by removing certain accounts from the nominal ledger and replacing them with **control accounts** much detailed work can be removed from the nominal ledger. Such work can then be delegated to more junior staff.

Day books act as an initial 'store' of information before the summarising and storing of that information in ledger accounts, including control accounts.

Diagram 1: Summary of stages of accounting

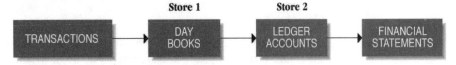

There are other advantages of dividing the ledger.

- Certain transactions can be kept confidential, i.e. access to the nominal ledger can be restricted as it only contains summary information. In some businesses this confidentiality is reflected in an alternative title to the nominal ledger, **the private ledger.**

- The computerisation of the accounting records can be done on part of the accounting system. Computerisation of the whole accounting system can be beneficial in many instances, but it may be of most benefit in those areas such as sales and purchases which have most of the business transactions. The creation of a separate sales ledger can allow its computerisation.

The only disadvantage of splitting the ledger is that more control is required to ensure all data is correctly recorded. The division should result in more control if handled properly, but if it is not correctly planned, it can make matters worse.

1.2   The nominal ledger

The nominal ledger is a summary of **all** transactions entered into by the business. In a well-structured accounting system the information in the nominal ledger alone is sufficient to produce the financial statements.

To avoid cluttering the nominal ledger, certain transactions of high frequency are recorded in detail in subsidiary records. Thus:

- sales to credit customers (and sales returns) are recorded in detail in the sales ledger

- purchases from credit suppliers (and purchases returns) are recorded in detail in the purchase ledger

- cash receipts and payments are recorded in detail in the cash book.

The nominal ledger contains only a summary record of such transactions, sufficient to produce the financial statements, but not sufficient, say, to identify how much money is owed by a particular debtor, or how much is owing to a particular creditor.

This is achieved by the use of **control accounts** in the nominal ledger.

- The sales ledger control account is a single account in the nominal ledger summarising all the transactions recorded in detail in the sales ledger.

- The purchase ledger control account is a single account in the nominal ledger summarising all the transactions recorded in detail in the purchase ledger.

- Many businesses also have a cash control account, being a single account in the nominal ledger summarising all the transactions recorded in detail in the cash book. However, other businesses prefer to regard the cash book itself as a part of the double entry system. In such cases there is no need for a separate cash control account in the nominal ledger.

1.3   The nature and purpose of the other ledgers

Sales ledger

The sales ledger has a ledger account for each debtor, which shows amounts owing by each debtor.

Purchase ledger

Similarly, the purchase ledger has an account for each creditor. The balances show the amounts owing to each creditor.

Cash book

Cash and cheque transactions form a major part of the total transactions of a business. Therefore it is appropriate to have a separate book which records these transactions.

1.4   The main books of prime entry

Transactions are summarised for posting into the control accounts by the use of books of prime entry. The main such books relevant to the syllabus are as follows.

- purchases day book

- purchases returns day book

- sales day book

- sales returns day book

- cash book

- petty cash book
- journal.

(All these items are dealt with in this chapter, except for the journal which is covered in a later chapter.)

Note particularly that in the modern business world many of these books, if not all of them, will take the form of computerised print-outs. Nevertheless, the same principles will apply.

2   Purchases day book

2.1   Purpose

The **purchases day book** is used to summarise the purchases made by a business, and will list the invoices received.

The purchases day book is not part of the double entry system. It is summarised periodically, and the totals posted to the relevant accounts in the nominal ledger (including the purchase ledger control account) and the **creditors ledger** (which has now been removed from the double entry system). The **creditors ledger** is the ledger which contains the personal accounts of the **individual** creditors. It is also known as the **purchases ledger** or **bought ledger**.

Note in the example which follows that the purchases day book deals with all types of purchases by a business – goods for resale, raw materials to be processed into goods for sale, and expenses of running the business. It therefore deals with items which will eventually find their way into either the purchases account or the various expense accounts.

The entries are made into the purchases day book from the suppliers' invoices received by the business. They must then be analysed, so that totals can be posted to the correct accounts.

Example of recording of transactions and posting to ledgers

During February 20X9 the purchases day book of a company appears as follows:

Date	Supplier	Ledger ref	Total	Purchases	Lighting and heating	Repairs and maintenance	Telephone	Sundry expenses
			£	£	£	£	£	£
5 Feb	British Telecom	B1	160				160	
8 Feb	J Smith	S13	80	80				
11 Feb	B Orange	O17	180	180				
14 Feb	Eastern Electricity	E12	138		138			
18 Feb	Wiggins Teape	W4	20					20
21 Feb	S Green	G7	100	100				
23 Feb	D Brown	B13	140	140				
25 Feb	Mendit Ltd	M1	40			40		
			858	500	138	40	160	20

Record the transactions in the appropriate ledgers.

Solution

(a) In the nominal ledger:

Purchases

20X9		£	20X9	£
Feb	Purchases day book	500		

Lighting and heating

20X9		£	20X9	£
Feb	Purchases day book	138		

Repairs and maintenance

20X9		£	20X9	£
Feb	Purchases day book	40		

Telephone

20X9		£	20X9	£
Feb	Purchases day book	160		

Sundry expenses

20X9		£	20X9	£
Feb	Purchases day book	20		

(b) In the creditors ledger:

British Telecom (B1)

20X9	£	20X9		£
		Feb	Purchases day book	160

D Brown (B13)

20X9	£	20X9		£
		Feb	Purchases day book	140

Eastern Electricity (E12)

20X9	£	20X9		£
		Feb	Purchases day book	138

S Green (G7)

20X9	£	20X9		£
		Feb	Purchases day book	100

Mendit Ltd (M1)

20X9	£	20X9		£
		Feb	Purchases day book	40

B Orange (O17)

20X9	£	20X9		£
		Feb	Purchases day book	180

J Smith (S13)

20X9	£	20X9		£
		Feb	Purchases day book	80

Wiggins Teape (W4)

20X9	£	20X9		£
		Feb	Purchases day book	20

KEY POINT

The credits to the purchases ledger accounts equal the debits in the nominal ledger accounts.

Notice that at this point the double entry is not complete. We have entered the debits in the nominal ledger, but the credits appear only in the purchase ledger which is not part of the double entry system. As we will see later, the credit entries are posted (as a summary total) to the purchase ledger control account in the nominal ledger, thus completing the double entry.

3   Other day books

3.1   How are transactions and their output dealt with?

The sales day book records sales invoices to credit customers. It is used as the source of postings to the individual debtor accounts in the sales ledger.

Sales returns and purchase returns are also logged in dedicated day books, and used as a further source of postings to the sales ledger and purchase ledger respectively.

The use of all these day books is summarised in the following table.

Day book	Transaction dealt with	Nominal ledger		Creditors or debtors ledger
		Debit	Credit	
Purchases	Invoices for goods or services purchased from suppliers	Expenditure accounts, e.g. purchases, lighting and heating, telephone	Purchase ledger control account	Entered on supplier's personal account on individual basis
Sales	Invoices for goods to customers	Sales ledger control account	Revenue accounts, e.g. sales, sundry income, rental income	Entered on customer's personal account on individual basis.
Purchases returns	Credit notes for goods returned to suppliers	Purchase ledger control account	Purchases returns	Entered on supplier's account on 'debit' side on individual basis
Sales returns	Credit notes for goods returned by customers	Sales returns	Sales ledger control account	Entered on customer's personal account on 'credit' side on individual basis

Using the purchases day book as a model, draft the layout of a sales day book.

Feedback to this activity is at the end of the chapter.

3.2   Contras

On occasion there may be a set-off between accounts in the debtors ledger and the creditors ledger. For instance, suppose a business both buys goods from and sells goods to Trollope. If at one time the creditors ledger shows that the business owes him £75 and the debtors ledger shows that he owes £50, there are two possible methods of approach.

1   The business pays Trollope £75 and he pays the business £50.

2   The business agrees with Trollope to pay him £25 and sets off the £50 owing to it in the debtors ledger with £50 of the £75 owing to Trollope in the creditors ledger. This procedure is called a 'contra entry'.

If the latter course is adopted the transactions should be recorded as follows.

1   In the creditors ledger (also known as the purchases ledger)

Trollope (T26)

	£		£
Sales ledger contra	50	Balance b/d	75
Balance c/d	25		
	——		——
	75		75
	——		——

2   In the debtors ledger (also known as the sales ledger)

Trollope (T17)

	£		£
Balance b/d	50	Purchases ledger contra	50
	——		——

The creditors ledger account now correctly shows the fact that we have agreed to pay Trollope only £25 as a result of the contra agreement. Clearly Trollope himself will make equivalent adjustments in his own books.

ACTIVITY 2

Why are there no columns for cash discounts allowed and received in the sales day book and purchases day book respectively?

Feedback to this activity is at the end of the chapter.

4   The cash book

4.1   Introduction

The name 'cash book' is something of a misnomer, because the book is used to summarise an organisation's bank transactions. A company's transactions in cash (i.e. notes and coins) are dealt with (in normal circumstances) through the petty cash book.

Many enterprises have two distinct cash books – a cash payments book and a cash receipts book – but for study and examination purposes it is convenient to think of it as a single book, the balance of which shows the cash at bank or overdraft.

4.2   The bookkeeping system summarised

The cash book is the cash account in the ledger treated as a separate record. As shown in earlier chapters the cash account transactions of a business are numerous and it is really the centre piece of the bookkeeping system, being involved in all sections of it:

- the sales ledger system when customers pay their accounts

- the purchases ledger system when suppliers' accounts are paid

- the nominal ledger system when expenses are paid or assets purchased, or when income is received or liabilities are paid off

For this reason it is convenient to regard the cash book as a book of prime entry, which in practice it is, because all cash received and paid is entered into it from the source documents.

The structure of the main elements of the bookkeeping system can now be presented thus.

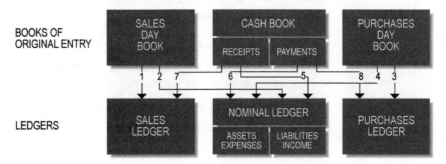

Each of the six arrows connecting these elements of the recording system is numbered. The explanations below clarify their meaning.

1   Sales day book → sales ledger

Individual credit sales are entered into the sales day book and into the sales ledger accounts of the credit customers. The arrow represents the entry from sales day book to the debit of the sales ledger account concerned.

2   Sales day book → nominal ledger (sales account)

The sales day book has two functions – to build up the total sales for a period to be credited to the sales account in the nominal ledger and to facilitate the debiting of the individual sales ledger accounts in the sales ledger. The second arrow represents the transfer of the sales day book total to the credit of the sales account. At this stage the double entry is incomplete: although debits have been made in the sales ledger, this does not form part of the double entry. The double entry is eventually completed by a debit entry in the sales ledger control account in the nominal ledger, the amount of the entry equalling the total of the debits posted to the individual accounts in the sales ledger.

3   Purchases day book → purchases ledger

This arrow represents the entries corresponding to arrow 1 above but for credit purchases – entered into the purchases day book and to the credit of the suppliers' accounts in the purchases ledger.

4   Purchases day book → nominal ledger (purchases account)

Arrow 4 corresponds to arrow 2. It is the transfer of the total purchases to the debit of purchases account in the nominal ledger. The purchases day book, like the sales day book, is not part of the double entry system but facilitates the making of the entries. The sum of the individual credits to purchases ledger accounts is equal to the single debit to purchases account. You saw in the example earlier that items other than the purchase of goods for resale may pass through the purchases day book.

5   Debit side of cash book → credit of nominal ledger accounts

The entries explained for arrow 6 below analyse the credits (payments) in the cash book. Arrow 5 indicates the corresponding process for the debits (receipts). Receipts could be sundry items of income, rental income for example, or the result of incurring a liability. When a business borrows money the entry in the cash book records the increased cash and the credit to the liability account in the nominal ledger records the obligation to repay the money in due course.

6   Credit side of cash book → debit of nominal ledger accounts

Arrow 6 is the analysis of payments made. The cash book records the payment of cash and thus the reduction in the cash balance, and the transfer to the appropriate nominal ledger account analyses the payment. The expense accounts in the nominal ledger collect all items relating to the same expense heading. Fixed asset accounts do the same for capital expenditure on different types of fixed asset.

7   Cash book→ sale ledger

Receipts from credit customers are entered into the cash book and to the credit side of the appropriate sales ledger account.

8   Cash book→ purchase ledger

Payments to suppliers are entered in the cash book and to the debit side of the appropriate purchase ledger account.

Remember that 7 and 8 are not part of double entry. Sales ledger and purchase ledger accounts are memorandum accounts only.

Example

The following transactions are recorded in the cash payments book of a company during February 20X9.

Date	Detail	Cheque no	Ledger ref	Bank £	Discount received £	Purchase ledger £	Wages £	Petty cash £	Sundry expenses £
2 Feb	Wages	124507	-	1,052			1,052		
5 Feb	J Smith	124508	S13	58	1	58			
9 Feb	B Jones	124509	-	120					120
16 Feb	Cash	124510	-	150				150	
23 Feb	S Green	124511	G7	80	6	80			
24 Feb	B Orange	124512	O17	100		100			
27 Feb	D Brown	124513	B13	119	2	119			
				1,679	9	357	1,052	150	120

Record the above transactions in the relevant ledger accounts.

Note: the above cash book illustrates the idea of analysis columns in the cash book. In its simplest form, the cash book consists of a single column on each side with an adjacent discount column. Every item of cash receipt or payment is then posted individually to the appropriate ledger account. It is often convenient to introduce analysis columns for expense and income items to enable monthly or other totals to be posted to the accounts. Although there is only one item in each of the expense columns in this cash book, it is important to realise that the postings to the accounts are of the **column totals** (£1,052, £150 and £120) and not the individual items.

For examination purposes you will nearly always need to work with the simple 'single column' type cash book with discount columns.

4.3   Discounts received

Before considering the double entry bookkeeping procedures here it is worth mentioning the discounts received column.

- It does not represent an amount paid in the period. The total of £1,679 is made up of the analysed column totals excluding discount received.

	£
Purchase ledger control	357
Wages	1,052
Petty cash	150
Sundry expenses	120
	1,679

- It is included in the cash payments book to show whether any cash discount has been taken for prompt payment and to facilitate its recording in both the nominal ledger and the creditors ledger.

Note that only cash (prompt payment) discounts will be included here, and not trade discounts. The distinction and different treatments are explained by the following table.

Term	Relates to	Bookkeeping implications
Cash discount	Discount for payment before a stated date	• Purchases are debited with the full invoice price.
		• On payment of the creditor, the difference between cash paid and the full invoice price of the invoice paid represents the cash discount.
Trade discount	Favourable price for people in the same trade.	Purchases are recorded at trade price (the lower price involved). The amount of the deduction does not appear in the ledger accounts.

Solution

Returning to the example, at the end of February the transactions are recorded as follows:

1   In the nominal ledger

Discount received

20X9		£	20X9		£
			Feb	Cash book	9

Wages

20X9		£	20X9	£
Feb	Cash book	1,052		

Petty cash

20X9		£	20X9	£
Feb	Cash book	150		

Sundry expenses

20X9		£	20X9	£
Feb	Cash book	120		

2   In the purchases ledger

D Brown (B13)

20X9		£	20X9	£
Feb	Cash book – discount	2		
	Cash book	119		

S Green (G7)

20X9		£	20X9	£
Feb	Cash book – discount	6		
	Cash book	80		

B Orange (O17)

20X9		£	20X9	£
Feb	Cash book	100		

J Smith (S13)

20X9		£	20X9	£
Feb	Cash book – discount	1		
	Cash book	58		

Note: the discount received is included on the 'debit' side of the creditor's personal account, representing a reduction in the amount owing to him.

Example

The following receipts are recorded in the cash book of a company during February 20X9.

Date	Detail	Ledger ref	Bank	Discount allowed	Sales ledger	Cash sales	Rental income	Sundry income
			£	£	£	£	£	£
2 Feb	Cash sales		140			140		
5 Feb	S Black	B7	75	5	75			
9 Feb	J Clark		5					5
16 Feb	Cash sales		100			100		
23 Feb	B Brown	B8	16	1	16			
24 Feb	Hire-it plc		80				80	
27 Feb	J Purple	P6	5		5			
			421	6	96	240	80	5

4.4   Discounts allowed

Once again the treatment of discounts merits close scrutiny. The discounts allowed column does not represent an amount received in the period, but is included in the cash receipts book to show whether any discount has been allowed and to facilitate its recording in both the nominal ledger and the debtors ledger.

ACTIVITY 3

Record the totals from the cash receipts book in the nominal ledger and the individual amounts in the sales ledger.

Feedback to this activity is at the end of the chapter.

5   Petty cash book

5.1   Purpose of petty cash system

The **petty cash system** is usually designed to deal with sundry small payments in cash made by a business, e.g. paying the milkman, purchasing biscuits, buying stationery or reimbursing travelling expenses.

The petty cash book is unlikely to impact on the purchase ledger and sales ledger systems, although the occasional purchase ledger payment might be made from petty cash.

5.2   Imprest system

The best way of dealing with petty cash is by means of an **imprest** system, which works as follows.

Step 1   To initiate the system, a round sum cheque is drawn. This will be dealt with through the cash payments book, the eventual debit being to petty cash and the credit to bank. This round sum amount will be referred to as the 'petty cash float'.

Step 2   As the petty cashier makes payments he records these in the petty cash book, which is not part of the double entry system.

KEY POINT

The **petty cash system** is usually designed to deal with sundry small payments in cash made by a business, e.g. paying the milkman, purchasing biscuits, buying stationery or reimbursing travelling expenses.

Step 3   When the petty cash runs low, a cheque is drawn to return the petty cash to the exact amount of the original float. At this stage vouchers should be produced by the petty cashier to the cheque signatory which will exactly equal the cheque required.

This aspect of control is the essential feature of the petty cash system. At any stage the float should be represented in the petty cash box by the actual cash therein, plus any vouchers in support of payments made since the last reimbursement.

Example

On 1 March 20X9 a petty cash float of £100 is introduced by Dialex. During March the following payments are made out of petty cash:

		£
2 March	Biscuits	10
8 March	Stationery	20
11 March	Bus fare	3
16 March	Train fare	5
25 March	Stationery	40

On 31 March the cash is reimbursed. Write up the petty cash book for the month.

Solution

Received	Date	Details	Voucher	Total	Stationery expenses	Sundry expenses	Travelling
£				£	£	£	£
100	1 Mar	Cash book					
	2 Mar	Gateway biscuits	1	10		10	
	8 Mar	Basildon Bond	2	20	20		
	11 Mar	Bus fares	3	3			3
	16 Mar	British Rail	4	5			5
	25 Mar	Office International	5	40	40		
				—	—	—	—
				78	60	10	8
				—	—	—	—
78	31 Mar	Cash					
		Balance c/d		100			
—				—			
178				178			
—				—			
100	1 Apr	Balance b/d					

5.3   Writing up the ledger accounts

No double entry bookkeeping entries are made from the receipts side of the petty cash book – in a good system the only receipt should be the reimbursement of the float and the double entry for that is dealt with in the posting of the cash book.

As regards the payments, the double entry in the nominal ledger is performed as follows:

Stationery

20X9		£	*20X9*	£
Mar	Petty cash book	60		

Sundry expenses

20X9		£	*20X9*	£
Mar	Petty cash book	10		

Travelling expenses

20X9		£	*20X9*	£
Mar	Petty cash book	8		

Conclusion

In this chapter the operation of the system of books of prime entry or day books has been studied. These are simply ways of summarising the money transactions of a business at suitable points in time and then posting these summaries to the relevant accounts in the nominal ledger.

SELF-TEST QUESTIONS

Division of ledgers

1   What is a book of prime entry? (1.1)

2   What is the sales ledger? (1.3)

Purchases day book

3   What is the purchases day book? (2.1)

Other day books

4   What documents are used to write up the sales returns book? (3.1)

5   What situation might cause a contra entry to take place? (3.2)

The cash book

6   Where is the total from the discount received column in the cash payments book posted to? (4.3)

7   What is the difference between a cash discount and a trade discount? (4.3)

Petty cash book

8   What is an imprest system? (5.2)

PRACTICE QUESTION

Heale

You are given the following information about the first month's trading of Heale:

			£
Sales details:			
	Credit sales	Jones	94
		Smith	118
		Turnip	141
		Clog	235
		Foul	353
Purchase details:			
	Credit purchases	Snell	80
		Ryan	100
		Ovett	150
		Coe	300
		Keino	100
		British Telecom	50
		British Gas	75

Cash book details:

Receipts from sales:		Jones	30
		Smith	60
		Turnip	110
		Foul	80
		Sundry income	10
Payments:		Petty cash	200
		Snell	70
		Ovett	30
		British Telecom	50
		Wages	300
		Sundry expenses	80

Petty cash book details:

Receipts	Cash	200
Payments	Stationery	16
	Postage	3
	Travelling	8
	Sundry expenses	12

(a)   Write up the sales day book, purchase day book, cash book and petty cash book.

(10 marks)

(b)   From the above books of prime entry, write up the nominal, sales and purchases ledgers.   **(20 marks)**

(c)   Extract a trial balance at the end of the month.   **(5 marks)**

(Total: 35 marks)

For the answer to this question, see the 'Answers' section at the end of the book.

FEEDBACK TO ACTIVITY 1

Sales day book

Date	Customer	Ledger ref	Total	Sales	Sundry income

FEEDBACK TO ACTIVITY 2

The sales day book records invoices sent out to customers and the purchases day book records invoices received from suppliers. At this stage it is not known whether cash discounts will be taken or not. It is only when the money is paid or received that this information is known.

FEEDBACK TO ACTIVITY 3

1   In the nominal ledger

Discount allowed

20X9		£	20X9		£
Feb	Cash book	6			

Cash sales

20X9		£	20X9		£
			Feb	Cash book	240

Rental income

20X9		£	20X9		£
			Feb	Cash book	80

Sundry income

20X9		£	20X9		£
			Feb	Cash book	5

Again it is worth noting the treatment of the discount, being debited to discount allowed and credited to sales ledger control account (reducing the amount owed to debtors).

2   Sales ledger

S Black (B7)

20X9		£	20X9		£
			Feb	Cash book – discount	5
				Cash book	75

B Brown (B8)

20X9		£	20X9		£
			Feb	Cash book – discount	1
				Cash book	16

J Purple (P6)

20X9		£	20X9		£
			Feb	Cash book	5

Here the discount is included on the 'credit' side of the debtor's personal account, representing a reduction in the amount owing by him.

The postings from the cash receipts book are to debit the bank account with the total and credit sales ledger accounts and income accounts.

Chapter 10
CONTROL ACCOUNT RECONCILIATIONS

The whole process of bookkeeping revolves around the idea that the records 'balance': every debit has a corresponding credit and the total of the debits equals the total of the credits. In other words, if there are no errors in the records, the trial balance will balance.

If the trial balance does not balance, the difference has to be found. In a system that is not computerised, it may take a lot of expensive time and effort to find the difference. However, there is a technique which simplifies the process considerably – balancing sections of the bookkeeping system separately.

As we have seen, the numerous transactions concerned with sales and purchases are not posted individually to the nominal ledger. Instead, they are dealt with in subsidiary ledgers (the sales and purchases ledger respectively). It is fairly easy to prove the accuracy of the sales ledger and the purchases ledger separately. The techniques for doing so are the subject of this chapter.

Objectives

By the time you have finished this chapter you should be able to:

- prepare control accounts proving the accuracy of the sales and purchases ledger.

1   Control account reconciliations

The objective of this chapter is to establish a technique for proving the correctness of a section of the bookkeeping system. Let us take the sales ledger first.

1.1   Proving the accuracy of the sales ledger entries

The total of the sales ledger balances is the key to the operation. Can we establish, independently of the sales ledger, a control total with which the total of these balances can be agreed?

The entries in the sales ledger come predominantly from the following sources:

Sales day book	–	credit sales
Cash book	–	cash received from customers
Cash book discount column	–	discounts allowed

There will be some other minor items such as bad debts written off and, of course, the balances brought forward from the previous period.

Is it possible to obtain the totals of these items without reference to the sales ledger? Yes. All the information is available.

Item	Source of total
Opening balances	List of last month's balances
Credit sales	Total of sales day book
Cash from customers	Sales ledger column in cash book (the analysed cash book was explained in the last chapter)
Sales returns	Total of sales returns day book
Discounts allowed	Discounts column in cash book

All these items are put together in a ledger account in the nominal ledger – the sales ledger control account. The advantage of this exercise is that it provides an independent check on the entries in the sales ledger. If all goes well, the balance on the sales ledger control at any time should equal the total of the individual balances in the sales ledger.

An example of a sales ledger control account appears below.

Sales ledger control account

		£			£
1 Jan	Balance b/d	108,000	31 Jan	Cash from customers	58,400
31 Jan	Sales for month	59,000		Discount allowed	300
				Sales returns	1,200
				Balance c/d	107,100
		£167,000			£167,000
1 Feb	Balance b/d	107,100			

Note that the items appear on the same side as that on which the individual items appear in the sales ledger.

The balance of £107,100 will then be agreed with the total of the sales ledger balances.

One important point must be thoroughly understood before proceeding. When we total the sales day book and post the figure of £59,000 to the debit of the control account we are duplicating individual debit entries in the sales ledger which in total amount to £59,000. In other words, we appear to be posting these debit entries twice, in breach of the normal rules of double entry. Similarly, with the credit entry of £58,400 cash from customers (and indeed with all other entries in the control account): the entry duplicates individual credit entries in the sales ledger which in total amount to £58,400.

The reason why this does not in fact breach the rules of double entry is that the sales ledger is **not part of the double entry system**. Neither is the purchases ledger. Only the entries in the nominal ledger (i.e. in the control accounts) form part of the double entry system. We say that the sales ledger and purchases ledger accounts are memorandum only, meaning that we maintain them only for administrative convenience, not as part of the double entry system. In some accounting systems the sales ledger and purchases ledger are part of the double entry system, and the control accounts are **memorandum only**, but this is less common.

1.2   Proving the accuracy of the purchases ledger

Exactly the same process is followed to agree the purchases ledger by preparing a purchases ledger control account which leads to a balance with which the total of the purchases ledger balances can be agreed.

An example of a purchases ledger control account appears below.

Purchases ledger control account

		£			£
31 Jan	Cash paid to creditors	36,000	1 Jan	Balance b/d	38,900
	Discount received	140	31 Jan	Purchases for month	18,200
	Purchases returns	215			
	Balance c/d	20,745			
		£57,100			£57,100
			1 Feb	Balance b/d	20,745

1.3   Additional items in control accounts

As well as the items covered so far, several others can appear:

Sales ledger control account	Purchases ledger control account
Cash refunds to customers Bad debts written off	Cash refunds from suppliers

One other additional item appears frequently in examination questions on control accounts – the **contra**. A contra is a transfer between two ledger accounts for the same person. It sometimes happens that a customer in the sales ledger is also a supplier in the purchases ledger. In many cases, the accounts are settled by each party paying the other in full for goods supplied. However, it is also possible to set off the balances and for the party with the greater balance to pay the difference.

Example

In the personal ledgers of X Ltd there is an account with Y Ltd in both the sales ledger and the purchases ledger:

Sales ledger
Y Ltd

	£		£
Goods	4,900		

Purchases ledger
Y Ltd

	£		£
		Goods	5,200

Instead of paying the £5,200 due to Y Ltd, X Ltd could pay £300 and cancel the remaining debt against the sales ledger balance due from Y Ltd. The ledger accounts would become:

Sales ledger
Y Ltd

	£		£
Goods	4,900	Contra purchases ledger	4,900

Purchases ledger
Y Ltd

	£		£
Cash	300	Goods	5,200
Contra sales ledger	4,900		
	5,200		5,200

KEY POINT

Contras must appear in both sales ledger and purchases ledger.

Both accounts are cleared. The vital point to grasp about contras is that they must appear in both sales ledger and purchases ledger, and therefore must necessarily be in both sales ledger control account and purchases ledger control account.

1.4   Reconciling items

In practice the balance on the control account may not agree with the total of the ledger accounts, and in such an instance the causes of the difference must be identified and adjustments made where necessary.

Such differences may be caused by:

• errors in the sales or purchases ledger control accounts

• errors in the debtors or creditors ledger

• errors in both the control accounts and the ledger accounts.

ACTIVITY 1

Suggest reasons why there might be a difference between the balance on the sales ledger control account and the total of the list of sales ledger balances.

Feedback to this activity is at the end of the chapter.

2   Agreement of the control account with the underlying accounts

Example

The following example illustrates the types of problem likely to arise in a system which seeks to ensure agreement of the control account balance with the sum of the balances on the underlying accounts. Full explanations of the amendments are given – such explanations would not normally be necessary in an examination question. This illustration and the entries to correct the errors are based on the purchases ledger control account being in the double entry system (whereas the purchases ledger accounts are memorandum only).

Alston's purchases ledger control account is an integral part of the double entry system. Individual ledger account balances are listed and totalled on a monthly basis, and reconciled to the control account balance. Information for the month of March is as follows:

1   Individual ledger account balances at 31 March have been listed out and totalled as follows:

	£
Total of debit balances	1,012
Total of credit balances	20,778

2   The purchases ledger control account balance at 31 March is £21,832 (net).

3   On further examination the following errors are discovered:

• The total of discount received for the month, amounting to £1,715, has not been entered in the control account.

• On listing-out, an individual credit balance of £205 has been incorrectly treated as a debit.

• A petty cash payment to a supplier amounting to £63 has been correctly treated in the control account, but no entry has been made in the supplier's individual ledger account.

• The purchases day book total for March has been undercast (understated) by £2,000.

• Contras (set-offs) with the sales ledger, amounting in total to £2,004, have been correctly treated in the individual ledger accounts, but no entry has been made in the control account.

You are required:

1   to prepare the part of the purchases ledger control account reflecting the above information

2   to prepare a statement reconciling the original total of the individual balances with the corrected balance on the control account.

Solution

The way to approach the question is to consider each of the above five points in turn and ask to what extent they affect (a) the purchases ledger control account and (b) the listing of purchases ledger balances.

Step 1

The **total of discount received in the cash book** is dealt with by debiting the purchases ledger control account and crediting discount received. Thus, if the posting has not been entered in either double entry account it clearly should be.

As the individual ledger accounts in the purchases ledger are posted individually from the cash payments book, the total of discount received will not feature in any postings to the purchases ledger; hence no amendment is required to the list of supplier balances.

Step 2

Individual credit balances are extracted from the purchases ledger. Here, this error affects the totals of the debit and credit balances of the ledger account balance. No adjustment is required to the control account.

Step 3

The question clearly states that the error has been made in the individual ledger accounts. Amendments should be made to the list of balances. Again, no amendment is required to the control account.

Step 4

The **total of the purchases day book** is posted by debiting purchases and crediting purchases ledger control account. If the total is understated the following bookkeeping entry must be made, posting the £2,000 understatement:

Dr   Purchases

Cr   Purchases ledger control

As the individual ledger accounts in the purchases ledger are posted individually from the purchases day book, the total of the day book being understated will not affect the listing of the balances in the purchases ledger.

Step 5

Here it is clear that the error affects the control account, not the purchases ledger. Correction should be made by the bookkeeping entry:

Dr   Purchases ledger control

Cr   Sales ledger control

Purchases ledger control account

	£			£
Discount received (S1)	1,715	31 Mar	Balance (net)	21,832
Sales ledger control (S5)	2,004		Purchase (S4)	2,000
Balance c/d	20,113			
	23,832			23,832

Reconciliation of individual balances with control account balance

	Dr £	Cr £
Balances as extracted	1,012	20,778
Credit balance incorrectly treated 2 × £205 (S2)		410
Petty cash payment (S3)	63	
		21,188
	1,075	1,075
Net total agreeing with control account		20,113

Conclusion

In this chapter we looked at the reasons why control account balances should be equal to the list of individual balances in the relevant ledger, and the reasons why these two totals are very often not equal. If the totals are not equal, then the reasons for the difference must be discovered, and the control account and list of individual balances amended accordingly.

SELF-TEST QUESTIONS

Control account reconciliations

1   Why should the balance on the purchase ledger control account equal the total of the balances in the purchases ledger? (1.2)

2   What three types of difference may cause control account reconciliation problems? (1.4)

Agreement of the control account with the underlying accounts

3   Would the miscasting of the sales day book affect the sales ledger balances? (2)

4   Is the opening balance on the purchase ledger control account a debit or a credit balance? (2)

5   What is the double entry for a discount received that has not been entered in the accounts? (2)

6   If a credit balance on a creditor's account had been included in the list of balances as a debit balance what amendment would be required? (2)

7   Is the entry in a creditor's individual account for a payment to him out of petty cash a debit or a credit entry? (2)

8   If the purchases day book is under-cast what would be the double entry to amend this? (2)

9   What is the double entry for a contra? (2)

MULTIPLE-
CHOICE
QUESTION

In a sales ledger control account, which of the following lists is composed only of items which would appear on the credit side of the account?

A   Cash received from customers, sales returns, bad debts written off, contras against amounts due to suppliers in the purchases ledger.

B   Sales, cash refunds to customers, bad debts written off, discounts allowed.

C   Cash received from customers, discounts allowed, interest charged on overdue accounts, bad debts written off.

D   Sales, cash refunds to customers, interest charged on overdue accounts, contras against amounts due to suppliers in the purchases ledger.

For the answer to this question, see the 'Answers' section at the end of the book.

PRACTICE
QUESTIONS

Question 1: Excel Stores Ltd

The book-keeper of Excel Stores Ltd prepared a schedule of balances of individual suppliers' accounts from the creditors ledger at 30 June 20X4 and arrived at a total of £86,538.28.

He passed the schedule over to the accountant who compared this total with the closing balance on the Purchases Ledger Control account reproduced below:

Purchases ledger control

20X4 June		£	20X4 June		£
30	Purchase returns	560.18	1	Balance b/d	89,271.13
30	Bank	96,312.70	30	Purchases	100,483.49
30	Balance c/d	84,688.31	30	Discount received	2,656.82
			30	Debtors ledger control (contras)	3,049.75
		192,561.19			195,261.19
			July 1	Balance b/d	84,688.31

During his investigation into the discrepancy between the two figures, the accountant discovered a number of errors in the control account and the individual ledger accounts and schedule. You may assume that the total of each item posted to the control account is correct except to the extent that they are dealt with in the list below:

1   One supplier had been paid £10.22 out of petty cash. This had been correctly posted to his personal account but has been omitted from the control account.

2   The credit side of one supplier's personal account had been under-added by £30.00.

3   A credit balance on a supplier's account had been transposed from £548.14 to £584.41 when extracted on to the schedule.

4   The balance on one supplier's account of £674.32 had been completely omitted from the schedule.

5   Discounts received of £12.56 and £8.13 had been posted to the wrong side of two individual creditors' accounts.

6   Goods costing £39.60 had been returned to the supplier but this transaction had been completely omitted from the returns day book.

(a) Prepare a statement starting with the original closing balance on the purchases ledger control account then identifying and correcting the errors in that account and concluding with an amended closing balance. **(9 marks)**

(b) Prepare a statement starting with the original total of the schedule of individual creditors then identifying and correcting errors in that schedule and concluding with an amended total. **(7 marks)**

(Total: 16 marks)

Question 2: DEF Ltd – Sales Ledger

DEF Ltd has a computerised sales ledger which is not integrated with the remainder of its accounting records which are kept manually.

A summary report (produced by totalling the individual customer accounts) from the computer system at 30 September 20X8 is as follows:

Sales Ledger control report 30 September 20X8

		£
Balance brought forward		15,438.00
Add:	Sales	74,691.00
	Repayments made	1,249.00
	Adjustments	23.00
Less:	Sales returns	2,347.00
	Payments received	71,203.00
	Bad debts written off	646.00
	Purchase ledger contra	139.00
	Discounts allowed	4,128.00
	Adjustments	58.00
Balance carried forward		12,880.00

The computerised customer records were inspected and two customers were found to have credit balances. These were:

B Green	£434.00
J Jones	£158.00

The balances on the manually prepared sales ledger control account in the nominal ledger at the same date were:

Debit   £12,814.00   Credit   £592.00

The accounts were reviewed and the following errors were found:

1 One of the pages in the sales day book had been over-added by £850.00.

2 The total on one page of the sales returns day book had been carried forward as £1,239 instead of £1,329.

3 XT Ltd had settled its account of £474 by purchase ledger contra. This had not been entered on a computer journal.

4 A sales return valued at £354 was entered in J Smith's account as a sale.

5 A repayment of £217 made to B Green was entered in his account as a payment received from him.

6 The balance on AS Ltd's account of £793 had been written off as a bad debt but was not entered on a computer journal.

7 A sale to CG Ltd for £919 was entered in EG Ltd's account.

8 Discount allowed to XYZ Ltd of £57 had not been entered in its account.

9 The total of the discount received column in the cash book was under-added by £100.

You are required:

(a) to restate the manual control account commencing with the balances given

(b) to show a corrected computerised control account using the format given

(c) explain the effect of each of items 1 to 9 above.   **(14 marks)**

For the answers to these questions, see the 'Answers' section at the end of the book.

FEEDBACK TO
ACTIVITY **1**

- The sales day book, sales returns book or cash receipts book have been incorrectly totalled.

- A total from a book of prime entry has been transferred to the control account as a different figure.

- An individual entry from a book of prime entry has been transferred to the individual debtor's account as a different figure.

- An entry in the control account or the individual debtor's account has been omitted or posted to the wrong side of the account.

- The double entry for a day book total has been incorrectly made.

- An individual debtor's account has been incorrectly balanced.

- The list of sales ledger balances has been incorrectly totalled.

- An entry has been made in either the control account or the individual debtor's account but not in both.

- An individual debtor's balance has been omitted from the list of balances.

Chapter 11
BANK RECONCILIATIONS

In this chapter the relationship between the balance in the cash book and the balance on the bank statement will be considered. The likely reasons for any differences will be investigated and a statement reconciling the two balances prepared.

Objectives

By the time you have finished this chapter you should be able to:

- amend the cash book for any errors or omissions

- prepare a statement reconciling the amended cash book balance with the bank statement balance.

1   The nature and purpose of a bank reconciliation statement

1.1   Bank statement and cash book

The **cash book** records all transactions with the bank.

The **bank statement** records all the bank's transactions with the business.

The contents of the cash book should be exactly the same as the record provided by the bank in the form of a bank statement, and therefore the business records should correspond with the bank statement.

This is in fact so, but with two important provisos.

- The ledger account maintained by the bank is the opposite way round to the cash book. This is because the bank records the balance in favour of an individual as a credit balance, i.e. a liability of the bank to the individual. From the individual's point of view it is, of course, an asset, i.e. a debit balance in his cash book.

- Timing differences must inevitably occur. A cheque payment is recorded in the cash book when the cheque is despatched. The bank only records such a cheque when it is cleared, which may be several days later.

The existence of the bank statement provides an important check on the most vulnerable of a company's assets – cash. However, the timing differences referred to above make it essential to reconcile the balance on the ledger account with that of the bank statement. This reconciliation takes the form of a bank reconciliation statement.

1.2   Why the bank statement and cash book balances may not agree

The reconciliation is carried out at frequent intervals, e.g. monthly.

Two types of items must be identified.

- Those which appear in the bank statement but which have not yet been entered in the cash book.

- Those which have been entered in the cash book but which have not yet appeared on the bank statement.

KEY POINTS

The **cash book** records all transactions with the bank. The **bank statement** records all the bank's transactions with the business.

DEFINITION

A **bank reconciliation statement** reconciles the balance on the ledger account with that of the bank statement.

1.3 Items not yet entered in the cash book

These may include:

- bank charges
- bank interest (on overdrafts)
- standing orders and direct debits
- credit transfers – where a receipt has been paid direct into the firm's bank account.

All of these items must eventually be entered in the cash book because they relate to cash transactions of the business. This will then bring the cash book in line with the bank statement.

1.4 Items not yet on the bank statement

These will be timing differences that include:

- **Outstanding or unpresented cheques**

  Suppose a cheque relating to a payment to a supplier of Poorboy Ltd is written, signed and posted on 29 March. It is also entered in Poorboy's cash book on the same day. By the time the supplier has received the cheque and paid it into his bank account, and by the time his bank has processed it through the clearing system, the cheque does not appear on Poorboy's bank statement until, say, 6 April. If Poorboy receives a bank statement made up to 31 March, it will show a discrepancy with the cash book, because the cash book will show the cheque whereas the bank statement will not. Poorboy will regard the cash book as showing the true position, and the bank statement as not being fully up to date.

- **Outstanding deposits**

  In a similar way, a trader may receive cheques by post on 31 March, enter them in the cash book and pay them into the bank on the same day. Nevertheless, the cheques may not appear on the bank statement until 2 April. Again the cash book would be regarded as showing the true position.

  Outstanding deposits are also known as **outstanding lodgements**.

The purpose of performing a bank reconciliation statement is not to adjust the cash book in order to match the bank statement (as students sometimes mistakenly suppose), but simply to confirm that the cash book is correct. The only adjustments that would need to be made in the cash book would relate to cases where the bank statement reveals that the cash book is incorrect or incomplete (e.g. where a direct debit payment appears in the bank statement and has not yet been entered in the cash book).

ACTIVITY 1

The balance in a business's cash book is £1,600 debit. That includes £200 of cheques that have been drawn but not yet presented to the bank and £350 of deposits which have not yet appeared on the bank statement. Once these timing differences have been dealt with the cash book and bank statement balances agree.

What is the bank statement balance?

Feedback to this activity is at the end of the chapter.

1.5 Errors

There might be errors by the bookkeeper. In this case the appropriate correcting entries should be put through the cash book.

There might also be errors by the bank. In this (rare) case, it is the bank statement which is wrong and where the correction must be made.

1.6 Dishonoured cheques

Consider an example. Suppose that for the past two months Patterdale's ledger balance has shown an amount owing to you of £28. He sends you a cheque for £28 on 3 June which you promptly enter in the cash book and pay into the bank. This increases cash and reduces debtors by £28. A week later the bank returns the cheque marked R/D (return to drawer), i.e. it has been dishonoured. Since Patterdale's bank account is heavily overdrawn, his own bank has refused to honour the cheque. What effect does this have? There are two points to consider.

- The overall effect on your bank statement is nil. The receipt of £28 shown earlier on the bank statement will be cancelled out by the subsequent reversing entry by the bank (shown on the payments side of the bank statement and marked as 'dishonoured cheque' or 'item advised').

- Patterdale still owes £28 – his earlier cheque was a worthless piece of paper. The receipt of the cheque will have been recorded in the cash receipts book in the usual way, and it will be included in the total posted by debiting bank and crediting sales ledger control account at the end of the month. This must now be corrected by debiting sales ledger control account and crediting bank.

Patterdale's account in the debtors ledger will appear as follows:

Patterdale

	£		£
Balance b/d	28	Bank	28
Dishonoured cheque	28	Balance c/d	28
	——		——
	56		56
	——		——

Example

On 31 July 20X7 Blyth's cash book showed a balance in hand of £52 compared with a balance of £134 shown by his bank statement. He discovered the following.

(a) Cheques drawn by Blyth during July, amounting to £356, £1,732 and £196, had been entered in the cash book but had not been presented at the bank by the end of the month.

(b) Blyth had forgotten to enter in the cash book a standing order of £50 relating to a trade subscription.

(c) The bank had incorrectly credited Blyth's account with a dividend receipt of £25 relating to another customer.

(d) Bank charges of £105 shown on the bank statement had not yet been entered in the cash book.

(e) Cheques received from customers amounting to £1,211 were entered in the cash book on 31 July but were not credited on the bank statement until 3 August.

(f) Direct credits from customers of £180 and £31 had been paid direct into the bank, but no entry had been made in the cash book.

(g) The payments side of the cash book for July had been undercast by £1,000 (this means that the total of the payments side is understated by £1,000).

(h) The statement shows an item 'return cheque £72'. This has not yet been accounted for in the cash book.

You are required to show adjustments to the cash book and to prepare the bank reconciliation statement at 31 July 20X7.

Solution

Step 1 Identify those items which have yet to be entered in the cash book. These include (b), (d), (f) and (h). The error by the bookkeeper (g) must be corrected through the cash book since the unadjusted balance of £52 has been affected by the addition error.

Step 2 Identify those items which appear in the cash book but not in the statement: these include (a) and (e). These will appear on the bank reconciliation statement.

Step 3 The error by the bank (c) will be adjusted on the face of the bank reconciliation statement.

Cash book

20X7		£	20X7		£
31 Jul	Balance b/d	52		(b) Subscriptions	50
	(f) Direct credit	180		(d) Bank charges	105
	(f) Direct credit	31		(g) Cash book	1,000
				(h) Dishonoured cheque	72
		263			
	Corrected balance c/d	964			
		1,227			1,227
				Corrected balance b/d (overdrawn)	964

Bank reconciliation statement at 31 July 20X7

	£	£
Balance per statement		134
Correction of error by bank – amount wrongly credited (c)		25
		109
Unpresented cheques:		
(a)	356	
(a)	1,732	
(a)	196	
	2,284	
		2,175 O/D
Outstanding deposits (e)		1,211
Balance per cash book (overdrawn)		964 O/D

Notes: the bank reconciliation statement is rather complicated because it starts with a balance in hand and ends up with an overdraft balance (O/D). The logic is as follows.

- If the £25 had been credited to the correct customer, Blyth's balance would have been only £109 (in hand).

- The three unpresented cheques are regarded as payments for July. Had they appeared in the bank statement in July, they would have had the effect of turning a £109 balance in hand into an overdraft of £2,175 (be careful with the arithmetic).

- Operating in the opposite direction, if the deposits of £1,211 had been included in the bank statement in the same month as the cash book, the overdraft would have been reduced from £2,175 to £964.

- This illustration shows how important it is to understand the processes rather than to memorise a layout.

The cash book and the bank statement balance have now been reconciled. A balance sheet at 31 July 20X7 would show a bank overdraft of £964 under the heading of current liabilities.

ACTIVITY 2

The cash book of a business shows an opening balance of £270, cash receipts of £4,600 and cash payments of £4,800. There is also a standing order of £40 that has been omitted from the cash book.

The cash book includes £60 of cheques written but not appearing on the bank statement, and £490 of deposits not yet appearing on the bank statement. The balance on the bank statement was £400 in debit.

Prepare the bank reconciliation statement.

Feedback to this activity is at the end of the chapter.

Conclusion

There are a number of reasons why the balance on an organisation's bank statement may not agree with the balance in its cash book. These differences will include errors or omissions in the cash book or by the bank and timing differences such as unpresented cheques and outstanding lodgements. As part of the system of control over the cash of the business it is important that a reconciliation is prepared on a regular basis between the cash book and bank statement balances.

An examination question will typically require you to produce an adjusted cash book and then a reconciliation of the bank statement figure to that adjusted balance. It is quite wrong to include adjustments which need to be made in the cash book in the bank reconciliation statement.

SELF-TEST QUESTIONS

The nature and purpose of a bank reconciliation statement

1   Why does the bank statement appear to be the opposite way round to a ledger account? (1.1)

2   What types of items might appear on the bank statement but not be in the cash book? (1.3)

3   What are the two types of timing difference that might cause there to be a difference between the cash book and the bank statement?(1.4)

4   What is another name for an outstanding deposit? (1.4)

5   What does a cheque marked R/D mean? (1.6)

6   What is the double entry for a dishonoured cheque? (1.6)

7   What is the net effect on the bank statement of a dishonoured cheque? (1.6)

8   What would be the treatment of bank charges omitted from the cash book? (1.6)

9   What is the treatment of direct credits, paid into the bank from customers, in the cash book? (1.6)

10 Is an opening overdraft a debit or a credit balance in the cash book? (1.6)

The following attempt at a bank reconciliation statement has been prepared by Q Limited.

	£
Overdraft per bank statement	38,600
Add: deposits not credited	41,200
	79,800
Less: outstanding cheques	3,300
Overdraft per cash book	76,500

Question 1

Assuming the bank statement balance of £38,600 to be correct, what *should* the cash book balance be?

A   £76,500 overdrawn, as stated

B   £5,900 overdrawn

C   £700 overdrawn

D   £5,900 cash at bank

Question 2

After checking a business cash book against the bank statement, which of the following items could require an entry in the cash book?

1   Bank charges

2   A cheque from a customer which was dishonoured

3   Cheque not presented

4   Deposits not credited

5   Credit transfer entered in bank statement

6   Standing order entered in bank statement.

A   1, 2, 5 and 6

B   3 and 4

C   1, 3, 4 and 6

D   3, 4, 5 and 6

Spanners Ltd

The following is a summary from the cash book of Spanners Ltd for the month of October:

Cash book

	£		£
Balance b/d	1,407	Payments	15,520
Receipts	15,073	Balance c/d	960
	16,480		16,480

On investigation you discover that:

1   Bank charges of £35 shown on the bank statement have not been entered in the cash book.

2   A cheque drawn for £47 has been entered in error as a receipt.

3   A cheque for £18 has been returned by the bank marked 'Refer to drawer', but it has not been written back in the cash book.

4   The balance brought forward should have been £1,470.

5   Three cheques paid to suppliers for £214, £370 and £30 have not yet been presented to the bank.

6   Takings of £1,542 were placed in a night safe deposit on 31 October but were not credited by the bank until 3 November.

7   The bank charged a cheque for £72 in error to the company's account.

8   The bank statement shows an overdraft of £124.

(a)   Show what adjustments you would make in the cash book.

(b)   Prepare a bank reconciliation statement as at 31 October.   **(12 marks)**

For the answers to these questions, see the 'Answers' section at the end of the book.

**FEEDBACK TO
ACTIVITY 1**

	£
Balance per bank statement	1,450
Less: Unpresented cheques	(200)
Add: Outstanding deposits	350
Balance per cash book	1,600

**FEEDBACK TO
ACTIVITY 2**

Cash book

	£		£
Balance b/d	270	Cash payments	4,800
Cash receipts	4,600	Standing order	40
		Balance c/d	30
	4,870		4,870
Balance b/d	30		

Bank reconciliation statement

	£
Balance per bank statement	400 O/D
Outstanding cheques	60
	460 O/D
Outstanding lodgements	490
Balance per cash book	30

Chapter 12

JOURNAL ENTRIES AND THE SUSPENSE ACCOUNT

Many entries to the nominal ledger concern sales, purchases, and cash receipts and payments. We have seen how the relevant day books function as the sources of such entries.

However, there are other transactions that do not originate in the above day books. Examples include annual depreciation charges, bad debt provisions and accruals and prepayments. To initiate entries such as these, appropriate instructions must be given to the bookkeeper. These instructions will involve the use of the journal, as we shall find out in this chapter.

Objectives

By the time you have finished this chapter you should be able to:

- draft journal entries

- correct errors in the ledger accounts

- clear the balance on a suspense account by the correction of errors and the application of double entry principles

- correct the profit for errors discovered.

1   The journal

1.1   The nature and purposes of a journal

Adjustments for things such as annual depreciation charges, bad debt provisions and accruals and prepayments require an amount to be transferred from one ledger account to another. Sometimes several accounts are involved, as when a number of bad debts are written off on the same date.

It is essential to keep an orderly record of such transfers because:

- the sales or purchases ledger control accounts will not agree with the underlying ledgers if the totals of transfers to or from these ledgers are not available

- transfers between ledger accounts are by definition non-routine items. They must all be properly authorised and capable of being checked – a record obviously facilitates this.

KEY POINT

- The **journal** is a book or other record containing details of non-routine ledger transfers.
- The journal is not part of the double entry – it is a record of double entries made in ledger accounts.

The record is in the form of a **journal** – an additional day book in the system designed to give details of all transfers between ledger accounts. Each entry in the journal consists of the names of the accounts involved and the debit and credit entries required.

Journal entries are also used in the correction of errors. If the error causes the trial balance not to balance, a **suspense account** is opened for the amount of the difference. The balance on the suspense account is cleared as the difference is found.

The journal is not part of the double entry – it is a record of double entries made in ledger accounts.

1.2   Presentation

A journal should be laid out in the following way:

Date/No	Details	Ledger folio	Dr £	Cr £
20X9				
6 Feb	Van account	V1	2,000	
	Motor expenses account	M3		2,000
	Purchase of van incorrectly debited to motor expenses			

Notice particularly that:

- in the 'details' column should be entered the names of the accounts to be debited and credited

- the debit entries should be entered before the credit entries

- the names of the accounts to be credited are often inset slightly from the names of the accounts to be debited

- the narrative explaining the journal should give a brief explanation of the entry – unless a question specifically states that no narrative is required. The narrative is included to aid comprehension if the journal is reconsidered at a later date

- in examination questions the ledger folio column is not needed.

Example

Journal entries for the following are required:

1   closing stock £3,500

2   motor expenses of £200 incorrectly debited to heat and light

3   telephone accrual £58

4   rates prepayment £78.

Solution

Date/No	Details	Dr £	Cr £
1	Stock (balance sheet)	3,500	
	Stock (trading account)		3,500
	Inclusion of closing stock in accounts.		
2	Motor expenses	200	
	Heat and light		200
	Invoice for motor expenses incorrectly charged to heat and light.		
3	Telephone expense	58	
	Accruals		58
	Accrual for telephone bills.		
4	Prepayments	78	
	Rates expense		78
	Prepayment of rates.		

A journal entry is simply a clear and comprehensible way of setting out a bookkeeping double entry that is to be made.

ACTIVITY 1

Draft the following journal entries.

(a) Increase in provision for doubtful debts from £200 to £300.

(b) Receipt of £1,000 for sale of fixed asset which originally cost £6,000 and has a net book value of £1,500.

Feedback to this activity is at the end of the chapter.

2   Suspense accounts

A **suspense account** is an account in which debits or credits are held temporarily until sufficient information is available for them to be posted to the correct accounts.

Suspense accounts are often encountered and must be dealt with according to the usual rules of double entry bookkeeping.

2.1   Creation of suspense accounts

There are two main reasons why suspense accounts may be created:

- On the extraction of a trial balance, the debits are not equal to the credits and the difference is put to a suspense account.

- When a bookkeeper performing double entry is not sure where to post one side of an entry, he may debit or credit a suspense account and leave the entry there until its ultimate destination is clarified.

2.2   Differences on trial balances

Before opening a suspense account the accountant will try to ascertain the reason why his trial balance does not balance. This may be the result of:

- errors in the double entry bookkeeping

- an error in the extraction of the trial balance.

If no error is discovered, he may set up a suspense account, so as to balance the trial balance. For example, if the credit side of the trial balance is greater than the debit side, the opening suspense account entry for the difference will be a debit.

2.3   Clearing suspense accounts

A suspense account should not remain permanently in the books of account, but as it forms a 'T' account it should be cleared by means of normal bookkeeping procedures.

Example

On extracting a trial balance the accountant of ETT discovered a suspense account with a debit balance of £1,075; he also found that the debits exceeded the credits by £957. He posted this difference to the suspense account and then investigated the situation. He discovered the following points.

(a)   A debit balance of £75 on the postages account had been incorrectly extracted on the trial balance as £750 debit.

(b)   A payment of £500 to a creditor, X, had been correctly entered in the cash book, but no entry had been made in the creditor's account.

(c)   When a motor vehicle had been purchased during the year the bookkeeper did not know what to do with the debit entry so he made the entry
Dr Suspense, Cr Bank £1,575.

(d)   A credit balance of £81 in the sundry income account had been incorrectly extracted on the trial balance as a debit balance.

(e)   A receipt of £5 from a debtor, Y, had been correctly posted to his account but had been entered in the cash account as £625.

(f)   The bookkeeper was not able to deal with the receipt of £500 from the owner's own bank account, and he made the entry Dr Bank and Cr Suspense.

(g)   No entry has been made for a cheque of £120 received from a debtor M.

(h)   A receipt of £50 from a debtor, N, had been entered into his account as £5 and into the cash book as £5.

Solution

Step 1 The £1,075 debit balance is already included in the books, whilst the £957 is entered on the credit side of the suspense account because the trial balance, as extracted, shows debits exceeding credits by £957. Although the two amounts arose in different ways they are both removed from suspense by the application of double entry.

Step 2 The incorrect extraction is corrected by amending the balance on the trial balance and debiting the suspense account with £675. In this case the 'credit' entry is only on the trial balance, as the postages account itself shows the correct balance, the error coming in putting that balance on the trial balance.

Step 3 The non-entry of the £500 to the debit of X's account causes the account to be incorrectly stated and the trial balance to be unbalanced. To correct matters Dr X, Cr Suspense, amending both X's ledger account and the trial balance.

Step 4 The suspense entry here arose from adherence to double entry procedures, rather than a numerical error. In this case the bookkeeper should have Dr Fixed asset – cost, Cr Bank instead of Dr Suspense, Cr Bank, so to correct matters the entry Dr Fixed asset – cost, Cr Suspense is made.

Step 5 Is similar to Step 2, but note that the incorrect extraction of a credit balance as a debit balance means that twice the amount involved has to be amended on the trial balance and debited to suspense account.

Step 6 Is similar to Step 3 – on this occasion Dr Suspense, Cr Cash, and amend the cash book balance on the trial balance.

Step 7 Is similar to Step 4. The bookkeeper should have Dr Bank, Cr Capital, but has instead Dr Bank, Cr Suspense, so to correct matters Dr Suspense, Cr Capital.

Step 8 Item (g) does not appear in the suspense account as the error does not affect the imbalance of the trial balance. As **no** entry has been made for the cheque, the correcting entry is:

		£	£
Dr	Cash	120	
Cr	Debtor M		120

Step 9 Item (h) also does not appear in the suspense account. Although an entry has been made in the books which was wrong, the entry was incorrect for both the debit and credit entry. The correcting entry is:

		£	£
Dr	Cash	45	
Cr	Debtor N		45

Suspense account

	£		£
Balance b/d (S1)	1,075	Trial balance – difference (S1)	957
Postages (trial balance only) (S2)	675	X (S3)	500
Sundry income (trial balance only)		Fixed asset – cost (S4)	1,575
(S5)	162		
Cash (S6)	620		
Capital account – ETT (S7)	500		
	3,032		3,032

Once a suspense account has been created it should be cleared by the application of double entry principles. Not all errors affect the suspense account. If no entry at all has been made for a transaction, then the trial balance still balances.

2.4   Transposition errors

Though not encountered in the example above, a common cause of bookkeeping error is through the transposition of digits, i.e. £527 is recorded at £725, (the 5 and 7 have been transposed). The difference the error creates is always divisible by 9.

3   Adjustments to profit

3.1   Introduction

You may be asked to alter a business's profit in the light of various adjustments that need to be made owing to information received after the accounts have been prepared. This is a good test of your double entry technique and also, of course, something that frequently happens in practice.

3.2   Example

D Tree has prepared the following summary of assets and liabilities at 31 March 20X5.

	£		£
Plant and machinery	3,105	Capital as on 1 April 20X4	4,070
Debtors	6,100	Profit for the year	1,735
Stock	4,250	Loan	3,000
Balance at bank	500	Creditors	5,150
	13,955		13,955

After examination of the books you ascertain the following:

1   Plant and machinery cost £5,500 and should have a net book value of £3,005.

2   Debtors were shown after deducting a doubtful debt of £75. It was agreed that this debt was bad and should be written off and that provision should be made for further debts amounting to £35, which were considered doubtful.

3   Ten tons of raw material had been valued for stock purposes at cost, £15 per ton, but was damaged and unsuitable for production. It was considered to be worth £3 per ton as scrap.

4   Goods sold for £30, which was 20% above stock valuation, had been included in sales. These goods awaited collection by the customer and had been included in stock at valuation.

5   Loan interest was outstanding for six months at 6% per annum.

6   Rent of £150 was due for the quarter ended 31 March 20X5.

7   The balance at bank as shown by the cash book was not in accordance with the bank statements on which the following debits had been made but not entered in the cash book.

	£
Bank charges	30
D Tree - drawings for the year	520

Required:

Prepare the following,

(a)   A statement showing the adjustments to the profit for the year

(b)   A balance sheet at 31 March 20X5.

3.3   Solution

Step 1

Examine the information in the question and decide which items will affect the year's profits, and which information will affect the balance sheet.

Step 2

Produce the required statement, starting with the original profit and making the appropriate adjustments as below.

(a)   **Profit and loss account adjustments for the year ended 31 March 20X5**

	£	£
Profit for the year per account		1,735
Less: Additional depreciation (£3,105 – £3,005)	100	
Provision for doubtful debts	35	
Stock adjustments:		
Revaluation (£150 – £30)	120	
Goods already sold to customer (£30 × $\frac{100}{120}$)	25	
Loan interest (6% for six months on £3,000)	90	
Rent	150	
Bank charges (remember, drawings do not affect profit)	30	
		550
Revised profit for the year		1,185

Step 3

Prepare the balance sheet.

(b) **Balance sheet at 31 March 20X5**

	Cost £	Depreciation £	Net £
Fixed assets	5,500	2,495	3,005
Current assets			
Stock (4,250 – 120 – 25)		4,105	
Debtors	6,100		
Less provision for doubtful debts	35		
		6,065	
		10,170	
Creditors: amounts falling due within one year			
Bank overdraft (500 – 30 – 5,20)		50	
Sundry creditors (5,150 + 150)		5,300	
Loan interest		90	
		5,440	
			4,730
Total assets less current liabilities			7,735
Creditors: amounts falling due in more than one year			
6% loan			(3,000)
			4,735
Capital account			
Balance at 1 April 20X4			4,070
Revised profit for the year		1,185	
Less drawings		520	
Retained profit for the year			665
Balance at 31 March 20X5			4,735

Conclusion

In order to put through many items of double entry bookkeeping and to correct errors, journal entries must often be drafted. Errors or omissions in the double entry bookkeeping system will often lead to the temporary creation of a suspense account. The reasons for the creation of this suspense account must be investigated and the balance cleared by correcting the error by applying double entry principles.

SELF-TEST QUESTIONS

The journal

1   What is a journal? (1.1)

2   How should a journal entry be set out? (1.2)

3   Why is a narrative required for a journal entry? (1.2)

4   What is the journal entry required for an accrual? (1.2)

Suspense accounts

5   What is a suspense account? (2)

6   What are the two ways in which a suspense account may be created? (2.1)

7   If the debits in a trial balance exceed the credits will the suspense account balance be a debit or a credit? (2.2)

8   If an entry is omitted from the ledger entirely will a suspense account be created? (2.3)

9   If a credit balance is extracted on the trial balance as a debit balance what will be the amending entry in the suspense account? (2.3)

MULTIPLE-CHOICE QUESTIONS

Question 1

Y purchased some plant on 1 January 20X0 for £38,000. The payment for the plant was correctly entered in the cash book but was entered on the debit side of plant repairs account.

Y charges depreciation on the straight line basis at 20% per year, with a proportionate charge in the year of acquisition and assuming no scrap value at the end of the life of the asset.

How will Y's profit for the year ended 31 March 20X0 be affected by the error?

A   Understated by £30,400

B   Understated by £36,100

C   Understated by £38,000

D   Overstated by £1,900

Question 2

The trial balance of Z failed to agree, the totals being: debit £836,200, credit £819,700.

A suspense account was opened for the amount of the difference and the following errors were found and corrected.

1   The totals of the cash discount columns in the cash book had not been posted to the discount accounts. The figures were Discount Allowed £3,900 and Discount Received £5,100.

2   A cheque for £19,000 received from a customer was correctly entered in the cash book but was posted to the customer's account as £9,100.

What will the remaining balance on the suspense account be *after* the correction of these errors?

A   £25,300 credit

B   £7,700 credit

C   £27,700 debit

D   £5,400 credit

Question 3

The trial balance of C Limited did not agree, and a suspense account was opened for the difference. Checking in the bookkeeping system revealed a number of errors.

1   £4,600 paid for motor van repairs was correctly treated in the cash book but was credited to motor vehicles asset account

2   £360 received from B, a customer, was credited in error to the account of BB

3   £9,500 paid for rent was debited to the rent account as £5,900

4   The total of the discount allowed column in the cash book had been debited in error to the discounts received account

5   No entries had been made to record a cash sale of £100.

Which of the errors above would require an entry to the suspense account as part of the process of correcting them?

A   3 and 4

B   1 and 3

C   2 and 5

D   2 and 3

For the answers to these questions, see the 'Answers' section at the end of the book.

EXAM-TYPE
QUESTIONS

Question 1: Journal Entries

Draft the journal entries for the following transactions:

(a)   Road fund tax of £150 on a new motor car had been incorrectly posted to cost of motor vehicles account, and an adjustment is required. (The point here is that road fund tax is not a part of the capital cost of the motor car, but a running expense, and should therefore be allocated to an appropriate expense account in the profit and loss account, not included in the asset account.)

(b)   Pimple agrees to offset £1,500 due on his sales ledger account against the amount owing on his purchase ledger account.

(c)   A customer, Black, owes £270 and is adjudicated bankrupt with no assets to his name – a provision for doubtful debts of £300 is also to be created.

The business does not have control accounts for sales and purchases. **(9 marks)**

Question 2: February

February, having been unable to balance his trial balance at 31 December, opened up a suspense account and entered in it the amount he was out of balance. The debits had exceeded the credits by £736.

The following errors were subsequently discovered.

(a)   An allowance of £265 to a debtor, January, was entered in his account as £256.

(b)   The total of the discount received column in the cash book for the month of December £237 had not been posted.

(c)   £500, representing the sale proceeds of a machine scrapped, had been passed through the sales account.

(d)   A balance of £268, owing by a debtor, March, had been omitted from the trial balance at 31 December.

(e)   The bank overdraft of £313 had been entered in the trial balance as £331.

(f)   Sale of goods for £1,000 to April on credit had been completely missed from the books.

(g)   Discounts received balance of £379 had been entered in the trial balance as £397 (debit balance).

Show the suspense account after the rectification of all errors and state the entries to be made to correct the errors which do not pass through the suspense account.
(13 marks)

For the answers to these questions, see the 'Answers' section at the end of the book.

	Date/No	Details	Dr £	Cr £
	1	Bad debts expense	100	
		Provision for doubtful debts		100
		Increase in provision for doubtful debts.		
	2	Cash	1,000	
		Fixed asset – accumulated depreciation		
		(6,000 – 1,500)	4,500	
		Profit and loss (loss on disposal)	500	
		Fixed asset at cost		6,000
		Disposal of fixed asset for £1,000.		

Chapter 13
APPLICATIONS OF INFORMATION TECHNOLOGY

This chapter is designed to provide a review of the uses of computers in financial accounting. It starts by looking at the different form accounting records might take, and then moves on to compare manual and computerised accounting systems.

We will then go on to consider each of the four main applications of information technology in the office environment, namely:

- financial accounting systems
- word processing
- spreadsheets
- database systems.

Practical experience of using computers for accounting and related tasks will obviously help you to appreciate the issues involved. Try to obtain this experience.

Objectives

By the time you have finished this chapter you should be able to:

- discuss the advantages and disadvantages of computerisation in a business
- discuss various practical applications of computer technology in business situations
- discuss the application of computers in areas of accounting.

1 The form of accounting records

1.1 A typical manual system

A typical manual system consists of the following elements.

- Separate books of original entry, which are the original accounting records of a business and are not part of the double entry.

- The nominal ledger, which is a book within which there is a page for each ledger account in the double entry system.

- Further ledgers, the main ones being the sales ledger, the purchase ledger and the cash book. These ledgers do not normally form part of the double entry.

Often these records are in the form of books, but they can equally be in some other form. For example a sales ledger may be a collection of individual cards with one or more cards for each customer. The advantage of cards lies in the ability to insert additional cards for customers who have a lot of transactions or cards for new customers and still retain the alphabetical order of customers.

Often the subsidiary ledgers may not be laid out as ledger accounts but as running totals of amounts owing. See the example below.

Sales ledger

Customer: I. Qasim

Date		Dr £	Cr £	Balance £
1 Mar.	Brought forward			3,978.45
19 Mar.	Invoice 2354	1,549.00		5,527.45
23 Mar.	Cash Receipt Book		3,978.45	1,549.00

Whatever the format, the reasons for the types of records and the double entry principles remain the same.

1.2   A typical computerised system

Computerised systems can vary in the form they take. All of the accounts may be computerised but in many businesses only some are. For example, a business may have just the sales ledger on computer.

A fully computerised system will operate under the same principles as a manual system except that all the records will be stored in one place, i.e. the hard disk of the computer. This does not necessarily mean that all accounting personnel have access to all records. The system will be broken down into sections in the same way as the manual system.

Another difference in a computerised system may be that when the data is printed out, the form of that information may look very different from a manual system particularly with regard to the nominal ledger. Whereas in a manual system the nominal ledger is a collection of 'T' accounts, the nominal ledger on a computer system will probably appear as an arithmetic listing of debits and credits. This does not mean however that the system is not performing double entry; it is.

2   Manual and computerised accounting systems

2.1   Advantages of computers

- **Speed** – The computer is very fast. This speed can be of value to the business in two ways:

  - High volumes of work can be handled by a computer.

  - Rapid turn-round and response can be achieved.

  Thus, one company might value a computer primarily for its ability to cope with large numbers of orders; another might be more interested in speeding up its order processing.

- **Stored programs** – Once the programs have been written and tested, the computer can perform large amounts of work with the minimum of labour costs. Only small teams of operators are needed for the largest machines. This is possible because the computer runs under the control of its stored program, and operator activity is limited to loading and unloading peripherals and indicating what work is to be done.

- **Decision-making capabilities** – The computer can be programmed to undertake complicated decision-making processes. It can handle work to a much higher degree of complexity than other office machines – and often more than the manager.

- **File storage and processing** – Large files of data can be stored on magnetic media which require very little space. More important, files thus stored can be reviewed and updated at high speeds, and information can be retrieved from them very quickly.

KEY POINT

Whatever the format, the reasons for the types of records and the double entry principles remain the same.

KEY POINT

Computerised accounting systems vary in form.
In some businesses, all the accounts are computerised, whereas in others, only part of the accounts are.

KEY POINT

Computers have **advantages** in terms of:
- speed
- stored programs
- decision-making capabilities
- file-storage and processing
- accuracy and reliability.

- **Accuracy and reliability** – The computer is very accurate (provided always that its programs are free from faults). It is also very reliable.

2.2 Disadvantages of computers

- **Lack of intelligence** – The computer is a machine. It cannot recognise errors made in its program, nor notice that data is incomplete or incorrect. Errors that would be detected by clerks in a manual system may go unnoticed in a computer-based system. The utmost care has to be devoted to the development of computer-based systems, to foresee every contingency and to test every instruction. Thus, system development is often both prolonged and costly.

- **Quantifiable decisions** – The program can only take decisions that can be quantified, e.g. that can be expressed as two numbers or amounts that can be compared with each other. It cannot make value judgements of the type involved in, for example, selecting personnel, or deciding whether to take legal action if debts are overdue. The solution indicated by the program may have to be modified because of intangible factors known to the manager but incapable of being expressed in the program.

- **Initial costs** – Initial costs, i.e. hardware, software, site preparation, training, etc. tend to be high. Note that today software costs often exceed hardware costs.

- **Inflexibility** – Because of the care and attention to detail needed in systems and program development and maintenance, computer systems tend to be inflexible. They take longer and cost more to alter than manual systems.

- **Vulnerability** – The more work an organisation transfers to a computer, the greater is its dependence on a single resource. If the machine breaks down or is damaged, or if computer staff take industrial action, many systems may be brought to a halt.

Many of these apparent disadvantages relate to 'bespoke' systems, i.e. systems developed by a particular business specifically for its own use. In practice, the difficulties are often overcome simply by purchasing an 'off-the-shelf' package, that is a system that has been developed by a specialist software development company and which is intended for use in any business. The cost of purchasing such a package is much less than the cost of developing a bespoke system. The purchaser also benefits from the fact that any bugs in the package will have been eliminated during the many years in which it has been used by numerous other businesses.

2.3 Examples of the benefits of computer systems

- **Reduced data processing costs** – The computer may provide a cheaper way of performing a given task.

- **Other cost savings** – Money may be saved even though the cost of processing data remains constant or even increases. For example fewer errors may be made by management once they have better information.

- **Increased throughput** – The computer can cope with increasing volumes of work better than manual systems.

- **Faster processing** – Transactions can be dealt with more rapidly.

- **Greater accuracy** – Fewer errors occur than in manual systems.

- **Staff shortage** – The computer can reduce the problems caused by shortage of office staff.

- **Improved control** – Constant high-speed monitoring of files often improves control.

- **Communication** – The use of terminals and data transmission facilities greatly improves communications.

- **Quantitative techniques** – A wide range of quantitative techniques becomes available to aid management decision-making.

- **Computer facilities** – The work of staff who require calculations to be made can be greatly facilitated (e.g. design staff, research staff, engineers, statisticians).

We will now go on to look at the four major applications of information technology in the office environment.

3   Financial accounting systems

3.1   Integrated accounting packages

The usual pattern for financial accounting has been for computerisation on a piecemeal basis, tackling the aspects involving most work first, e.g.:

- sales ledger
- purchase ledger
- payroll.

However, a number of integrated accounting packages now exist which handle all parts of the process and ultimately produce the financial statements. Each package varies, but the broad groups are described below.

Cash book systems

This group merely emulates a manual cash book. Such a system might be suitable for a small business which does not sell on credit and which either (i) provides a service or (ii) buys its stock for cash or on credit from a small number of suppliers.

Basic bookkeeping systems

These might be suitable for the smaller business selling mainly on a cash basis, requiring basic bookkeeping. Such a system will normally offer basic facilities for maintaining a sales ledger, a purchase ledger and a nominal ledger. There should be facilities for automatically producing quarterly VAT returns, a full print out of transactions and perhaps bank reconciliation statements. The package will also generate trial balances, profit and loss accounts and balance sheets.

Bookkeeping and accountancy systems

In addition to offering the basic facilities described above, these packages can cope with greater numbers of customer and supplier accounts and offer more sophisticated credit control facilities. They can generate invoices, print out customers' statements and produce ageing schedules of debtors. They may be able to produce standard letters automatically to send to customers whose accounts are overdue or who have exceeded their agreed credit limit.

Within this group the more advanced packages may incorporate stock control facilities. Separate records are maintained for each stock item recording units purchased and sold and the balance of stock in hand.

3.2   Micro-computer accounting package

Most micro-computer accounting packages are used by people who are not computer programmers or systems analysts. The users of such systems are normally accountants and their accounting staff. To run an accounting package, the user will normally have the program on a hard disk. Data may be on separate disks. The program will probably operate on a 'menu system', i.e. the user will select the required options from a list of choices (the menu). A typical initial menu would include the following options:

- Create new accounts
- Edit account data
- Post transactions
- Create report layouts
- Print reports
- Quit.

To select an option, the user will key in the appropriate number. For example, to create new accounts, number **1** would be keyed in.

Each of these options would involve another sub-menu. For example, having selected CREATE NEW ACCOUNTS, the operator would typically be offered a sub-menu displaying the following options

- New customer accounts
- New supplier accounts
- New income accounts
- New expense accounts
- New balance sheet accounts
- Return to main menu.

Thus, the initial set-up of a computerised accounting system is similar to a manual system, i.e. a sales ledger, purchase ledger and nominal ledger are set up and account codes allocated for each individual account. In the majority of cases, the bank account is contained within the nominal ledger.

The computer program will have been set up to 'recognise' different transaction types.

- Sales invoices
- Credit notes (re sales)
- Purchase invoices
- Credit notes (re purchases)
- Receipts
- Payments
- Journals.

To post to the ledger, the user would batch up the appropriate source documents (for example, sales invoices), and compute the batch total. The user would select the POST TO LEDGER option from the appropriate sub-menu and key-in the following data for each sales invoice:

- Customer account code
- Nominal ledger account code
- Date
- Invoice number
- Description
- Goods value
- VAT value
- Total value

Provided valid code numbers are used and the totals agree, the posting will be accepted, similarly the batch total will need to be verified before the program will actually post the transactions to the ledgers. An additional security measure is that of passwords, e.g. the user would have to know the appropriate password to load the system in the first place and possible different passwords for each ledger.

4   Word processing

4.1   Introduction

The second major application of information technology we will consider is word
processing. This is the name given to the process of producing a typescript using
computer facilities. The facilities are the ability to store text and to manipulate it on a
VDU screen.

The minimum hardware requirements are as follows:

- visual display unit and keyboard

- processor

- disk drive

- printer.

Word processing developed to overcome some of the problems of using a typewriter
for the production of typescript.

- **Repetition** – If several drafts of a document have to be produced, the whole
  document will have to be retyped each time.

- **Corrections** – Even with the advent of correcting fluid, correcting typing errors is
  a time consuming business and quite messy. A typed letter with several corrections
  on it does not create a good impression.

- **Checking** – Every time a document is retyped it must be checked in its entirety.

4.2   Features of word processing

Entering the text

Text is typed into the word processor using a visual display unit. Each 'document' is
assigned a reference so that it can be stored and subsequently retrieved. As the text is
typed in, it appears on the VDU screen to enable the 'typist' to check visually that
there are no typing errors. Any errors can be corrected by moving the cursor to the
error and over typing.

Storing the text

After the text has been typed in, it is stored on disk under its unique title (**file name**).
Once the text has been stored, a hard-copy of the text will be printed to be reviewed by
the author for errors or subsequent amendments.

Retrieving the text

If for any reason amendments need to be made to any stored text, it is retrieved from
store into the main memory of the word processor and displayed on the VDU screen.
Retrieval is by means of the unique file name.

Editing the text

This is the stage where the text is made ready for printing. There are two aspects:

- **Editing** – Any errors are corrected and any amendments made. Amendments may
  include changing the order of paragraphs, adding and deleting whole or parts of
  paragraphs.

- **Text formatting** – This means arranging the text to exactly how the author wishes
  it to appear. What size of paper (e.g. A4, A5) or special form (like a polling card) is
  to be used? How wide should the margins be, what line spacing, etc.?

All the instructions for editing and formatting are keyed in using the VDU. All word
processors enable 'on screen' editing – i.e. you can see the results of the amendments
on the VDU screen; most enable 'on screen' formatting (WYSIWYG – 'what you see
is what you get').

Printing the text

After all amendments have been made, the text is put back into store in its final form. A copy is printed to enable the author to ensure that his instructions have been carried out. Provided that the author is satisfied with the finished product, it can then be printed.

5   Spreadsheets

5.1   Introduction

A **spreadsheet** is a computer package that can be used for numerous 'modelling' type business applications.

A spreadsheet displays on the screen a series of rows and columns. The intersection of rows and columns form 'cells' into which the user can type information using the computer keyboard. Three types of information are entered.

- text, e.g. January, February, March, April
- numbers, e.g. 200, 300, 400, 500
- formulae, e.g. Sales – Costs = Profit.

When the content of any cell is altered, the effects of the alteration are reflected, using the formula, on all other cells.

Once a model has been entered into the computer using the spreadsheet, it can be stored on disk. It can then be recalled, altered and used with new data. The output can be printed in tabular form. Some spreadsheets allow data to be displayed and printed graphically.

The model on the spreadsheet is often too large to be displayed on the screen in its entirety and so the VDU can then be thought of as a 'window' which can be moved to the various parts of the spreadsheet.

5.2   Features of a spreadsheet

Spreadsheets contain the following features:

- **'What if?' analysis** – A major feature of a spreadsheet is its ability to calculate the effect of changes in the data or formula used in the model. This is sometimes described as the 'what if?' facility, e.g. what would be the profit if sales increased by 20%?

- **Conditional statements** – Calculations may be made dependent upon values in other cells, e.g. if sales are greater than £500,000 then costs are 10% of sales otherwise fixed costs are £50,000.

- **Look-up tables** – The value to be inserted in a specific cell can be selected from a range of values held in a table, e.g. tax rates at different levels of income.

- **Selective printing** – The user may specify a portion of the model to be printed rather than the whole of it.

- **Graphics** – Most spreadsheets can produce bar charts, pie-charts, etc., with shading and colour.

- **Goal seeking facility** – Some spreadsheets can provide all possible input value combinations which produce a specified bottom line output value.

- **Statistical function** – Most spreadsheets provide statistical analysis so that they are able to calculate values such as an average, sum, standard deviation, etc.

DEFINITION

A **spreadsheet** is a computer package that can be used for numerous 'modelling' type business applications.

- **Flexibility** – Spreadsheets should allow considerable flexibility to the user in designing the model, e.g. inserting blank rows and columns, deleting rows and columns and moving blocks of rows and columns to another part of the spreadsheet.

- **Databases** – Spreadsheets can be used as simple databases (see below).

ACTIVITY 1

Make a list of the ways in which you might think that spreadsheets could be used in business.

Feedback to this activity is at the end of the chapter.

6 Database systems

6.1 Introduction

DEFINITION

A **database** is a collection of information or data files which provides access to the common data to a number of different users with different needs.

A **database** is a collection of information or data files which provides access to the common data to a number of different users with different needs.

A database is analogous to an electronic card index. Each card contains some information, e.g. about a client. The items of information held (e.g. name, address, fees) are fields.

The advantages of a database over a card index are the following.

- They are expandable.

- Amount of information held in each record/field can be much larger than a card index.

- Calculations can be performed automatically, e.g. return on capital employed.

- Records may be sorted, or those matching a certain criterion selected, automatically, and in a variety of orders.

- Reports based on the information may be prepared and printed.

6.2 Database design

DEFINITION

Databases may be flat file, relational or programmable.

There are various ways of designing database systems so as to link the data together.

- A **flat file** database is a single file database. All records in this type of database are of a standard format. Data can be stored, accessed, sorted and updated.

- A **relational** database is one where files can be linked together and data can be accessed from any file.

- A **programmable** database is one which has its own programming language which enables the database to be tailored to individual needs.

Database systems will continue to be a major area of expansion of computer applications in the future.

6.3 Database management system

The software that runs the database is known as the database management system. The database management system organises the data input into the database and allows various application programs to use the database.

Conclusion

After studying this chapter you should be able to discuss applications of computers in business in general and in accounting in particular. Spreadsheets, databases and micro-computer accounting packages should now be familiar terms.

The form of accounting records

1   What are the three main parts of a typical manual system? (1.1)

Manual and computerised accounting systems

2   What are the five advantages of computers in business? (2.1)

Financial accounting systems

3   Which parts of an accounting system are normally computerised first? (3.1)

4   What do we call computerised accounting systems that can handle all parts of the accounting system? (3.1)

Spreadsheets

5   What is a 'cell' of a spreadsheet? (5.1)

6   What are the distinguishing features and uses of a spreadsheet? (5.2)

Database systems

7   What is a database? (6.1)

Question 1: Saavik Ltd

The company accountant of Saavik Ltd is interested in purchasing a spreadsheet type of financial modelling package. As his assistant with experience in using a spreadsheet during your recent examination training, he has asked you to explain the principal features of a spreadsheet.

Draft a memorandum to the company accountant to:

(a)   explain the principal features of a spreadsheet

(b)   list the main criteria that the company accountant should use to evaluate a spreadsheet package.   **(8 marks)**

Question 2: Database

(a)   Explain the term 'database' and how the operation of a data processing system using a database differs from one using conventional file structures.

(b)   What advantages are to be gained from using a database system?   **(10 marks)**

For the answers to these questions, see the 'Answers' section at the end of the book.

Possible uses of spreadsheet packages in practice in business might include the following:

- cash flow forecasting
- budgeting and control
- profit and loss accounts
- profit projections
- stock count records
- marketing analysis
- sales forecasting
- tax budgeting.

.

Chapter 14
ACCOUNTING CONVENTIONS AND POLICIES

With this chapter we turn to a different aspect of accounting – the concepts and conventions that underpin the practical work we have been concerned with so far. Some of the concepts we have met already, but the purpose of this chapter is to bring them all together and explain the two main regulatory statements issued by the ASB in this area:

- FRS 18 *Accounting policies*, issued in December 2000

- the *Statement of Principles for Financial Accounting*, issued in December 1999.

Before studying the rest of this chapter, it is important to realise that accounting is not an exact science – judgement and estimation are required to assess almost every item in the financial statements. For example, you have already met the need to use estimation techniques to arrive at depreciation charges and the provision for doubtful debts in accounts.

Much of the material in this chapter makes more sense in the context of limited company accounts. It will be a good idea to reread this chapter when you have finished Chapter 20.

Objectives

By the time you have finished this chapter you should be able to:

- explain a number of accounting conventions

- explain accounting policies, estimation techniques and measurement bases

- explain the purpose of each element of a conceptual framework.

1   Accounting conventions

1.1   The nature and purpose of accounting conventions

Accounting conventions are principles or accepted practice which apply generally to transactions.

Some accounting conventions are of more relevance to some transactions than to others, but all have an influence in determining:

- which assets and liabilities are recorded on a balance sheet

- how assets and liabilities are valued

- what income and expenditure is recorded in the profit and loss account

- at what amount income and expenditure is recorded.

It is useful to state and clarify the meaning of accounting conventions so that unusual transactions or situations can be dealt with.

DEFINITION

Accounting conventions are principles or accepted practice which apply generally to transactions.

1.2   Determination of value of each asset and liability separately

In **determining the aggregate amount of any item**, the amount of any individual asset or liability that falls to be taken into account shall be determined separately.

For example, when stock is valued at the lower of cost and net realisable value, the value must be determined for separate types of stock and then aggregated. In this way anticipated losses on one type of stock will not be offset against expected gains on another. This principle is identified in the Companies Act 1985.

1.3   Historical cost

The **historical cost** accounting system is a system of accounting in which all values are based on the historical costs incurred.

This is the basis of accounting prescribed by the Companies Act (although the Act does allow Alternative Accounting Rules that enable certain assets to be revalued and stated at their revalued amounts).

1.4   Stable monetary unit

Business activity involves the undertaking of all types of transactions. These diverse transactions are expressed in terms of a common unit of measurement, namely the monetary unit. Financial statements prepared on a historical cost basis make the assumption that the pound sterling is a stable monetary unit. This means, therefore, that 20X1 £s can be added to 20X9 £s and a meaningful result obtained.

Example

A company balance sheet states its plant and machinery at **cost less aggregate depreciation**, made up as follows.

	Cost	Aggregate depreciation	Net book value
	£	£	£
Assets acquired 20X1	80,000	24,000	56,000
Assets acquired 20X2	100,000	20,000	80,000
Assets acquired 20X3	60,000	6,000	54,000
	240,000	50,000	190,000

If the pound sterling is a stable unit of measurement, the above aggregation is meaningful. The problem arises, however, that even in periods of only gradual inflation, the pound sterling is not a stable unit of measurement. The purchasing power of a 20X2 £ is different from that of a 20X1 or 20X3 £. This is a severe criticism of accounts prepared on a conventional or historical cost basis (see below).

1.5   Money measurement

Money measurement: Accounts only record items to which a monetary value can be attributed.

All items, in theory, can have a monetary value attributed to them, but not all items can be measured owing to the practical difficulties of valuation. Can values be attributed to the worth of employees for example?

Some would argue that it is desirable to value employees and record them as an asset on the balance sheet but it is very difficult to arrive at a value.

1.6   Materiality

Materiality is the principle that financial statements should separately disclose items which are significant enough to affect evaluation or decisions.

The significance of an item stems from its importance in the overall context of the financial statements.

This convention ensures that only significant items are included in the financial statements in order to improve their clarity. The materiality test, i.e. what is and is not significant, will differ from organisation to organisation.

Materiality may be considered in the context of the financial statements as a whole or individual items within them. It may also be considered in relative or absolute terms depending upon the item concerned.

1.7   Realisation concept

The **realisation concept** states that a transaction should be recognised when the event from which the transaction stems has taken place and the receipt of cash from the transaction is reasonably certain.

A sale on credit is recognised when the sale is made and the invoice sent out rather than waiting until the cash from the sale is received.

1.8   Objectivity convention

This is the main basis of historical cost accounting. Certain aspects of historical cost accounting do, however, represent departures from the objectivity convention. For example, although the depreciation charge is often based on the original cost of an asset (objective) it depends also on the estimated useful life and estimated scrap value at the end of that useful life (subjective).

One advantage of the objectivity convention is that it reduces the extent to which financial statements may be influenced by subjective opinion. In the past great importance has been placed on objective or verifiable evidence. At the present time, particularly as a result of inflation, this approach is being increasingly brought into question.

1.9   Business entity

The **business entity concept** states that financial accounting information relates only to the activities of the business entity and not to the activities of its owner(s).

Under this concept accounting is seen as relating to an independent unit, the entity. The entity is seen as being separate from its owner(s), whatever its legal status. Thus, a company is both legally and for accounting purposes a separate entity distinct from its owners, the shareholders. On the other hand, the business of a sole trader is not a legal entity distinct from its proprietor; however, for accounting purposes, the business is regarded as being a separate entity and accounts are drawn up for the business separately from the trader's own personal financial dealings.

The entity concept is essential in order to be able to account for the business as a separate economic unit. Thus, flows of money between the business and the proprietors may be separately identified from other money flows.

DEFINITION

Duality: Every transaction has two effects.

1.10 Duality

Every transaction has two effects.

The duality concept underpins double entry and the balance sheet, which is why we have examined this principle in detail in earlier chapters.

DEFINITION

For accounting purposes the lifetime of the business is divided into arbitrary **periods** of a fixed length, usually one year.

1.11 Accounting period convention

For accounting purposes the lifetime of the business is divided into arbitrary **periods** of a fixed length, usually one year.

At the end of each arbitrary period, usually referred to as the accounting period, two financial statements are prepared:

- The **balance sheet**, showing the position of the business as at the end of the accounting period.

- The **profit and loss account** for the accounting period. Profit or loss is arrived at on the basis of the **matching** concept. We have already looked at the difficulties of matching revenues and associated costs, particularly in the case of expenditure on items such as research and development and fixed assets, where the benefits extend to more than one accounting period.

Some accountants argue that profit can only be meaningfully measured over the lifetime of a business, i.e. the period starting with the date the business is formed and ending with the date the business goes into liquidation. This is because, by avoiding the use of arbitrary accounting periods, the problem of matching does not arise. There is also certainty of income and expenditure.

In spite of the arbitrary nature of the accounting period convention, it is necessary to strike a compromise between theoretical accuracy and the needs of the financial community. These needs require periodic financial statements which will form the basis of subsequent financial decisions.

1.12 Substance over form convention

DEFINITION

Substance over form:
The economic substance of a transaction should be reflected in the accounts, rather than simply its legal form.

The economic substance of a transaction should be reflected in the accounts, rather than simply its legal form.

A good example of this convention is that of assets acquired on hire purchase terms. Despite the fact that such assets are not owned by the user until the final instalment has been paid, a fixed asset is recorded in his accounts at the start of the hire purchase agreement. The substance of the transaction is that the accounts should reflect the use of a fixed asset in a business.

More recently, it has become accepted practice for assets used under long-term leases to be accounted for as if they were owned by the user. This is despite the fact that for most long-term leases the user never becomes the legal owner of the asset.

ACTIVITY 1

Which accounting conventions would be likely to be used in the following situations?

(a) Determining which accounting period an item of expenditure relates to.

(b) Valuing an asset of the business that is to appear in the balance sheet.

(c) The accounting treatment of an asset being purchased by the business on hire purchase terms.

Feedback to this activity is at the end of the chapter.

1.13 The usefulness of these conventions

The conventions have the following uses:

- They are of some help in dealing with unusual transactions or situations as they provide some principles which can be applied to a specific transaction.

- They can help a user of accounting information to understand detailed accounting entries.

However, it can be argued that they are of limited use for the following reasons:

- Some are statements of the obvious.

- Some are too general to be of practical help.

- They would be much more helpful if integrated. As presented above they are mainly a listing of conventions which by and large are not related to each other. The ASB has integrated these principles into a **conceptual framework** – the *Statement of Principles for Financial Reporting*.

2   FRS 18 *Accounting policies*

2.1   Introduction

FRS 18 *Accounting Policies* was issued in December 2000 to replace SSAP 2 *Disclosure of Accounting Policies*.

2.2   Accounting policies

DEFINITION

Accounting policies are those principles, bases, conventions, rules and practices applied by an entity that specify how the effects of transactions and other events are to be reflected in financial statements.

Accounting policies are those principles, bases, conventions, rules and practices applied by an entity that specify how the effects of transactions and other events are to be reflected in financial statements.

Accounting policies are applied in:

- recognising
- selecting measurement bases for, and
- presenting

assets, liabilities, gains, losses and changes to capital.

Example

A company's accounting policy with regard to stock is to include it using FIFO. This is an accounting policy because it specifies the measurement basis to be used in arriving at cost of stock.

2.3   Measurement bases

DEFINITION

Measurement bases are the various values that an item may have, such as cost or realisable value.

Measurement bases are the various values that an item may have, such as cost or realisable value.

Measurement bases fall into two broad categories – those reflecting current values and those reflecting historical values.

For many items, a choice of measurement basis is available. For example, a company might carry its fixed assets at cost less depreciation or decide to revalue them to their current value.

Because a change of measurement basis could have a major impact on the financial statements, it counts as a change of accounting policy.

2.4   Estimation techniques

Estimation techniques are the methods used by an entity to arrive at estimated monetary amounts for assets, liabilities, gains, losses and changes in capital. For example, the various acceptable methods of depreciation include straight line, reducing balance, etc.

Estimation techniques are subordinate to accounting policies: an accounting policy will specify the basis on which an item is to be measured; where there is uncertainty over the amount corresponding to that basis, the amount will be arrived at using an estimation technique. A change in estimation technique is **not** a change in accounting policy.

2.5   Accounting policies and the true and fair view

The accounting policies adopted by an entity must be such that the financial statements show a true and fair view, consistent with accounting standards and the Companies Acts.

When there is a choice of policy available in an accounting standard, the most appropriate should be chosen. If a policy is adopted that does not conform to accounting standards or the Companies Acts, because conformity would mean that a true and fair view would not be given, the following disclosures must be made:

- a statement that a deviation has been made in order to show a true and fair view
- an explanation of the treatment that the accounting standard or legislation would normally require
- an explanation of why the normal treatment would not give a true and fair view
- an explanation of the difference between the position as reported and the position as it would have been if the standard or legislation had been complied with, including quantification, if possible.

2.6   Accounting concepts in FRS 18

FRS 18 identified two accounting concepts that play a pervasive role in financial statements and in the selection of accounting policies:

- the going concern concept
- the accruals concept.

These concepts must be applied in preparing financial statements (unless of course the entity is not a going concern, as explained earlier).

FRS 18 also mentions the importance of the realisation concept.

Going concern concept

The going concern concept means that the financial statements are drawn up on the assumption that there is no **intention** or **necessity** to **liquidate** or **curtail significantly the scale of operation**.

These words deserve careful reading. Circumstances where the going concern assumption would not be justified would include:

- where there is a specific intention to liquidate the business in the near future
- where there is a strong possibility that shortage of finance will force the business into liquidation – this may be revealed by preparing a cash flow forecast for the next twelve months where a month-by-month comparison of expected cash inflows and outflows indicates financing requirements that are unlikely to be satisfied by the bank or by outside lenders

- where there is a strong possibility that shortage of finance will result in the sale of a significant part of the business.

In the above circumstances the going concern assumption would not be valid, and the financial statements would be prepared on a basis which takes the likely consequences into account.

In most cases, however, financial statements will be prepared on a going concern basis and the directors will be able to justify the validity of this basis. The directors and auditors of a company both have a responsibility to ensure that the company is indeed a going concern if the going concern basis is adopted.

Accruals (or matching) concept

The **accruals** or **matching concept** states that costs and revenues should be matched one with the other and dealt with in the accounting period to which they relate.

The starting position should be to use the concept to determine the accounting period in which revenue (i.e. sales) is recognised.

Revenue is usually recognised when it is **realised**. The realisation of revenue is usually taken to occur on the date of sale rather than on the (usually later) date when the cash relating to the sale is received.

The efforts of expenditure in the past have led to the revenues accruing now. It is thus logical to match the costs or expenses of earning revenue with the revenue reported in any particular period. The operating profit determined in this way is supposed to indicate how efficiently the resources of the business have been utilised.

Although the accruals or matching principle is conceptually simple, it does run into practical difficulties.

For example, expenditure on fixed assets will provide benefits extending over several accounting periods. When a fixed asset is acquired it is necessary to estimate its useful life. The **service potential** of a fixed asset will diminish over its useful life, and this reduction is a cost or expense to be matched against the revenue of each period and is called **depreciation**.

2.7   Selection of accounting policies

The objectives against which a company needs to judge the appropriateness of its accounting policies are:

- relevance
- reliability
- comparability
- understandability.

It is also necessary to balance conflicting aspects and to balance the cost of providing information with the benefits to users.

The *Statement of Principles for Financial Reporting* provides more details of these four matters (see later in this chapter).

2.8   Reviewing and changing accounting policies

Accounting policies should be reviewed regularly to ensure that they remain appropriate. They should be changed if the benefit to users outweighs the disadvantages. The overriding consideration is to maintain a true and fair view.

Estimation techniques

Estimation techniques should be chosen with a view to enabling a true and fair view to be presented.

Accounting for changes in accounting policies and estimation techniques

You may be wondering why FRS 18 makes such a fuss about distinguishing between accounting policies (including measurement bases) and estimation techniques.

The point is that the method of accounting for the changes is normally different. A detailed consideration of this is deferred to near the end of Chapter 21 because the matter really relates only to company accounting.

2.9   Disclosure requirements

The following information should be disclosed in the financial statements:

- a description of each of the accounting policies that is material in the context of the entity's financial statements

- a description of significant estimation techniques

- details of any changes to the accounting policies that were followed in preparing financial statements for the preceding period, including:
  - a brief explanation of why each new accounting policy is thought more appropriate
  - where practicable, the effect of a prior period adjustment on the results for the preceding period, in accordance with FRS 3, *Reporting Financial Performance* (see Chapter 21)
  - where practicable, an indication of the effect of a change in accounting policy on the results for the current period.

- where the effect of a change to an estimation technique is material, a description of the change and, where practicable, the effect on the results for the current period.

If the application of the going concern basis is in doubt, or the going concern basis is not applied, the following additional disclosures are needed:

- any material uncertainties of which the directors are aware in making their assessment, related to events or conditions that may cast significant doubt upon the entity's ability to continue as a going concern

- where the foreseeable future considered by the directors has been limited to a period of less than one year from the date of approval of the financial statements, that fact

- when the financial statements are not prepared on a going concern basis, that fact, together with the basis on which the financial statements are prepared and the reason why the entity is not regarded as a going concern.

3   A conceptual framework

3.1   Nature and purposes

A conceptual framework is a statement of generally accepted theoretical principles which provide a frame of reference within a particular field of enquiry.

The UK's Accounting Standards Board started the development of its conceptual framework in the early 1990s. It was finally issued in December 1999 as the *Statement of Principles for Financial Reporting*. Its development was controversial and it was subject to much criticism in its exposure draft form because not everyone subscribes to the theoretical principles it embraces. For example, the Statement of Principles envisages a 'mixed measurement' approach to financial accounting in which a mixture of historical and current values are used. Many commentators have interpreted this as a commitment by the ASB to move towards a system of full current cost accounting, a move which would be highly controversial. The ASB denies that this is its intention.

3.2   The ASB Statement of Principles for Financial Reporting

The Statement of Principles is the UK's conceptual framework.

The purposes of the Statement of Principles are:

- to set out the principles that the ASB believes should underlie the preparation and presentation of the financial statements
- to provide a frame of reference to be used by the ASB in the development of future accounting standards and the review of existing accounting standards
- to clarify the conceptual underpinnings of proposed accounting standards, enabling standards to be developed on a consistent basis, and reducing the need to debate fundamental issues every time a standard is developed or revised
- to provide those who are interested in the work of the ASB with information about its approach to the formulation of accounting standards
- to assist preparers and users of financial statements in applying accounting standards and in dealing with topics that do not form the subject of an accounting standard.

The Statement of Principles is not an accounting standard. Nothing in the Statement overrides a specific accounting standard. It covers such issues as:

- the users and information needs of users
- the types of reports and information which best satisfy their needs
- the qualitative characteristics of financial statements.

3.3   The purpose of each part of the conceptual framework

The conceptual framework is broken down into a number of chapters. Only the first three are examinable in detail on Paper 1.1.

Chapter 1   The objective of financial statements

A conceptual framework needs to clarify what is the point of producing financial information. This would involve consideration of the various users of financial information and their needs. We examined this in Chapter 1.

Chapter 2   The reporting entity

This chapter focuses on the entities that ought to prepare and publish financial statements.

Chapter 3   The qualitative characteristics of financial information

Financial statements need to possess certain characteristics if the information is to be useful, e.g. the information needs to have the qualities of relevance, reliability, etc. This is the most important area in the statement for this syllabus and its main points are dealt with in below.

3.4   The potential benefits and drawbacks of an agreed conceptual framework

The potential benefits of a conceptual framework are related to the purposes stated by the ASB for the Statement of Principles. In summary, the benefits are as follows:

- It provides a framework for setting accounting standards.
- It provides a basis for resolving disputes.
- Fundamental principles do not have to be repeated in accounting standards.
- There should be a reduction in pressure from vested interests who wish to pursue a particular policy out of self interest rather than satisfying the general needs of users.

Drawbacks to a conceptual framework include the following:

- Owing to their general nature the principles may not, in practice, reduce the options available.
- There may be further disagreement as to the contents of the framework in addition to disagreement over the contents of standards.

4   Qualitative characteristics of financial information

4.1   Summary of characteristics

The Statement contains a rather complicated diagram (shown below) which summarises the factors which it regards as important features of financial statements.

The qualitative characteristics of financial information

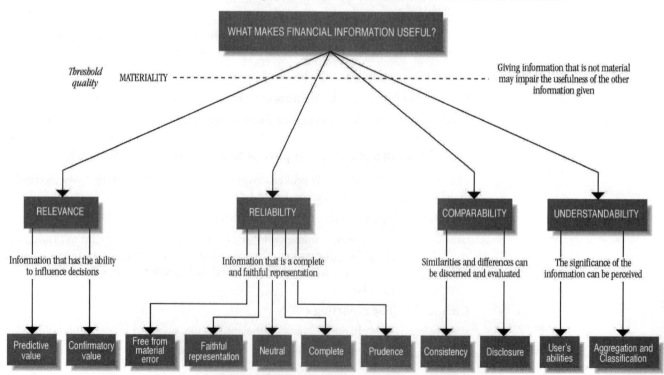

Each of these characteristics is briefly considered below.

KEY POINT

If information could influence users' decisions taken on the basis of financial statements, it is **material**.

4.2   Materiality

As you can see in the diagram, materiality is described as a 'threshold' quality. If information could influence users' decisions taken on the basis of financial statements, it is material. In the profit and loss account, an item is normally regarded as material – and therefore disclosable – if it is more than 5% of the normal level of pre-tax profit.

KEY POINT

Financial information is **relevant** if it can assist users' decision-making by helping them to evaluate past, present or future events or confirming, or correcting, their existing evaluations.

4.3   Relevance

Relevance is one of the basic requirements that financial information must have. Financial information is relevant if it can assist users' decision-making by helping them to evaluate past, present or future events or confirming, or correcting, their existing evaluations.

Relevant information may have predictive value or confirmatory value. That is, it helps users in assessing the future of the business or confirming past predictions.

KEY POINT

To be **reliable**, information must be free from bias and error.

4.4   Reliability

Information is obviously of limited use if it is unreliable. To be reliable, it must be free from bias and error. Some contingent items may by their nature be bound to be unreliable. FRS 12 gives guidance as to the extent to which such items should be recognised or disclosed.

The other subsidiary qualities which make information reliable are as follows:

- **Faithful representation** – Information must faithfully represent the effects of transactions and other events.
- **Neutrality** – Judgement is necessary in arriving at many items in the financial statements. Judgement is involved in fixing depreciation rates, valuing stock, determining the level of doubtful debt provisions and many others. Neutrality means that these judgements are made without bias.
- **Completeness** – Information presented in financial statements should be complete, subject to the constraints of materiality.
- **Prudence** – Caution must be exercised in preparing financial statements and in estimating the outcome of uncertain events. This does not mean, however, that the approach should be over-cautious. The aim should be to report the most likely outcome, with a slight element of caution, not to prepare financial statements on the most pessimistic basis. That could be seriously misleading.

KEY POINT

Comparability means that the financial statements should be comparable with the financial statements of other companies and with the financial statements of the same company for earlier periods.

4.5   Comparability

Comparability means that the financial statements should be comparable with the financial statements of other companies and with the financial statements of the same company for earlier periods.

To achieve comparability we need consistency and disclosure of accounting policies. Accounting standards contribute to comparability by reducing the options available to enterprises in their treatment of transactions. FRS 18's requirement that companies disclose their accounting policies helps with adjustments to allow for differences between companies. Also, if a company changes its accounting policies there must be full disclosure of the effect of the change.

KEY POINT

In making financial statements as **understandable** as possible, a reasonable knowledge of business and accounting on the part of the user has to be assumed.

4.6   Understandability

Companies differ greatly in the extent of the efforts they make to enable users to understand their financial statements. Understandability is dependent upon users' abilities, and the Statement suggests that a reasonable knowledge of business and accounting has to be assumed here. Aggregation and classification also have a role to play. The formats in the Companies Act 1985 and in some accounting standards provide some guidance.

4.7   Limiting factors

You can see that some of the characteristics discussed above conflict to some extent with others. Information that is more reliable can be less relevant and vice versa. In other words, a balance between characteristics needs to be achieved.

DEFINITION

A balance between different characteristics of information needs to be achieved.

Finally, benefit and cost have to be considered. As far as possible, the benefits from presenting the information should exceed the cost of providing it.

5   The elements of financial statements

For the Paper 1.1 syllabus we do not need to be concerned with the detail of this section of the Statement of Principles. However, it does contain three important definitions which you should know – definitions of assets, liabilities and ownership interest.

5.1   Assets

DEFINITIONS

Assets: 'rights or other access to future economic benefits controlled by an entity as a result of past transactions or events'.

Liabilities: 'obligations of an entity to transfer economic benefits as a result of past transactions or events'.

Ownership interest is the residual amount found by deducting all of the entity's liabilities from all of the entity's assets.

Assets: 'rights or other access to future economic benefits controlled by an entity as a result of past transactions or events'.

This very general definition requires some explanation. The first point to note is that ownership is not required. As long as the item is **controlled by** the entity it can be recognised as an asset.

Secondly, there is reference to future economic benefits. If an item does not yield benefits of some kind in the future (profit for example) it has no value as an asset.

Finally, the definition refers to past transactions or events. The commonest past transaction giving rise to an asset is the purchase of that asset.

5.2   Liabilities

Liabilities: 'obligations of an entity to transfer economic benefits as a result of past transactions or events'.

Note that some obligating event must already have taken place by the balance sheet date.

5.3   Ownership interest

Ownership interest is the residual amount found by deducting all of the entity's liabilities from all of the entity's assets.

The definition makes it clear that it is the owners of a business who benefit from increases in net assets, whether arising through operating profit or through revaluation.

Conclusion

This chapter provides the main coverage of accounting concepts and conventions, plus a detailed review of the relevant parts of the ASB's Statement of Principles. It is easy to underestimate these areas and to concentrate on the computational aspects of accounting. Remember that about 40% of your paper will deal with non-computational topics. About half of that 40% is likely to come from this chapter. Work at it!

Accounting conventions

1   What is the stable monetary unit convention? (1.4)

2   What is the money measurement convention? (1.5)

3   What is the objectivity convention? (1.8)

4   What is the business entity convention? (1.9)

5   What is the accounting period convention? (1.11)

FRS 18 *Accounting Policies*

6   What are measurement bases? (2.3)

7   What are estimation techniques? (2.4)

8   What are the two pervasive accounting concepts identified in FRS 18? (2.6)

9   In what circumstances should accounting policies be changed? (2.8)

A conceptual framework

10   What is a conceptual framework? (3.1)

11   What are the purposes of the ASB's *Statement of Principles for Financial Reporting*? (3.2)

12   What are the potential benefits and drawbacks of a conceptual framework? (3.4)

Qualitative characteristics of financial information

13   List the factors in financial statements which make information relevant. (4.3)

14   List the factors in financial statements which make information reliable. (4.4)

15   What qualities assist comparability of financial statements? (4.5)

The elements of financial statements

16   How does the Statement of Principles define:

 (a) assets (5.1)

 (b) liabilities (5.2)

 (c) ownership interest? (5.3)

The Accounting Standards Board's '*Statement of Principles for Financial Reporting*' gives five qualitative characteristics which make financial information reliable.

These five characteristics are:

A   Prudence, consistency, understandability, faithful representation, substance over form.

B   Accruals basis, going concern concept, consistency, prudence, true and fair view.

C   Faithful representation, neutrality, substance over form, completeness, consistency.

D   Freedom from material error, prudence, faithful representation, neutrality, completeness.

For the answer to this question, see the 'Answers' section at the end of the book.

EXAM-TYPE **QUESTION**	**Accounting concepts**

Accounting concepts

If the information in financial statements is to be useful, regard must be had to the following accounting concepts among others:

(a)   materiality   **(4 marks)**

(b)   substance over form   **(3 marks)**

(c)   money measurement.   **(3 marks)**

Explain the meaning of each of these concepts, including in your explanations one example of the application of each of them.   **(Total: 10 marks)**

For the answers to these questions, see the 'Answers' section at the end of the book.

FEEDBACK TO
ACTIVITY 1

(a)   Accruals or matching concept

Accounting period convention

(b)   Historical cost accounting convention

Objectivity convention

(c)   Substance over form convention

Chapter 15
INTANGIBLE FIXED ASSETS: GOODWILL AND RESEARCH AND DEVELOPMENT

This chapter considers two important types of intangible assets. Intangible fixed assets are assets which do not have a physical substance but have value to the business. In accounting terms they most commonly arise when the business has paid money to acquire them or has incurred expenditure which has created an intangible asset.

FRS 10 *Goodwill and Intangible Assets* was published in December 1997. Note that it is not examinable in full in this paper.

Objectives

By the time you have finished this chapter you should be able to:

- explain the nature and permissible accounting treatment of goodwill

- explain the methods of accounting for research and development costs laid down in SSAP 13.

1   Goodwill

1.1   The nature of goodwill

A common situation is that the owner of a business wishes to sell the business to someone else. The seller and the buyer must then agree a fair price for the transaction.

One approach might be to draw up a balance sheet of the business as at the date of sale. However, assets and liabilities in a balance sheet are usually stated on the basis of historical costs, and this may not be a fair indication of current market values.

An improvement on the basic idea might therefore be to list the tangible assets and liabilities to be taken over, and to value them at current market value. Surely then the total would be a good indication of the overall value of the business?

Even this, however, fails to take account of certain intangible assets that may be possessed by a business. In particular, it fails to take account of the fact that the business is already up and running, with established markets and customers, with a good reputation, with a track record of successful dealings. These intangible benefits are also acquired by the purchaser and they place him in a much stronger position than someone acquiring identical tangible assets but having to start a business from scratch.

DEFINITION

Purchased goodwill is the difference between the cost of an acquired entity and the aggregate of the fair values of that entity's identifiable assets and liabilities.

For this reason, when a business changes hands the price paid will commonly exceed the net value of the tangible assets owned by the business (even when these are valued at market prices). The difference is an intangible asset referred to as 'goodwill'. Goodwill has been defined as 'the advantage, whatever it may be, which a person gets by continuing to carry on, and being entitled to represent to the outside world that he is carrying on, a business which has been carried on for some time previously'.

Thus goodwill may be seen as the value of the going concern element of the business.

Consider why goodwill may exist.

Feedback to this activity is at the end of the chapter.

1.2   Purchased and non-purchased goodwill

Purchased goodwill arises as a result of a purchase transaction (e.g. when one business acquires another as a going concern). In such a case, the value of the goodwill can be computed by comparing the purchase price of the whole business with the market values of the separate net assets acquired.

Purchased goodwill will be recognised within the accounts because at a specific point in time the fact of purchase has established a figure of value for the business as a whole which can be compared with the fair value of the individual assets acquired, and this figure will be incorporated in the accounts of the acquiring business as the cost of the acquisition.

Notice that even before the business was purchased, the goodwill must have existed; that is why the purchaser was willing to pay for it. In other words, the goodwill is inherent in the business. This raises the question of why the previous owner of the business did not recognise the goodwill as an asset on his balance sheet.

The answer is that it is extremely difficult to place a value on such an intangible asset, and in practice no attempt is made to do so, except when it is particularly needed, usually when the business is being sold. Until that point, the inherent goodwill is simply ignored in the accounts. Not only is its value difficult to estimate, but also even if an estimate could be made at a particular moment the value would be likely to fluctuate frequently.

1.3   Valuation methods for goodwill

Valuing goodwill is a problem often faced by the accountant, who may be asked to value a business on behalf of a buyer, a seller, or as an independent third party. The difficulty is that there are no laid down rules to follow, and ultimately the value of goodwill is what someone will pay for it.

Nevertheless, some parameters of goodwill value can be set by the accountant. You are not expected to study these in detail at this stage, but an indication of the approach is given below. This is based on the idea of **superprofits**. The idea is that such excess profits are attributable to the intangible assets in the business, i.e. its goodwill.

	£
Average annual profits	30,000
Less: Time of manager/owner at normal salary	12,000
Interest on capital employed	5,000
	17,000
Superprofits	13,000

Goodwill might be valued at £13,000 × n

Where n represents the number of years by which 'superprofits' are multiplied, typically in the range 2 to 4.

Alternative methods are based on valuing the business as a whole and deducting the fair value of the tangible net assets of the business. This approach accords more with the definition of goodwill as the residual figure arising on the purchase of a business.

Thus in the above example, the value of the business as a whole may be computed by capitalising existing profits by a number, being an accepted number by the seller and purchaser. If that number is 10 then the business would be valued at $10 \times £30,000$ or £300,000.

If the fair value of the tangible net assets is £150,000, goodwill is valued at £150,000.

Clearly the assumptions used to calculate a value are crucial and need to be agreed between the two parties to the transaction.

Goodwill is valued differently from other assets because, by definition, it is not capable of being sold independently of the business. It is an integral part of the business. As we saw in the second example above the calculation of goodwill was calculated by reference to the value of the business as a whole.

1.4 Alternative accounting treatments of goodwill

Having placed a value on goodwill, we then need to consider how to account for the item. If we have paid for goodwill, the credit entry is cash, but what is the appropriate debit?

Below we discuss the normal accounting treatment required nowadays by accounting standards, and also one possible alternative.

1 *Carry as an asset, amortised over useful life through the profit and loss account*

Following the issue of FRS 10, this is now the normal method of accounting for goodwill.

Arguments for:

- Goodwill is an asset on which capital has been expended in exchange for benefits which will materialise in future periods. Although different in quality and character from other assets, it does exist and can be purchased or sold, and as such it should be treated as an asset.

- The expense of acquiring purchased goodwill should be matched against the extra earnings generated from its acquisition.

Arguments against:

- Comparability is lost when one type of goodwill ('purchased') is treated as an asset while another ('inherent' or 'non-purchased') is not recognised as such.

- The life of goodwill is indeterminate in the extreme, and even if determined, a single event may drastically alter that life. Any amortisation period is therefore too arbitrary to be realistic.

2 *Eliminate against profits on acquisition*

Following the issue of FRS 10, this is no longer an acceptable accounting treatment.

Arguments for:

- Goodwill is not an asset in the normal sense of the word; it is not independently realisable and many of the factors contributing to it are beyond the control of management. Thus, it is not prudent to carry goodwill as an asset in the balance sheet and, as a once-for-all expense of acquisition, it should be written off as it arises.

- Goodwill will usually be worthless in a forced liquidation.

Arguments against:

- Since consideration has been given, then clearly an asset existed. If so, then it would seem excessively prudent to write it off immediately.

- It is assumed that the accounts are prepared on a going concern basis, which renders this point irrelevant.

1.5   The standard accounting treatment of purchased goodwill

Goodwill is classified as an **intangible asset**, and the debit will be to a separate asset account called 'goodwill'.

In the balance sheet, goodwill will be shown in fixed assets, above tangible fixed assets such as land and buildings and plant and machinery.

Goodwill should be amortised over its estimated useful economic life, which is presumed to be twenty years or less in most cases. Amortisation is the same as depreciation, but is the appropriate term to use when referring to intangible assets. The straight line method will usually be the method of amortisation used.

Example

A company acquires the business of a sole trader for £5,000,000. The purchase price reflects the net assets at their current market valuation of £4,500,000, the remainder being attributable to goodwill. The company considers that it will continue to benefit from the good reputation of the sole trader for five years.

You are required to show how the goodwill will appear in the balance sheet of the company one year after the business was acquired.

Solution

	Cost	*Amortisation*	*Net book value*
	£000	£000	£000
Goodwill	500	100	400

2   Research and development costs

2.1   The classification of research and development costs

Some companies – e.g. those engaged in developing pharmaceuticals, or those in the high-tech electronic industries – spend very significant sums of money on research and development. By investing now, they hope eventually to develop products which will sell profitably. A problem arises in matching the expenditure on research and development activities with the revenues that will eventually be earned from sale of the finished products.

One argument, based on the prudence concept, is that such expenditure should be written off as an expense in the profit and loss account immediately. The argument is that the value of such expenditure is necessarily uncertain (after all, just think how many research ideas do *not* lead to profitable products), and therefore to treat it as an asset is not prudent.

The alternative argument is based on the accruals or matching concept. Since revenues will arise in later periods as a result of present expenditure, it is not appropriate to write off the expenditure until those later periods. In the meantime, it should be carried in the balance sheet as an asset.

Accounting standards are sympathetic to both of these arguments. Essentially, the required treatment is to write off research and development costs immediately (following the prudence concept), unless certain strict conditions are satisfied. Where expenditure does meet the criteria, it is permissible to carry it forward as an asset.

An essential first step is to distinguish between three categories of research and development expenditure.

Pure (or basic) research: original investigation undertaken in order to gain new scientific or technical knowledge and understanding. Basic research is not primarily directed towards any specific practical aim or application.

Applied research: original investigation undertaken in order to gain new scientific or technical knowledge and directed towards a specific practical aim or objective.

Development: the use of existing scientific or technical knowledge in order to produce new or substantially improved materials, devices, products, processes, systems or services prior to the commencement of commercial production.

2.2 Accounting treatment

There are two possible accounting treatments:

1 To treat the expenditure on research and development as a cost, and charge it in the profit and loss account with other expenses

2 To treat the expenditure as creating a fixed asset, and amortise it over the period for which benefits from the research and development expenditure continue to flow.

Example

ABC Ltd is developing a new product, the widget. This is expected to be sold over a three-year period starting in 20X2. The data is as follows:

	20X1 £000	20X2 £000	20X3 £000	20X4 £000
Net revenue from other activities	400	500	450	400
Net revenue from widgets	-	450	600	400
Development costs of widgets	(900)			

Solution

Profit treating development costs as expenses when incurred

	20X1 £000	20X2 £000	20X3 £000	20X4 £000
Other activities – Net revenue	400	500	450	400
Widgets – Net revenue	-	450	600	400
Development costs	(900)	-	-	-
Net profit/(loss)	(500)	950	1,050	800

Net profit amortising development cost over life of widgets

	20X1 £000	20X2 £000	20X3 £000	20X4 £000
Other activities – Net revenue	400	500	450	400
Widgets – Net revenue	-	450	600	400
Development costs of widgets $\frac{£900,000}{3}$	-	(300)	(300)	(300)
Net profit	400	650	750	500

2.3 SSAP 13 *Accounting for Research and Development*

It will be noted that there is a conflict between the conventions of prudence (write off R&D immediately) and accruals (match expenditure against income). In order to resolve the problem, SSAP 13 lays down some ground rules.

In general, research and development expenditure should be written off in the period in which it is incurred (i.e. treated as an expense). However, an exception is made for **development expenditure only** provided all of the following conditions are met:

1   There is a clearly defined project.

2   The related expenditure is separately identifiable.

3   The outcome of such a project has been assessed with reasonable certainty as to:

   (a) its technical feasibility

   (b) its ultimate commercial viability considered in the light of factors such as likely market conditions (including competing products), public opinion, consumer and environmental legislation.

4   If further development costs are to be incurred on the same project, the aggregate of such costs together with related production, selling and administration costs are reasonably expected to be more than covered by related future revenues.

5   Adequate resources exist, or are reasonably expected to be available, to enable the project to be completed and to provide any consequential increases in working capital.

Where these conditions are met, the development expenditure may be capitalised as an asset (called **deferred development expenditure**) and amortised as illustrated in the example above. Capitalised development expenditure must be reviewed annually and written off if circumstances no longer justify its continued capitalisation.

Research expenditure is never capitalised; it must always be written off immediately as an expense.

2.4   Disclosure in the financial statements

'The accounting policy should be stated and explained.

The total amount of research and development expenditure charged in the profit and loss account should be disclosed, analysed between the current year's expenditure and amounts amortised from deferred expenditure.

Movements on deferred development expenditure and the amount carried forward at the beginning and the end of the period should be disclosed. Deferred development expenditure should be disclosed under intangible fixed assets in the balance sheet.'

(SSAP 13)

The Companies Act 1985 requires deferred development expenditure to be included as an intangible fixed asset in company accounts.

An example of an appropriate note to the balance sheet would be as follows:

	£000	£000
Deferred development expenditure at beginning of period		320
Expenditure incurred in the period	70	
Expenditure written off in the period	(64)	
		6
Deferred development expenditure at end of period		326

The profit and loss account or a note to the profit and loss account would disclose the total amount of research and development expenditure. For example:

	£000
Research and development expenditure:	
Expenditure charged in year	130
Development expenditure amortised	64
	194

The £130,000 does not include the £70,000 appearing in the balance sheet note as it has not been charged in the profit and loss account.

Conclusion

This chapter has dealt with two types of intangible assets which may be recorded on a balance sheet. The crucial point about goodwill is its residuary nature – it cannot exist by itself. In the area of research and development expenditure, it is only development expenditure which can be carried forward and only then if certain conditions are satisfied.

In fact, few companies do capitalise development costs even when the conditions in SSAP 13 are satisfied.

SELF-TEST
QUESTIONS

Goodwill

1   What is goodwill? (1.1)

2   What is the accounting treatment for goodwill? (1.4)

Research and development costs

3   How many categories of research and development expenditure are there? (2.1)

4   What conditions need to be satisfied in order to carry forward research and development expenditure? (2.3)

MULTIPLE-
CHOICE
QUESTION

Which of the following statements concerning the accounting treatment of research and development expenditure are true, according to SSAP 13 *Accounting for research and development*?

1   If certain criteria are met, research expenditure may be recognised as an asset.

2   Research expenditure, other than capital expenditure on research facilities, should be recognised as an expense incurred.

3   In deciding whether development expenditure qualifies to be recognised as an asset, it is necessary to consider whether there will be adequate finance available to complete the project.

4   Development expenditure recognised as an asset must be amortised over a period of not more than five years.

5   The financial statements should disclose the total amount of research and development expenditure recognised as an expense during the period.

A   1, 4 and 5

B   2, 4 and 5

C   2, 3 and 4

D   2, 3 and 5

For the answer to this question, see the 'Answers' section at the end of the book.

EXAM-TYPE
QUESTION

Research and development expenditure

(a)   Explain the three classifications of research and development expenditure.

(6 marks)

(b)   Discuss the treatment of research and development expenditure
with special reference to relevant concepts of accounting.   **(9 marks)**

(Total: 15 marks)

For the answer to this question, see the 'Answers' section at the end of the book.

FEEDBACK TO
ACTIVITY 1

Goodwill may exist because of any combination of a number of possible factors:

(a)   reputation for quality and/or service

(b)   a good location

(c)   technical 'know-how' and experience

(d)   possession of favourable contracts

(e)   good management and/or technical personnel.

Chapter 16
POST BALANCE SHEET EVENTS AND CONTINGENCIES

Two further accounting standards are covered in this chapter and both relate to the problems of whether to include or not to include certain items in the accounts. It is important to learn the definitions contained in this chapter.

Objectives

By the time you have finished this chapter you should be able to:

- define and distinguish between different categories of post balance sheet events
- account for each category of post balance sheet event in line with SSAP 17
- define and distinguish between different types of contingency
- account for each type of contingency in line with FRS 12.

1   SSAP 17 *Post Balance Sheet Events*

1.1   Definition and categories

Suppose the year end of a company is 31 December 20X7 and the directors approve the financial statements at a board meeting held on 22 March 20X8. The date on which the financial statements are approved by the board of directors is the date the board of directors formally approves a set of documents as the financial statements.

Certain events occurring during the intervening period will provide information which will help in preparing the financial statements.

Post balance sheet events are those events, both favourable and unfavourable, which occur between the balance sheet date and the date on which the financial statements are approved by the board of directors.

These post balance sheet events fall into two categories: adjusting events and non-adjusting events, described below.

1.2   Adjusting events

Adjusting events provide additional evidence of conditions existing at the balance sheet date. For example, bad debts arising one or two months after the balance sheet date may help to quantify the bad debt provision as at the balance sheet date. Adjusting events may, therefore, affect the amount at which items are stated in the balance sheet.

Here are some examples:

- sales of stock at less than cost, necessitating a reduction in the valuation of closing stock
- bankruptcy of a debtor, requiring the debt to be written off in whole or in part
- amounts received or receivable in respect of insurance claims which were being negotiated at the balance sheet date.

DEFINITION

Post balance sheet events are those events, both favourable and unfavourable, which occur between the balance sheet date and the date on which the financial statements are approved by the board of directors.

DEFINITION

Adjusting events are post balance sheet events which provide additional evidence of conditions existing at the balance sheet date.

1.3 Non-adjusting events

These are events arising after the balance sheet date but which do not concern conditions existing at the balance sheet date. Such events will not, therefore, have any effect on items in the balance sheet or profit and loss account. However, in order to prevent the financial statements from presenting a misleading position, some form of additional disclosure is required if the events are material, by way of a note to the financial statements giving details of the event.

Examples of non-adjusting events include:

- the raising of new capital

- major changes in the composition of the business (for example, acquisitions of new businesses)

- financial consequences of losses of fixed assets or stock as a result of fires or floods.

1.4 'Window dressing'

'Window dressing' refers to the practice of entering into certain transactions before the year end and reversing those transactions after the year end. Thus no real transaction has occurred (i.e. no substance, only legal form), but the balance sheet reflects the transaction (as it primarily records the legal form of assets and liabilities). The hoped-for effect is to improve the appearance of the balance sheet.

SSAP 17 requires a **disclosure** of such transactions (if they are material) by way of a note to the accounts. They are *not*, however, adjusting events.

Example

UK plc is a bank and is concerned that it has over-lent to customers in the year to 31 December 20X8. As a result, its ratio of liquid assets to total assets is too low. It thus arranges a loan of £40 million from another company in December. The loan is repaid in January.

	(a)	*(b)*
	£m	£m
Liquid assets	10	50
Investments:		
Advances to customers	200	200
Fixed assets	20	20
Less: Creditors – amounts falling due within one year	(10)	(50)
Total assets less current liabilities	220	220

$$\frac{\text{Liquid assets}}{\text{Total assets less current liabilities}} \qquad \frac{10}{220} \times 100 \qquad \frac{50}{220} \times 100$$

$$= 5\% \qquad\qquad = 23\%$$

(a) refers to the balance sheet if the transaction had not been entered into; (b) shows the actual balance sheet at the year end. Clearly (b) looks better if an accepted measure of security/solvency is a 'liquidity' ratio such as calculated above.

1.5 Standard accounting practice – SSAP 17

SSAP 17 *Accounting for Post Balance Sheet Events* requires that:

> 'Financial statements should be prepared on the basis of conditions existing at the balance sheet date.

A material post balance sheet event requires changes in the amounts to be included in financial statements where:

(a)   it is an adjusting event; or

(b)   it indicates that application of the going concern concept to the whole or a material part of the company is not appropriate.

A material post balance sheet event should be disclosed where:

(a)   it is a non-adjusting event of such materiality that its non-disclosure would affect the ability of the users of financial statements to reach a proper understanding of the financial position; or

(b)   it is the reversal or maturity after the year-end of a transaction entered into before the year-end, the substance of which was primarily to alter the appearance of the company's balance sheet.

In respect of each post balance sheet event which is required to be disclosed above, the following information should be stated by way of notes in the financial statements:

(a)   the nature of the event

(b)   an estimate of the financial effect, or a statement that it is not practicable to make such an estimate.

The estimate of the financial effect should be disclosed before taking account of taxation, and the taxation implications should be explained where necessary for a proper understanding of the financial position.

The date on which the financial statements are approved by the board of directors should be disclosed in the financial statements.'

ACTIVITY 1

How would the following be dealt with?

When drafting the final accounts, a company's accountant includes a figure of £2,000 as the net realisable value of damaged items of stock.

The cost of these items was £3,000, and the normal selling price would be £4,000. Between the balance sheet date and the approval of the accounts the items are sold for £3,100.

ACTIVITY 2

A company is engaged in the construction of its own factory. The estimated value on completion is £200,000, costs to date are £80,000 and at the balance sheet date expected further costs to completion were £90,000.

After the balance sheet date serious defects – which must have existed unnoticed for some time – are discovered in the foundations of the building, necessitating partial demolition and rebuilding at an estimated cost of £70,000 (in addition to the estimated further costs to completion of £90,000).

How would this be dealt with in the accounts?

Feedback to these activities is at the end of the chapter.

2 FRS 12 *Provisions, Contingent Liabilities and Contingent Assets*

2.1 Definition of 'contingency'

A **contingency** is a condition which exists at the balance sheet date where the outcome will be confirmed only on the occurrence or non-occurrence of one or more uncertain future events not wholly within the entity's control.

A contingent gain or loss is a gain or loss dependent on a contingency. A contingent asset or liability is an asset or liability dependent on a contingency.

This definition is not intended to encompass normal accounting estimates. For instance, the correctness of the amount of a provision for doubtful debts will be confirmed (or otherwise) by future events; however, such adjustments to the value of assets are not addressed in FRS 12. Other examples of accounting estimates which are not to be treated as contingencies include the net realisable value of stocks and the depreciation of fixed assets.

An example of a condition which does fall within the definition arises in connection with bills of exchange. Essentially, a bill of exchange is a written promise by a debtor to pay a certain sum of money at a specified future date. When a company has received such a bill from a debtor it may discount it, i.e. sell it to a third party such as a bank, which will advance the money due to the company (subject to a deduction for interest and costs) and then collect the amount from the debtor on maturity (i.e. on the specified date). Should the debtor fail to pay, the bank would look to the company for reimbursement.

If a company has discounted bills in this way, which have not matured by the balance sheet date, then there is a contingent liability: if the debtor fails to pay, the company will have to reimburse the bank or other third party to whom it discounted the bills. The existence of such a liability will only be confirmed if the debtor fails to pay – an uncertain future event. This situation is, therefore, of the type envisaged by FRS 12.

2.2 Distinction between different types of contingency

Contingencies are distinguished in FRS 12 by reference to the likelihood or otherwise of the contingency becoming an actual event.

There are four categories of contingencies – depending on whether the likelihood is:

- remote
- possible
- probable
- virtually certain.

It is a matter for the business to decide into which category the contingency falls (and clearly the projected result can turn out differently). The distinction is important because different accounting treatments may result.

A reasonable way to interpret 'probable' is whether a contingency has a better than 50% chance of happening.

2.3 Accounting for each type of contingency

The choices in accounting for contingencies are as follows:

- Provide for the likely financial effect of the item in the accounts.
- Do not provide, but disclose the nature of the contingency in a note to the accounts.
- Do not provide and do not disclose the nature of the contingency in a note to the accounts.

The first treatment will affect the balance sheet and the profit and loss account (i.e. the other side of the entry of the contingency as an asset or liability will be to profit and loss account).

The second treatment means that the user of the accounts should be provided with information about the contingency as it is relevant information to him.

The third treatment means that the user of the accounts has no information about the contingency on the grounds that to try and tell the user everything that might possibly happen to a business would result in the accounts being very lengthy and it would be difficult to see the wood for the trees.

The following table summarises the accounting treatment of different types of contingency required by FRS 12. (The percentages are not in the FRS, but are added here for guidance.)

Likelihood of occurrence	Material contingent gain	Material contingent loss
Remote < 5%	No disclosure	No disclosure
Possible 5% – 50%	No disclosure	Disclose by note
Probable 51% – 95%	Disclose by note	Set up provision
Virtually certain > 95%	Accrual	Set up provision

(*Note:* If the likelihood of occurrence is virtually certain, then the asset or liability is not contingent.)

2.4   Disclosure of contingency

In respect of each contingency which is required to be disclosed by note, the following information should be stated by way of notes in financial statements:

- a brief description of the nature of the contingent liability or asset

- the uncertainties which are expected to affect the ultimate outcome

- an estimate of the financial effect, made at the date on which the financial statements are approved by the board of directors or a statement that it is not practicable to make such an estimate

- the possibility of any reimbursement.

Examples

In the following examples, the company's year end is 31 December and the directors approve the financial statements on 11 March.

1   X Ltd has guaranteed a loan of £10,000 granted to Y Ltd. At the time when the financial statements of X Ltd are being finalised, it is clear that Y Ltd is in financial difficulties and it is probable that X Ltd will have to meet the guarantee.

    Accounting treatment

    Since it is probable that the liability will arise, an accrual is necessary in the financial statements:

		£	£
Dr	Profit and loss account	10,000	
Cr	Creditors		10,000

2   X Ltd has guaranteed a loan of £5,000 granted to Y Ltd. At the date when the directors approve the financial statements of Y Ltd, it is possible, but not probable that the guarantee will be invoked.

Accounting treatment

Assuming that the amount of £5,000 is a material amount for X Ltd, the contingent liability should be disclosed by way of note to the financial statements.

3   X Ltd has guaranteed a loan of £20,000 granted to Y Ltd. After the balance sheet date of X Ltd but before the financial statements are approved by the directors, X Ltd receives notice that Y Ltd is in liquidation and that the guarantee will be invoked by the creditor of Y Ltd.

Accounting treatment

This is an adjusting post balance sheet event under SSAP 17. The amount should therefore be accrued in the financial statements.

A C T I V I T Y   3

A Ltd is suing B Ltd for £50,000 damages. At the date on which the financial statements are approved, counsel's opinion is that A Ltd is likely to win its case.

How should this matter be treated in the accounts?

A C T I V I T Y   4

The company is being sued for £100,000 damages. Counsel assesses the chances of losing the case as fifty-fifty.

How should this matter be treated in the accounts?

Feedback to these activities is at the end of the chapter.

Conclusion

The two accounting standards covered in this chapter both relate to the problems of whether to include or not to include certain items in the accounts. It is important to learn the definitions contained in this chapter and the accounting entries which result.

**S E L F - T E S T
Q U E S T I O N S**

SSAP 17 *Post Balance Sheet Events*

1   What is a post balance sheet event? (1.1)

2   What is the date on which the accounts are approved? (1.1)

3   Give two examples of adjusting events (1.2)

4   Give two examples of non-adjusting events (1.3)

5   What are the two circumstances when a material post balance sheet event requires the adjustment of amounts in the accounts? (1.5)

FRS 12 *Provisions, Contingent Liabilities and Contingent Assets*

6   What is a contingency? (2.1)

7   What are the four classifications of contingencies? (2.2)

8   When should contingencies be accrued in the financial statements? (2.3)

SSAP 17 *Accounting for Post Balance Sheet Events* regulates the extent to which events after the balance sheet date should be reflected in financial statements.

Which of the following lists of such events consists only of items that, according to SSAP 17, should normally be classified as non-adjusting?

A   Insolvency of a debtor whose balance was outstanding at the balance sheet date, issue of shares or debentures, a major merger with another company

B   Issue of shares or debentures, changes in foreign exchange rates, major purchases of fixed assets

C   A major merger with another company, destruction of a major fixed asset by fire, discovery of fraud or error which shows that the financial statements were incorrect

D   Sale of stock giving evidence about its value at the balance sheet date, issue of shares or debentures, destruction of a major fixed asset by fire.

EXAM-TYPE
QUESTIONS

Question 1: Events

In relation to SSAP 17 *Accounting for Post Balance Sheet Events*, you are required:

(a)   to define 'adjusting events' and 'non-adjusting events'

(b)   to give two examples of each

(c)   to state how material post balance sheet events should be incorporated into companies' financial statements.   **(15 marks)**

Question 2: Jurien Limited

The directors of Jurien Limited are considering the draft financial statements for the year ended 31 March 20X1.

Matters under discussion are:

(a)   After a party in February 20X0, 18 people died as a result of food poisoning from eating food manufactured by Jurien. At 31 March 20X1 the company was advised that there was probably no liability and the matter was disclosed as a contingent liability at that date. As the result of developments in the case, which is still not settled, the company was advised that it is now probable, as at 31 March 20X1, that the company will be found liable. Some directors consider that the matter should mean a contingent liability until the court case decides the matter, while others consider that provision should be made for it in the financial settlements for the year ended 31 March 20X1.   **(3 marks)**

(b)   No provision has yet been made for a trade debtor of £560,000 outstanding at 31 March 20X1. In June 20X1 the directors of Jurien became aware that the debtor was in financial difficulties. Directors are divided as to whether a provision should be made or not.   **(3 marks)**

(c)   The company's closing stock of finished goods is valued by taking the cost of labour and materials plus an allocation of overheads. One director has queried the basis on which the overheads are added and has asked for clarification of the relevant rules, with two examples of overheads which must be excluded.   **(4 marks)**

Write a memorandum to the directors advising them on the three points raised, explaining the authority for your advice in each case.   **(Total: 10 marks)**

For answers to these questions, see the 'Answers' section at the end of the book.

| FEEDBACK TO ACTIVITY 1 | The valuation in the accounts should be adjusted to £3,000, i.e. cost, since net realisable value has, in the event, turned out to be greater than cost. This is an adjusting post balance sheet event. |

| FEEDBACK TO ACTIVITY 2 | This is an adjusting post balance sheet event. There is an anticipated loss on the factory of £40,000 (value £200,000 less costs to date £80,000 less estimated further costs £160,000). The asset should, therefore, be valued at £40,000 (costs to date £80,000 less attributable loss £40,000). |

| FEEDBACK TO ACTIVITY 3 | This is a material contingent gain, which should be disclosed by way of note. |

| FEEDBACK TO ACTIVITY 4 | Since the chances are fifty-fifty, the loss is not 'probable'; the contingent loss should, therefore, be disclosed by way of note. This is clearly a borderline case. |

Chapter 17
INCOMPLETE RECORDS

So far in this text, the ledger accounting that has been encountered has been complete even if errors have been made. Many businesses, however, do not maintain a complete set of double entry books. The term 'incomplete records' refers to the varying situations that fall short of full double entry. In most cases this will occur with a sole trader rather than larger forms of business entity and therefore this chapter will concentrate on the approach and techniques required to prepare a trading and profit and loss account and balance sheet for a sole trader who does not keep a full set of double entry accounts.

Objectives

By the time you have finished this chapter you should be able to:

- calculate the profit of a business from information about its balance sheet only

- reconstruct the ledger accounts for a business from details of its transactions and prepare a set of financial statements

- understand gross profit margins and mark-ups and be able to use them in an incomplete records situation

1   Incomplete and limited accounting records

1.1   Distinction between incomplete and limited accounting records

Limited accounting records refers to the situation where a sole trader maintains records of his transactions, but not a full set of double entry books of account. Additional information is needed before final accounts can be prepared.

Incomplete accounting records are records which the trader has not fully completed or where no records at all have been kept of transactions.

DEFINITIONS

Limited accounting records refers to the situation where a sole trader maintains records of his transactions, but not a full set of double entry books of account. Additional information is needed before final accounts can be prepared.

Incomplete accounting records are records which the trader has not fully completed or where no records at all have been kept of transactions.

Many businesses fall into both of these categories. Many businesses keep limited accounting information, such as daily records of cash received, invoices paid (i.e. some form of purchase day book) and wages paid. They leave it to the accountant who prepares the annual financial statements to make sense of the information and to ask for other information when required.

With limited accounting records, the accountant thus has (generally) sufficient information to prepare the accounts but no ledger accounts have been prepared. We will look at the procedures used to prepare financial statements in this situation later in the chapter.

A trader who has kept very little information on his daily transactions is providing the accountant with the task of preparing financial statements from incomplete data. In this section we will see how it is possible to prepare financial statements even from very skimpy data. However these financial statements are more prone to error because of the incomplete records.

In practice, the term **incomplete records** is used to cover both situations.

1.2   Incomplete records: calculating net assets and profit

The most basic incomplete records situation of all is where one is required to calculate net profit, given details only of a sole trader's capital at the beginning and end of the year and of his drawings.

Example

A sole trader's capital position is as follows:

	31 December	
	20X6	*20X7*
	£	£
Motor vehicle:		
Cost	2,000	2,000
Depreciation	(800)	(1,200)
	1,200	800
Stock	2,040	2,960
Debtors	865	1,072
Bank	1,017	1,964
Cash	351	86
	5,473	6,882
Creditors	1,706	1,905
Net assets	3,767	4,977

The trader estimates that his drawings for the year have amounted to about £3,000. An estimate of his net profit for the year is required.

Solution

From the basic balance sheet equation: capital equals assets less liabilities. The trader's opening and closing capital account balances are £3,767 and £4,977 respectively. His net profit may be calculated by completing his capital account.

Capital account

20X7		£	*20X7*			£
	Drawings	3,000	1 Jan	Balance b/d		3,767
31 Dec	Balance c/d	4,977		Net profit (bal fig)		4,210
		7,977				7,977
			20X8			
			1 Jan	Balance b/d		4,977

Note that the net profit figure is very much an estimate and depends on the reliability of the drawings and the opening and closing net asset positions.

It also assumes that no new capital has been introduced by the owner during the year.

1.3 Alternative method

An alternative method of calculation is:

	£
Net assets this year end	4,977
Net assets last year end	3,767
Increase in net assets	1,210
Less: Capital introduced by owner	-
Add: Drawings	3,000
Profit for the year	4,210

The alternative method emphasises that profit represents an increase in the net assets of the business unless it is withdrawn by the owner.

> Profit for the year = Increase in net assets − Capital introduced + Drawings

On 1 January 20X5 B Freen commenced business. At that date he purchased a shop premises for £14,000 and paid £2,000 for interior fittings. He also paid £4,000 into the business bank account. On 31 December 20X6 he realised the need for a profit figure for the two years he had been in business, but his records were completely inadequate. At this date the assets he possessed in addition to the premises and fittings were as follows.

	£
Stock	6,000
Debtors	1,040
Motor lorry purchased 30 June 20X6 for	8,000
Cash at bank	2,500

He owed £1,400 to trade creditors and had borrowed £10,000 from a friend. Interest accrued but unpaid on the loan amounted to £200. Freen estimated that he was withdrawing £300 a month from the business.

Compute the net profit for the two years valuing the fixed assets at cost less depreciation (on a straight line basis): on premises at 2% p.a. and on fittings at 5% p.a. and on the motor lorry at 20% p.a.

Feedback to this activity is at the end of the chapter.

2   Final accounts from limited accounting records

2.1   Cash and bank transactions

In the first example above, no details were given of transactions taking place during the year. If basic information regarding receipts and payments is provided, it is possible to build up to a balance sheet and profit and loss account, although some important assumptions may well need to be made.

2.2   Basic procedure for limited records

The procedure suggested below is a full procedure suitable for a wide range of limited records questions and may be set out in basic steps. We will see later how some of these steps can be cut back for examination purposes.

Step 1

Set aside a sheet of paper for the trading and profit and loss account and another for the balance sheet. Some information can be inserted straight into the final accounts.

Step 2

Prepare the opening balance sheet from information on assets and liabilities.

The opening capital account balance can be calculated as a balancing figure (capital = assets less liabilities).

Step 3

Insert the opening balances in 'T' accounts. For example:

Balance	Account
Cash at bank	Cash at bank (bank)
Cash in hand	Cash in hand (cash)
Debtors	Sales control account
Creditors	Purchases control account
Accrued expenses	Separate account for each expense category
Prepayments	Separate account for each expense category

Purchases control account and sales control account have a similar layout to control accounts in a double entry system. The difference is that their key objective in incomplete records is often to calculate purchases and sales made in the accounting period which will be transferred to the trading and profit and loss account.

Alternative names given to these accounts in incomplete records are:

Sales control   =   Total sales account or
                                          Total debtors account

Purchases control   =   Total purchases account or
                                          Total creditors account.

Step 4

Information is almost certain to be given as regards cash and bank transactions. Accordingly the cash and bank accounts can be prepared, making use of double entry principles and completing the entries by debiting and crediting whichever accounts are appropriate.

Notes:

1   Cash withdrawn is cash taken out of the bank (Cr bank) and into cash in hand (Dr cash).

2   Cash banked operates in the opposite direction – it is a reduction of cash in hand (Cr Cash) and an increase in money at bank (Dr Bank).

Depending on the degree of incompleteness, cash is likely to contain one or two missing items of information. This aspect of the problem will receive more attention later.

Step 5

Insert into the accounts the closing balances provided in the question in respect of debtors, creditors, accrued expenses and prepayments. In simple questions the respective transfers to profit and loss may be calculated as balancing items.

Sales control account

	£		£
Opening debtors b/d	X	Cash	X
Sales (bal fig)	X	Closing debtors c/d	X
	X		X

Purchases control account

	£		£
Cash	X	Opening trade creditors b/d	X
Bank	X	Purchases (bal fig)	X
Closing trade creditors c/d	X		
	X		X

Rates account (assuming paid in advance)

	£		£
Opening prepayment b/d	X	Profit and loss (bal fig)	X
Bank	X	Closing prepayment c/d	X
	X		X

Step 6

Carry out any further adjustments as required, such as dealing with doubtful debts and depreciation.

ACTIVITY 2

A business has a cash float of £50 and the following expenses are paid out of the till before cash is banked:

	£
Purchases	20
Wages	100
Expenses	80

The bank statement shows that the takings banked in the period were £4,000.

Write up the cash account.

Feedback to this activity is at the end of the chapter.

ACTIVITY 3

The following information relates to a business's transactions for a month.

	£
Opening cash	100
Closing cash	50
Opening debtors	460
Closing debtors	420
Cash expenses	750
Bankings	4,220
Cash drawings	1,200
Cash sales	2,500
Credit sales	3,700
Bad debts written off	50
Discounts allowed	70

Write up the cash account and sales control account.

Feedback to this activity is at the end of the chapter.

Example

Yatton does not keep proper books of account. You ascertain that his bank payments and receipts during the year to 31 December 20X8 were as follows.

Bank account

	£		£
Balance 1 Jan 20X8	800	Cash withdrawn	200
Cheques for sales	2,500	Purchases	2,500
Cash banked	3,000	Expenses	800
		Drawings	1,300
		Delivery van	
		(bought 1 Oct 20X8)	1,000
		Balance 31 Dec 20X8	500
	6,300		6,300

From a cash notebook you ascertain the following details:

	£
Cash in hand 1 January 20X8	70
Cash takings	5,200
Purchases paid in cash	400
Expenses paid in cash	500
Cash in hand 31 December 20X8	30
Drawings by proprietor in cash	Unknown

You discover that assets and liabilities were as follows:

	1 Jan 20X8	31 Dec 20X8
	£	£
Debtors	300	450
Trade creditors	800	900
Expense creditors	100	150
Stock in hand	1,400	1,700

Yatton says that he has no hope of receiving an amount of £100 due from one customer and that a provision of 10% of debtors would be prudent. Depreciation on the van is to be provided at the rate of 20% per annum.

You are required to prepare a trading and profit and loss account for the year to 31 December 20X8 and a balance sheet at that date.

Solution

Step 1

The sheets set aside for the final accounts can be inserted with main headings, and certain information such as opening and closing stock can be inserted.

Step 2

The preparation of the opening balance sheet is usually achieved by drawing up a statement of opening capital using information given in the question about the opening balances. A careful scrutiny of the question reveals:

(W1)   **Statement of opening capital**

	Dr	Cr
	£	£
Bank	800	
Cash	70	
Debtors	300	
Trade creditors		800
Expense creditors		100
Stock	1,400	
	2,570	900
	900	
	1,670	

Thus debits (assets) exceed credits (liabilities) by £1,670. Accordingly Yatton's business has net assets of £1,670, represented on the balance sheet by his opening capital account.

Step 3

Insert the opening balances into T accounts if construction of the accounts is required. Leave plenty of space between the ledger accounts.

Thus a ledger account for Bank is not required as the question has already provided this. Accounts for stock and capital are not required as the information can be inserted immediately into the final accounts.

(W2)

Cash

	£		£
Balance b/d	70		

(W3)

Sales control account

	£		£
Balance b/d	300		

(W4)

Purchases control account

	£		£
		Balance b/d	800

(W5)

Creditors – expenses

	£		£
		Balance b/d	100

Step 4

Prepare the cash account, and post the cash and bank entries to the other accounts.

(W2)

Cash

	£		£
Balance b/d	70	Bank	3,000
Bank	200	Purchases control account	400
Sales control account	5,200	Expenses	500
		Drawings (bal fig)	1,540
		Balance c/d	30
	5,470		5,470

(W3)

Sales control account

	£		£
Balance b/d	300	Bank	2,500
		Cash	5,200

(W4)

Purchases control account

	£		£
Bank	2,500	Balance b/d	800
Cash	400		

(W5)

Expenses

	£		£
Bank	800	Balance b/d	100
Cash	500		

(W6)

Drawings

	£		£
Bank	1,300		
Cash	1,540		

(W7)

Van cost

	£		£
Bank	1,000		

Two points are worth noting at this stage:

1 The commentary above is designed to show what happens after each step; there is no question of writing out each account on more than one occasion.

2 If a question gives full details of the bank account (as this one does), there is no need to write it out again as part of your workings.

Step 5

Insert the closing balances and calculate the transfers to profit and loss.

(W4)

Purchases control account

	£		£
Bank	2,500	Balance b/d	800
Cash	400	Trading and profit and loss	
Balance c/d	900	(bal fig)	3,000
	———		———
	3,800		3,800
	———		———

(W5)

Expenses

	£		£
Bank	800	Balance b/d	100
Cash	500	Trading and profit and loss	
Balance c/d	150	(bal fig)	1,350
	———		———
	1,450		1,450
	———		———

The sales control account has not yet been closed, as there is an adjustment for bad debts still to be made.

Step 6

Carry out any further adjustments. These will be familiar, and the principles behind them are unchanged.

Bad debts

(W3)

Sales control account

	£		£
Balance b/d	300	Bank	2,500
Trading and profit and loss		Cash	5,200
(bal fig)	7,850	Bad debts	100
		Balance c/d (£450 − £100)	350
	———		———
	8,150		8,150
	———		———

(W8)   **Bad debts**

	£		£
Sales control account	100	Profit and loss	135
Provision for doubtful debts	35		
	135		135

(W9)   **Provision for doubtful debts**

	£		£
Balance c/d (10% × £350)	35	Balance b/d	Nil
		Bad debts	35
	35		35

Depreciation

(W7)   **Van cost**

	£		£
Bank	1,000	Balance c/d	1,000

(W10)   **Van accumulated depreciation**

	£		£
Balance c/d	50	Profit and loss	50

Charge 20% × 3 months × £1,000 = £50

Drawings

(W6)   **Drawings**

	£		£
Bank	1,300	Capital	2,840
Cash	1,540		
	2,840		2,840

The remaining figures can be inserted into the final accounts.

Yatton
Trading and profit and loss account
for year ended 31 December 20X8

	£	£
Sales (W3)		7,850
Cost of sales:		
Opening stock	1,400	
Purchases (W4)	3,000	
	4,400	
Less: Closing stock	1,700	
		2,700
Gross profit		5,150
Expenses (W5)	1,350	
Bad debts (W8)	135	
Depreciation of van (W10)	50	
		1,535
Net profit		3,615

Yatton
Balance sheet as at 31 December 20X8

	£	£	£
Fixed assets:			
Van at cost			1,000
Depreciation to date (W10)			50
			950
Current assets:			
Stocks		1,700	
Debtors (W3)	350		
Less: Provision for doubtful debts	35		
		315	
Cash at bank		500	
Cash in hand		30	
		2,545	
Less: Current liabilities:			
Trade creditors	900		
Expense creditors	150		
		1,050	
			1,495
			2,445
Capital account:			
Balance at 1 January 20X8 (W1)			1,670
Profit for year		3,615	
Less drawings (W6)		2,840	
Retained profit for the year (W6)			775
Balance at 31 December 20X8			2,445

3   Using ratios and percentages

In the example above, drawings was the only unknown in the cash account. What happens if there are two unknowns in the cash account – for example, drawings and takings? We can still construct the financial statements provided we are given some additional information.

3.1   Gross profit percentages

$$\text{Gross profit percentage} = \frac{\text{Gross profit}}{\text{Sales}} \times 100$$

For instance, if we know that sales total £8,000 and the gross profit percentage is 25%, the following can be deduced.

	£	%
Sales	8,000 (given)	100
Less: Cost of sales	6,000	75
	———	—
Gross profit	2,000	25 (given)
	———	—

ACTIVITY 4

Assume that we are told that the gross profit percentage is 30% and gross profit £6,000. What are sales and cost of sales?

Feedback to this activity is at the end of the chapter.

3.2   Margins and mark-ups

The gross profit percentage in the previous examples is also known as the **profit margin**. The percentage of profit is given by reference to sales.

Alternatively information on the **mark-up** may be given.

KEY POINT

Mark-up percentage = $\frac{\text{Gross profit}}{\text{Cost of sales}} \times 100$

$$\text{Mark-up percentage} = \frac{\text{Gross profit}}{\text{Cost of sales}} \times 100$$

Thus if we know that cost of sales is £6,000 and the mark-up is one third, we can set out the following:

	£	Ratio
Sales		
Cost of sales (given)	6,000	3
	———	—
Gross profit		1
	———	—

The 'ratio' is an alternative to using percentages. One third is awkward to work with in percentage terms.

In ratio terms gross profit is one part to three parts costs. Sales are therefore four parts $(1 + 3)$ so total sales $= \frac{4}{3} \times £6,000 = £8,000$.

	£	Ratio
Sales	8,000	4
Cost of sales	6,000	3
	———	—
Gross profit	2,000	1
	———	—

The sales of a business are £280,000 and there is a mark-up on cost of 40%. What are the figures for cost of sales and gross profit?

Feedback to this activity is at the end of the chapter.

3.3 Converting margins to mark-ups and vice versa

Suppose we have been told that sales are £60,000 and the mark-up is 25%. The information given can be set out:

	£	%
Sales	60,000	
Cost of sales		100
		—
Gross profit		25
		—

Laying out the information as above should show that gross profit and cost of sales can still be worked out. In percentage terms sales are 125% (100 + 25). Profit is therefore $\frac{25}{125} \times £60,000 = £12,000$.

	£	%
Sales	60,000	125
Cost of sales	48,000	100
	———	———
Gross profit	12,000	25
	———	———

To convert mark-up to margin (where figures are percentages):

$$\text{Margin} = \frac{\text{Mark-up}}{\text{Mark-up} + 100}$$

To convert margin to mark-up:

$$\text{Mark-up} = \frac{\text{Margin}}{100 - \text{Margin}}$$

Example

Kendal, a sole trader, has provided you with the following information relating to the year ended 31 December 20X5.

1   He has not made a note of drawings or of cash received. The following items were paid from takings prior to banking:

Purchases	£760
Sundry expenses	£400

2   Kendal has estimated that his gross profit percentage is 20%.

3   His summarised bank account was as follows.

Bank

20X5		£	20X5		£
1 Jan	Balance b/d	1,700		Rent	1,000
	Bankings	16,940		Electricity	235
				Purchases	16,140
				Drawings	265
			31 Dec	Balance c/d	1,000
		———			———
		18,640			18,640
		———			———

4   Assets and liabilities were as follows:

	31 Dec 20X5	31 Dec 20X4
	£	£
Stock	4,800	5,600
Debtors	1,650	2,100
Creditors:		
Goods	1,940	1,640
Electricity	65	-
Cash float	2,400	170

5   He started paying rent in 20X5. A year's rent was paid in advance on 1 April 20X5.

You are required to prepare:

* a trading and profit and loss account for the year ended 31 December 20X5

* a balance sheet at that date.

Solution

Step 1

Sheets are reserved for the profit and loss account and balance sheet. In particular, the trading account becomes a key working in situations where a margin or mark-up is given. Insert the opening and closing stock figures (if given) and also the margin percentages.

Step 2

In earlier examples the opening balance sheet has been completed in order to derive the opening capital balance. This working will now be done after the sales and purchases control accounts have been completed, as it only helps in finding one figure to go into the final accounts.

We need to recognise that there may be time pressure in the examination and therefore we should spend our time first on the control accounts.

Step 3

Insert the opening balances in 'T' accounts.

Step 4

Deal with the information given about cash and bank transactions. Note that the bank account is not included in the workings, full details being given in the question.

In addition, no ledger accounts have been shown for the various expenses. Instead workings have been shown on the face of the profit and loss account, e.g. rent.

There is a rent prepayment of £250 (three months rent). The expense is therefore £750. The derivation of the £750 (1,000 – 250) has been shown in brackets by the narrative on the profit and loss account

Where simple adjustments are to be made, this method allows the speedier preparation of the solution.

Step 5

Insert the closing balances into the accounts. At this point the figure for purchases can be calculated.

Having reached this far, a little more thought is now required.

The position as regards unknowns can be summarised as follows:

Debtors	–	The figures for sales and receipts from debtors are unknown.
Cash	–	The figures for drawings and receipts from debtors are unknown.

This is where the gross profit percentage is utilised as follows:

		£	£	%
Sales			22,500	100
Less:	Cost of goods sold:			
	Opening stock	5,600 (given)		
	Purchases	17,200 (calculation)		
		22,800		
Less:	Closing stock	4,800 (given)		
			18,000	80
Gross profit			4,500	20 (given)

The sales figure has now been derived, leaving only one unknown in the debtors account – receipts from debtors, which is calculated as a balancing figure.

The resulting double entry (Dr Cash £22,950, Cr Debtors £22,950) means that there is now only one unknown in the cash account, the drawings figure.

Workings

(W1)
Cash

	£		£
Balance b/d	170	Bank	16,940
Debtors	22,950	Creditors – goods	760
		Creditors – expenses	400
		Drawings (bal fig)	2,620
		Balance c/d	2,400
	23,120		23,120

(W2)
Sales control

	£		£
Balance b/d	2,100	Cash (bal fig)	22,950
Trading and profit and loss	22,500	Balance c/d	1,650
	24,600		24,600

(W3)
Purchases control

	£		£
Bank	16,140	Balance b/d	1,640
Cash	760	Trading and profit and loss	
Balance c/d	1,940	(bal fig)	17,200
	18,840		18,840

(W4)   **Drawings**

	£		£
Bank	265	Capital	2,885
Cash	2,620		
	2,885		2,885

(W5)   **Statement of opening capital**

	Dr	Cr
	£	£
Bank	1,700	
Stock	5,600	
Debtors	2,100	
Creditors – goods		1,640
Cash	170	
	9,570	1,640
	1,640	
	7,930	

(a)   **Trading and profit and loss account for the year ended**
                          31 December 20X5

	£	£	%
Sales		22,500	100
Opening stock	5,600		
Purchases	17,200		
	22,800		
Closing stock	4,800		
Cost of sales		18,000	80
Gross profit		4,500	20
Rent (1,000 – 250)	750		
Electricity (235 + 65)	300		
Sundry	400		
		1,450	
Net profit		3,050	

(b)   **Balance sheet as at 31 December 20X5**

	£	£
Current assets:		
Stock		4,800
Debtors		1,650
Prepayment		250
Bank		1,000
Cash		2,400
		10,100
Less: Current liabilities:		
Creditors:		
Goods	1,940	
Expenses	65	
		2,005
		8,095
Capital account:		
Opening capital		7,930
Net profit	3,050	
Less drawings	2,885	
Retained profit		165
Closing capital		8,095

3.4 Variations on the theme

No two incomplete records questions are the same. Two examples of possible variations are as follows:

- Suppose that stock was destroyed in a fire and that there was enough information to calculate sales, purchases and opening stock. The gross profit percentage would enable sales to be converted to cost of sales. Closing stock could then be calculated as a balancing figure.

- Suppose that a trader always received a rebate from his suppliers amounting to 1% of purchases, and that in the current year the rebate amounted to £172. Clearly this tells us that purchases were £17,200. If cash paid to suppliers was unknown, it could be calculated as a balancing figure.

The fact that all incomplete records questions are different, means that there is no universally correct way of attempting them. The key feature is to remember that double entry bookkeeping should be used to prepare the required financial statements. Therefore you should convert the incomplete records into suitable accounting form.

Conclusion

No two incomplete records situations are exactly the same. For examination questions, what is required is a knowledge of the techniques covered in this chapter for reconstructing financial statements from a variety of types of incomplete information, together with a thorough grasp and application of double entry bookkeeping.

The six-step approach set out in the chapter is a good starting point in most questions, although all six steps may not always be required. You should then be aware of the use of the cash and bank accounts, sales and purchases control accounts and any margins, mark-ups or other ratios that are given in the question. A good tip is that if a margin or mark-up is given in the question then it is highly likely that the only way to calculate either sales or purchases will be by applying this percentage to the information in the question.

Incomplete and limited accounting records

1   How can the profit of a business be measured if opening and closing net assets and drawings are known? (1.2)

Final accounts from limited accounting records

2   What are the six basic steps for the approach to an incomplete records question? (2.2)

Using ratios and percentages

3   How is the gross profit percentage calculated? (3.1)

4   How is a mark-up percentage calculated? (3.2)

5   How is a cost mark-up converted to a profit margin? (3.3)

6   If stock was destroyed in a fire but sales, purchases and opening stock could be calculated how would the figure for stock destroyed be estimated? (3.4)

MULTIPLE-
CHOICE
QUESTIONS

Question 1

The following information is relevant to the calculation of the sales figure for Alpha, a sole trader who does not keep proper accounting records:

	£
Opening debtors	29,100
Cash received from credit customers and paid into the bank	381,600
Expenses paid out of cash received from credit customers before banking	6,800
Bad debts written off	7,200
Refunds to credit customers	2,100
Discounts allowed to credit customers	9,400
Cash sales	112,900
Closing debtors	38,600

The figure which should appear in Alpha's trading account for sales is:

A   £525,300

B   £511,700

C   £529,500

D   £510,900

Question 2

A sole trader who does not keep full accounting records wishes to calculate her sales revenue for the year.

The information available is:

1	Opening stock	£17,000
2	Closing stock	£24,000
3	Purchases	£91,000
4	Standard gross profit percentage on sales revenue	40%

Which of the following is the sales figure for the year calculated from these figures?

A   £117,600

B   £108,000

C   £210,000

D   £140,000

Question 3

A business compiling its accounts for the year to 31 January each year, pays rent quarterly in advance on 1 January, 1 April, 1 July and 1 October each year. After remaining unchanged for some years, the rent was increased from £24,000 per year to £30,000 per year as from 1 July 20X0.

Which of the following figures is the rent expense which should appear in the profit and loss account for the year ended 31 January 20X1?

A   £27,500

B   £29,500

C   £28,000

D   £29,000

Question 4

On 31 December 20X0 the stock of V Limited was completely destroyed by fire.

The following information is available:

1   Stock at 1 December 20X0 at cost £28,400

2   Purchases for December 20X0 £49,600

3   Sales for December 20X0 £64,800

4   Standard gross profit percentage on sales revenue 30%.

Based on this information, which of the following is the amount of stock destroyed?

A   £45,360

B   £32,640

C   £40,971

D   £19,440

For answers to these questions, see the 'Answers' section at the end of the book.

Question 1: B Letitslide

B Letitslide is in business but does not keep proper books of account. In order to prepare his trading and profit and loss account for the year ended 31 December 20X5 you are given the following information:

	20X5 1 Jan £	20X5 31 Dec £
Stock on hand	1,310	1,623
Debtors	268	412
Creditors for goods	712	914
Creditors for expenses	116	103

In addition, you are able to prepare the following summary of his cash and bank transactions for the year.

Cash account

	£		£
Balance 1 Jan	62	Payments into bank	3,050
Shop takings	4,317	Purchases	316
Cheques cashed	200	Expenses	584
		Drawings	600
		Balance 31 Dec	29
	4,579		4,579

Bank account

	£		£
Balance 1 Jan	840	Cash withdrawn	200
Cheques from customers	1,416	Purchases	2,715
Cash paid in	3,050	Expenses	519
		Drawings	400
		Delivery van	
		(purchased 1 Sep)	900
		Balance 31 Dec	572
	5,306		5,306

In addition, Mr Letitslide says that he had taken goods for personal consumption and estimates those goods cost £100.

In considering the debtors, Mr Letitslide suggests that there is no hope of receiving an amount of £30 from one customer. There are other doubtful debts and a provision is to be made of 5% of the debtors after writing off the bad debt of £30.

Allowing depreciation on the delivery van of 20% per annum, prepare the trading and profit and loss account for the year ended 31 December 20X5 and a balance sheet as at 31 December 20X5.   **(25 marks)**

Question 2: Ben White

Ben White, a retailer, adds 25% to the cost of goods purchased for resale to arrive at his selling prices.

His financial position at 30 June 20X5 was:

	£
Assets:	
Plant and machinery (NBV)	5,000
Stock	3,825
Debtors	7,175
Cash at bank	2,200
Liabilities:	
Creditors	3,000
Loan from Z (interest-free)	2,000

During the year ended 30 June 20X6 he:

(1)   paid £11,675 for goods for resale (cheque)

(2)   repaid £500 of the loan from Z (cheque)

(3)   purchased a van for £700 (cheque) on the last day of the year

(4)   withdrew from the bank £80 per month personal expenses

(5)   paid into the bank a legacy of £300

(6)   paid income tax £600 (treat as drawings) (cheque)

(7)   withdrew an unspecified amount of cash from takings prior to banking.

At 30 June 20X6 stock at cost was £4,000, debtors totalled £7,000 and creditors were £3,500; the balance at bank amounted to £1,950. Depreciation of plant was 10% on reducing balance. No depreciation is to be provided on the van.

You are required to prepare:

(a) a trading and profit and loss account for the year ended 30 June 20X6

(b) the balance sheet as at 30 June 20X6. **(20 marks)**

For answers to these questions, see the 'Answers' section at the end of the book.

FEEDBACK TO ACTIVITY 1

Statement of affairs at:

	1 Jan 20X5	31 Dec 20X6	
	Assets	Liabilities	Assets
	£	£	£
Shop premises	14,000		14,000
Shop depreciation 2% × £14,000 × 2 years			(560)
Fittings	2,000		2,000
Fittings depreciation 5% × £2,000 × 2 years			(200)
Cash	4,000		2,500
Stock			6,000
Debtors			1,040
Motor lorry			8,000
Motor lorry depreciation 20% × £8,000 × 6 months			(800)
Trade creditors		1,400	
Loan		10,000	
Accrued interest		200	
		11,600	31,980
			(11,600)
Capital	20,000		20,380

Capital account

	£		£
Drawings 24 × £300	7,200	Opening capital	20,000
Closing capital	20,380	Net profit (bal fig)	7,580
	27,580		27,580

FEEDBACK TO ACTIVITY 2

Cash

	£		£
Balance b/d	50	Purchases	20
Cash takings (sales) (bal fig)	4,200	Wages	100
		Expenses	80
	4,250	Bankings	4,000
		Balance c/d	50
			4,250

FEEDBACK TO
ACTIVITY 3

Cash

	£		£
Balance b/d	100	Expenses	750
Sales	2,500	Bank (bankings)	4,220
Cash from debtors – sales		Drawings	1,200
control (bal fig)	3,620	Balance c/d	50
	———		———
	6,220		6,220
	———		———

Sales control

	£		£
Balance b/d	460	Bad debt	50
Sales	3,700	Discounts allowed	70
		Cash received	3,620
		Balance c/d	420
	———		———
	4,160		4,160
	———		———

FEEDBACK TO
ACTIVITY 4

	£	%
Sales	20,000	100
Less: Cost of sales	14,000	70
	———	———
Gross profit	6,000 (given)	30 (given)
	———	———

The percentages provided may have been calculated by reference to a similar business or from the previous years' results of this business.

FEEDBACK TO
ACTIVITY 5

	£	%
Sales	280,000	140
Cost of sales (280,000 × 100/140)	200,000	100
	———	———
Gross profit (280,000 × 40/140)	80,000	40
	———	———

The percentages provided may have been calculated by reference to a similar business or from the previous years' results of this business.

Chapter 18
PARTNERSHIP ACCOUNTS

In earlier chapters we have been concerned principally with the accounts of sole traders. When a business expands, a common first step is for the sole trader to invite another person, or persons, to join him in partnership. By doing so he takes advantage of the resources the other person(s) can bring to the business: management time, specialist expertise, financial capital. In return, he sacrifices a share of the business, in that his partner(s) will now be entitled to share in the profits and assets of the business.

The balance sheet of a partnership is identical to that of a sole trader in so far as assets and liabilities are concerned. It is in the capital section of the balance sheet that differences emerge. Similarly, the profit and loss account of a partnership is identical to that of a sole trader until we reach the net profit earned for the period. At that point the sole trader's profit and loss account comes to an end, whereas in a partnership we continue with an appropriation account showing how the net profit is divided among the partners.

Objectives

By the time you have finished this chapter you should be able to:

- divide profit between partners
- prepare partnership financial statements.

1 Partnerships: basic principles

1.1 Identification of partnership

DEFINITION

A partnership is a collection of individuals jointly carrying on business.

A partnership is a natural progression from a sole trader, the sole proprietor taking in one or more partners (co-proprietors) in common with a view to profit. A partnership is not a corporate entity, but a collection of individuals jointly carrying on business.

Although partnerships are covered by statutory rules, mainly by the Partnership Act 1890, the Act is far less demanding than the Companies Acts, and its provisions may be varied by agreement between the partners. Since no limitation of the liability of the partners is (usually) involved, there is no need for the detailed statutory rules to protect creditors typical of the Companies Act. Therefore, those matters which the partners agree between them provide the legal structure within which the partners operate.

1.2 Advantages and disadvantages of partnerships

KEY POINT

Partnerships - advantages:

- spread risk
- bring in special skills
- draw upon larger capital.

Comparing a partnership to sole trading, the **advantages** of operating as a partnership are as follows:

- business risks are spread among more than one person
- individual partners can develop special skills upon which the other partners can rely rather than being a jack of all trades
- certain partners may be able to draw upon larger capital resources to set up the partnership or expand the partnership.

KEY POINT

Partnerships - disadvantages:
- can lead to disputes
- share all liabilities.

The **disadvantages** of partnerships are as follows:

- There may be disputes between partners on matters such as the direction the business is taking or how much money individual partners are taking out of the business. Some partners may feel they are contributing more time and effort to the partnership than others and not being sufficiently rewarded financially as a result.

- A partner is 'jointly and severally liable' for his partners. This means that if one partner is being sued in relation to the business of the partnership, the other partners share in the responsibility.

A partnership has some advantages over a company, as the arrangement is less formal than setting up a company. If the partners wish to dissolve the business, that is an easier matter to achieve by a partnership rather than a company.

The advantage of a company is that the owners of the business – the shareholders – may be protected from the creditors of the company as regards the payment of outstanding debts. This point is looked at more closely when we examine company accounts in the next chapter.

1.3　Conventional methods of dividing profit

KEY POINT

Partnership agreements do not need to be written down.

A partnership agreement, which need not necessarily be in written form, will govern the relationships between the partners. Important matters to be covered include the following:

- name of firm, the type of business, and duration
- capital to be introduced by partners
- distribution of profits between partners
- drawings by partners
- arrangements for dissolution, or on the death or retirement of partners
- settling of disputes
- preparation and audit of accounts.

The division of profit stated in the partnership agreement may be quite complex in order to reflect the expected differing efforts and contributions of the partners. For example, some or all of the partners may be entitled to a salary to reflect the differing management involvement in the business. Interest on capital may be provided to reflect the differing amounts of capital contributed. The percentage profit shares may differ to reflect seniority or greater skills.

It is important to appreciate, however, that all of the above examples are means of dividing the profits of the partnership and are not expenses of the business. A partnership salary is merely a device for calculating the division of profit; it is not a salary in the normal meaning of the term.

1.4　Partnerships and sole traders

The accounting techniques developed for sole traders are generally applicable to partnerships, but there are certain important differences as shown in the following table.

Item	Sole trader's books	Partnership's books
Capital introduced	Capital account	Partners' fixed capital accounts
Drawings and share of the profit	Capital account	Partners' current accounts
Division of profits	Inapplicable – one proprietor only	Appropriation account

2   Preparing partnership financial statements

2.1   Capital accounts

At the commencement of the partnership, an agreement will have to be reached as to the amount of capital to be introduced. Capital may take the form of cash or other assets. Whatever the form of assets introduced and debited to asset accounts, it is normal to make the credit entry to fixed **capital accounts**. These are so-called because they are not then used to record drawings or shares of profits but only major changes in the relations between partners. In particular, fixed capital accounts are used to deal with:

- capital introduced or withdrawn by new or retiring partners
- revaluation adjustments.

The balances on fixed capital accounts do not necessarily bear any relation to the division of profits. However, to compensate partners who provide a larger share of the capital, it is common for notional interest on capital accounts to be paid to partners. This is dealt with through the appropriation account.

2.2   Partners' current accounts

Partners' current accounts are used to deal with the regular transactions between the partners and the firm, i.e. matters other than those sufficiently fundamental to be dealt with through the capital accounts. Most commonly these are:

- share of profits, interest on capital, and partners' salaries, usually computed annually
- monthly drawings against the annual share of profit.

2.3   Ledger accounts and balance sheet presentation

Example 1

Nab and Crag commenced business in partnership on 1 January 20X6, contributing as fixed capital £5,000 and £10,000 cash respectively. All profits and losses are shared equally. The profit for the year ended 31 December 20X6 amounted to £10,000. Drawings for Nab and Crag amounted to £3,000 and £4,000 respectively.

You are required to prepare the capital and current accounts and balance sheet extracts.

Partners' capital accounts

		Nab £	Crag £			Nab £	Crag £
				20X6			
				1 Jan	Cash	5,000	10,000

Partners' current accounts

		Nab £	Crag £			Nab £	Crag £
20X6				20X6			
31 Dec	Drawings	3,000	4,000	31 Dec	Share of profits	5,000	5,000
	Balance c/d	2,000	1,000				
		5,000	5,000			5,000	5,000
				20X7			
				1 Jan	Balance b/d	2,000	1,000

The above accounts are presented in a columnar format. This is quite common in a partnership set of books as each partner will have similar transactions during the year. A columnar format allows two (or more) separate accounts to be shown using the same narrative. It is important to remember though that each partner's account is separate from those of the other partner(s).

The balance sheet for the partners is drawn up as follows.

Balance sheet at 31 December 20X6 (extract)

	Capital accounts £	Current accounts £	£
Partners' accounts:			
Nab	5,000	2,000	7,000
Crag	10,000	1,000	11,000
	15,000	3,000	18,000

Note that the current account balances of £2,000 and £1,000 will be credited in the following year with profit shares and debited with drawings.

One of the main differences between the capital section of the balance sheet of a sole trader and a partnership is that the partnership balance sheet will often only give the closing balances, whereas the sole trader's movements in capital are shown. The main reason for the difference is simply one of space. Movements in the capital and current accounts for a few partners cannot be easily accommodated on the face of the balance sheet.

Example 2

In our second example, the information is the same as in Example 1, except that Nab's drawings are £5,300. The current accounts now become:

Partners' current accounts

		Nab £	Crag £			Nab £	Crag £
20X6				20X6			
	Drawings	5,300	4,000		Share of profits	5,000	5,000
31 Dec	Balance c/d		1,000	31 Dec	Balance c/d	300	
		5,300	5,000			5,300	5,000
20X7				20X7			
1 Jan	Balance b/d	300		1 Jan	Balance b/d		1,000

Note that Nab's current account is overdrawn. We present this in the balance sheet as follows.

Balance sheet at 31 December 20X6 (extract)

	Capital accounts £	Current accounts £	£
Partners' accounts:			
Nab	5,000	(300)	4,700
Crag	10,000	1,000	11,000
	15,000	700	15,700

2.4 Appropriation account

The appropriation account is a ledger account dealing with the allocation of net profit between the partners. In practice it is often included as the final part of the trading and profit and loss account.

An important point is that all allocations of profit to partners in their capacity as partners, and during the time they actually are partners, are made through the appropriation account. This applies even though such allocations may be described as partners' salaries, interest on capital or a share of profits.

Example 3

Pike and Scar are in partnership and have the following profit-sharing arrangements.

- interest on capital is to be provided at a rate of 8% per annum
- Pike and Scar are to receive salaries of £6,000 and £8,000 pa respectively
- the balance of profit or loss is to be divided between Pike and Scar in the ratio 3: 2.

Net profit for the year amounts to £20,000 and capital account balances are Pike £12,000 and Scar £9,000.

We are required to prepare:

- a statement showing the allocation of profit between the partners
- relevant entries in the trading and profit and loss and appropriation account.

Solution

Allocation of net profit of £20,000

	Pike		Scar		Total
	£		£		£
Interest on capital	960		720		1,680
Salaries	6,000		8,000		14,000
Balance of profits (£20,000 – £15,680) in ratio 3:2	2,592	(3/5)	1,728	(2/5)	4,320
Totals	9,552		10,448		20,000

Note that this is only a calculation of the allocation of profit and not part of the double entry bookkeeping system. It merely provides the figures for the appropriation account.

Extract from trading and profit and loss and appropriation account for the year ended ...

	£	£
Sales:		x
Cost of sales		x
Gross profit		x
Expenses		x
Net profit		20,000
Allocated to:		
Pike	9,552	
Scar	10,448	
		20,000

The profit and loss appropriation account is closed by transferring the profit shares to the credit of the partners' current accounts. The double entry is therefore as follows:

Debit	Credit	With
Profit and loss appropriation account	Pike's current account	£9,552
Profit and loss appropriation account	Scar's current account	£10,448

For the purposes of examinations (and in practice) parts (a) and (b) above can be amalgamated as follows:

Extract from trading and profit and loss and appropriation account for the year ended

	£
Sales:	x
Cost of sales	x
Gross profit	x
Expenses	x
Net profit	20,000

Appropriation statement

	Pike		Scar		Total
	£		£		£
Interest on capital	960		720		1,680
Salaries	6,000		8,000		14,000
Balance of profits (£20,000 – £15,680) in ratio 3: 2	2,592	(3/5)	1,728	(2/5)	4,320
Totals	9,552		10,448		20,000

The debits actually being made are as before (£9,552 and £10,448).

Example 4

The facts are the same as for Example 3, except that net profit is now only £3,680 and we need to show its allocation between the partners.

Allocation of net profit of £3,680

	Pike	Scar	Total
	£	£	£
Interest on capital	960	720	1,680
Salaries	6,000	8,000	14,000
Balance of loss £3,680 – £15,680 = (£12,000) to be shared in ratio 3: 2	(7,200)	(4,800)	(12,000)
Totals	(240)	3,920	3,680

The double entry in this case is as follows:

Debit	Credit	With
Profit and loss appropriation account	Scar's current account	£3,920
Pike's current account	Profit and loss appropriation account	£240

The relevant part of the profit and loss account would show:

	£	£
Net profit		3,680
Allocated to:		
Scar	3,920	
Pike	(240)	
		3,680

One point which regularly causes difficulties is the partners' salaries. The key is to remember at the outset that a partner's salary is an appropriation of profit, whereas a salary paid to an employee is an expense.

Accordingly a salary to which a partner is entitled is included as part of the appropriation statement. Questions sometimes state that a partner has withdrawn his salary. In this case:

- include the salary in the appropriation statement as usual; and
- quite separately, treat the withdrawal of the salary as drawings.

Debit	Credit	With
Partners' current account	Bank	Amount withdrawn

2.5 Guaranteed minimum profit share

In certain partnership agreements, a partner may be guaranteed a minimum share of profits. The appropriation of profit would proceed in the normal way. If the result is that the partner has less than this minimum, the deficit will be made good by the other partners (normally in profit-sharing ratio).

Example 5

Tessa, Laura and Jane are in partnership and have the following profit-sharing arrangements:

- Tessa and Laura are to receive salaries of £20,000 and £30,000 respectively.
- The balance of profit or loss is to be divided Tessa 1, Laura 2, Jane 3.
- Tessa is guaranteed a minimum profit share of £25,000.

The net profit for the year is £68,000. You are required to show the appropriation account for the year.

Appropriation account

	Tessa £	Laura £	Jane £	Total £
Net profit				68,000
Salaries	20,000	30,000	–	(50,000)
				18,000
Balance of profits in ratio 1: 2: 3	3,000	6,000	9,000	(18,000)
	23,000	36,000	9,000	
Adjustment	2,000			
Laura 2/5 × 2,000		(800)		
Jane 3/5 × 2,000			(1,200)	
Totals	25,000	35,200	7,800	68,000

2.6   Interest on drawings

Occasionally there is a provision in a partnership agreement for a notional interest charge on the drawings by each partner. The interest charges are merely a negative profit share – they are a means by which total profits are allocated between the partners.

The reason for an interest on drawings provision is that those partners who draw out more cash than their colleagues in the early part of an accounting period should suffer a cost.

Example

Dick and Dastardly are in partnership. The capital and current accounts as at 1 January 20X7 show the following.

	Capital £	Current £
Dick	50,000	2,500
Dastardly	20,000	3,000

The partnership agreement provides for the following.

- Profits and losses are shared between Dick and Dastardly in percentages 60 and 40.
- Interest on capital at 10% per annum is allowed.
- Interest on drawings is charged at 12% per annum.

Drawings for the year to 31 December 20X7 are as follows:

	Dick £	Dastardly £
1 February 20X7	5,000	2,000
30 September 20X7	2,000	5,000

The profit for the year is £20,000. You are required to prepare the appropriation account and the current accounts for the year ended 31 December 20X7.

Solution

Appropriation account for the year ended 31 December 20X7

	Dick £	Dastardly £	£
Profit for the year			20,000
Add: Interest on drawings (see working)	(610)	(370)	980
			20,980
Less: Interest on capital:			
50,000 × 10%	5,000		
20,000 × 10%		2,000	(7,000)
			13,980
Balance in profit-sharing ratio:			
13,980 × 60%	8,388		
13,980 × 40%		5,592	(13,980)
Total allocation	12,778	7,222	20,000

Current accounts

		Dick £	Dastardly £			Dick £	Dastardly £
20X7				*20X7*			
1 Feb	Drawings	5,000	2,000	1 Feb	Balance b/d	2,500	3,000
30 Sep	Drawings	2,000	5,000	31 Dec	Share of profits	12,778	7,222
	Balance c/d	8,278	3,222				
		15,278	10,222			15,278	10,222

Working

		Dick £	Dastardly £
Interest on drawings			
1 February 20X7	$5,000 \times 12\% \times 11/12$	550	
	$2,000 \times 12\% \times 11/12$		220
30 September 20X7	$2,000 \times 12\% \times 3/12$	60	
	$5,000 \times 12\% \times 3/12$		150
		610	370

2.7 Pulling the topics together

You should now be in a position to follow through from the trial balance stage, a full example of partnership accounts.

You are provided with the following information regarding the partnership of Dacre, Hutton and Tod.

(a) The trial balance is as follows:

The trial balance at 31 December 20X6

	Dr £	Cr £
Sales		50,000
Stock at 1 January 20X6	6,000	
Purchases	29,250	
Carriage inwards	250	
Carriage outwards	400	
Creditors		4,000
Cash at bank	3,900	
Current accounts:		
Dacre		900
Hutton		750
Tod		1,350
Capital accounts:		
Dacre		4,000
Hutton		5,000
Tod		6,000
Drawings:		
Dacre	2,000	
Hutton	3,000	
Tod	5,000	
Sundry expenses	2,800	
Debtors	13,000	
Shop fittings:		
Cost	8,000	
Accumulated depreciation		1,600
	73,600	73,600

(b) Closing stock is valued for accounts purposes at £5,500.

(c) Depreciation of £800 is to be provided on the shop fittings.

(d) The profit-sharing arrangements are as follows:

- Interest on capital is to be provided at a rate of 10% per annum.

- Dacre and Tod are to receive salaries of £3,000 and £4,000 per annum respectively.

- The balance of profit or loss is to be divided between Dacre, Hutton and Tod in the ratio of 3: 8: 4.

You are required to prepare final accounts together with current accounts of the partners.

Solution

Dacre, Hutton and Tod
Trading and profit and loss account for the year ended 31 December 20X6

	£	£
Sales		50,000
Opening stock	6,000	
Purchases	29,250	
Carriage inwards	250	
	35,500	
Less: Closing stock	5,500	
		30,000
Gross profit		20,000
Sundry expenses	2,800	
Carriage outwards	400	
Depreciation	800	
		4,000
Net profit		16,000
Allocated to:		
Dacre	4,900	
Hutton	4,500	
Tod	6,600	
		16,000

Balance sheet as at 31 December 20X6

	Cost	Acc dep'n	
	£	£	£
Fixed assets			
Shop fittings	8,000	2,400	5,600
Current assets			
Stock		5,500	
Debtors		13,000	
Cash		3,900	
		22,400	
Current liabilities			
Creditors		4,000	
Net current assets			18,400
			24,000

Partners' accounts

	Capital accounts £	Current accounts £	£
Dacre	4,000	3,800	7,800
Hutton	5,000	2,250	7,250
Tod	6,000	2,950	8,950
	15,000	9,000	24,000

Partners' current accounts

Current accounts

		Dacre £	Hutton £	Tod			Dacre £	Hutton £	Tod £
20X6					**20X6**				
	Drawings	2,000	3,000	5,000	1 Jan	Balance b/d	900	750	1,350
31 Dec	Balance c/d	3,800	2,250	2,950		P&L app	4,900	4,500	6,600
		5,800	5,250	7,950			5,800	5,250	7,950
					20X7				
					1 Jan	Balance b/d	3,800	2,250	2,950

Workings and commentary

The adjustments for stock and depreciation should by now be familiar.

The new development is that, having calculated the profit for the period, it has to be appropriated between Dacre, Hutton and Tod. To calculate their respective shares an appropriation statement is used as follows:

Appropriation account for the year ended 31 December 20X7

	Dacre £	Hutton £	Tod £	Total £
Interest on capital	400	500	600	1,500
Salaries	3,000	-	4,000	7,000
Balance of profit (£16,000 − £8,500) in ratio 3:8:4	1,500	4,000	2,000	7,500
	4,900	4,500	6,600	16,000

This gives us the figures for the double entry:

- Dr   Profit and loss appropriation
- Cr   Partners' current accounts.

A final point

The majority of examination questions specify separate capital and current accounts. Occasionally you may be faced with a question specifying only one account for each partner. Such an account acts as a capital and current account combined.

Conclusion

Accounting for partnerships is similar to accounting for sole traders in many respects, except that profit needs to be allocated between the partners and the capital section of the balance sheet is more complex.

Partnerships: basic principles

1   What is a partnership? (1.1)

2   What are the advantages and disadvantages of partnerships? (1.2)

Preparing partnership financial statements

3   What are the differences between capital and current accounts? (2.1, 2.2)

4   Is interest on drawings an expense of the partnership? (2.6)

D, E and F are in partnership, sharing profits in the ratio 5:3:2 respectively, after charging salaries for E and F of £24,000 each per year. On 1 July 20X0 they agreed to change the profit-sharing ratio to 3:1:1 and increase E's salary to £36,000 per year, F's salary continuing unchanged. For the year ended 31 December 20X0 the partnership profit amounted to £480,000.

Which of the following correctly states the partners' total profit shares for the year?

	D	E	F
A	£234,000	£136,800	£109,200
B	£213,000	£157,800	£109,200
C	£186,000	£171,600	£122,400
D	£237,600	£132,000	£110,400

For the answer to this question, see the 'Answers' section at the end of the book.

Oliver and Twist

Oliver and Twist are in partnership, sharing profits equally after Oliver has been allowed a salary of £5,000 per year. No interest is charged on drawings or allowed on current accounts, but interest of 10% pa is allowed on the opening capital account balances for each year. Their bookkeeper has been having trouble balancing the books and has eventually produced the following list of balances as at 31 December.

	£
Capital account:	
Oliver	9,000
Twist	10,000
10% loan account:	
Twist	5,000
Williams	6,000
Current account balance on 1 January:	
Oliver	1,000
Twist	2,000
Drawings:	
Oliver	6,500
Twist	5,500
Sales	113,100
Sales returns	3,000
Closing stock	17,000
Cost of goods sold	70,000
Sales ledger control account	30,000
Purchase ledger control account	25,000
Operating expenses	26,100

Fixed assets at cost	37,000
Provision for depreciation	18,000
Bank overdraft	3,000
Suspense account	?

You ascertain the following information:

(a) The sales ledger control account does not agree with the list of balances from the ledger. The following errors when corrected will remove the difference:

- the sales returns day book has been undercast by £100

- a contra entry with the creditors ledger for £200 has been omitted from the control accounts

- an invoice for £2,000 was incorrectly entered in the sales day book as £200.

(b) A fully depreciated fixed asset, original cost £5,000, was sold during the year. The proceeds of £1,000 were entered in the bank account only, and no other entries in connection with the disposal were made.

(c) It is agreed that hotel bills for £500 paid by Twist from his personal bank account are proper business expenses. Oliver has taken goods out of the business for his own use, costing £1,000. No entry has been made for either of these items.

(d) No interest of any kind has yet been paid or recorded.

(e) Any remaining balance on the suspense account cannot be traced, and is to be treated in the most suitable manner.

Required:

(a) Prepare a trial balance and establish the balance on the suspense account.

(4 marks)

(b) Incorporate the necessary adjustments, showing your workings clearly in any way you feel appropriate. **(8 marks)**

(c) Prepare final accounts for presentation to the partners. **(13 marks)**

(Total: 25 marks)

For the answer to this question, see the 'Answers' section at the end of the book.

Chapter 19
ACCOUNTING FOR LIMITED COMPANIES I

In this chapter we turn our attention to the special problems of accounting for limited companies.

Double entry bookkeeping and the recording of transactions in books of prime entry are exactly the same for a sole trader and a limited company. Even the financial statements of the two types of organisation are fairly similar.

However, there are some differences in the way that companies are financed and the way in which their profits are dealt with as compared with a sole trader. It is these areas that we cover in detail in this chapter.

Objectives

By the time you have finished this chapter you should be able to:

- discuss the different types of limited company that exist

- recognise different forms of company finance

- prepare financial statements for a company in a form that is suitable for internal usage within the company

- account for different types of share issues

- understand the uses of different reserves and be able to account for appropriations to reserves.

1 Types of limited company

1.1 Introduction

KEY POINT

The **limited company** is the main business form in the UK.

Companies are owned by **shareholders**.
Shareholders' **liability** is limited to what they paid for their shares.

Most companies are limited by **shares**. This means that in the event of the failure of a company, the amount the shareholders can lose is restricted to the amount they have paid for their shares. This is a consequence of the legal status of a limited company as a separate entity from its owners. If the assets of the company are insufficient to pay the company's debts, the shareholders cannot be called upon to make good the deficit from their personal assets.

It is important to appreciate that not all limited companies are large – they vary in size from the very small to the huge quoted company which operates world-wide.

1.2 Key factors distinguishing companies

KEY POINTS

Companies are **separate legal entities**.

Shareholders and managers are separated in law.

Shareholders have **limited liability**.

Companies must comply with **company rules**.

There are four key factors which distinguish companies from other forms of business enterprise:

- the fundamental concept of the **separate legal entity** of the company – the company is a separate entity in law. From this flow the next two points below.

- the **separation of the ownership** (shareholders) **from the management** (directors) of the company. It is most important to understand this. In some small companies, the directors and the shareholders may happen to be the same people. Even so, it is important to understand that in such a case the individuals concerned are performing two separate roles.

- the **limited liability** of shareholders for the debts of a company. Generally speaking their liability is limited to any portion of the nominal value of shares which is unpaid.

- the formalities required. A sole trader or partnership can operate with few or no formalities. In return for the privilege of limited liability, companies must comply with a great many rules, some of which are listed below.

Company rules

Company rules include the following:

- on formation, the company must lodge a number of documents with the Registrar of Companies. The most important of these documents are the **memorandum and articles of association** which set out the objects for which the company was formed, the powers and duties of the directors and many other matters.

- The company's annual profit and loss account and balance sheet must be lodged with the Registrar and are then available for public inspection.

Another formality required is that companies must generally appoint qualified auditors to report on the profit and loss account and balance sheet. However, small companies are exempted from this requirement.

1.3   Difference between sole traders and companies

These factors lead to differences between companies and sole traders in the following respects:

- the form of the capital accounts
- the form of loans to the company
- the way in which profits are withdrawn by the proprietors
- the form in which retained funds are presented.

The differences may be summarised as follows.

Item	Sole trader	Company
Capital introduced by proprietors	Capital account	Issued share capital
Loans from third parties	Loan account	Debentures or loan account
Profits withdrawn by proprietors	Drawings	Dividends
Profits retained in the business	Capital account	Reserves

1.4   Advantages and disadvantages of operating as a limited company

The advantages of operation as a limited company rather than as a sole trader can be as follows:

- The liability of the shareholders is limited to the capital already introduced by them.

- There is a formal separation of the business from the owners of the business, which may be helpful to the running of the business. For example, if several members of a family are the shareholders in a company but only two of the family are directors, it is clear to all concerned who is running the company.

- Ownership of the business can be shared between people more easily than other forms of business organisation, e.g. a partnership.

- Shares in the business can be transferred relatively easily.

- There may be tax advantages.

KEY POINT

The objects, powers and duties of a company are set out in its **memorandum and articles of association**.

The company's annual profit and loss account and balance sheet must be lodged with the Registrar of Companies.

KEY POINT

Advantages of limited company:
- limited liability
- formal separation of roles
- easier to share ownership
- easy to transfer shares
- may be tax advantages.

The disadvantages of operation as a limited company rather than as a sole trader can be as follows:

- There are the costs of formation of the company.

- There are the annual running costs of the company. Annual returns need to be completed and sent to the Registrar of Companies. The audit fee is a additional cost.

- Directors of a company are subject to greater legislative duties than others running an unincorporated business.

- It is difficult and expensive to return capital that is surplus to the business's requirements back to the shareholders.

- There may be tax disadvantages.

1.5   Types of company

The various types of limited company may be categorised as follows.

Private companies and public companies

Whether a particular company is private or public is a matter of law.

A **public company** must have a minimum allotted share capital of £50,000, of which at least one quarter of the nominal value and the whole of any share premium are paid up. Such a company has the letters 'plc' after its name; these stand for 'public limited company'.

A **private company** is a company that is not a public company; such a company has the letters 'Ltd' after its name.

Quoted and unquoted companies

A **quoted** (or listed) **company** is a company whose shares are traded on the London Stock Exchange. Clearly a quoted company must, by definition, be a public company, although of course not all public companies are quoted companies.

2   Company finance

2.1   Sources of finance

The way in which the assets of a company are financed will vary from one company to another. Part of the finance may be provided by the owners or proprietors of the company (referred to as shareholders), while part may be provided by outsiders including trade creditors, banks and other lenders of funds.

The principal sources of finance may be summarised as follows:

Share capital

- ordinary shares
- preference shares

Liabilities

- secured loan stock (debentures)
- unsecured loan stock (debentures)
- convertible loan stock
- bank overdraft
- trade creditors.

2.2   Share capital and reserves

Share capital represents part of the capital invested in the company by its shareholders.

Reserves represent the balance of net assets accruing to the shareholders and may include part of past issues of share capital (known as share premium), retained trading profits and revaluation gains on the revaluation of fixed assets.

The total of share capital and reserves represents the book value of the net assets of the company.

2.3   Nominal value and market value of share capital

Each share has a stated nominal (or par) value. This has little practical significance except as a base line price below which further shares may not generally be issued. The nominal value is also used as a means of calculating dividends to shareholders.

The market value of a share is not fixed at any particular date. The market value is related to the market value of the business of the company. For example, if a business is worth £100,000 and there are 1,000 £1 shares in issue in the company, the market value of each share is £100.

If the company is listed on a stock exchange, then a price will be quoted for the shares based upon recent transactions between purchasers and sellers of shares. This is also referred to as the market value of a share, but this may not be the same value that would apply if the entire business was sold and thus all the shares were sold as one transaction.

It is important to appreciate that the market value of a share quoted on the Stock Exchange has no direct relationship to the nominal value.

2.4   Types of share capital

The share capital of a company may be divided into various classes. The company's internal regulations (the Articles of Association) define the respective rights attached to the various shares, e.g. as regards dividend entitlement or voting at company meetings. The various classes of share capital are dealt with below. In practice it is usually only larger companies which have different classes of share capital.

Ordinary shares

DEFINITION

Ordinary shares are the normal shares issued by a company.

These are the normal shares issued by a company. The normal rights of ordinary shareholders are to vote at company meetings and to receive dividends paid out of profits earned by the company.

Ordinary shares are often referred to as equity shares. A special class of ordinary share is the redeemable ordinary share where the terms of issue specify that it is repayable by the company (i.e. the company undertakes to buy back the share from the shareholder).

Preference shares

DEFINITION

Preference shares are shares carrying a fixed rate of dividend.

Preference shares are shares carrying a fixed rate of dividend, the holders of which have a prior claim to any company profits available for distribution.

The rights and advantages of the shares will be specified in the Articles of Association. Special categories of preference shares include:

- participating preference shares – where shareholders are entitled to participate together to a specified extent in distributable profits and surpluses on liquidation.

- redeemable preference shares – the terms of issue specify that they are repayable by the company.

The following is a summary of the key differences between ordinary and preference shares:

Aspect	Ordinary shares	Preference shares
Voting power	Carry a vote.	Do not usually carry a vote.
Distribution of profits (dividends)	A dividend, which may vary from one year to the next, after the preference shareholders have received their dividend.	A fixed dividend (fixed percentage of nominal value) in priority to ordinary dividend.
Liquidation of the company	Entitled to surplus assets on liquidation, after liabilities and preference shares have been repaid.	Priority of repayment over ordinary shares but not usually entitled to share in surplus assets on liquidation.

2.5   Types of loan

Debentures or loan stock

A debenture is a written acknowledgement of a loan to a company, given under the company's seal, which carries a fixed rate of interest.

A debenture may relate to a loan from one person. Debenture stock, on the other hand, may be held by a large number of individuals.

Debentures are not part of a company's share capital – they are third party liabilities. Debenture interest is therefore a charge against profit and must be paid whether or not the company makes a profit.

Debenture or loan stock may be secured or unsecured. A debenture is secured if the holder has the right to sell the company's assets if it defaults on its payment obligations.

Convertible loan stock

A loan which gives the holder the right to convert to other securities, normally ordinary shares, at a predetermined rate and time.

This is a hybrid, having characteristics both of loan stock and of ordinary shares. On issue, the stock starts off with the characteristics of loan stock. The conditions of issue state that at certain specified future dates holders of the stock may, if they wish, convert their stock into a specified number of ordinary shares.

Bank overdraft

Often a bank overdraft is secured on specific assets of the company, thus taking the form of a secured loan.

3   Financial statements

3.1   Introduction

Two important considerations directly affect the financial statements of a company:

- The Companies Act 1985 (incorporating later additions and amendments introduced by the Companies Act 1989) contains detailed rules governing the form and content of company accounts.

- Financial Reporting Standards (FRSs) and Statements of Standard Accounting Practice (SSAPs) issued by the accountancy profession contain regulations in addition to those found in statute.

3.2   Purpose of financial statements

A distinction must be made between:

- financial statements which the Companies Acts require to be presented to shareholders, and lodged with the Registrar. These must comply with the requirements of the items mentioned above.

- financial statements which are prepared for internal purposes, e.g. for management. These statements need not comply with legal and accountancy requirements and will give more detail than the statutory accounts.

At this stage you need to know the detailed requirements of the Companies Act, FRSs or SSAPs only to the extent that they are covered in this text.

3.3   Balance sheet

A vertical form balance sheet of a company might appear as follows:

Balance sheet at 31 December 20X1

	£	£
Fixed assets:		
Intangible assets:		
Goodwill		50,000
Tangible assets:		
Freehold land and buildings	124,700	
Plant and machinery	29,750	
		154,450
		204,450
Investments		20,000
		224,450
Current assets:		
Stocks	59,670	
Debtors	49,350	
Cash at bank and in hand	4,645	
	113,665	
Creditors: amounts falling due within one year:		
Trade creditors	31,690	
Taxation	26,735	
Dividend payable	30,000	
	88,425	
Net current assets		25,240
Total assets less current liabilities c/f		249,690

Total assets less current liabilities b/f	249,690
Creditors: amounts falling due after more than one year:	
8% Debenture 20X4	100,000
	149,690
Capital and reserves	
Called up share capital – 50p ordinary shares	75,000
Profit and loss account	74,690
	149,690

The profit and loss account balance represents the retained profits of the company, i.e. those profits of the company which have not yet been paid out by way of dividend to the shareholders.

A term you have not met yet is **reserves**. In a sole trader's accounts, the proprietor's capital consists of the original capital introduced to set up the business plus, each year, the profit that has been made, minus drawings taken out.

In the case of a company, the initial capital is the share capital, and this is held in the balance sheet at the same figure year after year unless new shares are issued. The company's profit for the year minus dividends paid to the members is accumulated under the heading 'profit and loss account' in the balance sheet.

It is important to realise that the shareholders' interest in the company consists of the share capital plus reserves (£149,690 in the above example) and not merely the share capital figure.

The profit and loss account is an example of a **reserve.** Any balances in a company balance sheet representing profits or surpluses, whether they are realised or not, are collectively referred to as **reserves.** There is more about reserves later in this chapter.

It is helpful if you can produce company balance sheets in the form shown above when practising questions, highlighting the words shown in this particular example in bold.

ACTIVITY 1

List the ways in which the balance sheet shown above differs from that of a sole trader.

Feedback to this activity is at the end of the chapter.

3.4   The nature and purpose of a dividend

A dividend is a return of part of the profits made by the company to the shareholders.

Dividends can be stated as a percentage based on the nominal value of the share or alternatively as an amount per share, e.g. an 8p dividend on a £1 share can be expressed either as a dividend of 8% or as a dividend of 8p per share.

Modern practice tends to state dividends on a pence per share basis and not as a percentage.

Dividends are **declared** by the company in general meeting. This can only be done if the directors recommend payment of a dividend and the dividend declared cannot exceed the amount recommended by them. The directors on their own responsibility can declare an interim dividend during the accounting period on account of the total dividend for the year, provided this is allowed by the articles of the company.

The recording of dividends in the ledger accounts

The bookkeeping for payment of an interim dividend is as follows:

Debit	Credit	With
Profit and loss account (appropriation of profit)	Bank	Dividend

The bookkeeping for a proposed final dividend is as follows:

Debit	Credit	With
Profit and loss account (appropriation of profit)	Proposed dividend (shown as current liability on balance sheet)	Dividend

Both the interim and the final dividend appear in the profit and loss account. The final proposed dividend will appear as a creditor in the balance sheet.

Note that the current practice of including proposed dividends as liabilities in the balance sheet is likely to change in the future as the UK moves into line with international accounting standards. Eventually, proposed dividends will be shown by a note to the accounts.

ACTIVITY 2

How would an 8 pence dividend on a 50 pence share be expressed?

Feedback to this activity is at the end of the chapter.

3.5   Simple profit and loss account

The format of the profit and loss account for the year can vary. Costs can be analysed in different ways, but all that is required is the application of common sense as to a reasonable layout.

3.6   The nature of corporation tax

KEY POINT

Corporation tax is a tax levied on companies as a percentage of their taxable profits.

There is a special cost to a company which is not a cost to a sole trader business or a partnership – **corporation tax**.

Corporation tax is a tax levied on companies as a percentage of their taxable profits. Certain adjustments need to be made to adjust accounting profits to taxable profits (knowledge of these adjustments is not required at this stage).

Taxation is shown as a deduction from profit, and the balance of tax unpaid at the end of the year appears as a current liability in the balance sheet.

As shareholders' dividends are not tax deductible, taxation is shown **before** shareholders' dividends. Consider the following layout.

XY Ltd Profit and loss account for the year ended 20X9

	£	£
Sales		X
Costs – various analyses can be made		(X)
Net profit before taxation	Say	150,000
Corporation tax		48,000
Net profit after taxation		102,000
Dividends		
Preference dividend – paid	10,000	
Preference dividend – proposed	10,000	
Ordinary dividend – paid	18,000	
Ordinary dividend – proposed	36,000	
		74,000
Profit retained for the year		28,000

3.7   Recording taxation in the ledger accounts

Corporation tax is payable in most cases after the end of the accounting period. In order to agree the corporation tax payable, the company must submit the accounts to the Inland Revenue. Thus at the time of the preparation of the accounts the corporation tax is an estimate of the liability. The entry is as follows:

Debit	Credit	With
Profit and loss account	Tax creditor (shown as current liability on balance sheet)	Estimate of corporation tax charge

ACTIVITY 3

The trial balance (below) at 31 December 20X3 has been extracted from the books of Tefex Ltd

You are required:

(a)   to prepare a trading and profit and loss account for the year ended 31 December 20X3

(b)   to prepare a balance sheet at that date.

Additional information:

- Stock at 31 December 20X3 was £5,200.

- Machinery costing £1,200, on which £700 depreciation had been provided, was sold for £400 in the year.

- There were no fixed asset purchases in the year.

- Depreciation on machinery is provided on the reducing balance basis on the net book value at the end of the year at the rate of 10%.

- No depreciation is provided on land.

- The doubtful debt provision is to be £600.

Tefex Ltd Trial balance at 31 December 20X3

	Dr £	Cr £
Creditors		3,600
Debtors	8,300	
Land at cost	2,000	
Machinery at cost	12,000	
Proceeds of sale of machinery		400
Doubtful debt provision at 31 Dec 20X2		500
Depreciation provision at 31 Dec 20X2		4,500
Cash in hand	500	
Wages	2,400	
Insurance	600	
Interest paid	800	
Bank balance		4,300
Stock at 31 Dec 20X2	4,800	
Sales		24,200
Purchases	22,000	
Share capital		10,000
Profit and loss account at 31 Dec 20X2		5,900
	53,400	53,400

Feedback to this activity is at the end of the chapter.

4   Issue of shares

4.1   The terminology of share capital

The **authorised** share capital is the maximum number of shares a company may issue.

The **issued** share capital is the actual number of shares in issue at any point in time. It is the issued share capital which appears on a company's balance sheet.

The **called up** share capital is the amount of nominal value paid by shareholders on their issued shares plus further amounts agreed to be paid by shareholders on set dates in the future.

Most capital is issued on a fully called basis and it is the only type of share capital which we will have to deal with at this level of examinations.

Paid up share capital is the amount of nominal value paid at the current date.

Thus if there are further calls, the paid up share capital will be less than the called up share capital.

DEFINITIONS

Authorised share capital: the maximum number of shares a company may issue.
Issued share capital: the actual number of shares in issue at any point in time.
Called up share capital: the amount of nominal value paid by shareholders on their issued shares plus further amounts agreed to be paid by shareholders on set dates in the future.
Paid up share capital: the amount of nominal value paid at the current date.

4.2 Issues of shares at nominal value

A company issues 200,000 50p ordinary shares at their nominal value.

Cash book

	£		£
Ordinary share capital	100,000		

Ordinary share capital account

	£		£
		Cash	100,000

4.3 Issues at a value in excess of nominal value

In this case the amount by which the issue price exceeds the nominal value must by law be transferred to a share premium account.

A company issues 200,000 50p ordinary shares at an issue price of 75p.

Cash book

	£		£
Ordinary share capital	100,000		
Share premium	50,000		

Ordinary share capital account

	£		£
		Cash	100,000

Share premium account

	£		£
		Cash	50,000

Balance sheet extract:

	£
Capital and reserves:	
Called up share capital – 50p ordinary shares	100,000
Share premium account	50,000
Profit and loss account	X

The Companies Act 1985 prohibits the issue of shares at a discount – in other words at a value less than their nominal value.

4.4 Bonus issues

The issue of bonus shares (a bonus, scrip or capitalisation issue) is the issue of shares to existing shareholders in proportion to their existing holdings.

No cash or other consideration is passed from shareholders to the company.

Recording a bonus issue in ledger accounts

The bonus issue is financed internally by a capitalisation of reserves and recorded as follows:

Debit	Credit	With
Reserves	Share capital	Amount of bonus issue

Any reserve may be used to finance the bonus issue. Clearly a reserve which, by statute, cannot be distributed would be used in preference to reserves which can be distributed.

The advantages and disadvantages of a bonus issue

The effects of a bonus issue are threefold:

• issued share capital is brought more into line with the fixed assets employed in the company

• issued share capital is divided into a larger number of shares

• market price per share falls, although not necessarily pro rata to its bonus issue. The stock market usually interprets a bonus issue as a sign of strength.

The third effect is the main reason why bonus issues are made in the UK. It is felt that if the market price per share becomes very high, investors are more reluctant to purchase the shares. Of course, nothing has changed in terms of the real worth of the company – the effect is purely psychological.

4.5 Rights issues

A rights issue represents the offer of shares to existing shareholders in proportion to their existing holding at a stated price. Unlike the bonus issue, the shareholders do not have to take up their offer and have the alternative of selling their rights on the stock market.

These are recorded as follows:

Debit	Credit	With
Cash book		Proceeds
	Share capital	Nominal value
	Share premium	Premium (if any)

The advantages and disadvantages of rights issues

The advantages of a rights issue include the following:

• A rights issue is the cheapest way a company can raise further finance by the issue of shares.

• A rights issue to existing shareholders has a greater chance of success (i.e. actually finding buyers) compared to a share issue to the public.

• It may be more appropriate compared to issuing debentures if further profits will take a long time to arise from additional investment (i.e. interest does not have to be paid).

There are also the following disadvantages:

• A rights issue is more expensive than issuing debt.

• It may not be successful in raising the finance required.

(a) A plc has 200,000 50 pence ordinary shares in issue and makes a bonus issue of 50,000 50 pence ordinary shares. Its only available reserve is the profit and loss account balance of £230,000.

(b) B plc has 200,000 50 pence ordinary shares in issue and makes a rights issue of 50,000 50 pence shares at a price of 80 pence each and the issue is fully taken up.

Write up the ledger accounts for each transaction.

Feedback to this activity is at the end of the chapter.

5   Reserves

Prominently displayed on the balance sheet is the heading 'Capital and reserves'. We have already considered capital and this section will consider reserves.

5.1   Distinction between capital and revenue reserves

KEY POINT

Capital reserves must be established for:
- share premium account
- capital redemption reserve (not within the syllabus)
- revaluation reserve.

Capital reserves must be established in certain circumstances by law. They include:

- share premium account
- capital redemption reserve (not within the syllabus)
- revaluation reserve.

Revenue reserves arise when the company makes profits and does not pay out all the profits to the shareholders. There is no statutory requirement for a company to have any amounts in its revenue reserves.

5.2   The permitted uses of capital and revenue reserves

Revenue reserves can be used for any purpose by the company. The most important practical effect is that they can be distributed to shareholders as dividends.

Capital reserves cannot be so used but this does not mean they cannot be used for other things.

Share premium account

The share premium account arises on the issue of shares (i.e. it is a capital reserve). It follows that there should be restrictions as to its use.

KEY POINT

The share premium account may be used for:
- financing fully paid bonus shares
- writing off preliminary expenses
- writing off certain other expenses
- providing the premium payable on some share redemptions.

The share premium account may be used for the following purposes:

- financing the issue of fully paid bonus shares
- writing off preliminary expenses on the formation of a company
- writing off expenses, commission or discount on share or debenture issues
- providing the premium payable on the redemption of debentures and in certain cases on redeemable shares.

Note that the balance on share premium account is either a credit balance or nil – never a debit balance.

Revaluation reserve

The revaluation reserve arises from the revaluation of the fixed assets of a company and, as a revaluation is an unrealised gain, it cannot be used to support the payment of a cash dividend.

The reserve can be used to finance the issue of fully paid bonus shares.

If the asset(s) which were revalued are subsequently sold at or above the valuation figure, the amount(s) in the revaluation reserve become realised and thus can be distributed to shareholders as a dividend.

ACTIVITY 5

A company owns a building that was originally bought for £100,000. Since that date the accumulated depreciation on the building has totalled £30,000. The building has recently been revalued at £150,000.

How would this be reflected in the ledger accounts? (Refer back to the chapter on depreciation if you are unsure.)

Feedback to this activity is at the end of the chapter.

5.3   Revenue reserves

The profit for the year (after allowing for expenses and taxation) may be dealt with as follows:

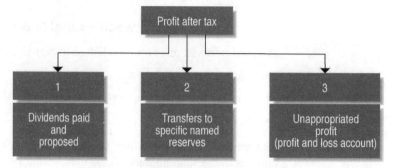

Where profit is transferred to a named reserve, the directors are indicating that these amounts are not currently regarded as available to support a dividend payment (although there is nothing in law to prevent their distribution).

Examples of reserves given special names or titles include the following.

Plant replacement reserve

During a period of rising prices the replacement cost of new plant will be far greater than its original cost, and consequently the assets representing the historical cost depreciation will fall short of the required amount. Setting up a plant replacement reserve will help to solve this problem. Each year profit is reduced by a further amount (over and above historical cost depreciation). The double entry each year is as follows:

Debit	Credit	With
Profit and loss account (appropriation of profit)	Plant replacement reserve	Additional depreciation

Stock replacement reserve

A similar problem arises with stock. During a period of increasing prices, each successive unit of stock costs more. By reducing distributable profits, amounts which might otherwise have been distributed as dividends are retained within the business. The double entry is as follows:

Debit	Credit	With
Profit and loss account (appropriation of profit)	Stock replacement reserve	Additional deduction relating to cost of sales

General reserve

Questions often state that, for example, 'the directors wish to transfer £3,000 to a general reserve' without indicating a specific purpose for the reserve. The double entry is as follows:

Debit	Credit	With
Profit and loss account (appropriation of profit)	General reserve	Transfer to general reserve

The use of a general reserve is now quite rare in practice.

5.4   Profit and loss account (reserve)

As shown in the diagram in the previous section any unappropriated profits remain in the profit and loss account. It is however important to distinguish between:

- the 'normal' profit and loss account, for the year, which is made up in a similar fashion to that of the sole trader; and

- the profit and loss account (reserve), which is the total accumulated unappropriated profit of the company to date – effectively, the amount the company regards as distributable to shareholders. It is this balance that appears in the balance sheet.

Note that there are detailed legal rules regarding distributable profits, but these are beyond the scope of this text.

5.5   Statement of reserves

In order to cope with the double entry involved in and disclosure of the transfers between various reserves, it is helpful to present the movement in the various reserves in columnar format. This statement can be put immediately below the profit and loss account for the year.

Example

ZZ Ltd's summarised balance sheet at 31 December 20X7 showed:

ZZ Ltd's summarised balance sheet at 31 December 20X7 (Extract)

	£
Net assets	280,000
Called up share capital:	
50p ordinary shares	75,000
£1 8% preference shares	60,000
Share premium account	25,000
Plant replacement reserve	30,000
Profit and loss account	90,000
	280,000

The net profit for the year to 31 December 20X8 has been computed as £180,000.

The following additional information is available:

- Corporation tax is estimated at £70,000.

- An interim dividend of 2p has been paid on the ordinary shares, and one half of the dividend on the preference shares.

- It is proposed to pay the remaining dividend on the preference shares and a final dividend of 5p on the ordinary shares.

- £20,000 is to be transferred to the plant replacement reserve.

You are required to:

- construct the profit and loss account for the year

- show the balance sheet at the end of the year to the extent that information is available.

Solution

Profit and loss account for the year ended 31 December 20X8

	£	£
Profit before taxation		180,000
Corporation tax		70,000
Profit after taxation		110,000
Dividends:		
Preference – paid (60,000 × 4%)	2,400	
Preference – proposed	2,400	
		(4,800)
Ordinary – paid (150,000 × 2p)	3,000	
Ordinary – proposed (150,000 × 5p)	7,500	
		(10,500)
Profit retained for the year		94,700

Balance sheet (extracts) as at 31 December 20X8

	£
Creditors: amounts falling due within one year:	
Corporation tax	70,000
Dividends (2,400 + 7,500)	9,900
Capital and reserves:	
Called up share capital	
50p ordinary shares	75,000
£1 8% preference shares	60,000
Share premium account	25,000
Plant replacement reserve	50,000
Profit and loss account	164,700
	374,700

Note: the total amount of capital and reserves (and thus the net assets) has increased by the amount of retained profits of the company, proved below.

	£
Net assets last year	280,000
Retained profit	94,700
Net assets this year	374,700

Statement of reserves

	Profit and loss	Plant replacement	Share premium
	£	£	£
Balance at 1 January 20X8	90,000	30,000	25,000
Profit for the year	94,700		
Transfer	(20,000)	20,000	
Balance at 31 December 20X8	164,700	50,000	25,000

6   Drafting financial statements of companies for internal use

The term **financial statements** includes the balance sheet and the profit and loss account (sometimes referred to as the 'income statement'). A detailed example is shown in this section.

6.1   Internal and external users

One of the questions we must ask is 'How much information should the financial statements include?' The answer to this depends on for whom the statements are required. For the sake of clarity, the users may be divided into two groups:

- **Internal users** – directors and management require a detailed profit and loss account and balance sheet. For the purpose of simplicity, it will be assumed that these are required on an annual basis.

- **External users** – the Companies Act requires shareholders to be presented with a balance sheet and profit and loss account. These statements are normally made up on an annual basis and the Companies Act sets out minimum disclosure requirements. Published accounts must also comply with the requirements of relevant accounting standards.

Example

You are provided with the following trial balance of Aysgarth Ltd at 31 December 20X6:

Aysgarth Ltd
Trial balance for the year ended 31 December 20X6

	Dr £	Cr £
Ordinary share capital (50p shares)		60,000
5% Preference share capital (£1 shares)		20,000
Sales		80,000
Discount allowed	400	
Discount received		200
Carriage inwards	1,000	
Carriage outwards	800	
Debtors and creditors	10,000	2,000
Stock at 1 January 20X6	10,000	
10% Debentures 20X9		50,000
Debenture interest paid	5,000	
Fixed assets, at cost	230,000	
Fixed assets, aggregate depreciation		100,000
Purchases	49,000	
Administrative expenses	4,000	
Salaries (excluding directors)	4,000	
Preference dividend paid	1,000	
Profit and loss account balance		8,000
Cash at bank	5,000	
	320,200	320,200

Adjustments are required for:

- stock at 31 December 20X6, at cost £15,000

- directors' salaries not yet paid £5,000

- corporation tax for the year £5,000

- proposed ordinary dividend 2.5 pence per share

- depreciation charge for the year £4,600

- accrued audit fee £1,000.

You are required to prepare a balance sheet and profit and loss account in vertical form, suitable for presentation to the directors.

Solution

Aysgarth Ltd
Profit and loss account for the year ended 31 December 20X6

	£	£
Sales		80,000
Opening stock	10,000	
Purchases	49,000	
Carriage inwards	1,000	
	60,000	
Less: Closing stock	15,000	
Cost of sales		45,000
Gross profit		35,000
Discount received		200
		35,200
Discount allowed	400	
Carriage outwards	800	
Administrative expenses	4,000	
Staff salaries	4,000	
Directors' salaries	5,000	
Audit fee	1,000	
Depreciation (W2)	4,600	
Debenture interest	5,000	
		24,800
Net profit before tax		10,400
Corporation tax		5,000
Net profit after tax		5,400
Preference dividend of 5% (paid)	1,000	
Ordinary dividend of 5% (proposed) (W1)	3,000	
		4,000
Retained profit		1,400
Retained profit at 31 December 20X7		8,000
Retained profit at 31 December 20X8		9,400

Aysgarth Ltd Balance sheet as at 31 December 20X6

	£	£	£
Fixed assets:			
Tangible assets:			
Freehold land and buildings			125,400
(£230,000 – 104,600 (W2))			
Current assets:			
Stock		15,000	
Trade debtors		10,000	
Cash at bank		5,000	
		30,000	
Creditors: amounts falling due within one year:			
Trade creditors	2,000		
Current taxation	5,000		
Dividend proposed (W1)	3,000		
Accruals (£5,000 + £1,000)	6,000		
		16,000	
Net current assets			14,000
Total assets less current liabilities			139,400
Creditors: amounts falling due after more than one year: 10% debentures 20X9			50,000
			89,400
Capital and reserves:			
Called up share capital:			
Ordinary 50p shares			60,000
5% £1 preference shares			20,000
Profit and loss account			9,400
			89,400

Workings

The format for the profit and loss account follows the format of the sole trader, until the net profit before taxation figure. At this point the taxation for the period is shown, leading to the net profit after taxation. Dividends reduce the profit after taxation to a retained profit figure which is added to the opening balance on the profit and loss account.

(W1)   Dividend payable

	£		£
Balance c/d	3,000	Profit and loss	3,000

Note that the figure of 2.5 pence per share relates to the number of shares in issue (£60,000 of 50p shares = 120,000 shares) × 2.5 pence = £3,000.

(W2)   Fixed assets – Accumulated depreciation

	£		£
		Balance b/d	100,000
Balance c/d	104,600	Profit and loss	4,600
	104,600		104,600

Conclusion

Limited companies are financed by a mixture of share capital and third party liabilities. Profits are appropriated to the owners of the business in the form of dividends, to the government in the form of taxes, and retained within the business by means of various reserves.

The preparation of financial statements for a company in a form that is suitable for internal use within the company is an important examination topic and the key to success with this topic is to have a clear picture of the required format for the balance sheet and profit and loss account together with plenty of question practice.

SELF-TEST QUESTIONS

Types of limited company

1   What are four key factors that distinguish a company from a sole trader? (1.2)

2   Who are the owners of a company? (1.2)

3   Who are the managers of a company? (1.2)

4   What is the difference between a private company and a public company? (1.5)

Company finance

5   What is the relationship between the nominal value and the market value of a company's shares? (2.3)

6   What are preference shares? (2.4)

7   What are debentures? (2.5)

Financial statements

8   What is the double entry for a proposed final dividend? (3.4)

Issue of shares

9   How is an issue of shares at a price in excess of their nominal value accounted for? (4.3)

Reserves

10   What are the names of three capital reserves? (5.1)

MULTIPLE-CHOICE QUESTION

Bonus issues

At 1 January 200X the capital structure of Q Limited was as follows:

Issued share capital 1,000,000 ordinary shares of 50p each	£500,000
Share premium account	£300,000

On 1 April 200X the company made an issue of 200,000 50p shares at £1.30 each, and on 1 July the company made a bonus (capitalisation) issue of one share for every four in issue at the time, using the share premium account for the purpose.

Which of the following correctly states the company's share capital and share premium account at 31 December 200X?

	Share capital	Share premium account
A	£750,000	£230,000
B	£875,000	£285,000
C	£750,000	£310,000
D	£750,000	£610,000

For the answer to this question, see the 'Answers' section at the end of the book.

Question 1: Floyd Ltd

You are presented with the summarised trial balance of Floyd Ltd in respect of the year ended 31 March 20X5 as set out below.

The following final adjustments are required:

- The provision for doubtful debts is to be adjusted to 5% of the debtors figure. The charge is to be included in administrative costs.

- Corporation tax on the current year profits is estimated at £31,200.

- Depreciation at 10% of cost is to be provided. The charge is to be included in cost of sales.

- The directors propose a final dividend of 3 pence per share.

- Interest for the year ended 31 March 20X5 was paid on 1 April 20X5. No accrual has been made.

You are required to prepare a profit and loss account for the year ended 31 March 20X5, and a balance sheet as at that date, in so far as information permits.

(20 marks)

Floyd Ltd
Trial balance for the year ended 31 March 20X5

	£	£
Ordinary share capital (25p shares)		100,000
Plant and machinery:		
Cost	307,400	
Depreciation (1 Apr 20X4)		84,600
Debtors	52,030	
Creditors		38,274
Stock	61,070	
Profit and loss b/d		45,910
Cash at bank	41,118	
Cash in hand	126	
Share premium account		20,000
Sales		998,600
Interim dividend paid	2,500	
Provision for doubtful debts		1,860
9% debenture stock 20X9		75,000
Cost of sales	800,000	
Administrative costs	100,000	
	1,364,244	1,364,244

Question 2: Nimrod Co Ltd

The balances below have been extracted from the books of the Nimrod Co Ltd as at 30 September 20X7.

The following additional information is available:

- Stock on hand at 30 September 20X7 was £46,638.

- Insurance paid in advance is £300.

- Wages owing are £840.

- Depreciation is to be provided at 10% on cost of buildings and at 20% on the written down value of furniture and fittings.

- Provision for doubtful debts is to be reduced to 5% of debtors.

- Debenture interest outstanding is £1,200.

- The directors propose to pay a 5% ordinary dividend and the final preference dividend, and to transfer £24,000 to general reserve.

- The corporation tax charge for the year is £20,000.

You are required to prepare the trading, profit and loss and appropriation account for the year ended 30 September 20X7 and a balance sheet as at that date.

(25 marks)

Nimrod Co Ltd

	£	£
Creditors		18,900
Sales		240,000
Land at cost		54,000
Buildings at cost		114,000
Furniture and fittings at cost		66,000
Bank (credit balance)		18,000
Depreciation Buildings		18,000
Furniture and fittings		30,000
Discounts received		5,292
Unappropriated profit at 1 Oct 20X6		6,000
Provision for doubtful debts		2,448
Goodwill		49,200
Cash in hand		696
Stock at 1 Oct 20X6		42,744
Interim dividend on preference shares		1,800
Rates		6,372
Wages and salaries		24,000
Insurance		5,688
Returns inwards		1,116
General expenses		1,308
Debtors		37,920
Purchases		131,568
Debenture interest		1,200
Bad debts		2,028
5% debentures		48,000
6% £1 preference shares		60,000
£1 ordinary shares		60,000
General reserve		30,000
Share premium account		3,000

For the answers to these questions, see the 'Answers' section at the end of the book.

FEEDBACK TO
ACTIVITY 1

The differences that you should have noted are:

- Fixed assets are divided into tangible assets and intangible assets.

- Current liabilities are described as 'Creditors: amounts falling due within one year'.

- There are creditors for taxation and dividend payable.

- Long-term creditors are described as 'Creditors: amounts falling due after more than one year'.

- There is a capital and reserves section.

- There is a called up share capital heading.

- There is a profit and loss account heading.

FEEDBACK TO
ACTIVITY 2

16%, i.e. $(8/50 \times 100\%)$ or 8 pence per share.

FEEDBACK TO
ACTIVITY 3

The solution to this activity is as follows:

Tefex Ltd
Trading and profit and loss account for the year ended
31 December 20X3

	£	£
Sales		24,200
Opening stock	4,800	
Purchases	22,000	
	26,800	
Closing stock	5,200	
Cost of goods sold		21,600
Gross profit		2,600
Expenses:		
Wages	2,400	
Insurance	600	
Interest	800	
Depreciation (Working (1))	700	
Loss on sale (Working (2))	100	
Bad debts (600 – 500)	100	
		4,700
Loss for year		(2,100)
Profit and loss account b/d		5,900
Profit and loss account c/d		3,800

Workings

(W1)   **Depreciation**

	Cost £	Dep'n £
Opening balances	12,000	4,500
Sale	(1,200)	(700)
	10,800	3,800
	(3,800)	
NBV	7,000	
Depreciation charge 10% × £7,000 = £700		
Balance after sale	10,800	3,800
Depreciation charge for year		700
	10,800	4,500

(W2)   **Loss on sale of machinery**

	£
Cost	1,200
Depreciation	700
	500
Sold for	400
Loss	100

Tefex Ltd
Balance sheet as at 31 December 20X3

	Cost £	Dep'n £	£
Fixed assets:			
Tangible assets:			
Land	2,000	-	2,000
Machinery (working 1)	10,800	4,500	6,300
	12,800	4,500	8,300
Current assets:			
Stock		5,200	
Debtors (£8,300 – 600)		7,700	
Cash		500	
		13,400	
Creditors: amounts falling due within one year:			
Bank overdraft		4,300	
Trade creditors		3,600	
		7,900	
Net current assets			5,500
Total assets less current liabilities			13,800
Capital and reserves:			
Called up share capital			10,000
Profit and loss account			3,800
			13,800

FEEDBACK TO
ACTIVITY 4

The solution to this activity is as follows:

(a)

Share capital

	£		£
Balance c/d	125,000	Balance b/d (200,000 × 50p)	100,000
		Profit and loss (50,000 × 50p)	25,000
	125,000		125,000

Profit and loss

	£		£
Share capital	25,000	Balance b/d	230,000
Balance c/d	205,000		
	230,000		230,000

(b)

Bank

	£		£
Share capital	25,000		
Share premium	15,000		

Share capital

	£		£
Balance c/d	125,000	Balance b/d	100,000
		Bank	25,000
	125,000		125,000

Share premium

	£		£
		Bank	15,000

FEEDBACK TO
ACTIVITY 5

The solution to this activity is as follows:

Building – cost

	£		£
Balance b/d	100,000	Building – valuation	100,000

Building – accumulated depreciation

	£		£
Building – valuation	30,000	Balance b/d	30,000

Building – valuation

	£		£
Building – cost	100,000	Building – acc dep'n	30,000
		Balance c/d	70,000
	100,000		100,000
Balance b/d	70,000	Balance c/d	150,000
Revaluation reserve	80,000		
	150,000		150,000

Revaluation reserve

	£		£
		Building – valuation	80,000

Chapter 20

ACCOUNTING FOR LIMITED COMPANIES II

This chapter considers the framework of laws and other rules which govern the way in which directors of limited companies must account for the activities of those companies.

There are three main sources of corporate accounting rules:

- statute law, contained in the Companies Acts

- accounting standards, established by the Accounting Standards Board

- requirements of the listing rules, which are contributed by the Financial Services Authority (FSA).

Not all of the accounting rules apply to all companies. Smaller companies are exempt from many of the provisions of all three sources. Not surprisingly, companies whose shares are not traded on the Stock Exchange will not be bound by its set of rules.

The overriding principle of the law surrounding corporate accounting is that each company's directors should produce and publish (make public) final accounts which show 'a true and fair view' of the company's performance and position. In pursuit of this objective, the Companies Acts lay down a set of items of information which must be disclosed as a minimum. This information must be disclosed in a prescribed format. (A company is free to publish additional information if they wish to do so, and in practice many do.)

Objectives

By the time you have finished this chapter you should be able to:

- explain the statutory framework for accounting for limited companies

- describe the statutory formats for the balance sheet and the profit and loss account

- be familiar with the contents of a directors' report

- describe the conditions causing a company to qualify as small or medium-sized

- appreciate the consequences of satisfying the conditions to be a small or medium-sized company.

1   The background to regulation

1.1   Introduction

It has long been accepted that limited companies should be required to publish information about themselves. Most countries with a developed commercial infrastructure have limited companies, and most of these have a framework of regulations surrounding them. These frameworks are a combination of **statutory** and **non-statutory rules.** In the UK and the USA, the role of non-statutory rules is extensive. This is also true of countries whose law and customs are, or were, heavily influenced by the UK or the USA, such as many Commonwealth countries. However, most continental European countries, and countries with links or former links with them, tend to favour a system of regulation where the law is more far-reaching. These differences of emphasis are purely cultural and historical.

Originally the law in the UK was mainly, if not totally, concerned with protecting those who had financial claims against the company (creditors and shareholders) from unscrupulous directors. As other groups were recognised as having a stake in the company, the role and scope of regulation has been expanded.

1.2 The need for regulation

Currently, in the UK regulation is seen as necessary for three main reasons:

- **Separation of ownership from control** – Except for very small companies, most companies are managed by directors who do not own all of the shares. This means that those who own shares, but are not directors, have a moral right to receive a periodic account of the stewardship of the directors. This right is also enshrined in law.

- **Limited liability status** – Shareholders cannot normally be required to contribute additional funds to meet unsatisfied creditors' claims against an insolvent company. Potential creditors need certain assurances about a company's future before they will be prepared to lend money or to provide goods or services on credit. To some extent they can obtain these assurances from accounting information provided by the company.

- **Economic power** – Certain large companies wield extensive economic power and influence, which affects society generally, as well as affecting those normally seen as having a direct stake in the those companies. For example, a large manufacturing company could employ a significant proportion of the wage earners in a particular locality. If the company were to go out of business, those living in the locality, even though not employed by the company, could be greatly affected by the closedown. House prices might fall, retailers might be forced to close down and a general economic malaise could pervade the area. Many people would argue that the general economic power of certain companies requires that there is a relatively high degree of accountability by companies to society generally.

Clearly not all of these points apply to companies of all sizes. In particular, they do not all apply to smaller companies, and the regulations reflect this.

Though regulation may be seen by companies as irksome, in fact a vigorous private sector cannot really exist without it. Unless companies provide accounting information they will find it very difficult to attract investors, lenders and suppliers who will provide goods and services on credit. They may also find it more difficult to attract employees and, in some cases, customers. They may also find resistance by society to accept certain companies operating at all. It is interesting to note that the USA, which is widely seen as a bastion of private enterprise, has one of the strictest and most far-reaching accounting regulatory frameworks. Regulation should not be seen as the enemy of the private sector, rather the opposite.

2 The legal framework

2.1 Introduction

The current law is set out in the Companies Acts of 1985 and 1989. These pieces of legislation lay down the legal position of a company in detail, from formation to liquidation and extinction.

KEY POINT

Directors must:

• keep accounting records which are sufficient to show and to explain the company's transactions

• prepare and publish a profit and loss account on an annual basis, a balance sheet and a directors' report.

The Acts also state the legal rules on company accounting. These require the directors to:

• keep accounting records which are sufficient to show and to explain the company's transactions. The accounting records should also be sufficient to enable the directors to be able to prepare final accounts.

• prepare and publish a **profit and loss account** on an annual basis, a **balance sheet** as at the last day of the company's accounting year (the 'final accounts') and a directors' report, which provides additional financial and other information. The accounts are required to show a true and fair view of the company's trading results and position.

The legislation does not specify what is meant by 'accounting records'. There is no suggestion that these need to be sophisticated, provided that they meet the objectives of being sufficient to show and explain the company's transactions and form a reliable basis for the preparation of the final accounts. In practice, the size and complexity of the company will dictate the necessary level of sophistication. For very small companies, and there are many such companies, very basic, hand-written records, perhaps not even written in double-entry form, will be all that is necessary. For other, larger, companies a computerised system might be absolutely essential to meet the objectives of the accounting records.

KEY POINT

Published accounts must present a 'true and fair view'.

2.2   The profit and loss account and balance sheet

What is meant by a 'true and fair view'? The answer to this question is not contained in the legislation. It cannot mean a totally correct view. You have already seen that in areas like stock valuation and depreciation, there is no such thing as complete correctness. All accounting statements contain judgements. While those who prepare accounts can use their judgement honestly and logically, this does not make the judgements correct. However, accounts that show 'a true and fair view' will not mislead readers into a false view of the company's trading and position.

KEY POINT

Published accounts must follow the stipulated formats.
There are four formats for profit and loss accounts.
There are two formats for balance sheets.

The published final accounts must be set out in one of the formats stipulated in the legislation. These are shown later in this chapter. There are four profit and loss account formats and two balance sheet ones. As you will see, each of these sets out the information in slightly different ways. It is up to the company's directors to select a format for each statement. Format 1 for both the profit and loss account and the balance sheet is probably the most popular in practice. Format 1 for the balance sheet is the one which this book tends to follow, whenever the vertical form is used. In the examination, profit and loss account Format 1 will probably be examined more frequently than Format 2, but both are in the syllabus. Companies may select whichever format they prefer to use, but having selected a particular format they must continue to use it from year to year. If there are valid reasons for changing the format, it is possible to change, but the reasons for the change must be clearly disclosed in the accounts.

The objective of having legally prescribed formats is to make it easier for users of the final accounts to find the items in which they are particularly interested. They also facilitate making comparisons between different companies and between different time periods for the same company.

Format 1 for the profit and loss account contains some items which perhaps need some explanation. Unfortunately the Companies Acts do not provide any explanation of them, but the popular interpretation is as follows:

Cost of sales	This includes all production expenses, including materials used, productive labour, production overheads and so on.
Distribution costs	These are all of the costs concerned with selling and delivering the products or services which the company provides.
Administrative expenses	This 'mops up' all expenses which are not included in cost of sales, distribution costs or in any other specified expense items (such as interest charges).
Other operating income	This is all income of the company which is not included under any other specific heading.

Where a company has nothing to put into one of the categories in the final account formats, it would normally ignore the item in the accounts. It would not show a nil figure. Companies do not need to show the letters and numbers which appear in the formats shown later.

2.3 Examples of the formats

The formats that you will meet later in this chapter do not look very much like balance sheets and profit and loss accounts since they contain neither figures nor rulings for sub-totals and totals. The following is an example of a profit and loss account and balance sheet for a company, using Format 1 in each case.

Example of profit and loss account: Format 1

Ducat plc
Profit and loss account for the year ended 31 December 20X3

	£m	£m
Turnover		623
Cost of sales		414
Gross profit		209
Distribution costs	73	
Administrative expenses	32	105
		104
Other operating income		8
		112
Income from other fixed asset investments	2	
Other interest receivable and similar income	16	18
		130
Interest payable and similar charges		15
		115
Tax on profit on ordinary activities		35
Profit on ordinary activities after taxation		80
Transfer to general reserve	40	
Proposed dividend on ordinary shares	50	90
Retained loss for the year		(10)
Retained profit brought forward from last year		46
Retained profit carried forward		36

Note: 'Comparative figures' showing the equivalent figures for the previous year must also be included in practice. Note that not all of the items in Format 1 appear in this profit and loss account. This is simply because they do not apply to this company for this year or for the previous one. The several lines after 'Profit on ordinary activities after taxation' are not included in Format 1, but they are required to be included under the Companies Acts.

Example of balance sheet: Format 1

Ducat plc
Balance sheet as at 31 December 20X3

	£m	£m	£m
Fixed assets			
Intangible assets:			
Development costs		35	
Tangible assets:			
Land and buildings	220		
Plant and machinery	103		
Fixtures, fittings, tools and equipment	149	472	507
Current assets			
Stocks:			
Raw materials and consumables	11		
Work in progress	6		
Finished goods and goods for resale	34	51	
Debtors:			
Trade debtors	106		
Prepayments and accrued income	12	118	
Cash at bank and in hand		23	
		192	
Creditors: amounts falling due within one year			
Trade creditors	20		
Other creditors including taxation and social security	43		
Accruals and deferred income	13	76	
Net current assets			116
Total assets less current liabilities			623
Creditors: amounts falling due after more than one year			
Debenture loans		110	
Provisions for liabilities and charges			
Pensions		47	157
			466
Capital and reserves:			
Called up share capital			200
Share premium account			40
Revaluation reserve			70
Capital redemption reserve			120
Profit and loss account			36
			466

Note: Again 'comparative figures' have been omitted, but they should be there in practice. Where there is no asset or claim under any of the Format 1 items, that item has been omitted.

The data below is an extract from the trial balance of Unity plc at 31 March 20X4, after the necessary year-end adjustments had been made.

Show the first part of the published profit and loss account of the company using Format 1.

Extract from the trial balance of Unity plc at 31 March 20X4

	Dr £'000	Cr £'000
Cost of sales	1,823	
Distribution costs	547	
Sales		4,050
Rents receivable		437
Loan stock interest	647	
Administrative expenses	974	

Feedback to this activity is at the end of the chapter.

ACTIVITY 2

The directors of Unity plc (see previous activity) are interested to see how the company's profit and loss account would look if it were prepared following Format 2. You discover that the sum of cost of sales, distribution and administrative expenses which appears in the original profit and loss account as 3,344 (1,823 + 547 + 974) can be alternatively analysed as set out below.

Show the profit and loss account for Unity plc as it would appear if it were to be produced following Format 2. (See section 3.1 later in the chapter for Format 2.)

Unity plc

	£'000
Decrease in stocks of finished goods and work in progress	52
Raw materials and consumables	875
Depreciation	943
Staff costs	1,065
Other operating charges	409
	3,344

Feedback to this activity is at the end of the chapter.

2.4 Notes to the accounts

In addition to those items which are specified in the formats, the final published accounts are required by the Companies Act or accounting standards to disclose other information by way of notes. Full details of the disclosure notes required are given later in this chapter, but your syllabus requires seven of them, the notes detailing:

- fixed asset movements
- disclosable expenses
- reserve movements
- exceptional and extraordinary items (see Chapter 21)
- post balance sheet events
- contingent liabilities and contingent assets
- research and development expenditure.

Though the formats and the additional requirements add up to quite a lot of information, there is other information which could be given, or given in more detail. To simplify the basic accounting statements, many companies give only the information in outline on the face of the statements, using supporting notes to fill in the detail.

The law also specifies certain accounting conventions which must be followed in preparing the accounts. These are:

- **Going concern:** Unless the contrary is known to be true, it is assumed that the business of the company will continue indefinitely.

- **Consistency:** Where different accounting treatments could be made of a particular type of transaction, the one selected should be applied consistently.

- **Prudence:** Where the outcome of a transaction is not known, a degree of caution must be exercised in accounting for it.

- **Accruals:** Profit is the difference between revenues and expenses, not the difference between cash receipts and payments.

In addition, published company final accounts must comply with the following rules:

- Each component of an asset or liability must be looked at separately in deducing the aggregate figure which must be used in the published final accounts.

- Assets and liabilities must not be netted against one another to arrive at a net figure to be shown in the published balance sheet. This could have the effect of masking the extent of the company's borrowing, an effect which the directors might see as desirable.

These conventions, or other points, can be departed from if, in the opinion of the directors, they prevent a true and fair view being presented. In such a case, the directors will need to give a note of details of the departure with the reason for it.

2.5   The directors' report

The directors must publish a directors' report which contains further information of both a financial and a non-financial nature. This report is a narrative review of the development of the company's business for the year under review. The items which must be included in the directors' report are listed later in this chapter. The legislation does not require that the directors' report is set out in any particular format.

Many companies also produce a **Chairman's statement.** Though this can be a valuable source of information to readers, it is not a legal requirement.

2.6   Small and medium-sized companies

The need to publish full final accounts and a directors' report is reduced for small and medium-sized companies. To qualify, a company must satisfy any two out of the three tests relating to turnover, balance sheet totals and employee numbers. The limits shown apply to financial years ending on or after 30 January 2004. The old limits are shown in brackets. The objective of relaxing the requirements for smaller companies is partly an attempt to limit the cost burden of complying with legislation. It is also a recognition by the legislators that there is certain information which companies may prefer not to disclose and which, in the case of smaller companies, it is reasonable not to make them disclose.

Criteria	Small	Medium
Turnover	≤ £5.6 million (£2.8m)	≤ £22.8 million (£11.2m)
Assets	≤ £2.8 million (£1.4m)	≤ £11.4 million (£5.6m)
No of employees	< 50	≤ 250

The published final accounts (including the directors' report, except for small companies) must normally be produced with respect to the same accounting year-end each year. The financial year for which the profit and loss account is prepared must begin on the day following the date to which the last accounts were prepared and must end on the last day of the company's normal financial year. The financial year-end must coincide with, or fall not more than seven days before or after, the accounting reference date of the company notified to the Registrar of Companies.

Each shareholder and debenture holder is entitled to receive a copy of the accounts and a copy must be laid before the annual general meeting of the company. The company must also send a copy of the accounts to the Registrar of Companies which must then be readily available to anyone who wishes to inspect it.

2.7   Audit

The Companies Acts require companies (other than very small companies) to have qualified **auditors.** The role of the auditors is to carry out an independent review of the company's published final accounts and accounting records. The auditors' report expresses the auditors' opinion as to whether:

- the published profit and loss account and balance sheet show a true and fair view of the company's trading and position

- the published final accounts comply with the form and content prescribed by the Companies Acts

- the company has maintained accounting records sufficient to show and explain the company's transactions and to enable the published final accounts to be prepared

- accounting standards have been complied with, where appropriate

- the content of the directors' report is consistent with the published final accounts.

Where the auditors are of the opinion that the company is deficient in any of these respects, they must make this clear in their report. The auditors play a very important role in the regulation of accounting in the UK.

Clearly the role of the auditors requires that they are completely independent of the company and its directors. The auditors are, in effect, acting as a watchdog for the shareholders, and possibly for society generally, over financial statements produced by the directors.

Internal auditors

Many companies employ internal auditors (which is not a statutory requirement) as well as external auditors (which is). The role of internal auditors is rather different from that of the externals. The work of the internal auditor might well include going beyond that which is necessary to form an opinion about the truth and fairness of the final accounts. The internal auditors are usually concerned with the quality of the information which the company's accounting information system provides to management. They are ultimately responsible to the directors and will undertake tasks dictated by the company's senior management. The external auditors, on the other hand, are responsible to the shareholders and their task is defined by law. The directors cannot limit the definition of the task undertaken by the external auditors.

3   Company published final accounts formats

These formats for the published profit and loss account and balance sheet are those shown in the Companies Act 1985. For examination purposes, the formats shown above in our examples are more useful, but you need to be aware of the possible items which could appear. Formats 3 and 4 of the profit and loss account are rare in the UK, so are not illustrated here.

3.1   The profit and loss account

Format 1

1 Turnover
2 Cost of sales
3 Gross profit or loss
4 Distribution costs
5 Administrative expenses
6 Other operating income
7 Income from shares in group undertakings
8 Income from shares in participating interests
9 Income from other fixed asset investments
10 Other interest receivable and similar income
11 Amounts written off investments
12 Interest payable and similar charges
13 Tax on profit or loss on ordinary activities
14 Profit or loss on ordinary activities after taxation
15 Extraordinary income
16 Extraordinary charges
17 Extraordinary profit or loss
18 Tax on extraordinary profit or loss
19 Other taxes not shown under the above items
20 Profit or loss for the financial year

Format 2

Format 2 classifies expenses slightly differently and in a little more detail. For example, staff costs are shown separately rather than included in cost of sales, distribution costs or administrative costs, as appropriate.

1 Turnover
2 Change in stocks of finished goods and work in progress
3 Own work capitalised
4 Other operating income
5 (a) Raw materials and consumables
   (b) Other external charges
6 Staff costs:
   (a) wages and salaries
   (b) social security costs
   (c) other pension costs
7 (a) Depreciation and other amounts written off tangible and intangible fixed assets
   (b) Exceptional amounts written off current assets
8 Other operating charges
9 Income from shares in group undertakings
10 Income from shares in participating interests
11 Income from other fixed asset investments
12 Other interest receivable and similar income
13 Amounts written off investments
14 Interest payable and similar charges
15 Tax on profit or loss on ordinary activities
16 Profit or loss on ordinary activities after taxation
17 Extraordinary income
18 Extraordinary charges
19 Extraordinary profit or loss
20 Tax on extraordinary profit or loss
21 Other taxes not shown under the above items
22 Profit or loss for the financial year

Note that from item 9 onwards Format 2 is identical to Format 1.

3.2 Balance sheet format

A Called up share capital not paid

B Fixed assets

    I Intangible assets

        1 Development costs

        2 Concessions, patents, licences, trade marks and similar rights and assets

        3 Goodwill

        4 Payments on account

    II Tangible assets

        1 Land and buildings

        2 Plant and machinery

        3 Fixtures, fittings, tools and equipment

        4 Payments on account and assets in course of construction

    III Investments

        1 Shares in group undertakings

        2 Loans to group undertakings

        3 Shares in participating interests

        4 Loans to participating interests

        5 Other investments other than loans

        6 Other loans

        7 Own shares

C Current assets

    I Stocks

        1 Raw materials and consumables

        2 Work in progress

        3 Finished goods and goods for resale

        4 Payments on account

    II Debtors

        1 Trade debtors

        2 Amounts owed by group undertakings

        3 Amounts owed by participating interests

        4 Other debtors

        5 Called up share capital not paid

        6 Prepayments and accrued income

    III Investments

        1 Shares in group undertakings

        2 Own shares

        3 Other investments

    IV Cash at bank and in hand

D Prepayments and accrued income

E Creditors: amounts falling due within one year

        1 Debenture loans

        2 Bank loans and overdrafts

        3 Payments received on account

        4 Trade creditors

        5 Bills of exchange payable

        6 Amounts owed to group undertakings

        7 Amounts owed to participating interests

        8 Other creditors including taxation and social security

        9 Accruals and deferred income

F Net current assets (liabilities)

G Total assets less current liabilities

H Creditors: amounts falling due after more than one year

        1 Debenture loans

        2 Bank loans and overdrafts

        3 Payments received on account

        4 Trade creditors
        5 Bills of exchange payable
        6 Amounts owed to group undertakings
        7 Amounts owed to participating interests
        8 Other creditors including taxation and social security
        9 Accruals and deferred income

I   **Provisions for liabilities and charges**
        1 Pensions and similar obligations
        2 Taxation, including deferred taxation
        3 Other provisions

J   **Accruals and deferred income**

K   **Capital and reserves**
    I   Called up share capital
    II   Share premium account
    III   Revaluation reserve
    IV   Other reserves
        1 Capital redemption reserve
        2 Reserve for own shares
        3 Reserves provided for by the articles of association
        4 Other reserves
    V   Profit and loss account

Notes

- 'Called up share capital not paid' can appear either at A or as a debtor at C.
- 'Prepayments and accrued income' can appear either as a debtor at C or at D.
- 'Accruals and deferred income' can appear either as a creditor at E or at J.

4   Notes to the final published accounts

4.1   Disclosure of supporting information

The Companies Act 1985 requires the disclosure of a great deal of supporting information by note to the accounts. Examples of these are given below.

Note to the profit and loss account detailing the amounts of certain expenses
- directors' remuneration
- amortisation of intangible fixed assets
- depreciation of tangible fixed assets (Format 1)
- auditors' remuneration, including expenses
- staff costs (with average number of staff also)
- exceptional items.

Note to the balance sheet detailing movements on fixed assets

This note will state, for each class of fixed asset:

Cost or valuation
- balance at beginning of year
- additions during the year
- cost of assets disposed of during the year
- revaluations during the year.

Aggregate depreciation
- balance at beginning of year
- charge for the year
- elimination for disposals during the year.

Illustration

The normal format of the note detailing fixed asset movements is shown below:

Tangible fixed assets: Land and buildings

	Freehold £m	Long leasehold £m	Short leasehold £m	Plant, equipment and vehicles £m	Total £m
Cost:					
Beginning of year	2,042.4	273.7	183.2	817.5	3,316.8
Additions	302.1	5.3	5.5	110.6	423.5
Disposals	(6.6)	(1.3)	(9.0)	(48.2)	(65.1)
End of year	2,337.9	277.7	179.7	879.9	3,675.2
Depreciation:					
Beginning of year	72.4	24.0	81.2	432.2	609.8
Charged during year	40.7	5.3	4.3	88.5	138.8
Disposals	(1.5)	(0.7)	(5.4)	(46.6)	(54.2)
End of year	111.6	28.6	80.1	474.1	694.4
Net book value:					
Beginning of year	1,970.0	249.7	102.0	385.3	2,707.0
End of year	2,226.3	249.1	99.6	405.8	2,980.8

A similar table will show the movements on intangible fixed assets if the company owns any.

Note detailing reserve movements

Opening and closing amounts must be disclosed, with details of movements during the year. The note is usually presented in columnar form as shown in the following illustration.

Note on reserves

	Share premium account £000	Revaluation reserve £000	Profit and loss account £000	Total £000
At 1 January 20X0	30,138	938	102,525	133,601
Goodwill eliminated on current year acquisitions	-	-	(5,906)	(5,906)
Arising on issue of shares	32,493	-	-	32,493
Retained profit for the year	-	-	26,056	26,056
At 31 December 20X0	62,631	938	122,675	186,244

Note that the retained profit for the year is included here from the profit and loss account to build up the figure of 122,675 for the balance sheet. It is not really correct to show the opening balance brought forward in the profit and loss account.

Other notes

In addition to the notes explained in detail above, the Companies Act 1985 requires many more. Some of the more important ones are:

- details of **directors' emoluments**

- details of **directors' loans**

- analysis of **interest payable** showing the break-down between interest on short-term loans (repayable within five years) and long-term loans (repayable after more than five years).

5   Contents of the directors' report

The content of the directors' report is as follows:

Content	Explanation
Principal activities	What these are and how they have changed over the period.
Review	A review of the development of the business of the company over the period.
Future developments	Some indication of the company's plans for the future.
Dividends	Amount proposed.
Post balance sheet events	Any significant events which have occurred since the end of the accounting period.
Research and development	Some indication of the activities of the company in this regard.
Fixed assets	The difference between book and market value of land and buildings, if significant.
Charitable and political	If in excess of £200, separate totals for each donations category. If political donations exceed £200, the names of recipients and amounts must be given.
Own shares acquired	Details of any shares in itself which the company has acquired.
Employees	Information on health, safety, training and welfare. Where employees number 250 or more, also information on company policy towards disabled people.
Directors	(a) Names of those who held office at any time during the period (b) Directors' interests in contracts of third parties and the company (c) Each director's shares and debenture holdings (including a 'nil' return where relevant): • at the start of the accounting period • at the end of the accounting period • at the date of appointment for directors appointed during the accounting period.
Supplier payment policy	A statement of the company's policy in terms of the payment of its suppliers (public companies and some large private companies only).

Conclusion

This chapter has examined aspects of the legal regulation of company accounting in the UK. The need for extensive regulation arises for three principal reasons: the separation of control and ownership which is characteristic of limited companies; limited liability status; and the economic power which is wielded by companies (especially the larger ones).

The legal framework of accounting has been examined, with particular reference to the format in which company accounts are presented.

The background to regulation

1   What are the three sources of rules which make up the 'regulatory framework' of accounting in the UK? (Introduction)

2   What are the three major reasons for it being regarded as necessary that a regulatory framework exists? (1.2)

The legal framework

3   What two requirements are imposed on directors of UK limited companies in the context of accounting? (2.1)

4   Which one of the following is the precise wording of the Companies Act 1985 in its requirement of what the published accounts of UK companies should show?

    (a)   'a fair and reasonable view'
    (b)   'a true and reasonable view'
    (c)   'a true and fair view'
    (d)   'a correct and fair view'. (2.2)

5   What are the three tests used to determine whether a company is small or medium sized? (2.6)

Content of the directors' report

6   Which one of the following is not required to be included in the directors' report?

    (a)   a review of the development of the business of the company over the period
    (b)   amount of dividend proposed
    (c)   total amount of the company's tax liability for the year
    (d)   details of own shares acquired. (5)

General Warehouses plc

The trial balance (see below) of General Warehouses plc shows the following balances at 31 December 20X3.

The following final adjustments need to be made:

*   stock of goods for resale at 31 December 20X3, £50m

*   provide annual depreciation of £16m on warehouse plant and machinery

*   provide for corporation tax, due 30 September 20X4, £25m

*   proposed dividend, £30m.

Prepare the published profit and loss account and balance sheet for the 20X3 financial year. The directors consider that Format 2 should be used.   **(20 marks)**

General Warehouses plc

	Dr £m	Cr £m
Ordinary share capital		150
Share premium account		10
General reserve		10
Profit and loss account		25
Stock at 1 January 20X3	30	
Sales		500
Purchases	270	
Purchase returns		13
Sales returns	14	
Carriage outwards	14	
Warehouse wages	40	
Salespersons' salaries	30	

Administrative wages	20	
Warehouse plant and machinery	63	
Delivery vehicle hire	10	
Provision for depreciation – plant and machinery		25
Goodwill	50	
Distribution expenses	5	
Administrative expenses	15	
Directors' salaries (charge to administrative expenses)	15	
Rents receivable		8
Trade debtors	165	
Cash at bank	30	
Trade creditors (payable by 28/2/20X4)		30
	771	771

EXAM-TYPE
QUESTIONS

General Warehouses plc

Question 1: Board of Directors

After the directors of General Warehouses plc (see Practice Question) had seen the draft profit and loss account and balance sheet for the 20X3 financial year they concluded that the profit and loss showed too much analysis of their expenses.

Prepare a further profit and loss account for publication purposes using Format 1, for comparison by the Board of Directors of General Warehouses plc.

(10 marks)

Question 2: Ople plc

The profit and loss account (below) for the year to 31 March 20X2 has been prepared for the management of Ople public limited company. The following additional information is available:

- Wages and salaries (other than those for directors) are to be apportioned as follows:

Distribution	80%
Office expenses	20%

- The company's issued and fully paid up share capital is as follows:

	£'000
Ordinary shares of £1 each	8,000
10% Preference shares of £1 each	1,000

You are required, in so far as the information permits, to prepare Ople plc's profit and loss account for the year to 31 March 20X2 in accordance with the requirements of the Companies Act 1985 and related accounting standards.

(15 marks)

Ople plc
Profit and loss account to 31 March 20X2

	£'000		£'000
Opening stock	500	Sales	8,500
Purchases	4,400	Closing stock	700
Gross profit c/d	4,300		
	9,200		9,200
Auditors' remuneration	50	Gross profit b/d	4,300
Depreciation		Dividends received	240
Delivery vans	40		
Office furniture	20		
Plant and machinery	85		
Directors' salaries	95		
Distribution expenses	425		
Factory expenses	970		

Hire of plant and machinery	15	
Office expenses	190	
Legal expenses	35	
Rent and rates (warehouse)	65	
Wages and salaries	1,200	
Net profit c/d	1,350	
	4,540	4,540
Provision for corporation tax	380	Net profit b/d 1,350
Net profit after tax c/d	1,000	Over-provision of last year's corporation tax 30
	1,380	1,380
Preference dividend paid	100	Net profit after tax b/d 1,000
Ordinary dividend		
Paid	200	
Proposed	200	
Retained profit for year	500	
	1,000	1,000

Question 3: Small plc

Small plc is a quoted company with an authorised share capital of £250,000, consisting of ordinary shares of £1 each. The company prepares its accounts as on 31 March in each year and the trial balance, before final adjustments, extracted on 31 March 20X5 is shown below.

You ascertain that:

- the debenture stock is repayable at par by six equal annual drawings starting on 31 December 20X5

- annual depreciation on leasehold factory: 2% on cost

- annual depreciation on plant and machinery: 20% reducing balance on NBV as at 31 March 20X4 plus additions less disposals in the year

- plant disposed of originally cost £16,000. Accumulated depreciation is £3,200

- stock has been valued consistently at the lower of cost and net realisable value

- A dividend of 20% is proposed.

You are required to prepare, in a form suitable for publication and in conformity with the provisions of the Companies Act 1985, the balance sheet as on 31 March 20X5.

(15 marks)

Small plc

	£	£
Ordinary share capital, issued and fully paid		200,000
Retained profits as on 1 April 20X4		61,000
6% Debenture stock (secured on leasehold factory)		60,000
Leasehold factory:		
Cost at beginning of year	200,000	
Accumulated depreciation at beginning of year		76,000
Plant and machinery:		
Cost at beginning of year	80,000	
Accumulated depreciation		30,000
Additions in year	10,000	
Creditors and accrued expenses		170,000
Stock as on 31 March 20X5	160,000	
Debtors	100,000	
Prepayments	80,000	
Balance at bank	90,000	
Profit for the year (subject to any items in the above notes)		111,000
Proceeds of sale of plant		12,000
	£720,000	£720,000

Question 4: Pride Ltd

The following extracts have been taken from the trial balance of Pride Limited at 31 March 20X7.

The profit and loss account balance of £34,000 shown is the final balance of retained profit for the year and may be incorporated into your answer as such.

Notes

- The balance on the suspense account is made up as follows:

	£000
Receipt of cash on 8 January 20X7 on the issue of 200,000 ordinary shares of 50p each at a premium of 30p per share	160
Proceeds of sale of plant*	6
	166

*This plant had originally cost £18,000 and had been written down to £6,000 at 31 March 20X6.

- The company's policy is to provide depreciation for a full year in the year of acquisition of assets and none in the year of sale.

- Depreciation is to be provided on the straight line basis at the following annual rates:

Land	Nil
Buildings	2%
Plant and Equipment	20%

- The provision for doubtful debts is to be increased to £12,000.

- Payments and accruals at 31 March 20X7 were:

	£000
Prepayments	8,000
Accruals	4,000

- The closing stock was £180,000.

Prepare the balance sheet of Pride Limited as at 31 March 20X7 for publication, complying as far as possible with the provisions of the Companies Acts.

(10 marks)

Pride Ltd Trial balance at 31 March 20X7

	£000	£000
Issued share capital:		
500,000 ordinary shares of 50p each		250
Share premium account 1 April 20X6		180
Profit and loss account 31 March 20X7		34
Land at cost	210	
Building:		
Cost 1 April 20X6	200	
Accumulated depreciation at 1 April 20X6		120
Plant and equipment:		
Cost	318	
Accumulated depreciation at 1 April 20X6		88
Debtors	146	
Cash at bank	50	
Creditors		94
10% debentures issued 20X1		100
Allowance for doubtful debts		10
Suspense account		166

For the answers to these questions, see the 'Answers' section at the end of the book.

The profit and loss account of Unity plc for the year ended 31 March 20X4, using Format 1 is as follows:

Unity plc
Profit and loss account for the year ended
31 March 20X4

	£000	£000
Turnover		4,050
Cost of sales		1,823
Gross profit		2,227
Distribution costs	547	
Administrative expenses	974	1,521
Profit from trading activities		706
Income from other fixed asset investments		437
		1,143
Interest payable on loans		647
Profit on ordinary activities before tax		496

The profit and loss account of Unity plc for the year ended 31 March 20X4, using Format 2 would be as follows:

Unity plc
Profit and loss account for the year ended
31 March 20X4

	£000	£000
Turnover		4,050
Decrease in stocks of finished goods and work in progress		52
		3,998
Raw materials and consumables		875
		3,123
Staff costs	1,065	
Depreciation	943	
Other operating charges	409	
		2,417
Profit from trading activities		706
Income from other fixed asset investments		437
		1,143
Interest payable on loans		647
Profit on ordinary activities before tax		496

Chapter 21

FRS 3 REPORTING FINANCIAL PERFORMANCE

FRS 3 *Reporting Financial Performance* is an important accounting standard which sets out radical changes to the way in which financial performance must be reported. The standard represents an attempt to shift the emphasis of the profit and loss account away from the final profit figure, by ensuring that users are provided with a more complete picture of the various gains and losses arising during the year.

FRS 3 introduced two major changes. The first is concerned with the **format of the profit and loss account**. The second is that a number of **statements and notes to the accounts** must be prepared in order to provide a more complete picture of the movements in wealth during the period.

Objectives

By the time you have finished this chapter you should be able to:

- discuss the profit and loss account disclosures required by FRS 3

- prepare profit and loss accounts including FRS 3 disclosures

- understand and state the purposes of the statements required by FRS 3.

1   Profit and loss account format

1.1   Disclosures

Various elements of financial performance must be shown separately in the profit and loss account. These elements are as follows:

Results of continuing operations

These should include any operations acquired during the period.

Results of discontinued operations

The analysis between continuing and discontinued operations should be disclosed, starting with turnover and continuing down to the level of operating profit. The minimum disclosure requirements are to show separate analysis of turnover and operating profit for continuing operations (including acquisitions) and discontinued operations.

Operations are classed as discontinued if the sale or termination of the operation is completed within the accounting period or within the three months following the end of the period.

Certain exceptional items

These are:

- gains or losses on the sale or termination of an operation

- gains or losses on the disposal of fixed assets

- any costs incurred in relation to fundamental reorganisation and restructuring.

To distinguish them from 'normal' exceptional items discussed below, these three are sometimes referred to as **super-exceptional items**.

Exceptional items are material items which fall within the ordinary activities of the business but which need to be disclosed because of their size or incidence. Although the three exceptional items listed above must be shown separately in the profit and loss account, other forms of exceptional item should be included under the statutory headings to which they relate. This requirement is designed to ensure that users do not place too much emphasis on the profit figure *excluding* exceptional items. The exceptional items that do not fall within the three categories listed above should be disclosed separately in a note to the accounts, or, if the amount is of sufficient importance, it can be given more prominence by placing it on the face of the profit and loss account.

DEFINITION

Extraordinary items are abnormal items which are not part of the normal operations of the reporting entity and are not likely to recur.

Extraordinary items

These are abnormal items which are not part of the normal operations of the reporting entity and are not likely to recur. They do not include exceptional items such as those listed above. FRS 3 points out that extraordinary items would be very unusual and offers no examples of items which may fall within this category. This item is expected to appear in financial reports very rarely, if at all. Before FRS 3 was published, extraordinary items regularly appeared in the accounts of companies and became, according to one member of the ASB, '… a convenient repository for all unwanted costs'. As a result, comparisons of performance between years and between companies became difficult.

The layout required for the profit and loss account can be illustrated diagrammatically as follows:

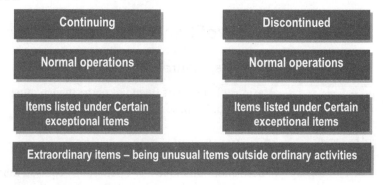

ACTIVITY **1**

Why is it necessary to show separately the different elements of financial performance? How might this be of value to users?

Feedback to this activity is at the end of the chapter.

1.2 Earnings per share

The earnings per share (EPS) of a listed company must be shown on the face of the profit and loss account. EPS is an important investor ratio which is considered later in this text. The ratio divides the total profit attributable to ordinary shareholders by the number of ordinary shares in issue in order to derive a measure of share return. FRS 3 states that the profit attributable to ordinary shareholders must be derived after taking into account extraordinary items and preference dividends. If an additional measure of EPS, based on another measure of profit, is shown, this must be calculated on a consistent basis and must be reconciled with the figure calculated in accordance with FRS 3. The EPS figure as required by FRS 3 must be at least as prominent in the accounts as any additional EPS measure and the reasons for calculating the additional measure must be explained.

1.3   Acceptable formats

FRS 3 provides illustrative examples of acceptable profit and loss account formats which include the presentation of earnings per share.

A slightly simplified version is shown below.

Profit and loss account

| | Continuing operations | | | |
	Existing	*New acquisitions*	*Discontinued operations*	*Total*
	£m	*£m*	*£m*	*£m*
Turnover	550	50	175	775
Cost of sales	415	40	165	620
Gross profit	135	10	10	155
Distribution costs and administrative expenses	65	4	25	94
Operating profit	70	6	(15)	61
Profit on sale of properties in continuing operations	9			9
Loss on disposal of discontinued operations			(7)	(7)
Profit on ordinary activities before interest	79	6	(22)	63
Interest payable				(18)
Profit on ordinary activities after interest				45
Taxation				(16)
Profit for financial year				29
Dividends				(8)
Retained profit for the financial year				21
Earnings per share				39p

2   Additional financial statements and notes

2.1   Introduction

The following additional financial statements and notes provide a number of benefits to users. In particular, they:

- bring together related and relevant information which appears in different parts of the financial statements

- provide additional information for evaluation and comparison purposes

- show the effect of movements in wealth on shareholders' funds.

2.2   Statement of total recognised gains and losses

This statement brings together the recognised gains (both realised and unrealised) which have arisen during the period from whatever source. It is important as it enables users to see the total gains and losses which have been recorded since the last accounts; not all gains and losses may pass through the profit and loss account.

Illustration

An illustration of the required statement of total recognised gains and losses is set out in FRS 3 and is reproduced below:

Statement of total recognised gains and losses 20X3

	£m
Profit for the financial year	29
Unrealised surplus on revaluation of properties	4
Unrealised loss on trade investments	(3)
Total gains and losses recognised since last annual report	30

2.3 Note of historical cost profits and losses

Companies which revalue their fixed assets will depreciate those assets on the revalued amount rather than on the original cost of the assets. This can create problems when making comparisons between companies. FRS 3 aims to make comparisons easier by requiring a note, or memorandum, to the accounts. This memorandum restates the accounts, in abbreviated form, on the basis of depreciation being charged according to the historical cost of assets rather than their revalued amounts.

The note is required where there is a material difference between the results shown in the profit and loss account and the results on an unmodified historical cost basis. This note, or memorandum, must be presented immediately after the profit and loss account or the statement of total recognised gains and losses.

An illustration of the required note of historical cost profits and losses is set out in FRS 3 and is shown below:

Note of historical cost profits and losses 20X3

	£m
Reported profit on ordinary activities before taxation	45
Realisation of property revaluation gains of previous years	9
Difference between a historical cost depreciation charge and the actual depreciation charge of the year calculated on the revalued amount	5
Historical cost profit on ordinary activities before taxation	59
Historical cost profit for the year retained after taxation and dividends	35

2.4 Reconciliation of movements in shareholders' funds

FRS 3 points out that the profit and loss account and the statement of total recognised gains and losses reflect the performance of the company for the period. However, other changes may occur to the shareholders' funds which can be important in understanding the financial position of the company. The reconciliation of movements in shareholders' funds sets out the effect on shareholders' funds of the various changes that occurred during the period, which may include dividends announced and the issue and redemption of shares.

An illustration of this statement is set out in FRS 3 and is reproduced below:

Reconciliation of movements in shareholders' funds 20X3

	£m
Profit for the financial year	29
Dividends	(8)
	21
Other recognised gains and losses relating to the year (net)	1
New share capital subscribed	18
Net addition to shareholders' funds	40
Opening shareholders' funds (originally £375m, before deducting prior year adjustment of £10m)	365
Closing shareholders' funds	405

3   Prior period adjustments

3.1   Routine adjustments

Often adjustments which relate to prior periods are shown in the accounts for the current period. In most cases, these adjustments arise because, in practice, it is necessary to make estimates when preparing accounts. When these estimates turn out to be incorrect, an adjustment is required. These adjustments are dealt with in the profit and loss account of the period in which the need for adjustment is identified and do not represent exceptional or extraordinary items.

A C T I V I T Y **2**

Identify three expense items where estimates have to be made when preparing accounts and where some adjustment may be necessary in future periods.

Feedback to this activity is at the end of the chapter.

3.2   Adjustments made against reserves

In some cases, prior period adjustments should not be passed through the profit and loss account, but instead should be adjusted against the opening balance on retained profits or reserves. This would be appropriate where the adjustment arose from a change in accounting policy or from a fundamental error.

FRS 18 distinguishes a change in accounting policy from a change in estimating techniques, such as a change of depreciation method. These are only adjusted against the opening balance of reserves if they involve a fundamental error, or an accounting standard or legislation requires them to be adjusted in this way. If the effect of a change in estimating techniques has a material effect on the results of a period, details should be disclosed by note.

Changes in accounting policy should not be made lightly as this interferes with comparability. Change is only justified if the new policy provides a fairer presentation of the results of the company than the old policy. Similarly, fundamental errors which may destroy the validity of the published financial statements of prior periods are not expected to be a common event.

FRS 18 contains some examples of changes to assist in understanding the difference between a change of accounting policy and a change in an estimation technique.

In each example, three questions are asked – does the change involve a change to:

- recognition?
- presentation?
- measurement basis?

If the answer to one or more of the questions is 'yes', then the change is to an accounting policy and must be accounted for as a prior period adjustment against opening reserves.

Example 1: Classification of overheads

An entity has previously shown certain overheads within cost of sales. It now proposed to show these overheads within administrative expenses.

Does this involve a change to:

- recognition?   x
- presentation?   ✓
- measurement basis?   x

Explanation – Although there is no change to the recognition and measurement of costs, they are being presented differently.

Conclusion – This is a change of accounting policy.

Example 2: Depreciation of vehicles

An entity has previously depreciated vehicles using the reducing balance method at 40 per cent per year. It now proposes to depreciate vehicles using the straight-line method over five years, since it believes this better reflects the pattern of consumption of economic benefits.

Does this involve a change to:

- recognition?   x
- presentation?   x
- measurement basis?   x

Explanation – Vehicles are being recognised and presented in the same way as before, and using the same, historical cost measurement basis. The only change is to the estimation technique used to measure the unexpired portion of each vehicle's economic benefit.

Conclusion – This is not a change of accounting policy. Paragraph 82 of FRS 15 also states that a change from one method of providing depreciation to another does not constitute a change of accounting policy.

Example 3: Depreciation of vehicles

An entity has previously depreciated vehicles using the reducing balance method at 40 per cent per year. It now proposes to depreciate vehicles using the straight-line method over five years. In addition, it has previously recorded the depreciation charge within cost of sales, but now proposes to include it within administrative expenses.

Does this involve a change to:

- recognition?   x
- presentation?   ✓
- measurement basis?   x

Explanation – This accounting change involves both a change to presentation, as in Example 1, and a change of estimation technique, as in Example 2. For the reasons set out in those examples, the former is a change of accounting policy, but the latter is not.

Conclusion – The two changes are accounted for separately. No change is made to the amount of depreciation charged in earlier periods, but the profit and loss account for the preceding period is restated to move the depreciation charge from cost of sales to administrative expenses.

An illustrative example of movements on the reserves, including prior period adjustments is given in FRS 3 and is reproduced below.

Reserves

	Share premium account	Revaluation reserve	Profit & loss account	Total
	£m	£m	£m	£m
At beginning of year as previously stated	44	200	120	364
Prior year adjustment			(10)	(10)
At beginning of year as restated	44	200	110	354
Premium on issue of shares (nominal value £7m)	11			11
Transfer from profit and loss account of the year			21	21
Decrease in value of trade investment		(3)		(3)
Surplus on property revaluations		4		4
At end of year	55	201	131	387

Note: Nominal share capital at end of year £18m (20X2 £11m).

This chapter concludes your study of company financial statements. It will be helpful now to go back and reread Chapter 14, *Accounting Conventions and Policies*, as many of the points made in that chapter are important for company accounting, especially the provisions of FRS 18.

Conclusion

This is a short but important chapter. When preparing financial statements for examination purposes, you need to read the question carefully to see how far FRS 3 is involved, if at all.

SELF-TEST
QUESTIONS

Profit and loss account format

1   What are the three 'super-exceptional' items defined in FRS 3 and requiring separate disclosure in the profit and loss account? (1.1)

2   How are turnover and expenses to be analysed in the profit and loss account to comply with FRS 3? (1.1)

Additional financial statements and notes

3   What items besides the profit for the financial year may appear in the statement of recognised gains and losses? (2.2)

4   Name two other statements required by FRS 3. (2.3, 2.4)

MULTIPLE-
CHOICE
QUESTION

A company compiles its accounts for the year to 31 March. In May 20X0 the company sold its northern division, making a profit of £4m. The company's trading profit for the year to 31 March 20X0 was £11m, to which the northern division had contributed £3m.

Which of the following treatments of the profit on the sale of the northern division and of its trading results is correct according to FRS 3 *Reporting financial performance*?

	Trading results of northern division in profit and loss account for year ended 31 March 20X0 as:	*Profit on sale of northern division in profit and loss account as an exceptional item separately disclosed for year ended:*
A	Discontinuing activity	31 March 20X0
B	Discontinuing activity	31 March 20X1
C	Part of continuing activities	31 March 20X0
D	Part of continuing activities	31 March 20X1

For the answer to this question, see the 'Answers' section at the end of the book.

EXAM-TYPE
QUESTION

Reporting financial performance

S Limited operates through three divisions and compiles its accounts to 31 March each year. In the year ended 31 March 20X1 one division was sold. The other two were reorganised but continued in operation.

Divisional information for the year ended 31 March 20X1 is given below.

During the year ended 31 March 20X1 the company had interest charges of £80m, tax is estimated at £124m, and a dividend of £120m is proposed.

Prepare the company's profit and loss account for the year ended 31 March 20X1 in accordance with FRS3, so far as is possible from the information provided.

Divisional information for the year ended 31 March 20X1

	Division 1 (Sold during year) £1m	Division 2 £1m	Division 3 £1m
Sales	200	280	1,366
Operating expenses	(182)	(218)	(642)
Reorganisation costs:			
Redundancy costs	(20)	(50)	(20)
Closure costs	(30)	(8)	(6)
Loss on disposal	(160)		
Loss of disposal of assets as a result of reorganisation		(10)	(16)

(15 marks)

For the answer to this question, see the 'Answers' section at the end of the book.

FEEDBACK TO
ACTIVITY **1**

Different elements of the company's activities may differ in respect to stability, risk and predictability. Disclosure of each element separately should give users a better understanding of the results for the period and should help them in deciding the extent to which past results are a guide to the future.

FEEDBACK TO
ACTIVITY **2**

Three examples of such expense items are:

- provision for doubtful debts
- bad debts written off
- provision for depreciation.

Chapter 22
BASIC CONSOLIDATED ACCOUNTS

So far we have been looking at the financial statements of individual companies. In practice, most large companies operate as groups of companies. In its simplest form, a group consists of one company which owns a controlling interest in another. The controlling company is referred to as the **parent company** or **holding company** and the controlled company as its **subsidiary**. The balance sheet combining the two companies is referred to as a **consolidated balance sheet**.

Objectives

By the time you have finished this chapter you should be able to:

- prepare a consolidated balance sheet for a company with one subsidiary

- make appropriate adjustments for goodwill and minority interests

- understand the provisions of the Companies Acts and FRS 2 *Accounting for Subsidiary Undertakings* regarding subsidiaries to be consolidated.

1   What are consolidated accounts?

1.1   Investment and control

When one company invests in another, the investment appears as an asset in its balance sheet and dividends received are credited to profit and loss account. As long as the investment remains a small percentage of the total share capital of the company in which the shares are held, no one would want to quarrel with this treatment.

KEY POINT

When a company owns most or all of another, the two companies can be regarded as a single entity. **Consolidated accounts** are used in this case.

Suppose, however, that the holding represents all or most of the total share capital. Now the investing company is in a position to **control** the other company, and for all practical purposes is entitled to the whole or most of its profit, whether or not these profits are actually paid out in the form of dividends. Also, the increase in value of its assets over the years, reflecting retained profits, accrues ultimately to the investing company.

In these circumstances, the accounting treatment described above does not reflect the true nature of the relationship between the parent company and the subsidiary. In reality, the two companies can be regarded as a single entity because the subsidiary is controlled by the parent. **Consolidated accounts** is the name given to the accounting techniques which seek to reflect the true position, as regards both profits and assets, when one company controls another.

DEFINITIONS

Parent company: a company owning a controlling interest in another.

Subsidiary company: a company which is controlled by a parent company.

Group: a parent company plus its subsidiaries.

Consolidated accounts aggregate the profits and losses of all group's undertakings.

Minority interest: any third company owning a part of a subsidiary.

- **Parent company** – A company owning a controlling interest (e.g. more than 50% of equity) in another.

- **Subsidiary company** – A company which is controlled by a parent company.

- **Group of companies** – A parent company plus its subsidiaries.

- **Consolidated accounts** – Consolidated accounts consist of a **consolidated balance sheet**, in which all assets and liabilities of group undertakings are aggregated, and a **consolidated profit and loss account** aggregating the profits and losses of all group undertakings. (For Paper 1.1 we are concerned only with the consolidated balance sheet.)

- **Minority interest** – If the subsidiary is not wholly owned by the parent, the 'outside' interest is referred to as the 'minority interest'.

2 The basic balance sheet consolidation procedure

2.1 A basic example

P Ltd was incorporated on 1 January 20X1. On 1 January 20X3 it acquired 100% of the ordinary shares in S Ltd which was incorporated on that day. Five years later, on 31 December 20X7, the balance sheets of the two companies were as follows.

P Ltd and S Ltd balance sheets

	P Ltd £	S Ltd £
Fixed assets	10,000	5,000
Investment in S Ltd: 5,000 £1 shares	5,000	
Net current assets	5,000	3,000
	20,000	8,000
Share capital: ordinary shares of £1 each	10,000	5,000
Profit and loss account	10,000	3,000
	20,000	8,000

Prepare a consolidated balance sheet for P Ltd and its subsidiary.

Discussion

Preparing a consolidated balance sheet really means 'adding together' the two balance sheets. In doing so the £5,000 investment in S Ltd appearing in the P Ltd balance sheet is cancelled by the £5,000 share capital in the balance sheet of S Ltd.

ACTIVITY 1   Try to produce your own answer using common sense, then check with our solution.

Feedback to this activity is at the end of the chapter.

It was possible to answer that simple question without proper workings. For more complex questions we need a systematic approach to workings. We begin by looking at the working for goodwill on consolidation.

2.2 Goodwill on consolidation

If the parent pays more for the investment in the subsidiary than the value of the subsidiary's net assets, the difference represents the amount paid for the unrecorded goodwill in the subsidiary.

In the example above, the amount paid for 100% of the shares in S Ltd, £5,000, exactly equalled the net assets of S, and no goodwill arose.

Let us modify the example to illustrate what happens when the amount paid for the shares exceeds the value of the net assets acquired. Our approach is to calculate the net value of the subsidiary's assets on the date it was acquired, which of course is equal to its share capital and accumulated reserves as on that date. We compare this with the amount paid by the parent company, and the difference represents goodwill.

The facts are as above, except that P paid £6,000 for the shares. The balance sheets of the two companies are now as follows:

Balance sheets at 31 December 20X7

	P Ltd	S Ltd
	£	£
Tangible fixed assets	10,000	5,000
Investment in S Ltd: 5,000 £1 shares	6,000	
Net current assets	4,000	3,000
	20,000	8,000
Share capital: ordinary shares of £1 each	10,000	5,000
Profit and loss account	10,000	3,000
	20,000	8,000

The net current assets of P Ltd are reduced by £1,000 to reflect the higher price paid for the shares.

When we set the cost of the investment off against the net assets of the subsidiary, a goodwill balance of £1,000 emerges. (Remember that we calculate the net assets by adding the share capital and reserves. By the balance sheet equation, this total always equals the net assets, and it is usually a simpler calculation than adding all the net assets separately.)

Setting off investment against subsidiary's net assets

	£	£
Cost of investment in S		6,000
Share of net assets acquired		
Share capital	5,000	
Profit and loss account (at acquisition)	nil	
	5,000	
P's interest	100%	5,000
Goodwill on acquisition		£1,000

This is the standard working for goodwill.

The calculation shows that P paid £1,000 more than their net book value for the assets of S. The difference is **goodwill**, defined as the difference between the cost of an entity and the fair value of that entity's net assets.

The calculation above depends on the fact that share capital plus reserves equals net assets. In our example, the reserves of S are nil because P acquired the shares on the day S Ltd was incorporated. S had not had any time to build up reserves.

ACTIVITY 2

Calculate the goodwill arising on acquisition in each of the following cases.

1   P Limited acquired 100% of the shares of T Limited for £126,000, when the net assets of T Limited were valued at £94,000.

2   Q Limited acquired 100% of the shares of V Limited for £250,000. At the time of the acquisition, the share capital and reserves of V Limited were as follows:

	£
Ordinary shares of £1 each	80,000
Share premium	45,000
Profit and loss account reserve	92,000
	217,000

The balance sheet value of the assets of T Limited reflect their fair value.

3   R Limited acquired 75% of the shares of X Limited for £300,000, when the value of the net assets of X Limited was £364,000.

Feedback to this activity is at the end of the chapter.

2.3 Amortisation of goodwill

Goodwill can be described as the additional value obtained from an acquisition over and above the value of the net assets acquired.

This additional value does not last for ever. In other words goodwill does not retain its value. Like other long-term assets, its value erodes over time. It is therefore appropriate to depreciate or amortise goodwill over a number of years after a subsidary has been acquired. When goodwill is amortised:

- The charge for amortisation each year is treated as a expense in the consolidated profits and loss account.

- The value of goodwill in the consolidated balance sheet is its original value minus accumulated amortisation.

In the example above the goodwill on acquisition amounted to £1,000. Look back at the original example and you will see that we are preparing a consolidated balance sheet five years after the acquisition. The goodwill arising at acquisition must be amortised (depreciated) over its estimated economic life, through the consolidated profit and loss account. If we assume a life of ten years for this goodwill, the consolidated balance sheet at 31 December 20X7 will be as follows:

P Ltd and its subsidiary
Consolidated balance sheet as at 31 December 20X7

	£	£
Fixed assets:		
Goodwill	1,000	
Less: amortisation	500	
		500
Sundry		15,000
		15,500
Net current assets		7,000
		22,500
Share capital-ordinary shares of £1 each		10,000
Profit and loss account (10,000 + 3,000-500)		12,500
		22,500

The amortisation through the profit and loss account at £100 per year has reduced the profit and loss reserve balance.

ACTIVITY 3

Peter has prepared a consolidated balance sheet for the AVP Group as at 31 December 20X4 as follows:

	£
Tangible fixed assets	600,000
Goodwill	120,000
Net current assets	80,000
	800,000
Ordinary shares of £1	200,000
Share premium	140,000
Profit and loss reserves	460,000
	800,000

AVP Limited acquired 100% of ZZ Limited on 1 January 20X4 for £260,000, when the fair value of the net assets of ZZ Limited was £140,000. Peter's boss sees that Peter has forgotten to provide for amortisation of the goodwill. Goodwill should be amortised straight line over 10 years.

Required:

Adjust the balance sheet to provide for the amortisation of goodwill.

Feedback to this activity is at the end of the chapter.

2.4   Minority interests

What if a parent company does not buy 100% of the shares in the subsidiary? As long as it owns more than 50%, the company is a subsidiary. If the parent company owns, say, 80% of the ordinary share capital, the holders of the remaining 20% are referred to as the **minority**, or **minority interest**. Total assets and liabilities are shown exactly as before, but a new item representing the minority interest must be introduced into the share capital and reserves of the subsidiary. The minority interest can be calculated by taking the appropriate percentage of the net assets at the balance sheet date, but net assets will again equal share capital plus reserves and it is convenient to calculate the minority interest by dividing up the share capital and reserves. The example below shows the technique.

The facts are as before, but P paid £4,800 for 80% of the share capital of S.

Balance sheets at 31 December 20X7

	P Ltd	S Ltd
	£	£
Fixed assets	10,000	5,000
Investment in S: 4,000 £1 shares	4,800	
Net current assets	5,200	3,000
	20,000	8,000
Share capital: ordinary shares of £1 each	10,000	5,000
Profit and loss account	10,000	3,000
	20,000	8,000

Before calculating the minority interest, let us calculate the goodwill in this example.

Goodwill calculation

	£	£
Cost of investment in S		4,800
Share of net assets acquired:		
Share capital	5,000	
Profit and loss account (as before)	nil	
	5,000	
P's interest	80%	4,000
Goodwill on acquisition		£800

The minority interest

The minority interest is calculated as at the current balance sheet date and not as at acquisition like the goodwill. The calculation is as follows:

Minority interest calculation

	£	£
Net assets of S at the balance sheet date		
Share capital	5,000	
Profit and loss account	3,000	
	8,000	
Minority interest 20%		1,600

The consolidated balance sheet is now as follows:

Consolidated balance sheet

	£	£
Fixed assets		
Goodwill at cost	800	
Amortisation	400	400
Sundry		15,000
		15,400
Net current assets		8,200
		23,600
Share capital – ordinary shares of £1 each		10,000
Profit and loss account 10,000 + (80% × 3,000) – 400		12,000
		22,000
Minority interest		1,600
		23,600

2.5 Pre-acquisition profit

There is one final adjustment to consider. In the examples so far, the subsidiary was acquired at its formation. It had had no chance to trade and earn profits before the acquisition.

If a subsidiary is acquired after its formation and has accumulated some retained profit, only the **post-acquisition** profit may be combined with the parent's profit and loss account balance. The pre-acquisition portion represents assets at the date of acquisition, and so must form part of the calculation of goodwill.

Here is an example to illustrate the adjustment for pre-acquisition profit.

Example

Q Limited acquired 80% of the share capital of T Limited on 1 January 20X1 for £10,000, when the profit and loss account balance of T Limited was £4,000.

At 31 December 20X3, three years later, the companies' balance sheets were as follows:

Balance sheets at 31 December 20X3

	Q Ltd £	T Ltd £
Fixed assets	8,000	11,000
Investment in T at cost	10,000	
Net current assets	4,000	3,000
	22,000	14,000
Ordinary share capital (shares of £1 each)	10,000	5,000
Profit and loss account	12,000	9,000
	22,000	14,000

Goodwill is to be amortised on the straight line basis over five years.

Goodwill calculation

	£	£
Cost of investment in T		10,000
Share of net assets acquired:		
Share capital	5,000	
Profit and loss account	4,000	
	9,000	
Q's interest	80%	7,200
Goodwill on acquisition		2,800
Amortisation $3 \times 20\% = 60\% \times £2,800$		1,680
Balance at 31 December 20X3		1,120

Calculation of minority interest

	£	£
Net assets of T at the balance sheet date		
Share capital	5,000	
Profit and loss account	9,000	
	14,000	
Minority interest 20%		2,800

Calculation of post-acquisition profit

	£
Q Ltd – all	12,000
T Ltd – $80\% \times (9,000 - 4,000)$	4,000
	16,000
Amortisation of goodwill (see working above)	1,680
	£14,320

Q Ltd and its subsidiary
Consolidated balance sheet as at 31 December 20X3

	£
Fixed assets (8,000 + 11,000)	19,000
Goodwill (See working above)	1,120
Net current assets	7,000
	27,120
Share capital	10,000
Profit and loss account (See working above)	14,320
	24,320
Minority interest (See working above)	2,800
	27,120

ACTIVITY 4

The balance sheet of A Limited and B Limited as at 1 May 20X4 were as follows:

	A Limited £	B Limited £
Net fixed assets	100,000	60,000
Net current assets, including cash	180,000	5,000
	280,000	65,000
Ordinary shares of £1	100,000	20,000
Share premium	40,000	15,000
Profit and loss account	140,000	30,000
	280,000	65,000

On 1 May 20X4, A Limited acquired all the shares in B Limited for £80,000 paying for them in cash.

Required:

Prepare a consolidated balance sheet for the A Limited Group immediately after the acquisition has taken place.

Feedback to this activity is at the end of the chapter.

3   The Companies Acts and FRS 2 *Accounting for Subsidiary Undertakings*

The preparation of consolidated financial statements is governed by the Companies Acts and FRS 2 *Accounting for Subsidiary Undertakings*. At this basic level you do not need to study all their detailed requirements. The only provisions requiring study are those defining which companies must be consolidated.

3.1   Requirement to prepare consolidated financial statements

The Companies Act 1985 requires companies with subsidiaries to prepare consolidated financial statements, and states that a company is a subsidiary of another company if that other company:

(a)   holds more than half of its equity share capital (this is the main criterion)

(b)   is a member of the company and has the power to appoint or remove a majority of its directors or controls a majority of the voting rights in the company

(c)   has the right to exercise a dominant influence over the company.

Points (b) and (c) show that control is the vital point, and that it can be exercised in more ways than by ownership of more than half of the share capital.

FRS 2 also contains these requirements.

3.2   Exemptions from consolidation

Both the Companies Act and FRS 2 contain exemptions from the general requirement to consolidate all subsidiaries. The FRS cannot override the Companies Act, but it can and does tighten the requirements.

The main points are summarised below.

(a)   Severe long-term restrictions on control

The Companies Act states that a subsidiary **may** be excluded from consolidation if there are severe long-term restrictions on control. FRS 2 **requires** exclusion on these grounds.

(b) Disproportionate expense or delay

The Companies Act allows exclusion on this ground but FRS 2 rejects this except for non-material subsidiaries.

(c) Investment is held for resale and the company has never been consolidated

If shares in a subsidiary are held temporarily, the Companies Act **allows** its exclusion.

Once again FRS 2 **requires** exclusion.

(d) Different activities

The Companies Act requires exclusion if the activities of parent and subsidiary are so different that the true and fair view of the group as a whole would be impaired if they were consolidated.

As this is a requirement under the Companies Act, FRS 2 has to accept it, but stipulates that it should be applied only in exceptional circumstances.

3.3   Exemption from the obligation to prepare consolidated financial statements

In addition to the grounds for exemption of single subsidiaries explained in section 3.2, a parent company can be exempted from preparing consolidated financial statements at all if any of the following conditions are met:

(a) The size of the group (as measured in the consolidated financial statements) is below the medium-sized limits in the Companies Act:

   (i)   turnover not exceeding £22.8m (previously £11.2m)

   (ii) balance sheet total not exceeding £11.4m (previously £5.6m)

   (iii) average number of employees not exceeding 250.

   The exemption applies if the company is within any two of these three limits. The limits apply to financial years ending on or after 30 January 2004. The previous limits are shown in brackets.

(b) The parent is itself a wholly owned subsidiary of another European Union company which prepares consolidated financial statements for the whole group.

(c) The parent is a majority owned subsidiary of an EU company and the minority shareholders have not requested consolidated financial statements.

All of these exemptions are in FRS 2 also.

The exemption from preparing consolidated accounts is not available to:

(i)   public companies

(ii)   banking and insurance companies

(iii) authorised persons under the Financial Services Act 1986

(iv)   companies belonging to a group containing a member of the above classes of undertaking.

SELF-TEST
QUESTIONS

Balance sheet consolidation procedure

1   How is goodwill calculated? (2.2)

2   What is the required treatment for purchased goodwill? (2.3)

3   Why must a distinction be drawn between a subsidiary's pre-acquisition and post-acquisition reserves? (2.5)

The Companies Acts and FRS 2 *Accounting for subsidiary undertakings*

4   What are the conditions making a company the subsidiary of another? (3.1)

5   What are the grounds exempting a subsidiary from consolidation? (3.2)

6   In what circumstances is a parent company not required to prepare consolidated financial statements? (3.3)

MULTIPLE-
CHOICE
QUESTIONS

Question 1

At 1 January 20X1 H Ltd acquired 80% of the share capital of S for £160,000. At that date the share capital of S consisted of 100,000 ordinary shares of £1 each and its reserves were £40,000. Goodwill on acquisition of subsidiaries is amortised on the straight line basis over five years.

In the consolidated balance sheet of H and its subsidiary S at 31 December 20X3 the amount appearing for goodwill should be:

A   £16,000

B   £19,200

C   £28,800

D   £4,000

Questions 2

At 1 January 20X1 H Ltd acquired 60% of the share capital of S for £180,000. At that date the share capital of S consisted of 200,000 shares of 50p each. The reserves of H and S are:

	At 1 Jan 20X1 £	At 31 Dec 20X3 £
H	280,000	340,000
S	50,000	180,000

In the consolidated balance sheet of H and its subsidiary S at 31 December 20X3, what amount should appear for the minority interest in S?

A   £92,000

B   £280,000

C   £152,000

D   £112,000

Question 3

H Ltd acquired 75% of the share capital of S for £280,000 on 1 January 20X1. Goodwill arising on consolidation has been fully amortised. Details of the share capital and reserves of S are as follows:

	At 1 Jan 20X1 £	At 31 Dec 20X7 £
Share capital	200,000	200,000
Profit and loss account reserve	120,000	180,000

H Ltd's reserves at 31 December 20X7 are £480,000.

What figure should appear in the consolidated balance sheet of H and S for the profit and loss account reserve at 31 December 20X7?

A   £530,000
B   £525,000
C   £485,000
D   £575,000

Question 1: Park Ltd and Gate Ltd

The balances below relate to Park Ltd and Gate Ltd at 31 December 20X4.

Park Ltd acquired its shares in Gate Ltd on 31 December 20X3.

Prepare the consolidated balance sheet of the group at 31 December 20X4. Goodwill should be amortised over five years on the straight line basis.

(15 marks)

Park Ltd and Gate Ltd

	Park Ltd £	Gate Ltd £
Freehold property, net of depreciation	-	99,000
Other fixed assets, net of depreciation	182,300	35,000
48,000 shares in Gate Ltd at cost	72,000	-
Current assets	62,100	68,000
	316,400	202,000
Issued share capital (£1 ordinary shares)	200,000	80,000
Retained profits at 31 December 20X3	45,100	37,500
Profit for 20X4	17,600	28,500
Unsecured loan repayable 20X8	-	30,000
Current liabilities	53,700	26,000
	316,400	202,000

Question 2: Redan Ltd and Pyrton Ltd

On 1 July 20X4, Redan Ltd acquired 70% of the ordinary share capital of Pyrton Ltd for £140,000. At that date Pyrton Ltd had a profit and loss account of £50,000.

The balance sheets below have been prepared at 30 June 20X8.

You are required to prepare the consolidated balance sheet of Redan Ltd and its subsidiary as at 30 June 20X8. Goodwill is amortised over five years on the straight line basis. **(10 marks)**

Redan Ltd and Pyrton Ltd

	Redan Ltd £	Redan Ltd £	Pyrton Ltd £	Pyrton Ltd £
Fixed assets:				
Tangible assets		190,000		170,000
Investments: shares in Pyrton		140,000		
		330,000		
Current assets	270,000		186,000	
Creditors: amount falling due within one year	225,000		137,000	
Net current assets		45,000		49,000
Total assets less current liabilities		375,000		219,000

Capital and reserves:		
Called up share capital:		
Ordinary shares of £1 each	200,000	130,000
Profit and loss account	175,000	89,000
	375,000	219,000

For the answers to these questions, see the 'Answers' section at the end of the book.

FEEDBACK TO ACTIVITY 1

Your solution should have been as follows:

The effect of the consolidation has really been to extend the balance sheet of the parent company. The investment in the subsidiary has been replaced by the underlying net assets of the subsidiary. The £3,000 increase in value of the assets since acquisition is represented by the £3,000 post-acquisition reserves of S, which are combined with those of P in the consolidated balance sheet.

Note that the share capital of the subsidiary company *never* appears as part of the figure of the share capital in the consolidated balance sheet.

P Ltd and its subsidiary
Consolidated balance sheet as at 31 December 20X7

	£
Fixed assets	15,000
Net current assets	8,000
	23,000
Share capital	10,000
Profit and loss account	13,000
	23,000

FEEDBACK TO ACTIVITY 2

1 £32,000 (£126,000 – £94,000)

2 £33,000 (£250,000 – £217,000)

3 Value of net assets acquired

= 75% of £364,000 = £273,000

So goodwill = £300,000 – £273,000

= £27,000

FEEDBACK TO ACTIVITY 3

Amortisation of goodwill for the year should be £120,000/10 = £12,000

Corrected consolidated balance sheet:

	£
Tangible fixed assets	600,000
Goodwill (120,000–12,000)	108,000
Net current assets	80,000
	788,000
Ordinary share of £1	200,000
Share premium	140,000
Profit and loss reserves	448,000
(460,000–12,000)	788,000

Goodwill = £80,000 – £65,000 = £15,000

A Limited Group
Consolidated balance sheet

	£
Net fixed assets (100,000 + 60,000)	160,000
Goodwill	15,000
Net current assets (180,000 – 80,000 + 5,000)	<u>105,000</u>
	<u>280,000</u>
Ordinary shares of £1 (A Ltd only)	100,000
Share premium (A Ltd only)	40,000
Profit and loss account	<u>140,000</u>
(exclude pre-acquisition profits of B Ltd)	<u>280,000</u>

Chapter 23

CASH FLOW STATEMENTS

Large companies are required by FRS 1 to include a cash flow statement in their financial statements. The cash flow statement is given the same importance as the profit and loss account and balance sheet.

Smaller companies are encouraged to produce a cash flow statement as it provides useful additional information to the users of accounts.

Objectives

By the time you have finished this chapter you should be able to:

- classify cash flows into appropriate headings
- prepare a cash flow statement from various data sources
- understand the link between profits and cash
- comment on the advantages of a cash flow statement to the user of accounts.

1 Cash flow statements

1.1 Profit versus liquidity

The accounting concepts of accruals and matching are used to compute a profit figure which shows the additional wealth created for the owners of the business during an accounting period. However, it is important for a business to generate cash as well as making profits. The two do not necessarily go hand in hand.

Profit represents the increase in net assets in a business during an accounting period. The increase in net assets may take the form of additional cash resources, or it may be tied up in other (less liquid) assets. For example:

- fixed assets may have been purchased
- there may be an increased amount of debtors
- there may be increased investment in stock
- the liabilities of the business may have decreased, i.e. more cash has been spent this year in paying off creditors more quickly than was the case last year.

We can reconcile profit to cash in an accounting period by taking into account these and other factors. This reconciliation is examined in detail later in the chapter.

1.2 The need for a cash flow statement

A cash flow statement is needed as a consequence of the differences between profits and cash. It helps to:

- provide additional information on business activities
- assess the current liquidity of the business
- allow the user to see the major types of cash flows into and out of the business
- estimate future cash flows
- determine cash flows generated from trading transactions as opposed to other sources of cash flows.

1.3 Outline of the requirements of FRS 1 *Cash flow statements*

FRS 1: *Cash flow statements* requires large companies to include a cash flow statement in their accounts. Smaller entities are encouraged to produce the statement as well.

KEY POINT

Increased profit may not mean increased cash. The additional assets may be in some other, less liquid form.

A cash flow statement can be presented in a number of ways. A cash flow statement is simply a summary of the cash receipts and payments of a business. Thus a summarised cash book would be one (very simple) form of cash flow statement.

FRS 1, however, requires a cash flow statement to be presented using standard headings. The objective of the standard headings is to ensure that cash flows are reported in a form that highlights the significant components of cash flow and facilitates comparison of the cash flow performance of different businesses.

The standard headings shown in the statement are as follows:

- cash flow from operating activities
- returns on investments and servicing of finance
- taxation
- capital expenditure
- equity dividends paid
- management of liquid resources
- financing.

The figure at the bottom is the resultant increase or decrease in cash during the accounting period.

Cash includes cash in hand, plus deposits in the bank which are repayable on demand, less overdrafts repayable on demand.

The illustrative cash flow statement from FRS 1 is shown below, with some minor changes to try to ease understanding.

Study the items in conjunction with the explanatory notes which follow the statement. The numbers to the left refer to the explanatory notes.

Cash flow statement for the year ended 31 December 20X0

		£000	£000
1	Net cash inflow from operating activities		6,889
2	Returns on investments and servicing of finance		
	Interest received	2,911	
	Dividends received	100	
	Interest paid	(12)	
			2,999
3	Taxation		(2,922)
4	Capital expenditure		
	Payments to acquire:		
	Intangible fixed assets	(71)	
	Tangible fixed assets	(1,496)	
	Proceeds from sale of tangible fixed assets	42	
			(1,525)
			5,441
5	Equity dividends paid		(2,417)
			3,024
6	Management of liquid resources		
	Purchase of current asset investment		(450)
7	Financing		
	Issue of ordinary share capital	206	
	Redemption of debentures	(149)	
			57
8	Increase in cash		2,631

9   Reconciliation of operating profit to net cash
        inflow from operating activities

	£000	£000
Operating profit		6,022
Depreciation charges		899
Increase in stocks		(194)
Increase in debtors		(72)
Increase in creditors		234
Net cash inflow from operating activities		6,889

Explanatory notes

1   *Net cash inflow from operating activities*

The cash flow statement opens with the cash inflow from operations, calculated in the reconciliation with operating profit (see note 9 below).

2   *Returns on investments and servicing of finance*

The main item here is likely to be interest paid on borrowings. Dividends and interest received are netted off, but ordinary dividends *paid* appear later in the statement.

3   *Taxation*

The cash flow statement deals with cash received and paid, so this item is likely to be mainly the corporation tax liability for the previous year, paid in the current year.

4   *Capital expenditure*

This is the cash paid out during the year to buy tangible and intangible assets. The cash inflow from the **proceeds of sale** of assets sold also appears here.

5   *Equity dividends paid*

The equity dividends *paid* in the year appear here. These are likely to be last year's final dividend plus this year's interim dividend.

Dividends paid would be regarded as being part of servicing of a company's finance, but when FRS 1 was revised in 1996 this separate heading was introduced, the reason being that dividends paid are more discretionary than interest. Note that preference dividends are shown as part of servicing of finance. It is only ordinary (equity) dividends paid which appear under this separate heading.

6   *Management of liquid resources*

Under this heading we show movement in 'current asset investments held as readily disposable stores of value'. To qualify, the investments must be readily disposable without curtailing or disrupting the company's business and readily convertible into known amounts of cash at or close to its carrying amount. Movements in any investments not meeting both these conditions will have to appear instead under capital expenditure.

7   *Financing*

Typical items appearing here are the proceeds of the issue of shares or new long-term borrowings and also any repayments of loans or redemptions of shares or debentures.

8   *Increase (or decrease) in cash*

This is the final balance of the cash flow statement and shows the increase or decrease in cash during the period covered by the cash flow statement. Only cash balances and overdrafts repayable on demand may be included. Movements in short-term investments will appear under **Management of liquid resources** if they qualify.

9　*Reconciliation of operating profit to net cash inflow from operating activities*

In a note to the cash flow statement, we show how the operating cash flow of £6,889 can be reconciled with the operating profit. You will find it convenient to prepare this note before doing the cash flow statement itself.

The reconciliation opens with the operating profit of £6,022. We have to add on the depreciation because this is a non-cash expense.

We then adjust for the movements during the year in the operating assets and liabilities – stock, debtors and creditors.

These items are explained in section 2.2 below.

Notice the use of brackets here and throughout the cash flow statement. Inflows or pluses are shown without brackets, while outflows or minuses are in brackets.

Study the format and the notes explaining the items until it becomes familiar to you.

2　Preparation of a cash flow statement

2.1　Direct and indirect methods

Figures for the cash flow statement will be derived either from the accounting records or from the other financial accounting statements – the balance sheets for the current period and the previous period and the profit and loss account for the period.

The item requiring most work will often be the net cash flow from operating activities. The two alternative methods of calculation are shown below:

Direct method		*Indirect method*	
	£000		£000
Cash received from customers	15,424	Operating profit	6,022
Cash payments to suppliers	(5,824)	Depreciation charges	899
Cash paid to and on behalf of employees	(2,200)		
Other cash payments	(511)	Increase in stocks	(194)
		Increase in debtors	(72)
		Increase in creditors	234
Net cash inflow from operating activities	6,889		6,889

DEFINITION

Direct method: records the gross trading cash flows.
Indirect method: makes adjustments to profit.

The **direct method** is so called because it records the gross trading cash flows. The **indirect method** starts with profit and adjusts for the non-cash expense of depreciation (added to profit) and for the movements in working capital items.

The information for the direct method could be found in the accounting records or derived from the other financial statements. The information for the indirect method is found in the other financial statements. For example, we shall need to calculate the operating cash flow from the profit, as shown in the example below.

Example of calculations using the indirect method

The summarised balance sheets of Grasmere Ltd at 31 December 20X4 and 20X5 were as follows:

Grasmere Ltd

	20X4 £	20X5 £
Plant and machinery, at cost	15,000	16,500
Less: Depreciation	8,000	10,000
	7,000	6,500
Stock	20,000	23,500
Debtors	10,000	15,000
Cash	5,000	2,000
	42,000	47,000
Share capital	20,000	20,000
Reserves	17,000	21,000
Creditors	5,000	6,000
	42,000	47,000

No fixed assets have been sold during the period under review. Depreciation provided for the year amounted to £2,000. There is no interest paid, dividends paid or taxation paid.

You are required to prepare a cash flow statement for the year ended 31 December 20X5.

Discussion

Examination questions usually present two balance sheets like this, from which you are to prepare a cash flow statement. At first sight there may seem to be no connection between the balance sheets and the company's cash flows, but there is. Take the first item in these balance sheets – the plant and machinery. The cost has risen from £15,000 to £16,500. This must mean that £1,500 has been spent on new plant during the year, a cash outflow of £1,500 under investing activities. All the other differences between the opening and closing balances are various types of cash flow, or are otherwise required to produce the cash flow statement.

Using the indirect method, we need to calculate the operating cash flow by adjusting the profit figure for non-cash expenses like depreciation and for the movements in the working capital items stock, debtors and creditors. FRS 1 requires us to show the reconciliation of operating profit and operating cash flow as a note to the cash flow statement.

If a question gives you a profit and loss account you obviously have the operating profit figure. If you only have the balance sheets, it is still possible to calculate operating profit, by using the increase in the retained profit (£21,000 minus £17,000, i.e. £4,000) and adding back dividends, tax and interest paid to arrive at operating profit. In the simplified Grasmere situation there are no dividends, tax or interest, and the operating profit must be £4,000.

A possible way of preparing a cash flow statement from examination-style information is to begin by setting up a format consisting of the five headings number (1) to (5) in the specimen layout that you met at the start of this chapter, leaving plenty of space between them. Then go through the given balance sheets from the top entering the differences in the correct positions in the format.

You will also need a format for the reconciliation of operating profit to net cash inflow or outflow from operating activities. The analysis of changes in net debt can be added at the end if it is asked for.

Try to produce Grasmere's cash flow statement before looking at the answer below.

(As there is no tax or dividends, the movement in reserves per the balance sheets represents operating profit for the year.)

Feedback to this activity is at the end of the chapter.

The example shows the important information that can be directly given by a cash flow statement. Despite making a profit of £4,000 in the period, the business has suffered a £3,000 reduction in cash. This is largely due to the amount of profit tied up in increased working capital (stock, debtors, less creditors).

2.2   Reconciliation of profit and cash flow

The main categories of items in the profit and loss account and on a balance sheet, which form part of the reconciliation between operating profit and net cash flow from operating activities are listed below.

Depreciation

Depreciation is a book write-off of capital expenditure. Capital expenditure will be recorded under 'capital expenditure and financial investment' at the time of the cash outflow. Depreciation therefore represents an addition to operating profit in deriving cash flow.

Profit/loss on disposal of fixed asset

The cash inflow from a sale is recorded under 'capital expenditure'. As a consequence any profit or loss on a disposal included within operating profit needs to be removed. An alternative name for loss on sale is 'depreciation under provided on disposal'; thus, like depreciation, a loss is added to operating profit. A profit on sale is a deduction from operating profit. (Following the issue of FRS 3 *Reporting Financial Performance*, profits and losses on disposal are unlikely to be included in operating profit, but are normally disclosed as exceptional items on the face of the profit and loss account.)

Balance sheet change in debtors

A sale creates income irrespective of the date of cash receipt. If the cash has not been received by the balance sheet date however, there is no cash inflow from operating activities for the current accounting period. Similarly, opening debtors represent sales of a previous accounting period most of which will be cash receipts in the current period.

The change between opening and closing debtors will thus represent the adjustment required to move from operating profit to net cash inflow:

- An increase in debtors is a deduction from operating profit. The company is owed more and thus has less cash.

- A decrease in debtors is an addition to operating profit.

Balance sheet change in stocks

Stock at the balance sheet date represents a purchase which has not actually been charged against current operating profits. As, however, cash was spent on its purchase or a creditor incurred, it does represent an actual or potential cash outflow.

Balance sheet change in creditors

If creditors are greater at the end of the year than at the beginning, the company must have more cash:

- An increase in creditors between two balance sheet dates is an addition to operating profit in calculating cash flow
- A decrease in creditors is a deduction from operating profit.

A further example

The balance sheets of Fox Limited as at 31 December were as follows:

Fox Limited

	20X8		20X7	
	£000	£000	£000	£000
Fixed assets				
Freehold property (as revalued)		22,000		12,000
Plant and machinery				
Cost	10,000		5,000	
Aggregate depreciation	2,250	7,750	2,000	3,000
		29,750		15,000
Trade investment at cost		-		7,000
		29,750		22,000
Current assets				
Stock	16,000		11,000	
Debtors	9,950		2,700	
Cash	-		1,300	
	25,950		15,000	
Less:				
Creditors: amounts falling due within one year				
Trade creditors	(8,000)		(11,000)	
Bank overdraft	(11,700)	6,250	-	4,000
Total assets less current liabilities		36,000		26,000
Less:				
Creditors: amounts falling due after more than one year				
10% debentures		(6,000)		(10,000)
		30,000		16,000
Called up share capital		16,000		14,000
Revaluation reserve		4,000		-
Profit and loss account		10,000		2,000
		30,000		16,000

Notes

- At the beginning of the year machinery, which had cost £1,000,000, and which had a book value of £250,000, was sold for £350,000.
- In addition to the interest on the debentures, interest paid on the overdraft amounted to £800,000.
- £4,000,000 of debentures were redeemed on 31 December 20X8.
- The trade investment was sold for £10,000,000 during the year. No dividends were received from it.

You are required to prepare a cash flow statement for the company for the year ended 31 December 20X8 complying with the requirements of FRS 1.

Discussion

With this question we meet a new problem – sales of fixed assets. It is now not possible to calculate all the figures needed from the balance sheets without some further workings. The clue to this is that further information is given below the balance sheet. In the case of fixed asset sales, three working ledger accounts will be needed:

- fixed asset – cost
- fixed asset – aggregate depreciation
- fixed asset – disposal.

The technique is to enter the opening and closing balances from the balance sheets, then record the additional information given in the notes below the balance sheet. Note that a double entry is required for all additional information – either an entry between two working accounts or an entry between one working and the cash flow statement. In using these three working accounts you are simply reconstructing the fixed asset accounts as they would be in the underlying records.

Solution

Fox Ltd
Cash flow statement for the year ended
31 December 20X8

	£000
Operating profit (W4)	6,800
Depreciation charges (W2)	1,000
Profit on sale of plant (W3)	(100)
Increase in stocks	(5,000)
Increase in debtors	(7,250)
Decrease in creditors	(3,000)
Net cash outflow from operating activities	(7,550)

Cash flow statement

	£000	£000
Net cash outflow from operating activities		(7,550)
Returns on investments and servicing of finance		
Interest paid (800 + 1,000)		(1,800)
Capital expenditure		
Payments to acquire tangible fixed assets:		
Plant and machinery (W1)	(6,000)	
Freehold property (10,000 – 4,000)	(6,000)	
Receipts from sale of investments	10,000	
Receipts from sale of plant	350	(1,650)
		(11,000)
Financing		
Issue of ordinary share capital	2,000	
Redemption of debentures	(4,000)	(2,000)
Reduction in cash (1,300 + 11,700)		(13,000)

Workings

(W1)   Plant and machinery – cost

	£000		£000
Balance b/d	5,000	Transfer – disposal	1,000
Additions during year			
(balancing figure)	6,000	Balance c/d	10,000
	11,000		11,000

(W2)   Plant and machinery – aggregate depreciation

	£000		£000
Depreciation: disposals		Balance b/d	2,000
during year £(1,000 –	750		
250)			
		Depreciation provided for	
Balance c/d	2,250	year (bal fig)	1,000
	3,000		3,000

(W3)   Plant and machinery – disposal

	£		£
Cost of disposals	1,000	Depreciation on disposals	750
Profit on sale	100	Sale proceeds	350
	1,100		1,100

(W4)   Calculation of operating profit

	£000
Profit for year (10,000 – 2,000)	8,000
Profit on sale of trade investment	(3,000)
Interest paid (800 + 1,000)	1,800
	6,800

That was quite a difficult example. Points to note are:

- In the calculation of the operating profit (W4) the retained profit has increased by £8,000,000. To calculate operating profit it is necessary to deduct the profit on sale of the trade investment and to add back the interest, which is shown separately in the cash flow statement under **Returns on investments and servicing of finance.**

- In the workings necessary to calculate the movement on the fixed assets, the opening and closing balances for cost and aggregate depreciation were first entered. Then from Note 1 to the question, we inserted the transfers from those accounts for the disposal. The balancing figure on the cost account is then the additions during the year, and the balance on the depreciation account is the depreciation charge for the year. Finally, in the disposal account, the inclusion of the sale proceeds allows us to calculate the profit on the sale which has to be eliminated from the profit in the reconciliation of profit and cash flow.

- The fact that the debentures were redeemed at the end of the year means that debenture interest at 10% must have been paid on the whole £10,000,000.

2.3   Example of calculations using direct method

As previously stated, gross cash flows from operating activities can be used to compute net cash flow from operating activities. The gross cash flows can be derived from:

- the accounting records of the entity by totalling the cash receipts and payments directly, or
- the opening and closing balance sheets and profit and loss account for the year by constructing summary control accounts for:
    - sales (to derive cash received from customers)
    - purchases (to derive cash payments to suppliers)
    - wages (to derive cash paid to and on behalf of employees).

2.4   Example using control accounts

The balance sheets of a business are:

Balance sheets

	Last year £	This year £
Fixed assets	153,364	149,364
Stocks	-	-
Debtors	265,840	346,000
Cash	-	165,166
Creditors	(219,204)	(318,890)
	200,000	341,640
Share capital	200,000	200,000
Reserves	-	141,640
	200,000	341,640

Extracts from the profit and loss account for the year are:

Profit and loss account

	£	£
Sales		1,589,447
Cost of sales		
Purchases (no stocks)	1,021,830	
Wages and salaries	145,900	
Depreciation	84,000	
		(1,251,730)
Administration		
Purchases	96,077	
Salaries	100,000	
		(196,077)
Operating profit and retained profit for the year		141,640

Additional information

1   Creditors consist of:

	Last year £	This year £
Creditors from purchases ledger		
Re fixed assets	-	46,000
Other	210,564	258,240
PAYE/NI creditor	8,640	14,650

2   Purchase invoices relating to fixed assets totalling £80,000 have been posted to the purchases ledger during the year.

Prepare the cash flow statement showing gross cash flow from operating activities and a note reconciling operating profit to net cash inflow from operating activities.

Solution

Cash flow statement

	£
Operating activities	
Cash received from customers (W1)	1,509,287
Cash payments to suppliers (W2)	(1,070,231)
Cash paid to and on behalf of employees (W3)	(239,890)
Net cash inflow from operating activities	199,166
Capital expenditure	
Purchase of fixed assets (W4)	(34,000)
Increase in cash	165,166

Workings

(W1)   **Sales ledger control**

	£		£
Balance b/d – Debtors	265,840	Cash receipts (balancing fig)	1,509,287
Sales	1,589,447	Balance c/d – Debtors	346,000
	1,855,287		1,855,287

(W2)   Purchases ledger control (excluding fixed asset purchases)

	£		£
Cash paid (bal fig)	1,070,231	Balance b/d – Creditors	210,564
Balance c/d	258,240	Purchases	
		Cost of sales	1,021,830
		Administration	96,077
	1,328,471		1,328,471

Note. Information relating to fixed assets is not included in the purchases ledger control account above in order to compute cash paid to suppliers of operating costs.

(W3)   **Wages control**

	£		£
Net wages and PAYE/NI		Balance b/d	
paid (bal fig)	239,890	PAYE and NI	8,640
		Cost of sales	145,900
Balance c/d PAYE and	14,650	Administration	100,000
NI			
	254,540		254,540

(W4)   **Fixed asset expenditure**

	£		£
Balance b/d	153,364	Depreciation charge	84,000
Addition (bal fig)	80,000	Balance c/d	149,364
	233,364		233,364

Cash paid for fixed assets is $80,000 - 46,000 = £34,000$. The £80,000 invoices agrees with the movement in fixed assets per the balance sheets.

Note. If gross cash flows from operating activities had not been requested, net cash inflow from operating activities could have been derived from operating profit as follows:

**Reconciliation of operating profit to net cash inflow
from operating activities**

	£
Operating profit	141,640
Depreciation charges	84,000
Increase in stock	-
Increase in debtors	(80,160)
Increase in creditors (excluding fixed asset creditors)	53,686
	199,166

This disclosure note is required in any case, so it may be helpful to do it anyway, both to help you with the calculation of the gross cash flows and to enable you to balance the remainder of the statement.

2.5　How to approach an examination question

In this section we will work through an examination question to show you the approach that you should take.

The summarised financial statements of Charlton Ltd are as follows:

Balance sheets at 31 December

	20X5	20X6
	£	£
Fixed assets (net book value)	40,406	47,759
Stock	27,200	30,918
Debtors	15,132	18,363
Bank	4,016	2,124
	86,754	99,164
Share capital	40,000	50,000
Share premium	8,000	10,000
Profit and loss account	13,533	16,748
Debenture stock	10,000	-
Creditors	3,621	10,416
Taxation	5,200	6,000
Proposed dividend	6,400	6,000
	86,754	99,164

Profit and loss account for the year ended 31 December 20X6

	£	£
Trading profit (after charging depreciation of £2,363 and interest of £900)		17,215
Taxation		6,000
Profit after tax		11,215
Dividends		
Paid	2,000	
Proposed	6,000	
		8,000
Retained profit		3,215
Balance b/d		13,533
Balance c/d		16,748

An item of machinery with a net book value of £1,195 was sold for £1,614. The depreciation charge of £2,363 does not include the profit/loss on the sale of the fixed asset.

You are required to prepare a cash flow statement for the year ended 31 December 20X6.

Solution

The steps of your solution should be as follows:

1 Allocate a page to the cash flow statement so that easily identifiable cash flows can be inserted. Use a separate page if the main statement is likely to be long. Allocate a further page to workings.

2 Go through the balance sheets and take the balance sheet movements to the cash flow statement, the reconciliation note or to workings as appropriate. Tick off the information in the balance sheets once it has been used.

3 Go through the additional information provided and deal with it as in Step 2.

4 The amounts transferred to workings can now be reconciled so that the remaining cash flows can be inserted on the statement or in the profit reconciliation note.

5 The profit reconciliation note can now be totalled, the operating cash flow transferred to the cash flow statement and the cash flow statement completed.

Cash flow statement for the year ended 31 December 20X6

	£	£
Net cash inflow from operating activities		19,905
Returns on investments and servicing of finance		
Interest paid	(900)	
Net cash outflow from servicing of finance		(900)
Tax paid (W2)		(5,200)
Capital expenditure		
Payments to acquire tangible fixed assets (W1)	(10,911)	
Receipts from sales of tangible fixed assets	1,614	
Net cash outflow from capital expenditure		(9,297)
		4,508
Equity dividends paid (W3)		(8,400)
Net cash outflow before financing		(3,892)
Financing		
Issue of shares (10,000 + 2,000)	12,000	
Redemption of debentures	(10,000)	
Net cash inflow from financing		2,000
Decrease in cash		(1,892)

Reconciliation of operating profit to net cash inflow from operating activities

	£
Operating profit (17,215 + 900)	18,115
Depreciation charge	2,363
Profit on sale of fixed asset (W1)	(419)
Increase in stocks	(3,718)
Increase in debtors	(3,231)
Increase in creditors (10,416 − 3,621)	6,795
Net cash inflow from operating activities	19,905

Workings

(W1a)   **Fixed assets – NBV**

	£		£
Balance b/d	40,406	Fixed assets disposal	1,195
Bank (bal fig)	10,911	Depreciation (profit and loss)	2,363
		Balance c/d	47,759
	51,317		51,317

Note. The above account summarises the balances and transactions relating to fixed assets during the year. It was necessary to combine fixed asset cost and fixed asset depreciation in one account because only the net book values were given.

The account is required in order to derive the expenditure on fixed assets for the year.

(W1b)   **Fixed assets disposal**

	£		£
Fixed assets – NBV	1,195	Bank	1,614
Profit on sale (profit and loss)	419		
	1,614		1,614

(W2)   **Taxation**

	£		£
Bank (bal fig)	5,200	Balance b/d	5,200
Balance c/d	6,000	Profit and loss	6,000
	11,200		11,200

Note. The taxation paid in the year has been last year's charge. Often there will be a change from last year's estimate and thus a ledger account will derive the correct figure paid.

(W3)   **Dividends**

	£		£
Bank (bal fig)	8,400	Balance b/d	6,400
Balance c/d	6,000	Profit and loss	8,000
	14,400		14,400

Note. The dividends paid this year will be:

- last year's proposed
- this year's interim.

This question is probably harder than any you will get in the examination. All of the problems in it could arise, but it is unlikely that they will all arise in one question.

3   Interpretation using the cash flow statement

The next chapter deals with the interpretation of financial statements, using ratios largely based on the profit and loss account and balance sheet. To conclude this chapter on cash flow statements we shall review the information users may derive from the cash flow statement.

3.1   Objective of FRS 1

The objective of FRS 1 is to ensure that companies within its scope:

- report the cash generation and cash absorption for a period, highlighting the different components of cash flow in a way that facilitates comparison of the cash flow performance of different businesses

- provide information that assists in the assessment of their liquidity, solvency and financial adaptability.

3.2   Information revealed by the cash flow statement

The cash flow statement will reveal:

- whether the overall activities reveal a positive cash flow

- whether the operating activities yield a positive cash flow

- the manner in which the capital expenditure has been financed (for example, whether it has come from internally-generated resources, borrowings, issues of shares or from the cash balances).

3.3   An appraisal of the requirements of FRS 1

FRS 1 does not apply to all companies and therefore it could be argued that it is given less importance as a result. However small companies are encouraged to adopt its requirements.

The formats of a cash flow statement are strictly laid down by the standard. This has the advantage of assisting comparability between companies. However, there may be different interpretations between companies as to the items to be included in the various definitions.

It is important to refer to notes accompanying a cash flow statement, as non-cash transactions may be significant in an accounting period and notes should show information on these.

Conclusion

This chapter has concentrated on the computational techniques involved in the preparation of a cash flow statement. If such a question comes up in the examination, you should find that most of the marks are fairly easy to obtain. Practice on the examples in the chapter will result in the FRS 1 format becoming second nature.

Do not ignore, however, the possibility of a written question. The information above will be useful in this regard.

SELF-TEST QUESTIONS

Cash flow statements

1   What are the standard headings in a cash flow statement? (1.3)

2   What are the main categories of items to adjust profit for in order to arrive at net cash flow from operating activities? (1.3)

Preparation of a cash flow statement

3   Is an increase in stocks a deduction from or addition to operating profit. (2.2)

4   Is a decrease in creditors a deduction from or addition to operating profit. (2.2)

---

5   Is a decrease in debtors a deduction from or addition to operating profit. (2.2)

6   Are receipts from the sale of fixed assets an investing activity or a financing activity? (2.2)

7   Is a surplus on the revaluation of property included in the cash flow statement? (2.2)

8   Under the direct method do wages paid include PAYE paid? (2.3)

FRS 1 *Cash Flow Statements* requires the cash flow statement to be accompanied by a note reconciling operating profit to net operating cash flow.

Which of the following lists consists only of items which could appear in such a reconciliation?

A   Depreciation, increase in debtors, decrease in creditors, interest paid, increase in stocks.

B   Increase in creditors, decrease in stocks, profit on sale of plant, depreciation, decrease in debtors.

C   Increase in creditors, equity dividends paid, depreciation, decrease in debtors, increase in stocks.

D   Depreciation, interest paid, equity dividends paid, decrease in stocks.

For the answer to this question, see the 'Answers' section at the end of the book.

Question 1: Bogdanovitch plc

The summarised financial statements of Bogdanovitch plc are as follows.

Balance sheet as at 31 December

	20X8		20X9	
	£	£	£	£
Fixed assets:				
Plant and machinery		2,086		2,103
Fixtures and fittings		1,381		1,296
		3,467		3,399
Current assets:				
Stock	1,292		1,952	
Debtors	1,763		2,086	
Cash	197		512	
		3,252		4,550
Creditors: amounts falling due within one year:				
Proposed dividends	132		154	
Taxation	257		312	
Trade creditors	899		903	
		(1,288)		(1,369)
		5,431		6,580
Capital and reserves:				
Share capital		4,200		4,500
Share premium		800		900
Profit and loss account		431		1,180
		5,431		6,580

Profit and loss account for year ended 31 December 20X9

	£	£
Profit before taxation		1,381
Taxation		310
Profit after taxation		1,071
Less dividends:		
Paid	168	
Proposed	154	
		322
Retained profit		749
Profit and loss account b/f		431
Profit and loss account c/f		1,180

You are informed that:

- plant and machinery with a net book value of £184 was disposed of for £203, whilst a new item of plant was purchased for £312

- fixtures and fittings with a net book value of £100 were disposed of for £95. Depreciation provided on fixtures and fittings amounted to £351.

You are required to prepare a cash flow statement for the year ended 31 December 20X9. **(20 marks)**

Question 2: Algernon Ltd

You are given below, in summarised form, the accounts of Algernon Ltd for 20X6 and 20X7:

Algernon Ltd

	20X6			20X7		
	Balance sheet			Balance sheet		
	Cost	Dep'n	Net	Cost	Dep'n	Net
	£	£	£	£	£	£
Plant	10,000	4,000	6,000	11,000	5,000	6,000
Buildings	50,000	10,000	40,000	90,000	11,000	79,000
			46,000			85,000
Investments at cost			50,000			80,000
Land			43,000			63,000
Stock			55,000			65,000
Debtors			40,000			50,000
Bank			3,000			–
			237,000			343,000
Ordinary shares of £1 each			40,000			50,000
Share premium			12,000			14,000
Revaluation reserve (land)			-			20,000
Profit and loss account			25,000			25,000
10% debentures			100,000			150,000
Creditors			40,000			60,000
Proposed dividend			20,000			20,000
Bank			-			4,000
			237,000			343,000

	20X6 Profit and loss account	20X7 Profit and loss account
	£	£
Sales	200,000	200,000
Cost of sales	100,000	120,000
	100,000	80,000
Expenses	50,000	47,000
	50,000	33,000
Interest	10,000	13,000
Dividends	20,000	20,000
	20,000	-
Balance b/f	5,000	25,000
Balance c/f	25,000	25,000

You are required:

(a) To prepare a cash flow statement for Algernon Ltd for 20X7, to explain as far as possible the movement in the bank balance. The cash flow statement should show gross cash flows from operating activities.

(10 marks)

(b) Using the summarised accounts given, and the statement you have just prepared, comment on the position, progress and direction of Algernon Ltd.

(8 marks)

(Total: 18 marks)

EXAM-TYPE
QUESTION

Crash Ltd

Prepare a cash flow statement for Crash Ltd for the year ended 31 March 20X6 using the indirect method, complying as far as possible with the requirements of FRS 1 *Cash Flow Statements*.

The balance sheets and notes are given below.   **(10 marks)**

Notes

1 Fixed assets

During the year fixed assets, which had cost £1,500,000 and which had a book value of £300,000 at 31 March 20X5, were sold for £375,000.

Land acquired in 20X2 was revalued upwards by £750,000 in preparing the balance sheet at 31 March 20X6.

2 Debentures

Interest is due half-yearly on 30 September and 31 March and was paid on the due dates.

The company repaid £750,000 debentures on 31 March 20X6.

3 Profit and dividends

Profit before interest for the year ended 31 March 20X6 was £555,000. No dividends were paid during the year.

4 Ignore taxation

The balance sheets of Crash Limited
at 31 March 20X6 and 31 March 20X5

	31 March 20X5		31 March 20X6	
	£000	£000	£000	£000
Fixed assets (Note 1)				
Cost or valuation	9,000		10,950	
Accumulated depreciation	(3,300)	5,700	(3,600)	7,350
Current assets				
Stock	1,215		1,350	
Debtors	1,350		1,290	
Cash	60		105	
	2,625		2,745	
Less current liabilities				
Trade creditors	(990)		(1,080)	
Bank overdraft	(195)		(270)	
	(1,185)		(1,350)	
Net current assets		1,440		1,395
		7,140		8,745
Less: 10% debentures		(1,500)		(750)
		5,640		7,995
Called up share capital		2,250		3,000
Share premium account		750		1,200
Revaluation reserve		-		750
Profit and loss account		2,640		3,045
		5,640		7,995

For the answers to these questions, see the 'Answers' section at the end of the book.

**FEEDBACK TO
ACTIVITY 1**

Your solution should have been as follows:

Grasmere Ltd Cash flow statement for the year ended
31 December 20X5

	£
Operating profit for the year (21,000 – 17,000)	4,000
Depreciation (10,000 – 8,000)	2,000
Increase in stock	(3,500)
Increase in debtors	(5,000)
Increase in creditors	1,000
Net cash outflow from operating activities	(1,500)

Cash flow statement

	£
Net cash outflow from operating activities (working)	(1,500)
Capital expenditure: payments to acquire fixed assets	(1,500)
Decrease in cash	(3,000)

Chapter 24
INTERPRETATION OF FINANCIAL STATEMENTS

Financial statements are prepared not as an end in themselves but in order that users can use them to make decisions. The financial statements therefore need to be interpreted. The calculation of ratios allows the relationships between different parts of the financial statements to be more clearly seen.

Objectives

By the time you have finished this chapter you should be able to:

- calculate accounting ratios
- interpret the ratios
- suggest possible reasons for the results obtained.

1   Analysis of accounting statements and use of ratios

1.1   Information relevant to each user group

The various users of financial statements require information for quite different purposes. There are a large number of ratios, not all of which will be relevant to a particular situation. It is therefore important to determine the precise information needs of the user, and the decisions he has to take after analysing the relevant information.

The needs of the three main users may be summarised as follows:

User	Needs information for
Management	Control of costs, improved profitability
Lenders	Borrowing and credit purposes
Shareholders and investment analysts	Investment decisions – buying and selling shares

KEY POINT

Key questions on use of information:
- What decision is being made?
- What information is relevant to that decision?

In order to identify what information a particular user needs, you can ask 'What decision is being made?' and 'What information is relevant to that decision?'

1.2   The shortcomings of interpretation

For many users, the main function of the financial statements is to aid decisions relating to the future. However, the financial statements are historical in nature: they describe what has happened in the period just ended. This is not necessarily a good indication of what may happen in the future. There is thus a significant shortcoming in any interpretation as to its effectiveness in estimating the future.

Even if the needs of the user are more concerned with historical stewardship of the business, there are limitations of interpretation, as the information presented to the user is of necessity summarised. The summarisation process may have the effect of distorting the nature of some of the information. For example, creditors will be classified into those payable within one year and those payable beyond one year. Two loans which have two days difference in their payment date may well as a consequence be classified under separate headings. The user, unless he is provided with further information, will tend to take the two resultant totals at face value.

Finally, it should be noted that the emphasis on information produced by an undertaking is financial. In many cases, non-financial data would be useful in order to see a complete picture of the state of the organisation. Non-financial data includes, for example, the number of employees in the organisation and the type of skills they possess, or indicators of efficiency with which the organisation addresses complaints from customers.

1.3   Why financial statements should be understandable

A user needs to understand information in order to draw valid conclusions from it. He needs to understand the basis upon which it is prepared and this is an area where the accountant can advise the user.

Understanding the information presented will allow the user to determine when more information is required, i.e. what information is missing. Also, the user may need to re-analyse the data so that it is relevant to his particular needs. Financial information is presented in a certain way in order to satisfy a range of user needs and therefore it follows that it may need to be adapted for certain specific needs.

1.4   The major techniques of interpretation

The syllabus at this level of accounting emphasises the use of ratios to interpret information but this is only one stage in the interpretation process. A most important first step is to understand the environment in which the business operates.

Factors that need to be considered include the following.

Markets in which the business operates

Consideration must be given to the growth opportunities in the market. Is it a new and expanding market or is there an expectation that the market is contracting? It is far easier to make profits in a market which is expanding than in one which is contracting.

General economic conditions

The state of the economy in which the business operates will affect the ability of the business to make sales. If the economy is in recession, then it will be harder for a business which sells goods to the public to make profits.

Size of business in relation to competitors

The success or failure of a business can be related to its size relative to its competitors in the market. In some markets it is necessary to be large in order to benefit from economies of scale such as advertising branded products. Other markets may suit small units of operation which can be more flexible to the needs of customers.

In the context of examination questions much of this information is not available, so in this chapter we will start at the calculation stage of ratios.

KEY POINT

When calculating ratios:
- calculate only those ratios relevant to the user
- state the definitions used.

When calculating ratios, the two main points to bear in mind are as follows.

- calculate only those ratios which are relevant to the needs of the user
- state the definitions used.

Some ratios can be calculated in different ways and therefore it is important to define the terms used.

Having calculated the ratios, the results must be analysed. Consideration needs to be given to such matters as these:

- If a ratio has been computed over a number of time periods, does it show a worsening or an improving situation?
- Can the ratio be compared to an objective standard? That is, can it be compared with an 'ideal' ratio?
- Do all the ratios when taken together support the conclusions drawn from each individual ratio?

The final stage of interpretation is the critical review.

The limitations of the data used to calculate the ratios must be considered so that a prudent overall conclusion can be reached.

1.5   The technique of ratio analysis and its potential shortcomings

KEY POINT

Ratios allow us to compare:
- with previous years
- with the same year (budgeted or planned)
- with other businesses.

The information gathered by calculating ratios will allow comparisons with:

- the performance of the business in previous years
- the budgeted or planned performance in the current year
- the performance of similar businesses.

The ratios themselves do not tell one what to do, but they do help to point one in the right direction. Ratios should, therefore, make it easier to make better decisions.

It must be emphasised that accounting ratios are only a means to an end; they are not an end in themselves. By comparing the relationship between figures, they merely highlight significant features or trends in the accounts. Indeed, they may well create more problems than they solve. The real art of interpreting accounts lies in defining the reasons for the features and fluctuations disclosed. To do this effectively, you may need more information and a deeper insight into the affairs of the business. You also need to bear in mind the following points:

- The date at which the accounts are drawn up. Accurate information can only be obtained with any degree of certainty from up-to-date figures. Furthermore, seasonal variations in the particular trade should be taken into account. Final accounts tend to be drawn up at the end of seasonal trade when the picture they present is of the business at its strongest point financially.

- The accuracy of the position shown in the balance sheet. The arrangement of certain matters can be misleading and present a more favourable picture, e.g. such 'window-dressing' operations as:

  – making a special effort to collect debts just before the year-end in order to show a larger cash balance and lower debtors than is normal

  – ordering goods to be delivered just after the year-end so that stocks and creditors can be kept as low as possible.

- Interim accounts. Whenever possible, interested parties should examine accounts prepared on a monthly basis, as a clearer picture of the trends and fluctuations will emerge from these than from the annual financial statements.

- Accounting ratios are based on accounting information and are, therefore, only as accurate as the underlying accounting information. At a time, as at present, when traditional accounting procedures are coming in for heavy criticism, students should remember that ratios based on those procedures can be easily criticised.

- The accounting ratios of one company must be compared with those of another similar company in order to draw meaningful conclusions. These conclusions will only be valid if that other company's trade is similar.

2   Using ratios

2.1   Types of ratios

Ratios fall into several groups, the relevance of particular ratios depending on the purpose for which they are required. The groups to be considered here are as follows:

- operating ratios

- short-term liquidity ratios

- working capital efficiency

- medium and long-term solvency ratios

- investor ratios.

Illustration

The above ratios will be illustrated by reference to the following financial statements:

Summarised balance sheets at 30 June

	20X7		20X6	
	£000	£000	£000	£000
Fixed assets (net book value)		130		139
Current assets:				
Stock	42		37	
Debtors	29		23	
Bank	3		5	
	74		65	
Creditors: amounts falling due within one year:				
Trade creditors	36		55	
Taxation	10		10	
	46		65	
Net current assets		28		-
Total assets less current liabilities		158		139
Creditors: amounts falling due beyond one year:				
5% secured loan stock		40		40
		118		99
Ordinary share capital (50p shares)		35		35
8% Preference shares (£1 shares)		25		25
Share premium account		17		17
Revaluation reserve		10		-
Profit and loss account		31		22
		118		99

Summarised profit and loss account for the year ended 30 June

	20X7 £000	20X7 £000	20X6 £000	20X6 £000
Sales		209		196
Opening stock	37		29	
Purchases	162		159	
	199		188	
Closing stock	42		37	
		157		151
Gross profit		52		45
Interest	2		2	
Depreciation	9		9	
Sundry expenses	14		11	
		25		22
Net profit		27		23
Taxation		10		10
Net profit after taxation		17		13
Dividends:				
Ordinary shares	6		5	
Preference shares	2		2	
		8		7
Retained profit		9		6

2.2   The ratios which primarily measure profitability

There are several ratios which attempt to assess the profitability of a business. These are most conveniently expressed in percentage form and include those listed below.

The gross profit percentage

DEFINITION

The **gross profit percentage:** Gross profit is expressed as a percentage of sales.

Gross profit is expressed as a percentage of sales, i.e.:

$$\text{Gross profit percentage} = \frac{\text{Profit}}{\text{Sales}} \times 100$$

This is a very popular ratio and is used by even the smallest of businesses. In the illustration the ratios for the two years are as follows:

Example	*20X7*	*20X6*
Gross profit percentage	$\frac{52}{209} \times 100 = 24.9\%$	$\frac{45}{196} \times 100 = 23.0\%$

What can be learned from these figures? Clearly, the gross profit percentage has improved, but it is not known why. Nor is it obvious whether these figures are better or worse than those which would be expected in a similar type of business. Before coming to definite conclusions one would need further information. For example, most businesses sell a wide range of products, usually with different gross profit percentages (or profit margins). It may be that in 20X7 the **sales mix** changed and that a larger proportion of items with a high profit percentage were sold, thus increasing the overall gross profit percentage of the business.

It is relevant to consider the change in sales at this point. This is measured by:

$$\text{Percentage growth in sales} = \frac{\text{Sales this year} - \text{Sales last year}}{\text{Sales last year}} \times 100$$

Example

$$\text{Percentage change in sales} = \frac{209 - 196}{196} \times 100 = 6.6\%$$

This is probably not a significant increase.

Net profit as a percentage of sales

This ratio is defined as:

$$\frac{\text{Net profit}}{\text{Sales}} \times 100$$

Example	*20X7*	*20X6*
Net profit as % sales	$\dfrac{27}{209} \times 100 = 12.9\%$	$\dfrac{23}{196} \times 100 = 11.7\%$

What conclusions can be drawn from this apparent improvement? Very few! Since net profit equals gross profit less expenses, it would be useful to tabulate, for each of the two years, the various expenses and express them as a percentage of sales. A suitable tabulation might be:

Expenses as a percentage of sales

	20X7		*20X6*	
	£000	%	£000	%
Sales	209	100.0	196	100.0
Cost of sales	157	75.1	151	77.0
Gross profit	52	24.9	45	23.0
Interest	(2)	(1.0)	(2)	(1.1)
Depreciation	(9)	(4.3)	(9)	(4.6)
Sundry expenses	(14)	(6.7)	(11)	(5.6)
Net profit	27	12.9	23	11.7

Given a detailed trading and profit and loss account, the above type of summary could be very useful. Care must be taken in interpreting the results, particularly since sales (£) are used as the denominator. An increase in sales (£) could be due to a combination of price and quantity effects.

Return on capital employed (ROCE)

This is an important ratio as it relates profit to the capital invested in a business. Finance for a business is only available at a cost – loan stock finance requires interest payments and further finance from shareholders requires either the immediate payment of dividends or the expectation of higher dividends in the future. Therefore a business needs to maximise the profits per £ of capital employed.

Owing to its importance the ROCE is sometimes referred to as the **primary ratio**.

There are several ways of measuring ROCE, but the essential point is to relate the profit figure used to its capital base. In other words, the profit figure shown at the top of the fraction must relate to the sources of finance shown at the bottom. As an example, if the profit figure chosen is the profit available to ordinary shareholders (i.e. the profit after payment of loan interest and preference dividends), then the bottom line of the fraction must be the funds provided by the ordinary shareholders, namely ordinary share capital plus reserves.

Total capital employed in the business

$$\text{ROCE (1)} = \frac{\text{Profit before interest and tax}}{\text{Share capital} + \text{Reserves} + \text{Long term liabilities}} \times 100$$

The denominator in this version of the ratio could alternatively be calculated as total assets less current liabilities.

Equity shareholders' capital employed

$$\text{ROCE (2)} = \frac{\text{Profit after interest and preference dividend but before tax}}{\text{Ordinary share capital} + \text{Reserves}} \times 100$$

Points to note:

- The interest referred to is the interest payable on the long-term liabilities. Any interest on short-term liabilities, such as a bank overdraft, is deducted from the profit, i.e. the numerator and the denominator must be computed on a consistent basis.

- The denominator in this second version of the ratio could alternatively be calculated as net assets less preference shares.

- Although it is better to base the calculation on average capital employed during the year, the calculation is often based on year-end capital employed (because there is insufficient data for all years to compute an average).

ACTIVITY 1

Calculate ROCE for 20X6 and 20X7 using each of these alternatives and comment on the results of your calculations.

Feedback to this activity is at the end of the chapter.

2.3   Structure of operating ratios

Various ratios are related to each other as is illustrated in the following figure:

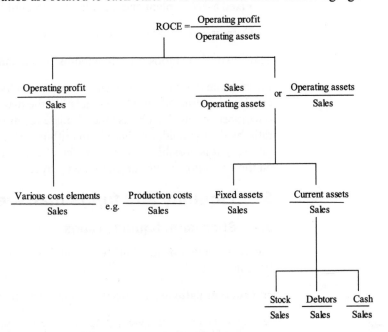

2.4   Factors affecting return on capital employed

There are two factors relevant here:

- profitability of sales
- rate of asset utilisation.

The product of these two gives the return on capital employed:

$$\frac{\text{Operating profit}}{\text{Sales}} \times \frac{\text{Sales}}{\text{Operating assets}} = \frac{\text{Operating profit}}{\text{Operating assets}} = \text{ROCE}$$

In the example for 20X7:

$$\frac{\text{Operating profit}}{\text{Sales}} = \frac{£29,000}{£209,000} = 13.9\%$$

$$\frac{\text{Sales}}{\text{Operating assets}} = \frac{£209,000}{£158,000} = 1.32$$

Note

$13.9\% \times 1.32 \times 100 = 18.3\%$, i.e. ROCE subject to a rounding difference.

2.5 Factors affecting operating profit/sales

This ratio may be subdivided as far as detail in our profit and loss account permits, since:

$$\frac{\text{Operating assets}}{\text{Sales}} + \frac{\text{Cost elements}}{\text{Sales}} = 1$$

Cost elements may include production, marketing, distribution, administration and so on.

2.6 Factors affecting operating assets/sales

In the first place, operating assets may be subdivided into fixed and current assets, since:

$$\frac{\text{Operating assets}}{\text{Sales}} = \frac{\text{Fixed assets}}{\text{Sales}} + \frac{\text{Current assets}}{\text{Sales}}$$

Each of these may be appropriately subdivided, e.g.:

Fixed assets = plant and machinery + freehold land + etc.

Current assets = stock + debtors + cash + etc.

Thus, two of the ratios give the months' stock and debtors carried by the company.

From the analysis it becomes clear that the subdivision of the key ratio, return on capital employed, is limited only by the detail in the data available. The important point to remember is that in each case the ultimate result is directly related to each individual ratio by the pyramid, i.e. there is an arithmetical relationship between all the pyramid ratios, so it is possible to determine the effect that a change in one of the ratios will have on the key ratio – return on capital employed.

3   Liquidity and funds management

3.1   Short-term liquidity ratios

The two main ratios for short-term liquidity are the current ratio and the liquidity (or quick) ratio.

DEFINITION

The **current ratio** is assets/liabilities.

The **current ratio** is the ratio of current assets to current liabilities, i.e.:

$$\text{Current ratio} = \frac{\text{Current assets}}{\text{Current liabilities}}$$

In the case of our example, the ratios for the two years are:

Example	*20X7*	*20X6*
Current ratio	$\dfrac{74}{46} = 1.61$	$\dfrac{65}{65} = 1.0$

The current ratio is sometimes referred to as the working capital ratio.

DEFINITION

The **liquid** (or **quick**) **ratio** is assets (less stock)/ liabilities.

The **liquid (or quick) ratio** is the ratio of current assets, excluding stock, to current liabilities, i.e.:

$$\text{Quick ratio} = \frac{\text{Current assets (less stock)}}{\text{Current liabilities}}$$

In the case of our example, the ratios for the two years are:

Example	*20X7*	*20X6*
Liquid (quick) ratio	$\dfrac{32}{46} = 0.7$	$\dfrac{28}{65} = 0.43$

Both of these ratios show a strengthening.

The extent of the change between the two years seems surprising and would require further investigation.

It would also be useful to know how these ratios compare with those of a similar business, since typical ratios for supermarkets are quite different from those for heavy engineering firms.

What can be said is that in 20X7 the current liabilities were well covered by current assets. Liabilities payable in the near future (creditors), however, are only half covered by cash and debtors (a liquid asset, close to cash).

Conventional wisdom has it that an ideal current ratio is 2 and an ideal quick ratio is 1. It is very tempting to draw definite conclusions from limited information or to say that the current ratio *should* be 2, or that the liquid ratio *should* be 1. However, this is not very meaningful without taking into account the type of ratio expected in a similar business.

It should also be noted that a high current or liquid ratio is not necessarily a good thing. It may indicate that working capital is not being used efficiently. The next group of ratios can help to identify whether or not this is the case.

3.2 Elements of working capital

It is necessary to consider three ratios concerned with current assets and current liabilities:

Stock turnover ratio

Companies have to strike a balance between being able to satisfy customers' requirements out of stock and the cost of having too much capital tied up in stock.

DEFINITION

The **stock turnover ratio** is the cost of sales divided by the average level of stock during the year.

The stock turnover ratio is the cost of sales divided by the average level of stock during the year, i.e.:

$$\text{Stock turnover ratio} = \frac{\text{Cost of sales}}{\text{Average stock level}}$$

For our example, the figures are as follows:

Example	*20X7*	*20X6*
Stock turnover ratio	$\dfrac{157}{1/2(37 + 42)} = 4.0$ times pa	$\dfrac{151}{1/2(29 + 37)} = 4.6$ times pa

The stock turnover ratio has fallen.

Note

The average of opening and closing stocks is used here, but examination questions frequently do not provide the opening stock figure and the *closing* stock has to be taken instead of the average stock. In any case, the average of opening and closing stock will not necessarily give the true average level of stock during the year if the stock fluctuates a lot from month to month.

Unless the nature of the business is known, it is not possible to say whether either 4.6 or 4.0 is satisfactory or unsatisfactory. A jeweller will have a low stock turnover ratio, but a fishmonger selling fresh fish should have a very high turnover ratio.

An alternative calculation of the stock turnover ratio is to show the result in days. The calculation is as follows:

$$\text{Stock turnover ratio} = \frac{\text{Average stock during the accounting period}}{\text{Cost of sales}} \times 365$$

Where 365 days is the length of accounting period.

So, for our example, the periods are:

Example	*20X7*	*20X6*
Stock turnover ratio	$\dfrac{(37 + 42)/2}{157} \times 365 = 92$ days	$\dfrac{(29 + 37)/2}{151} \times 365 = 80$ days

Debt collection period (or average period of credit allowed to customers)

Businesses which sell goods on credit terms specify a credit period. Failure to send out invoices on time or to follow up late payers will have an adverse effect on the cash flow of the business.

The quickest way to compute the debt collection period is to use the formula:

$$\frac{\text{Closing trade debtors}}{\text{Credit sales for year}} \times 365$$

Example	*20X7*	*20X6*
Debt collection period	$\dfrac{29,000}{209,000} \times 365 = 50.6$ days	$\dfrac{23,000}{196,000} \times 365 = 42.8$ days

Both of these levels are good. A level of 60 days is normally taken as a reasonable practical target. Nevertheless, the collection period has worsened and an investigation to discover the cause is needed. The increase could be the result of poorer credit control, or inadequate procedures to check up on new customers.

In interpreting this ratio, remember that if the trade is seasonal, it may be unusually high or low for this reason. The balance sheet date in our example is 30 June, and if sales peaked in May and June, the ratio would necessarily be higher.

Average period of credit allowed by suppliers

This is a similar calculation to that for trade debtors, showing the period of credit taken by the business from its suppliers. The calculation is:

$$\frac{\text{Closing trade creditors}}{\text{Credit purchases for year}} \times 365$$

This gives us:

	20X7	*20X6*
Example		
Creditor payment period	$\frac{36,000}{162,000} \times 365 = 81.1$ days	$\frac{55,000}{159,000} \times 365 = 126.3$ days

The average period of credit allowed has fallen substantially from last year. It is, however, in absolute terms still a high figure.

Often, suppliers request payment within thirty days. The company is taking nearly three months. Trade creditors are thus financing much of the working capital requirements of the business which is beneficial to the company.

However, there are three potential disadvantages of extending the credit period:

- Future supplies may be endangered.
- Possibility of cash discounts is lost.
- Suppliers may quote a higher price for the goods knowing the extended credit taken by the company.

3.3 The working capital cycle

The investment made in working capital is largely a function of sales and, therefore, it is useful to consider the problem in terms of a firm's working capital (or **cash operating**) cycle, which is illustrated in the figure below.

The cycle reflects a firm's investment in working capital as it moves through the production process towards sales. The investment in working capital gradually increases, firstly being only in raw materials, but then in labour and overhead as production progresses. This investment must be maintained throughout the production process, the finished goods holding period, and up to the final collection of cash from trade debtors. Note that the net investment can be reduced by taking trade credit from suppliers.

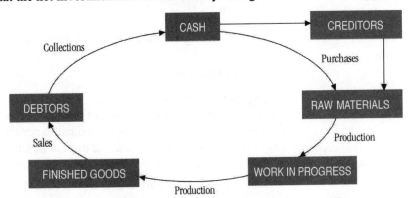

The faster a firm can 'push' items around the operating cycle, the lower its investment in working capital will be. However, too little investment in working capital can lose sales since customers will generally prefer to buy from suppliers who are prepared to extend trade credit, and if items are not held in stock when required by customers, sales may be lost.

With some fairly basic financial information, it is possible to measure the length of the working capital cycle for a given firm.

Example

The table below shows extracts from the profit and loss account for the year and the balance sheet as at the end of the year for a company. Assume all sales and purchases are on credit terms and calculate the working capital cycle.

Profit and loss account and balance sheet extracts

	£
Sales	250,000
Cost of goods sold	210,000
Purchases	140,000
Debtors	31,250
Creditors	21,000
Stock	92,500

Solution

Creditors

$$\text{Average payment collection period} = \left(365 \times \frac{\text{Creditors}}{\text{Purchases}}\right)$$

$$= 365 \times \frac{21}{140} = 55 \text{ days}$$

Debtors

$$\text{Average collection period} = \left(365 \times \frac{\text{Debtors}}{\text{Sales}}\right)$$

$$= 365 \times \frac{31.25}{250} = 46 \text{ days}$$

Stock turnover

$$= 365 \times \frac{\text{Stock}}{\text{Cost of goods sold}}$$

$$= 365 \times \frac{92.5}{210} = 161 \text{ days}$$

Length of working capital cycle = 152 days (46 + 161 − 55).

3.4 Overtrading

An expanding business may find itself short of working capital. If increased sales on credit are made, receivables rise and the business is likely to have difficulty in finding the cash to pay suppliers, wages and other expenses as it has to wait for customers to pay. The term 'overtrading' may be used to describe the condition of such a business. Several steps are available to remedy the situation:

- obtain a bank overdraft to smooth out cash flows

- issue extra shares to increase cash resources or, for a sole trader or partnership, have the owners introduce more capital

- make longer term borrowings, again to increase cash resources

- negotiate longer credit terms from major suppliers

- sell non-trading assets such as investments

- offer customers discounts for prompt payment

- try to make cash sales as well as credit sales.

Movements in accounting ratios or figures in the balance sheet can indicate overtrading. Points to look for include:

- deterioration in quick ratio or current ratio

- overdraft at or near its limit

- increase in trade payables as payments to suppliers are delayed

- increase in sales revenue and trade receivables.

3.5   Medium and long-term solvency ratios

Consider the various forms of long-term finance. The table below lists their priorities as regards the distribution of profits and repayment on liquidation. These priorities will be specified in the articles of association.

Source of finance	Priority in relation to profit	Priority on liquidation
Secured loan stock (debentures)	Interest must be paid whether or not the company makes a profit.	Secured by a fixed or floating charge – first claim on assets.
Unsecured loan stock	Interest must be paid whether or not the company makes a profit.	Ranks as unsecured creditor.
Preference share capital (assumed non-participating)	If the company makes a profit, the preference dividend has a priority over the ordinary dividend.	Cannot be repaid until all liabilities have been met. Has priority over ordinary shareholders.
Ordinary share capital	Dividends paid after debenture interest and fixed preference dividends have been paid.	Ranks behind all the above but usually entitled to surplus assets in a liquidation.

The various ratios can now be considered.

Gearing

Gearing is a very important concept in interpreting financial statements. It refers to the proportion of a company's total capital provided by loan capital as opposed to equity. The higher the proportion of loan capital, the more vulnerable a company is to a downturn in profits. This is because the interest on the loan has to be paid regardless of the level of profit. There are various methods of measuring a company's gearing; we begin by looking at the ratio of debt to equity.

Debt to equity ratio

This ratio shows the relationship between debt and equity. A ratio of 1 means that debt and equity are equal. Below 1, debt is less than equity; above 1, debt exceeds equity. Preference shares are regarded as equivalent to loans, and the equity interest must include all reserves as well as the share capital itself.

The debt to equity ratios in our example are as follows:

Example	*20X7*	*20X6*
Debt to equity ratio	$\dfrac{25 + 40}{118 - 25} = 0.699$	$\dfrac{25 + 40}{99 - 25} = 0.878$

Precisely when a company becomes highly geared is hard to define, and will vary from industry to industry. In the UK, a level of debt exceeding half the share capital, could probably be taken as a rough guide to the onset of medium to high gearing. (This means a debt to equity ratio of 0.5.)

Total gearing

This is the measure of gearing preferred by most accountants, and shows the percentage of total capital represented by loans.

Example	*20X7*	*20X6*
Total gearing	$\left(\dfrac{25+40}{118+40}\right) \times 100 = 41.1\%$	$\left(\dfrac{25+40}{99+40}\right) \times 100 = 46.8\%$

Applying the same criterion as that suggested above, medium/high gearing could be said to begin when the percentage exceeds 33 $^1/_3$%.

3.6 The advantages and disadvantages of raising finance by issuing debentures

Gearing may have an important effect on the distribution of profits. For example, consider two companies with the same profit record but different capital structures. The return of the ordinary shareholders can vary considerably.

Gearing comparison of companies A and B

	A Ltd £	B Ltd £
Capital structure:		
10% Loan stock	20,000	-
Ordinary share capital and reserves	10,000	30,000
	30,000	30,000
Therefore, gearing		
	Highly geared	No gearing
Year 1 Profits £4,000 before interest		
∴ Returns:		
10% Interest	2,000	-
Ordinary shares – balance	2,000	4,000
	4,000	4,000
Year 2 Profits double to £8,000 before interest		
∴ Returns:		
10% Interest	2,000	-
Ordinary shares – balance	6,000	8,000
	8,000	8,000
Therefore, increase in return to ordinary shareholders	3 times	2 times

Thus, the doubling of the profits in year 2 has the effect of tripling the return to the equity shareholders in the highly-geared company. The effect would be even more dramatic if the profits fell below £2,000 because then there would be no return at all to the ordinary shareholders in A Ltd. Thus an investment in ordinary shares in a highly-geared company is a far more speculative investment than a purchase of ordinary shares in a low-geared company.

3.7 Interest cover

Interest on loan stock (debenture stock) must be paid whether or not the company makes a profit. The ratio emphasises the cover (or security) for the interest by relating profit before interest and tax to interest paid.

Example	*20X7*	*20X6*
Interest cover	$\dfrac{29}{2} = 14.5$ times	$\dfrac{25}{2} = 12.5$ times

From the point of view of medium and long-term solvency, the company is in a strong position as regards the payment of interest. Profit would have to drop considerably before any problem arose in paying interest.

4   Ratios for investment appraisal

4.1   Information required by investors

Investors are interested in the income earned by the company for them and the return on their investment (the income earned related to the market price of the investment).

An investor in ordinary shares can look to the earnings of the company available to pay the ordinary dividend or to the actual ordinary dividend paid as a measure of the income earned by the company for him. The ratios he would compute in each case would be:

For dividends:

● dividend per share

● times covered

● dividend yield.

For earnings:

● earnings per share

● price earnings ratio.

Suppose that the company in the illustration is quoted on the Stock Exchange and that the market value of each ordinary share is 204 pence.

Dividend per share

This relates to ordinary shares and is calculated as follows:

$$\text{Dividend per share} = \frac{\text{Dividend paid}}{\text{Number of shares}}$$

Example	*20X7*	*20X6*
Dividend per share	$\frac{£6,000}{70,000} = 8.6\text{p per share}$	$\frac{£5,000}{70,000} = 7.1\text{p per share}$

Dividend cover

This is calculated by dividing profit available for ordinary shareholders by the dividend for the year (i.e. interim plus final) as follows:

$$\text{Dividend cover} = \frac{\text{Profit} - \text{Payment to preference shareholders}}{\text{Dividend paid}}$$

Example	*20X7*	*20X6*
Dividend cover	$\frac{£17,000 - £2,000}{£6,000}$	$\frac{£13,000 - £2,000}{£5,000}$
	$= 2.5 \text{ times}$	$= 2.2 \text{ times}$

Note that the profits available for ordinary shareholders are after the deduction of the preference dividend. The cover represents the 'security' for the ordinary dividend – in this company the cover is reasonable.

Dividend yield

This expresses dividend per share as a percentage of the current share price. The net yield at today's date is as follows:

$$\frac{8.6p}{204p} \times 100 = 4.2\%$$

Earnings per share (EPS)

When a company pays a dividend, the directors take many factors into account, including the need to retain profits for future expansion. Earnings per share looks at the profits which could in theory be paid to each ordinary shareholder.

Earnings are profits after tax and preference dividends, but before ordinary dividends. The denominator is the number of equity shares in issue during the accounting period:

$$\text{Earnings per share} = \frac{\text{Profit} - \text{Payment to preference shareholders}}{\text{Number of shares}}$$

FRS 14 requires earnings per share to be disclosed on the face of the profit and loss account of quoted companies.

Example	20X7	20X6
Earnings per share (EPS)	$\dfrac{£17,000 - £2,000}{70,000}$ $= 21.4p$ per share	$\dfrac{£13,000 - £2,000}{70,000}$ $= 15.7p$ per share

Price earnings ratio (P/E ratio)

This is regarded by many as the most important ratio. It expresses the current share price (market value) as a multiple of the earnings per share. For 20X7, the price earnings ratio is as follows.

$$\frac{204p}{21.4p} = 9.5$$

The ratio of 9.5 implies that if the current rate of EPS is maintained it will take nine and a half years to repay the cost of investing. The higher the PE ratio the longer the payback period. Thus we could conclude that the lower the PE ratio, the better investment it is. However, this is not generally the case. High PE ratios are generally viewed as better than low ones.

The apparent paradox is resolved if the forward looking nature of stock exchange investments is considered. The PE ratio is based on *current* EPS but the stock market is pricing the share on expectations of *future* EPS. If the market considers that a company has significant growth prospects, the market price of the share will rise.

Earnings yield

This term is not often referred to these days. It expresses the earnings per share as a percentage of the current share price, i.e.:

$$\text{Earnings yield} = \frac{21.4p}{204p} \times 100 = 10.5\%$$

It is merely the reciprocal of the PE ratio:

$$\frac{1}{\text{PE ratio}} = \text{Earnings yield}$$

$$\frac{1}{9.5} = 0.105, \text{ i.e. } 10.5\%$$

5   Appraising the position and prospects of a business

5.1   Introduction

Interpretation of accounts is a difficult area for which to prepare, as a wide variety of situations can be encountered. Here are the key points to remember:

- If a ratio is computed, define what items have been included in the numerator and denominator, as for some ratios definitions vary.

- Only compute a few ratios. Ratios are only a means to an end, i.e. they are computed in order that a comment can be made. The marks are gained by making the comments.

- Show the ratio in the 'normal' form, e.g. a ratio based on a profit figure is normally expressed as a percentage.

- Do not be frightened of making what may be regarded as an obvious comment. Thus, a statement that 'the gross profit to sales ratio has increased from last year' is stating something important – that the business is more profitable. It is only an obvious comment because the computation of a ratio made it so obvious. That is the main point of ratios – to highlight trends.

Example

A Ltd has been trading steadily for many years as ski shoe manufacturers. In 20X4 a surge in skiing increased the level of A Ltd's turnover significantly. The summarised balance sheets of the last two years are given below:

A Ltd Balance sheets

	20X4		20X3	
	£000	£000	£000	£000
Fixed assets:				
Intangible assets		30		40
Tangible assets:				
Property		640		216
Plant		174		142
		844		398
Current assets:				
Stock	540		140	
Debtors	440		170	
Investments	-		120	
Cash at bank	4		150	
	984		580	
Creditors: amounts falling due within one year:				
Trade creditors	520		250	
Taxation	70		80	
Dividend proposed	60		20	
	650		350	
Net current assets		334		230
Total assets less current liabilities		1,178		628
Creditors: amounts falling due after more than one year:				
10% debentures		120		-
		1,058		628

Capital and reserves:		
Called up share capital:		
Ordinary 50p shares	300	250
Revaluation reserve	270	-
Capital redemption reserve	-	50
Profit and loss account	488	328
	1,058	628

The sales for 20X4 and 20X3 respectively were £1,600,000 and £1,150,000. The cost of goods sold for 20X4 and 20X3 respectively were £1,196,000 and £880,000.

Given that this is the only information available, you are required to comment as fully as you can on A Ltd's financial position.

Solution: Comments on A Ltd – Financial position

Profitability and growth

Profit and loss accounts have not been given, but laying these out as far as they are available:

Profit and loss

	20X4	20X3
	£	£
Sales	1,600,000	1,150,000
Cost of sales	1,196,000	880,000
Gross profit	404,000	270,000

Profit margin

$$\frac{\text{Gross profit}}{\text{Sales}} \times 100$$

	20X4	20X3
	25.25%	23.48%

Return on capital employed

$$\frac{\text{Gross profit}}{\text{Share capital} + \text{Reserves} + \text{Debt}} \times 100$$

	20X4	20X3
	404,000	270,000
	1,178,000	898,000
	= 34.30%	= 30.07%

(Average capital employed should be used but year-end figures have been taken so that a figure for 20X3 can be computed. It is assumed that property was worth £270,000 more than its book value in 20X3 also.)

The ROCE figures have been computed in a rough and ready fashion but they indicate an improvement in 20X4 compared with 20X3. The gross profit/sales also shows a (slight) improvement. This would appear to be encouraging as the sales have grown considerably.

	20X4	20X3
Sales	£1,600,000	£1,150,000
Percentage increase	39.13%	

Solvency: long-term – Gearing

There was no debt in 20X3. The 10% debentures issued in 20X4 were to enable the investment to be made to finance growth.

The year-end gearing is as follows:

$$\frac{\text{Debt}}{\text{Capital employed (as above)}} \times 100$$

$$= \frac{120,000}{1,178,000} \times 100$$

$$= 10.19\%.$$

In absolute terms this is a low figure.

Solvency: short-term

Current ratio

	20X4	20X3
$\dfrac{\text{Current assets}}{\text{Current liabilities}}$	$\dfrac{984,000}{650,000} = 1.5$	$\dfrac{580,000}{350,000} = 1.7$

Quick ratio

	20X4	20X3
$\dfrac{\text{Current assets} - \text{Stock}}{\text{Current liabilities}}$	$\dfrac{444,000}{650,000} = 0.7$	$\dfrac{440,000}{350,000} = 1.3$

Both ratios have shown a decline – particularly the quick ratio. Conventional opinion states that for many businesses an ideal current ratio is 2 and an ideal quick ratio is 1. However, the ideal ratio will depend on the type of business that a company is engaged in. More important is the constancy of the ratio over time (assuming that the ratios reflect the efficient use of working capital).

The decline should not be viewed with alarm, particularly as the 20X3 figures include current assets which were surplus to the working capital requirements of the business at that time, i.e. the investments and cash. Both these items have been spent in purchasing new fixed assets. The quick ratio is, however, now low and should be watched carefully.

Short-term solvency: working capital efficiency

Example

	20X4	20X3
Stock turnover $=$ $\dfrac{\text{Cost of sales}}{\text{Year end stocks}}$	$\dfrac{1,196,000}{540,000} = 2.2$ times pa	$\dfrac{880,000}{140,000} = 6.3$ times pa

Year-end stock has been taken so that the 20X3 figure can be computed.

This is a very significant fall in stock turnover. It may indicate that:

- the growth in sales has been made by offering many more types of shoes, some of which are not selling quickly; or

- further growth in sales is expected so that the company has stepped up production to anticipate this.

A closer look at this area is required.

Example

	20X4	20X3
Debtor collection period $=$ $\dfrac{\text{Year end trade debtors}}{\text{Sales}} \times 365$	$\dfrac{444,000}{1,600,000} \times 365$ $= 100.4$ days	$\dfrac{170,000}{1,150,000} \times 365$ $= 54.0$ days

Fifty-four days to collect debts is not very impressive – 100 days is potentially disastrous. Immediate action is required to ensure prompter payment, although the situation may not be as bad as it appears if it is the case that the growth in sales took place shortly before the year end rather than throughout the year. Debtors at the year end would then not be typical of the sales throughout the whole year.

6 Appraising information for users

6.1 The nature and purpose of financial accounting

The nature of financial accounting is the reporting of transactions which can be expressed in monetary terms.

The purpose of such an exercise is to inform users of such information and to satisfy their needs.

6.2 The validity of the information

There are limitations in achieving the purpose of financial accounting, such as:

- Non-financial information may be just as important and helps in obtaining a complete picture of the state of the organisation. It includes, for example, the number of employees in the organisation and the types of skills they possess or indicators of efficiency with which the organisation addresses complaints from customers.

- The information is backward looking. Most users are concerned with the future.

- There is a tendency in financial accounting for increased complexity. This results from the continuing need to satisfy user needs for information, but the end result may be that users do not understand the more detailed information presented.

- The changing purchasing power of money is not dealt with.

Conclusion

The number of ratios that can be calculated may easily lead to confusion. Try to organise your thoughts in this area by mentally using the categories into which this chapter is broken down: operating ratios; liquidity, working capital and solvency; and stock exchange ratios.

Remember above all that the ratios are not an end in themselves. The examiner is interested in your ability to draw conclusions from accounts. Calculating a ratio is not the same as drawing a conclusion, but it can point you towards a conclusion.

SELF-TEST
QUESTIONS

Analysis of accounting statements

1   Name three different user groups of financial statements and state the particular interests of each group. (1.1)

Using ratios

2   How do you calculate the return on capital employed for a company? (2.2)

3   Show how two important ratios can be multiplied together to give the return on capital employed. (2.4)

Liquidity and funds management

4   What are the two key ratios to assess a company's liquidity? (3.1)

5   How would you assess whether a company's debt collection procedures were improving or deteriorating? (3.2)

6   Which is the more risky – investment in a highly geared company or a company with low gearing? (3.6)

Investment appraisal

7   What is the formula to calculate the dividend yield? (4.1)

8   How are the earnings of a company defined for EPS? (4.1)

Question 1

An analysis of its financial statements revealed that the debtor collection period of R Limited was 100 days, when 60 days is a reasonable figure.

Which one of the following could NOT account for the high level of 100 days?

A   Poor performance in R's credit control department.

B   A large credit sale made just before the balance sheet date.

C   R's trade is seasonal.

D   A downturn in R's trade in the last quarter of the year.

Question 2

Which of the following correctly defines working capital?

A   Fixed assets plus current assets minus current liabilities.

B   Current assets minus current liabilities.

C   Fixed assets plus current assets.

D   Share capital plus reserves.

For the answers to these questions, see the 'Answers' section at the end of the book

Question 1: Calculating ratios

You are given summarised results of an electrical engineering business, as below. All figures are in £'000.

You are required:

(a)   To prepare a table of the following 12 ratios, calculated for both years, clearly showing the figures used in the calculations:

- current ratio
- quick assets ratio
- stock turnover in days
- debtors turnover in days
- creditors turnover in days
- gross profit %
- net profit % (before taxation)
- interest cover
- dividend cover
- return on owners' equity (before taxation)
- return on capital employed
- gearing. **(12 marks)**

(b)   Making full use of the information given in the question, of your table of ratios, and your common sense, comment on the actions of the management.

(8 marks)

(Total: 20 marks)

Profit and loss account

	Year ended	
	31.12.20X1	*31.12.20X0*
Turnover	60,000	50,000
Cost of sales	42,000	34,000
Gross profit	18,000	16,000
Operating expenses	15,500	13,000
	2,500	3,000
Interest payable	2,200	1,300
Profit before taxation	300	1,700
Taxation	350	600
(Loss) profit after taxation	(50)	1,100
Dividends	600	600
Transfer (from) to reserves	(650)	500

Balance sheet

Fixed assets		
Intangible	500	-
Tangible	12,000	11,000
	12,500	11,000
Current assets		
Stocks	14,000	13,000
Debtors	16,000	15,000
Bank and cash	500	500
	30,500	28,500
Creditors due within one year	24,000	20,000
Net current assets	6,500	8,500
Total assets less current liabilities	19,000	19,500
Creditors due after one year	6,000	5,500
	13,000	14,000
Capital and reserves		
Share capital	1,300	1,300
Share premium	3,300	3,300
Revaluation reserve	2,000	2,000
Profit and loss	6,400	7,400
	13,000	14,000

Question 2: B Ltd

The following are the summarised accounts for B Ltd, a company with an accounting year ending on 30 September:

You are required:

(a) to calculate, for each year, two ratios for each of the following user groups, which are of particular significance to them:

- shareholders
- trade creditors
- internal management. **(12 marks)**

(b) to make brief comments upon the changes, between the two years, in the ratios calculated in (a) above. **(8 marks)**

(Total: 20 marks)

Summarised balance sheets

	20X1		20X2	
	£000	£000	£000	£000
Tangible fixed assets – at cost less depreciation		4,995		12,700
Current assets:				
Stocks	40,145		50,455	
Debtors	40,210		43,370	
Cash at bank	12,092		5,790	
	92,447		99,615	
Creditors: amounts falling due within one year:				
Trade creditors	32,604		37,230	
Taxation	2,473		3,260	
Proposed dividend	1,785		1,985	
	36,862		42,475	
Net current assets		55,585		57,140
Total assets less current liabilities		60,580		69,840
Creditors: amounts falling due after more than one year:				
10% debentures 20X6/20X9		19,840		19,840
		40,740		50,000
Capital and reserves:				
Called up share capital of 25p per share		9,920		9,920
Profit and loss account		30,820		40,080
Shareholders' funds		40,740		50,000

Summarised profit and loss accounts

	20X1	20X2
	£000	£000
Turnover	486,300	583,900
Operating profit	17,238	20,670
Interest payable	1,984	1,984
Profit on ordinary activities before taxation	15,254	18,686
Tax on profit on ordinary activities	5,734	7,026
Profit for the financial year	9,520	11,660
Dividends	2,240	2,400
	7,280	9,260
Retained profit brought forward	23,540	30,820
Retained profit carried forward	30,820	40,080

For the answers to these questions, see the 'Answers' section at the end of the book

Question 3: Brood Ltd

The balance sheets and summarised profit and loss accounts (ignoring tax) of Brood Limited at 30 April 20X0 and 30 April 20X1 are given below.

You are required to:

(a) Calculate the following ratios for each of the two years:

- return on total capital employed
- return on owner's equity
- current ratio
- quick ratio (acid test)
- gearing (leverage).

Use year-end figures for all ratios. **(5 marks)**

(b) Comment briefly on the movements in these ratios between the two years.

(5 marks)

(Total: 10 marks)

Brood Ltd Balance sheets

	30 April 20X0		30 April 20X1	
	£000	£000	£000	£000
Assets				
Tangible fixed assets				
Cost or valuation	51,000		63,000	
Accumulated depreciation	(12,500)	38,500	(16,300)	46,700
Current Assets				
Stocks	16,400		18,400	
Trade debtors	19,100		20,600	
Sundry debtors and prepayments	3,100		4,000	
Total assets	38,600		43,000	
Less: Current liabilities				
Trade creditors	(11,400)		(8,400)	
Accruals	(3,400)		(4,200)	
Overdraft at bank	(13,700)		(4,800)	
	28,500		17,400	
Net current assets		10,100		25,600
		48,600		72,300
Less: 7% Debentures (£20m issued 1 May 20X0)		(20,000)		(40,000)
		28,600		32,300
Called up share capital		10,000		10,000
Share premium account		5,000		5,000
Revaluation reserve		5,000		5,000
Profit and loss account		8,600		12,300
		28,600		32,300

Brood Ltd Profit and loss accounts

	20X0	20X1
	£000	£000
Sales	58,000	66,000
Cost of sales	(43,000)	(49,000)
Gross profit	15,000	17,000
Operating expenses	(10,000)	(10,500)
Profit from operations	5,000	6,500
Interest payable	(1,400)	(2,800)
Net profit for the period	3,600	3,700

For the answers to these questions, see the 'Answers' section at the end of the book

FEEDBACK TO
ACTIVITY 1

Total capital employed

$$20X6 \quad \frac{23+2}{139} \times 100 = 18.0\%$$

$$20X7 \quad \frac{27+2}{158} \times 100 = 18.4\%$$

Equity capital employed

$$20X6 \quad \frac{23-2}{99-25} \times 100 = 28.4\%$$

$$20X7 \quad \frac{27-2}{118-25} \times 100 = 26.9\%$$

There is a slight improvement in total ROCE and a falling off in equity ROCE.

A reason for the variation is the revaluation of fixed assets during the year. This has the effect of increasing the denominator in 20X7 relative to 20X6 and creates an unfair comparison as it is likely that the fixed assets were worth more than their book value last year as well.

The differences in returns for equity compared to total capital employed are large. It means that equity shareholders have had a significant increase in their return because of the company's using fixed interest finance to enlarge the capital employed in the business.

Chapter 25

THE THEORETICAL AND OPERATIONAL ADEQUACY OF FINANCIAL REPORTING

Despite its widespread use, historical cost accounting has a number of problems. These are discussed in this chapter, whilst noting the advantages of the method as well.

The chapter also discusses two alternatives to historical cost accounting.

Objectives

By the time you have finished this chapter you should be able to:

- understand some of the limitations of conventional financial reporting

- be aware of the possible means of addressing such limitations.

1   Limitations of historical cost accounting

Virtually everything you have studied so far in this book has been based on **historical cost accounting**. Under historical cost accounting, assets are recorded at the amount of cash or cash equivalents paid, or the fair value of the consideration given for them.

Liabilities are recorded at the amount of proceeds received in exchange for the obligation. This method of accounting has advantages, but it also has serious disadvantages.

KEY POINT

Historical cost accounting:
- assets are recorded at the amount paid
- liabilities are recorded at the amount received.

1.1   Advantages of historical cost accounting

The advantages of historical cost accounting include:

- Records are based on objectively verifiable amounts (actual cost of assets, etc.).

- It is simple and cheap.

- The profit concept is well understood.

- Within limits, historical cost figures provide a basis for comparison with the results of other companies for the same period or similar periods, with the results of the same company for previous periods and with budgets.

- No acceptable alternative has been developed, in the UK at any rate.

KEY POINT

Advantages of historical cost accounting:
- based on objectively verifiable amounts
- simple and cheap
- profit well understood
- provide a basis for comparison
- no acceptable alternative.

1.2   Disadvantages of historical cost accounting

The disadvantages of historical cost accounting include:

- It overstates profits when prices are rising through inflation. Several factors contribute to this. For example, if assets are maintained at their original cost, depreciation is based on that cost. As inflation pushes prices up, the true value to the business of the use of the asset becomes progressively more than the depreciation charge. This disadvantage can be overcome by revaluing fixed assets. FRS 15 *Tangible fixed assets* then requires depreciation to be based on the revalued amount.

- It maintains financial capital but does not maintain physical capital. If a business makes a profit it must necessarily have more net assets. If the whole of that profit is distributed as dividend by a company, or withdrawn from the business by a sole trader, the business has the same capital at the end of the year as it had at the beginning. In other words, it has maintained its financial capital. However, it will not have maintained its physical capital if prices have risen through inflation during the year, because the financial capital will not buy the same stock and other assets to enable the business to continue operating at the same level.

- The balance sheet does not show the value of the business. A balance sheet summarises the assets and liabilities of the business, but there are several reasons why it does not represent the true value of the business. One reason for this could be that the use of historical cost accounting means that assets are included at cost less depreciation based on that cost rather than at current value. (Another reason is, of course, that not all the assets are included in the balance sheet – for example, internally generated goodwill will not appear).

- It provides a poor basis for assessing performance. The profit is overstated, as explained above, while assets are understated. The result is that return on capital employed is doubly distorted and exaggerated.

- It does not recognise the loss suffered through holding monetary assets while prices are rising. A business holding cash or debtors through a period of inflation suffers a loss as its purchasing power declines.

These factors are developed and illustrated in the next section.

2   The impact of changing prices

2.1   Problems of historical cost accounting in times of changing prices

When prices are not changing, historical cost accounting (HCA) does accurately and fairly show profits made by the business and the value to the business of the assets less liabilities.

When prices are changing, however, there are problems. We discuss three of these below.

Depreciation

Under a system of HCA, the purpose of depreciation is simply to allocate the original cost of a fixed asset (less estimated residual value) over its estimated useful life. If depreciation is charged in the profit and loss account, then by reducing the amount which can be paid out as a dividend, funds are retained within the company rather than paid to the shareholders. When the time comes to replace the asset, management must ensure that those funds are available in a sufficiently liquid form.

When inflation is taken into account, we can note the following points.

- The depreciation charge is based on the original cost of the asset measured in terms of historical £s, whereas the revenues against which depreciation is matched are measured in terms of current £s. The profit figure we calculate is not meaningful as it ignores price changes which have taken place since the asset was purchased.

- Although the concept of depreciation ensures that the capital of the business is maintained intact in money terms, it does not ensure that the capital of the business is maintained intact in real terms (see Examples below).

- The depreciation provision at the end of the asset's useful life will fall short of its replacement cost.

Example 1

A business starts off with £1,000 cash and buys two machines at a cost of £500 each. All profits are distributed to the owners. At the end of ten years the company has no machines and £1,000 cash.

Thus the capital of the business has been maintained intact in money terms. Suppose at the end of ten years the current replacement cost of one machine is £1,000. Therefore the £1,000 cash at the end of the ten years will buy only one machine. In real terms the capital at the end of the period is half that at the beginning of the period.

Profit has been over-distributed. If profit is a true surplus, the owners should be able to withdraw all the profit and be in exactly the same position as before in real terms.

Stock and cost of sales

Assume a company values stock on a historical cost basis using the FIFO method. During a period of inflation the effect of this method is to overstate the real profit of a business, since sales (in current terms) are matched with cost of sales (in historical terms). If the company distributed the whole of its historical cost profit, it would not be maintaining the capital of the business intact in real terms.

Example 2

A business starts off on 1 January 20X7 with £1,000 cash (contributed by the proprietor). On the same day it purchased 500 motors at £2 each. These are sold on 31 March 20X7 for proceeds of £1,650. At this date the replacement cost of an identical motor is £2.20.

Under HCA the profit for the three months is £650 (£1,650 – £1,000). If the proprietor withdraws this profit, the closing balance sheet at 31 March would show capital account £1,000 represented by cash of £1,000.

Although capital has been maintained intact in money terms (it was £1,000 at 1 January), it has not been maintained intact in real terms. At 31 March £1,000 cash will buy only 455 (approximately!) motors.

Comparability of data over time

Example 3

We saw earlier in the chapter a need for users of accounts to be able to compare the results of the business over a number of years so that trends could be identified. Thus if sales were £100,000 four years ago and £130,000 in the current year, we could conclude that sales have increased by 30%. However, in real terms the increase may not be this amount as price levels may have changed in the previous four years. If price levels have risen by 40% in the last four years, then the sales should be £140,000 in the current year in order to maintain the real value of sales. There has therefore been a real decline.

2.2   Alternatives to historical cost accounting

Alternatives to HCA mainly fall into one of two categories: (a) **Current purchasing power accounting** and (b) **Current cost accounting**. These are discussed below.

Current purchasing power accounting (CPP)

CPP involves adjusting the historical cost accounts using a general price index (the Retail Price Index) so that all items are expressed in £s of year-end purchasing power.

The method has been rejected, most notably because many accountants felt it misleading to adjust specific assets such as stock and fixed assets by means of a general price index which was far more relevant to the spending power of a family than that of a trader.

Current cost accounting (CCA)

CCA involves taking account of specific price changes as they affect a particular business and will result in a separate set of financial statements, distinct from the historical cost financial statements.

KEY POINT

Current purchasing power accounting involves adjusting the historical cost accounts using a general price index.

KEY POINT

Current cost accounting involves taking account of specific price changes as they affect a particular business.

Although accountants generally believe CCA is superior to CPP, the profession has as yet to agree on any single method of accounting for inflation (or indeed, some people would even argue, on the need to do so).

CCA can be argued to be the best solution to the first two problems of HCA involving fixed assets and stock. By charging the current worth of these items against profits, the amount of operating profit recorded in the profit and loss account will be reduced. Thus the amount of dividends will tend to be reduced owing to the lower profits and more sums will be retained in the business to finance the increased replacement price of these assets.

Example 4

Continuing with example 2 above, we could measure profit by comparing the sale proceeds with the replacement cost of the stock at the time of sale.

Sale of stock

	£
Proceeds of sale	1,650
Current (or replacement) cost at the date of sale	1,100
Current cost profit	550

Note that the terms 'current cost' and 'replacement cost' mean the same, though the term current cost tends to be used more frequently.

If the proprietor withdrew £550, the closing balance sheet would appear as follows:

Sale of stock – continued

	£
Assets – Cash	1,100
Capital account:	
Balance at 1 January 20X7	1,000
Add: Net profit	650
	1,650
Less: Drawings	550
	1,100

This cash is now sufficient to buy 500 motors at the new price of £2.20 per motor. The trader can continue trading at the same level of business – capital has been maintained intact in real terms.

The comparability of data over a period of time is generally best handled by a CPP approach. Financial data from earlier years is uplifted to current price levels by the fraction:

$$\frac{\text{Retail price index in current year}}{\text{Retail price index in year when item originated}} \times \text{Amount at which item stated in accounts in earlier year}$$

Thus sales of £100,000 in example 3 above would be restated at £140,000 in current year price levels.

2.3   The usefulness of historical cost accounting

In terms of examinations at this level, questions are going to concern themselves with HCA accounting and you will only need to appreciate that historical cost accounts do not account for changing prices, as clearly shown by the examples above.

In practice it is largely accepted that HCA accounts have very severe limitations, but it is very difficult to persuade those who prepare accounts to take account of changing prices. Attempts to impose a system CPP or CCA have at best met with indifference, and at present there is no requirement to prepare either.

Most organisations seem content to prepare HCA accounts, presumably considering that they (and the users of financial statements) are aware of the inherent limitations therein. Indeed, the only regularly adopted practice in financial statements is to revalue land and buildings periodically and include such values in the financial statements.

In conclusion, the debate on accounting for changing prices is likely to continue in years to come, but at this stage you merely need to be aware (in broad outline) of the limitations of HCA.

Conclusion

The chapter has addressed a number of issues relating to the adequacy of financial reporting. The other approaches to financial statements consist of further statements being produced or financial statements being produced which incorporate the effect of changing prices.

SELF-TEST
QUESTIONS

Limitations of historical cost accounting

1   What are the advantages of historical cost accounting? (1.1)

2   What are the limitations of historical cost accounting? (1.2)

Alternatives to historical cost accounting

3   What does CPP stand for? (2.2)

4   What does CCA stand for? (2.2)

Answers to end-of-chapter questions

CHAPTER 1

EXAM-TYPE QUESTION

Financial statements

(a) The information in the financial statements is to be communicated to:

- **Shareholders** – the owners of the company, existing and potential, including persons or groups interested in take-overs and mergers.

- **Providers of external finance**, long and short-term, such as debenture holders and finance companies, both existing and potential.

- **Employees** past, present and potential.

- **Suppliers of goods and services, and customers,** past, present and prospective.

- **Tax authorities**.

- **Trade agencies, local authorities, environmental pressure groups** and any other members of the public who may require such information as is normally and legally contained in the financial statements.

- **Analysts and advisers**, both of investors (stockbrokers, economists, statisticians and journalists) and of employees (trade unions).

(b) The information contained in the financial statements should be:

- **Relevant** – to the needs of users

- **Reliable** – so that conclusions drawn may be 'true and fair'.

- **Comparable** – the information contained in one period's financial statements should be, as far as possible, calculated and presented on the same bases as in previous periods, so that comparisons are relevant.

- **Understandable** – material matters should be disclosed without unnecessary complex detail.

- **Complete** – if an unbalanced or biased view is presented, readers will be unable to make sound judgements.

- **Objective** – an unbiased view of the company's affairs, without regard to the interests of particular groups of interested parties, should be put forward.

- **Up-to-date** – companies are required to prepare their financial statements annually, and this is important from the point of view of investors and those advising them, for evaluation purposes.

(c) The kind of information required by two of the groups is:

- **Shareholders** – Shareholders are interested in the future performance of the business but require past figures as a guide to the future. Therefore, they need information about the performance and financial position of the business. In addition, any general indication given in the financial statements as to future prospects is relevant.

- **Tax authorities** – require past figures as a basis for computing tax liabilities.

CHAPTER 2

PRACTICE QUESTION

The Frog Shop

(a)   **Balance sheets at end of:**

Day one

	£		£
Cash	2,000	Capital	2,000

Day two

	£		£
Motor van	1,000	Capital	2,000
Shop fittings	800		
Cash	200		
	2,000		2,000

Day three

	£		£
Motor van	1,000	Capital	2,000
Shop fittings	800	Creditor	500
Stock	500		
Cash	200		
	2,500		2,500

Day four

	£		£
Motor van	1,000	Capital	2,000
Shop fittings	800	Add: Profit	400
Stock	250		
Cash	850		2,400
		Creditor	500
	2,900		2,900

Day five

	£		£
Motor van	1,000	Capital	2,000
Shop fittings	800	Add: Profit	400
Stock	250		
Cash	350		
	2,400		2,400

Day six

	£		£
Motor van	1,000	Capital	2,000
Shop fittings	800	Add: Profit	400
Stock	250		
Cash	300		2,400
		Less: Drawings	50
	2,350		2,350

Note: the capital could be shown in total as £2,350 without showing how it is made up.

Day seven

	£		£
Motor van	1,000	Capital	2,350
Shop fittings	800	Creditor	1,000
Stock	1,250		
Cash	300		
	3,350		3,350

Day eight

	£		£
Motor van	1,000	Capital (2,350 + 300)	2,650
Shop fittings	800	Creditor	1,000
Stock	350		
Debtors	1,200		
Cash	300		
	3,650		3,650

Day nine

	£		£
Motor van	1,000	Capital	2,650
Shop fittings	800	Creditor	1,000
Stock	350		
Debtors	700		
Cash	800		
	3,650		3,650

Day ten

	£		£
Motor van	1,000	Capital (2,650 − 100)	2,550
Shop fittings	800	Creditor	1,000
Stock	350		
Debtors	700		
Cash	700		
	3,550		3,550

(b) **Trading and profit and loss account for the ten days ended Day 10**

	£	£
Sales (650 + 1,200)		1,850
Purchases (500 + 1,000)	1,500	
Less: Closing stock	350	1,150
Gross profit		700
Wages		100
Net profit		600

Note: the link between the profit and loss account and the balance sheet amount of capital. Capital has moved during the ten days as follows:

	£
Opening capital	2,000
Add: Net profit for the period	600
Less: Drawings	50
	2,550

CHAPTER 3   EXAM-TYPE QUESTION

Grace

Bank (or cash)

	£		£
Capital	5,000	Purchases	1,000
Sales	1,200	Fixtures	900
Tom	1,900	Wages	100
Sales	500	Eileen	1,500
Trevor	500	Purchases	700
Guy – loan	1,000	Wages	150
		Eric	850
		Leasehold premises	4,000
		Wages	150
		Balance c/d	750
	10,100		10,100
Balance b/d	750		

Car

	£		£
Capital	4,500		

Capital

	£		£
Balance c/d	9,500	Cash	5,000
		Car	4,500
	9,500		9,500
		Balance b/d	9,500

Purchases

	£		£
Cash	1,000	Balance c/d	4,050
Eileen	1,500		
Eric	850		
Cash	700		
	4,050		4,050
Balance b/d	4,050		

Sales

	£		£
Balance c/d	4,400	Cash	1,200
		Tom	900
		Trevor	800
		Tom	1,000
		Cash	500
	4,400		4,400
		Balance b/d	4,400

Fixtures and fittings

	£		£
Cash	900		

Eileen – Creditor

	£		£
Cash	1,500	Purchases	1,500

Tom – Debtor

	£		£
Sales	900	Cash	1,900
Sales	1,000		
	1,900		1,900

Eric – Creditor

	£		£
Cash	850	Purchases	850

Trevor – Debtor

	£		£
Sales	800	Cash	500
		Balance c/d	300
	800		800
Balance b/d	300		

Wages

	£		£
Cash	100	Balance c/d	400
Cash	150		
Cash	150		
	——		——
	400		400
	——		——
Balance b/d	400		

Guy – Loan

	£		£
		Cash	1,000

Leasehold premises

	£		£
Cash	4,000		

Grace – Trial balance as at 30 June 20X9

Account	Dr	Cr
	£	£
Cash at bank	750	
Car	4,500	
Capital		9,500
Purchases	4,050	
Sales		4,400
Fixtures	900	
Trevor – Debtor	300	
Wages	400	
Guy – Loan		1,000
Leasehold premises	4,000	
	——	——
	14,900	14,900
	——	——

CHAPTER 4   MULTIPLE-CHOICE QUESTIONS

Question 1

C Carriage outwards and cost of storage are not allowed by SSAP 9.

Question 2

C 400 items   £

Cost $400 \times £4$ 1,600

NRV $(400 \times £3) - £200$ 1,000

Therefore use NRV.

200 items   £

Cost $200 \times £30$ 6,000

NRV $(200 \times £35) - £1,200 - £300$ 5,500

Therefore use NRV.

Total stock figure = £116,400 + £1,000 + £5,500 = £122,900

EXAM-TYPE QUESTION

Blabbermouth

Trading and profit and loss account for the year ended 31 March 20X7

	£	£
Sales:		25,375
Less: Cost of goods sold:		
Opening stock	4,100	
Purchases	17,280	
	21,380	
Less: Closing stock	5,200	
		16,180
Gross profit		9,195
Less: Expenses:		
Postage and stationery	727	
Rent and rates	500	
Light and heat	100	
Wages	8,237	
		9,564
Net loss		(369)

Note: the expenses of the business exceed gross profit therefore a net loss has been made.

Balance sheet as at 31 March 20X7

	£	£
Fixed assets:		
Fixtures and fittings		2,100
Current assets:		
Stock	5,200	
Debtors	8,250	
Cash	6,078	
	19,528	
Current liabilities:		
Creditors	7,247	
		12,281
		14,381
Capital employed:		
Balance at 1 April 20X6		18,250
Loss for year	369	
Drawings	3,500	
Retained loss		(3,869)
		14,381

PRACTICE QUESTION

Alpha

Trading and profit and loss account for year to 31 December

	£	£
Sales		39,468
Opening stock	3,655	
Purchases (working 2)	27,101	
	30,756	
Less: Closing stock	3,123	
		27,633
Gross profit		11,835
Insurance	580	
Plant repairs	110	
Rent and rates	1,782	
Wages	3,563	
Discount allowed	437	
Motor van expenses	1,019	
General expenses	522	
		8,013
Net profit		3,822

Balance sheet as at 31 December

	£	£	£
Fixed assets:			
Motor van			980
Plant			2,380
Shop fittings			1,020
			4,380
Current assets:			
Stock		3,123	
Debtors		3,324	
Cash on hand		212	
		6,659	
Current liabilities:			
Bank overdraft (working 1)	3,424		
Creditors	4,370		
		7,794	
			(1,135)
			3,245

Capital:

Balance at 1 Jan		2,463
Profit for year	3,822	
Drawings (working 2)	3,040	
Retained profit		782
Balance at 31 December		3,245

Workings

(W1)   **Trial balance at 31 December**

	Dr	Cr
	£	£
Sales		39,468
Insurance	580	
Plant repairs	110	
Rent and rates	1,782	
Motor van	980	
Plant	2,380	
Purchases	27,321	
Stock at 1 Jan (opening)	3,655	
Wages	3,563	
Discount allowed	437	
Motor van expenses	1,019	
Shop fittings	1,020	
General expenses	522	
Capital account at 1 Jan		2,463
Sundry debtors	3,324	
Sundry creditors		4,370
Cash on hand	212	
Personal drawings	2,820	
	49,725	46,301
Bank overdraft (balancing figure)		3,424
	49,725	49,725

(W2)   **Goods for own use:**

	£
Drawings per trial balance	2,820
Add: Goods for own use	220
	3,040
Purchases per trial balance	27,321
Less: Goods for own use	220
	27,101

Note: if stock is taken from the business by the proprietor for his personal use, the double entry is to debit drawings and credit purchases. No entry is made in the stock account.

CHAPTER 5

EXAM-TYPE QUESTIONS

Question 1: Dundee Engineering

Motor expenses and insurance

20X7–8		£	20X7–8		£
1 May	Bal b/d – insurance	290	1 May	Bal b/d – garage bills	478
30 June	Cash	698			
1 Sept	Cash	3,480	30 Apr	Profit and loss (bal fig)	4,811
1 Dec	Cash	3,900	30 Apr	Bal c/d – insurance (W1)	3,435
30 Apr	Bal c/d – garage bills	356			
		8,724			8,724
1 May	Bal b/d	3,435	1 May	Bal b/d	356

Workings

(W1)	Insurance prepayment	
		£
$3,480 \times \frac{4}{12}$		1,160
$3,900 \times \frac{7}{12}$		2,275
		3,435

Question 2: Heilbronn Properties

Interest payable

20X4–5		£	20X4–5		£
1 Aug	Bal b/d Interest prepaid	8,000	1 Aug	Bal b/d Interest payable	12,000
31 July	Cash paid (bal fig)	51,900	31 July	Profit and loss	56,000
31 July	Bal c/d Interest payable	14,500	31 July	Bal c/d Interest prepaid	6,400
		74,400			74,400
1 Aug	Bal b/d	6,400	1 Aug	Bal b/d	14,500

Rental income

20X4–5		£	20X4–5		£
1 Aug	Bal b/d Rental due	15,000	1 Aug	Bal b/d Rental in advance	3,000
31 July	Profit and loss (bal fig)	120,500	31 July	Cash received	116,000
31 July	Bal c/d Rental in advance	2,500	31 July	Bal c/d Rental due	19,000
		138,000			138,000
1 Aug	Bal b/d	19,000	1 Aug	Bal b/d	2,500

CHAPTER **6**   EXAM-TYPE QUESTION

Harry Evans

Provision for doubtful debt

20X0		£	20X0		£
31 Dec	Balance c/d (4% × £6,200)	248	31 Dec	Bad debts expense a/c	248
			20X1		
20X1			1 Jan	Balance b/d	248
31 Dec	Balance c/d (2% × £6,900)	138			
	Bad debts expense a/c	110			
		248			248
20X2			20X2		
31 Dec	Balance c/d (£350 + 2% × £5900)	468	1 Jan	Balance b/d	138
			31 Dec	Bad debts expense a/c	330
		468			468
			20X3		
			1 Jan	Balance b/d	468

Bad debts expense account

20X0		£	20X0		£
31 Dec	Bad debts	370	31 Dec	P&L a/c	618
	Doubtful debts	248			
		618			618
20X1			20X1		
31 Dec	Bad debts	1,500	31 Dec	Doubtful debts	110
				P&L a/c	1,390
		1,500			1,500
20X2			20X2		
31 Dec	Doubtful debts	330	31 Dec	P&L a/c	330

CHAPTER **7**   MULTIPLE-CHOICE QUESTION

B $\dfrac{£30,000 - 6000}{4} \times \dfrac{5}{12} = £2,500$

Question 1: Depreciation 1

Usually, with the exception of land, fixed assets have a limited number of years of useful life. When a fixed asset is purchased and later scrapped or disposed of by the firm, that part of the original cost not recovered on disposal is called depreciation. Depreciation is thus the part of the cost of the fixed asset consumed during its working life. Accordingly, it is a cost for services in the same way as an expense is a cost. Depreciation is, therefore, a revenue expense item and will be charged annually in the profit and loss account. The depreciation cost apportionable to each year of the asset's life is estimated in advance of disposal and accounted for by making annual provisions to reduce the asset from cost to the written down value, at the end of each year of its life.

An example of a method of computing the annual depreciation of an asset is the **straight-line method** which is outlined below:

$$\frac{\text{Cost} - \text{Residual value}}{\text{Number of years of expected life}} = \text{Depreciation charge pa}$$

e.g. $\dfrac{\pounds 1,000 - \text{Nil}}{10 \text{ years}} = \pounds 100 \text{ pa}$

Question 2: Depreciation 2

Motor cars – cost account

20X4		£	20X4		£
1 Jan	Cash – Car A	800	31 Dec	Balance c/d	2,000
1 Jul	Cash – Car B	1,200			
		2,000			2,000
20X5			20X5		
1 Jan	Balance b/d	2,000	1 Jul	Motor car disposal account (Car A)	800
			31 Dec	Balance c/d	1,200
		2,000			2,000
20X6					
1 Jan	Balance b/d	1,200			

Motor cars – accumulated depreciation account

20X4		£	20X4			£
31 Dec	Balance c/d	280	31 Dec	P&L account dep'n charge:		
				Car A		160
				Car B		120
		280				280
20X5			20X5			
1 Jul	Motor car disposal account (accumulated dep'n on Car A (160 + 80))	240	1 Jan	Balance b/d		280
				P&L account – dep'n charge:		
31 Dec	Balance c/d	360		Car A	80	

			Car B	240
				—
				320
		600		—
		—		600
20X6				—
31 Dec	Balance c/d	600	*20X6*	
			1 Jan　Balance b/d	360
			P&L account –	
		—	dep'n charge on Car B	240
		600		—
		—		600
				—

Motor cars – disposals account

20X5		£	*20X5*		£
1 Jul	Cost of disposal	800	1 Jul	Accumulated dep'n	240
	P&L account – dep'n			Cash account	
	over-provided on				
	disposal (bal fig)	40		(proceeds)	600
		—			—
		840			840
		—			—

Balance sheet (extract) as at 31 December 20X5

Fixed assets	*Cost*	*Accumulated dep'n*	*NBV*
	£	£	£
Motor cars	1,200	360	840

Question 3: Grasmere

Motor van – cost

20X2		£	*20X2*		£
Cash		2,400	Balance c/d		2,400
		—			—
		2,400			2,400
		—			—
20X3			*20X3*		
Balance b/d		2,400	Balance c/d		2,400
		—			—
		2,400			2,400
		—			—
20X4			*20X4*		
Balance b/d		2,400	Disposals		2,400
		—			—
		2,400			2,400
		—			—

Motor van – accumulated depreciation

20X2	£	20X2	£
Balance c/d	210	Profit and loss	210
	___		___
	210		210
	___		___
20X3		20X3	
Balance c/d	630	Balance b/d	210
		Profit and loss	420
	___		___
	630		630
	___		___
20X4		20X4	
Disposal	735	Balance b/d	630
		Profit and loss	105
	___		___
	735		735
	___		___

Motor van disposals

20X4	£	20X4	£
Cost	2,400	Accumulated depreciation	735
Profit and loss (bal fig)	135	Cash	1,800
	___		___
	2,535		2,535
	___		___

Workings

$$\text{Depreciation charge pa} = \frac{£2,400 - £300}{5} = £420 \text{ pa}$$

Charge for 20X2	=	(6m) 6/12 × £420	=	£210
Charge for 20X3	=	(12m)	=	£420
Charge for 20X4	=	(3m) 3/12 × £420	=	£105

Effect on financial statements

(a) *Profit and loss account:*

	£
20X2 Depreciation charge (Dr)	210
20X3 Depreciation charge (Dr)	420
20X4 Depreciation charge (Dr)	105
20X4 Depreciation over provided (Cr)	135

Note: the net effect of the two items in 20X4 would be combined with the depreciation charge on other fixed assets.

(b) *Balance sheet:*

	20X2	31 Dec 20X3	20X4
	£	£	£
Cost	2,400	2,400	-
Less: Accumulated depreciation	210	630	-
	___	___	___
Net book value	2,190	1,770	-
	___	___	___

CHAPTER 8	PRACTICE QUESTION

Delta

Trading and profit and loss account for the year to 31 December 20X9

	£	£	£
Sales			124,450
Less: Returns			186
			124,264
Opening stock		8,000	
Add: Purchases	86,046		
Less: Returns	135		
	85,911		
Carriage inwards	156		
Wages	8,250		
		94,317	
Less: Closing stock		(7,550)	
			94,767
Gross profit			29,497
Discount received			138
			29,635
Salaries		3,500	
Travellers' salaries		5,480	
Travelling expenses		1,040	
Discounts allowed		48	
General expenses		2,056	
Gas, electricity and water		2,560	
Rent (Working 2)		1,750	
Carriage outwards		546	
Printing and stationery		640	
Bad debts (Working 4)		485	
Loan interest (Working 1)		100	
Depreciation (Working 3)		575	
Bank charges		120	
			18,900
Net profit			10,735

Balance sheet as at 31 December 20X9

	Cost £	Dep'n £	£
Fixed assets			
Premises	8,000	-	8,000
Plant and machinery	5,500	550	4,950
Furniture and fittings	500	25	475
	14,000	575	13,425
Current assets			
Stock		7,550	
Debtors	20,280		
Less: Provision (Working 4)	1,014		
		19,266	
Prepayments		250	
Cash at bank		650	
		27,716	
Current liabilities			
Creditors	10,056		
Accruals – loan interest	100		
		10,156	
			17,560
			30,985
Loan – Omega			2,000
			28,985
Capital: balance at 1 Jan 20X9			20,000
Profit for the year		10,735	
Drawings		1,750	
Retained profit for the year			8,985
Capital: balance at 31 December 20X9			28,985

Workings

(W1)   **Loan interest**

Accrual required   = 5% × £2,000
                    = £100

Interest payable account

	£		£
Balance c/d	100	Profit and loss account	100
	100		100
		Balance b/d	100

Note: it is not necessary to show the writing up of the ledger account as above where there have been no previous expenses stored up in the ledger account during the year.

It is more important to understand the effect of the adjustment – a Dr to profit and loss account and a Cr on the balance sheet.

(W2) **Rent**

	£		£
Cash	2,000	Profit and loss account	1,750
		Prepayment c/d	250
	————		————
	2,000		2,000
	————		————
Prepayment b/d	250		

(W3) **Depreciation**

Plant and machinery 10% × £5,500	550
Furniture and fittings 5% × £500	25
	————
	575
	————

Note: as with working (1) it is not necessary to write up the ledger accounts. The effect of the calculations can be inserted into the profit and loss account and the balance sheet.

Dr	Depreciation (Profit and loss account)	= Expense
Cr	Accumulated depreciation (Balance sheet)	= Reduction in asset

(W4) **Bad debts**

Bad debts account

	£		£
Balance b/d (per trial balance)		Balance b/d (per trial balance)	
Bad debts	256	Bad debts recovered	45
Provision for doubtful debts	274	Profit and loss account	485
	————		————
	530		530
	————		————

Provision for doubtful debts account

	£		£
Balance required c/d		Balance b/d (per trial balance)	740
5% × £20,280	1,014	Bad debts account	274
	————		————
	1,014		1,014
	————		————

Note: no workings/ledger accounts have been shown for stock, as the opening and closing stock figures can be inserted into the final accounts without further adjustments.

CHAPTER 9

PRACTICE QUESTION

Heale

(a)

Sales day book

	£
Jones	94
Smith	118
Turnip	141
Clog	235
Foul	353
	___
	941
	___

Purchases day book

	Total	Purchases	Telephone	Gas
	£	£	£	£
Snell	80	80	-	-
Ryan	100	100	-	-
Ovett	150	150	-	-
Coe	300	300	-	-
Keino	100	100	-	-
British Telecom	50	-	50	-
British Gas	75	-	-	75
	___	___	___	___
	855	730	50	75
	___	___	___	___

Cash book

	£		£
Jones – sale	30	Petty cash	200
Smith – sale	60	Snell – purchases ledger	70
Turnip – sale	110	Ovett – purchases ledger	30
Foul – sale	80	British Telecom (purchases ledger)	50
Sundry income	10	Wages	300
Balance c/d	440	Sundry expenses	80
	___		___
	730		730
	___		___
		Balance b/d (overdrawn)	440

Petty cash book

Received		Total	Stationery	Postage	Travelling	Sundry expenses
£		£	£	£	£	£
200	Cash	-	-	-	-	
-	Stationery	16	16	-	-	-
-	Postage	3	-	3	-	-
-	Travelling	8	-	-	8	-
-	Sundry expenses	12	-	-	-	12
		___	___	___	___	___
		39	16	3	8	12
		___	___	___	___	___

(b)   **Nominal ledger**

Sales

	£		£
Trading account	941	Sales day book	941
	___		___
	941		941
	___		___

Note: the sales account has been closed off by transferring the balance to the trading and profit and loss account. Strictly this would only be done after a trial balance had been extracted and journals entries made to put through adjustments for the final accounts. The same applies to all the income and expense accounts set out below.

Purchases

	£		£
Purchase day book	730	Trading account	730
	___		___
	730		730
	___		___

Telephone

	£		£
Purchase day book	50	Profit and loss	50
	___		___
	50		50
	___		___

Heating and lighting

	£		£
Purchase day book	75	Profit and loss	75
	___		___
	75		75
	___		___

Sundry income

	£		£
Profit and loss	10	Cash book	10
	___		___
	10		10
	___		___

Wages

	£		£
Cash book	300	Profit and loss	300
	___		___
	300		300
	___		___

Sundry expenses

	£		£
Cash book	80	Profit and loss	92
Petty cash book	12		
	___		___
	92		92
	___		___

Stationery

	£		£
Petty cash book	16	Profit and loss	16
	——		——
	16		16
	——		——

Postage

	£		£
Petty cash book	3	Profit and loss	3
	——		——
	3		3
	——		——

Travelling

	£		£
Petty cash book	8	Profit and loss	8
	——		——
	8		8
	——		——

Sales ledger:
Jones

	£		£
Sales day book	94	Cash book	30
		Balance c/d	64
	——		——
	94		94
	——		——

Smith

	£		£
Sales day book	118	Cash book	60
		Balance c/d	58
	——		——
	118		118
	——		——

Turnip

	£		£
Sales day book	141	Cash book	110
		Balance c/d	31
	——		——
	141		141
	——		——

Clog

	£		£
Sales day book	235	Balance c/d	235
	——		——
	235		235
	——		——

Foul

	£		£
Sales day book	353	Cash book	80
		Balance c/d	273
	———		———
	353		353
	———		———

Purchase ledger:

Snell

	£		£
Cash book	70	Purchase day book	80
Balance c/d	10		
	———		———
	80		80
	———		———

Ryan

	£		£
Balance c/d	100	Purchase day book	100
	———		———
	100		100
	———		———

Ovett

	£		£
Cash book	30	Purchase day book	150
Balance c/d	120		
	———		———
	150		150
	———		———

Coe

	£		£
Balance c/d	300	Purchase day book	300
	———		———
	300		300
	———		———

Keino

	£		£
Balance c/d	100	Purchase day book	100
	———		———
	100		100
	———		———

British Telecom

	£		£
Cash book	50	Purchase day book	50
	———		———
	50		50
	———		———

British Gas

	£		£
Balance c/d	75	Purchase day book	75
	75		75

(c)   **Trial balance**

	Dr	Cr
	£	£
Sales ledger balances (total)	661	
Sales		941
Purchases ledger balances (total)		705
Purchases	730	
Telephone	50	
Heating and lighting	75	
Bank		440
Sundry income		10
Petty cash	161	
Wages	300	
Sundry expenses	92	
Stationery	16	
Postage	3	
Travelling	8	
	2,096	2,096

Note: the trial balance in part (c) has been extracted before closing off the income and expense accounts to the trading and profit and loss account.

CHAPTER **10**   MULTIPLE-CHOICE QUESTION

A   Cash refunds and interest charged on overdue accounts appear on the debit side of the account.

CHAPTER **10**   EXAM-TYPE QUESTIONS

Question 1: Excel Stores Ltd

(a)

	£	£
	−	+
Balance on control account at 30 June 20X4		84,688.31
Error in deriving closing balance (addition of debit side incorrect)		11,000.00
Items posted to wrong side of account:		
Discount received	2,656.82	
	2,656.82	
Contras	3,049.75	
	3,049.75	
Purchase returns omitted	39.60	

Error in credit side total		
(£195,461.19 − £195,261.19)		200.00
Transposition error in debit side total		
(£195,261.19 − £192,561.19)		2,700.00
Petty cash payment omitted	10.22	
	11,462.96	98,588.31
		11,462.96
Amended balance		87,125.35

Note: in this question you must spot the errors in the control account itself.

Given the number of errors in the control account, it would be easier to write it out again! However, the question asked for a statement reconciling the original and correct balances, and the answer has been produced in that format. Normally, a ledger account format should be used to emphasise that the adjustments form part of the double entry system.

(b)

		£	£
		−	+
Individual creditors at 30 June 20X4			86,538.28
Item:			
1	No effect		
2			30.00
3	584.41 − 548.14	36.27	
4			674.32
5	12.56 + 8.13	20.69	
		20.69	
6		39.60	
		117.25	87,242.60
			117.25
Amended listing			87,125.35

Question 2: DEF Ltd – Sales Ledger

(a)

Sales ledger control

	£		£
30.9.X8 Balance b/d	12,814	30.9.X8 Balance b/d	592
		Sales overstated (1)	850
		Returns understated (2)	90
30.9.X8 Balance c/d	158	30.9.X8 Balance c/d	11,440
	12,972		12,972
1.10.X8 Balance b/d	11,440	1.10.X8 Balance b/d	158

Note: net balance £11,282 (£11,440 − 158).

(b)

Sales ledger control report – 30 Sept 20X8

		£	
Balance brought forward		15,438	
Add:	Sales (74,691 – 354)	74,337	(4)
	Repayments made (1,249 + 217)	1,466	(5)
	Adjustments	23	
Less:	Sales returns (2,347 + 354)	2,701	(4)
	Payments received (71,203 – 217)	70,986	(5)
	Bad debts written off (646 + 793)	1,439	(6)
	Purchase ledger contra (139 + 474)	613	(3)
	Discounts allowed (4,128 + 57)	4,185	(8)
	Adjustments	58	
Balance carried forward		11,282	

(c) (1) The sales figure in the accounting system is overstated by £850.

(2) The sales returns figure in the accounting system is understated by £90.

(3) The computer individual account summary purchase ledger contra, is understated by £474.

(4) The individual account is overstated by £354 × 2 = £708.

(5) The individual account is understated by £217 × 2 = £434.

(6) The computer individual account summary bad debts are understated by £793.

(7) The individual accounts need adjusting:

   Dr   CG Ltd £919

   Cr   EG Ltd   £919

(8) The individual account is overstated by £57.

(9) There is no effect on the sales ledger control as the error affects the purchases ledger.

CHAPTER 11   MULTIPLE-CHOICE QUESTIONS

Question 1

C The bank reconciliation should have been calculated as follows:

	£
Overdraft per bank statement	(38,600)
Add deposits not yet credited	41,200
	2,600
Less outstanding cheques	(3,300)
Overdraft per cash book	(700)

Question 2

A Items 3 and 4 relate to timing differences only and would appear in the bank reconciliation. They do not require an entry in the cash book, because they have already been entered.

CHAPTER **11**   EXAM-TYPE QUESTION

Spanners Ltd

(a)   **Cash book adjustments**

Cash book

	£				£
Balance b/d	960	(1)	Bank charges		35
(4) Correction of balance b/d	63	(2)	Reversal of error		
			2 × £47		94
		(3)	Returned cheque		18
			Balance c/d		876
	1,023				1,023
Balance b/d	876				

(b)   **Bank reconciliation at 31 October**

	£	£
Balance per bank statement (overdrawn)		124 o/d
Add: Unpresented cheques (5) £(214 + 370 + 30)		614
		738 o/d
Less: Outstanding lodgement (6)	1,542	
Cheque charged in error (7)	72	
		1,614
Balance per cash book (in hand)		876

CHAPTER **12**   MULTIPLE-CHOICE QUESTIONS

Question 1

B   The profit will be understated by the following amount

	£
Amount charged in error to the repairs account	38,000
Less depreciation chargeable on the plant	
$(3/12 \times 20\% \times £38,000)$	(1,900)
	£36,100

Question 2

D

	£
Opening balance on suspense account	
(836,200 − £819,700)	16,500
Difference remaining after postings to the discount	
accounts (£5,100 − £3,900)	(1,200)
Difference from cheque incorrectly posted	
(£19,000 − £9,100)	(9,900)
	£5,400

Question 3

B Items 1 and 3 would result in an imbalance in the trial balance and therefore require an entry to the suspense account. Items 2, 4 and 5 do not affect the balancing of the accounts.

Question 1: Journal entries

Details	Dr £	Cr £
(a) Motor expenses	150	
Motor vehicles		150
Road fund tax transferred to correct account		

	Dr £	Cr £
(b) Pimple purchase ledger account	1,500	
Pimple sales ledger account		1,500
Contra on Pimple's purchase and sales ledger accounts		

	Dr £	Cr £
(c) Bad debts	570	
Black		270
Provision for doubtful debts		300
	570	570

Closure of Black's sales ledger account following notification of bankruptcy and creation of doubtful debts provision.

Note: as the business does not have control accounts for sales and purchases the double entry for debtors and creditors is in their individual accounts.

Question 2: February

Suspense account

		£			£
(a)	January – Debtor account	9	31 Dec Trial balance difference		736
(b)	Discount received	237	(d) Debtors in trial balance		268
(g)	Discount received in trial balance (397 + 379)	776	(e) Bank overdraft in trial balance		18
		1,022			1,022

(c) The correcting journal entry is as follows:

	Dr £	Cr £
Dr Sales account	500	
Cr Disposal account		500

Note: as a Dr and Cr had originally been made, the trial balance is not out of balance as a result of this transaction. In order to complete the accounts, further entries would be required to transfer the cost and accumulated depreciation on the machine to the disposal account.

(f)   Dr   April – Debtor account   1,000
       Cr   Sales account   1,000

Note: as no Dr and Cr had been made, the trial balance still balances!

CHAPTER **13**   EXAM-TYPE QUESTIONS

Question 1: Saavik Ltd

MEMORANDUM

To: The Company Accountant

From: Assistant Accountant

Date: X-X-20XX

Subject: Principal features of a spreadsheet financial modelling package

As requested in our recent discussion concerning the development of the accounting system of the company, I set out below the principal features of a spreadsheet financial modelling package.

(a) **Principal features of a spreadsheet package**

   (i)   **Overview**

   A spreadsheet is a large accounting worksheet comprising a matrix of columns (numbered A, B, C etc) and rows. The intersection of each row and column is called a cell. Each cell can contain any of the following:

   (1)   a description of an item, e.g. 'sales'

   (2)   a value, e.g. '3,000'

   (3)   a calculation, e.g. SUM(B3..B6).

   By carefully inserting data into the spreadsheet in these cells, a model of the business can be created. It is normal to have time periods represented by the columns, and items of income and expenditure represented by the rows.

   (ii)   **Storage and viewing of the spreadsheet**

   The spreadsheet will be stored on disk, and called into the computer's memory by the spreadsheet application program when the user wants to work on the spreadsheet. The VDU, however, cannot show all of the spreadsheet at any one time, and so the spreadsheet can be scrolled up/down and right/left using command keys or the computer's mouse if it has one.

   A full picture of the spreadsheet can, though, be printed out as a 'hard copy' whenever this is required.

   (iii)   **Use of the spreadsheet**

   When the model of the company has been built up on the spreadsheet, then it will permit 'what if?' analysis to be carried out on it. The user of the spreadsheet can alter the variables in the spreadsheet to see what effect this has on other parts of the model. For example, sales value for all product lines could be altered and the results on gross and net profit be seen. This type of analysis would normally take many hours using a manual system and gives a spreadsheet a distinct advantage over purely manual systems.

(b) **Criteria to be considered when evaluating a spreadsheet package**

   (i)   Size of spreadsheet – is the spreadsheet large enough for the company's requirements?

   (ii)   Other applications needed within the spreadsheet – does the spreadsheet need a separate database?

   (iii)   Manual – is there a well-written, easy to use reference manual?

(iv) Supplier support – does the supplier provide telephone hot-line support to sort out problems?

(v) Is the spreadsheet display easy to understand?

(vi) Does the spreadsheet contain all the arithmetical functions needed?

(vii) Is there an adequate help facility in the software?

(viii) Is split screen working allowed?

Note: it is important to make sure that your answer is in the format required, in this case a memorandum.

Question 2: Database

(a) *Database* is the term used to describe a sophisticated management information concept, based on the use of computers. It uses a comprehensive file of data so structured that individual applications, e.g. sales ledger, production control, management accounting, can draw on information from the file and update it but do not themselves constrain the file's design or its contents.

Whereas in conventional systems the programmer is concerned with the structure of files and methods of access, in a database system he can work independently of the file.

Between him and the file is a software interface known as the *database management system* (DBMS) which is responsible for providing the data as and when required by the particular application program.

(b) Advantages to be gained from using such a system include the following:

(i) The total needs of the company are taken into account in the design of the centralised file, in contrast to individual files serving the needs of each application.

(ii) Reports should be more comprehensive and meaningful because management information is based on all the data available.

(iii) More effective utilisation of programmers is possible because they are no longer concerned with data management as such. Also, they are no longer constrained by the need to consider file structure, etc.

(iv) Flexibility is increased because the DBMS can effect changes in the file independently of application programs.

CHAPTER **14**	MULTIPLE-CHOICE QUESTION

D The other three contain items which are not considered to contribute towards reliability.

CHAPTER **14**	EXAM TYPE QUESTION

Accounting concepts

(a) **Materiality**

The ASB 'Statement of Principles for Financial Reporting' defines materiality as follows:

> Information is material to the financial statements if its mistreatment or omission might reasonably be expected to influence the economic decisions of users of those financial statements, including their assessment of management's stewardship.

Example: A small item of office equipment, such as a stapler, might be regarded as a fixed asset because it remains in the business for several accounting periods. However, the record keeping involved is not worthwhile for such an insignificant item, and in practice its cost is recorded as an expense in the profit and loss account. Because the cost is immaterial, this is acceptable.

(b) **Substance over form**

In many cases the strict legal form of a transaction differs from its true economic substance. In such cases, the real nature (substance) of the transaction should be recognised whenever legally possible.

Example: An asset being acquired on hire purchase or finance lease terms should be recognised as an asset when the contract begins, even though ownership does not pass until the end of the contract, if at all.

(c) **Money measurement**

Accounts are stated in monetary terms, and can only deal with items to which a monetary value can be attributed. This is the money measurement concept. If an asset cannot be valued with reasonable accuracy, it cannot be included in the balance sheet.

Example: Most businesses make no attempt to include the value of their human resources on the balance sheet, because it is impractical to value skills, knowledge, etc., in a reliable way.

CHAPTER **15**	MULTIPLE-CHOICE QUESTION

D Statements 2,3 and 5 are correct. Statement 1 is incorrect: the SSAP 13 criteria relate to development expenditure, not research expenditure. Statement 4 is incorrect because SSAP 13 does not specify a particular number of years.

CHAPTER **15**	EXAM-TYPE QUESTION

Research and development expenditure

Note: when this (compulsory) question was set many students did not attempt it. It is not a difficult question but it does reinforce the need to ensure that all parts of the syllabus are covered.

(a) **Pure research:** Original work which is not primarily directed towards any specific aim or application.

Applied research: Original work directed towards a specific practical aim or objective.

Development: The use of scientific or technical knowledge to produce new or substantially improved products.

(b) The two accounting concepts which are particularly relevant here are the accruals concept and the prudence concept.

The accruals concept requires costs to be matched with the relevant revenue. This implies that costs which have been incurred but have not yet resulted in sales should be carried forward as assets at the year end so that they can be matched with sales when they do arise.

Under this concept all development costs would be carried forward.

Prudence however, requires costs to be written off unless it is reasonably certain that sales will be made in the future which will fully cover those costs.

Under this concept research expenditure would be written off as there is no clear link between the expenditure and the commercial sale of a product. Some development expenditure would also be written off if by the end of the accounting period it is not reasonably certain that profitable production will ensue. Only part of development expenditure would thus be carried forward.

CHAPTER 16	MULTIPLE-CHOICE QUESTION

B   The other lists contain adjusting items.

CHAPTER 16	EXAM-TYPE QUESTIONS

Question 1: Events

(a) SSAP17 *Accounting for post balance sheet events* offers the following definitions of events occurring between the balance sheet date and the date on which the financial statements are approved by the board of directors:

   (i)   Adjusting events are post balance sheet events which provide additional evidence of conditions existing at the balance sheet date. They include events which, because of statutory or conventional requirements, are reflected in financial statements.

   (ii) Non-adjusting events are post balance sheet events which concern conditions which did not exist at the balance sheet date.

(b) Any two from the following lists.

ADJUSTING EVENTS

The following are examples of post balance sheet events which normally should be classified as adjusting events:

Fixed assets. The subsequent determination of the purchase price or of the proceeds of sale of assets purchased or sold before the year end.

Property. A valuation which provides evidence of an impairment in value.

Investments. The receipt of a copy of the financial statements or other information in respect of an unlisted company which provides evidence of an impairment in the value of a long-term investment.

Stocks and work-in-progress

   (i)   The receipt of proceeds of sales after the balance sheet date or other evidence concerning the net realisable value of stocks.

   (ii) The receipt of evidence that the previous estimate of accrued profit on a long-term contract was materially inaccurate.

Debtors. The renegotiation of amounts owing by debtors, or the insolvency of a debtor.

Dividends receivable. The declaration of dividends by subsidiaries and associated companies relating to periods prior to the balance sheet date of the holding company.

Taxation. The receipt of information regarding rates of taxation.

Claims. Amounts received or receivable in respect of insurance claims which were in the course of negotiation at the balance sheet date.

Discoveries. The discovery of errors or frauds which show that the financial statements were incorrect.

NON-ADJUSTING EVENTS

The following are examples of post balance sheet events which normally should be classified as non-adjusting events:

Mergers and acquisitions.

Reconstructions and proposed reconstructions.

Issues of shares and debentures.

Purchases and sales of fixed assets and investments.

Losses of fixed assets or stocks as a result of a catastrophe such as fire or flood.

Opening new trading activities or extending existing trading activities.

Closing a significant part of the trading activities if this was not anticipated at the year end.

Decline in the value of property and investments held as fixed assets, if it can be demonstrated that the decline occurred after the year end.

Changes in rates of foreign exchange.

Government action, such as nationalisation.

Strikes and other labour disputes.

Augmentation of pension benefits.

(c) A material post balance sheet event requires changes in the amounts to be included in financial statements where:

(i)   it is an adjusting event; or

(ii) it indicates that application of the going concern concept to the whole or a material part of the company is not appropriate.

A material post balance sheet event should be disclosed where:

(i)   it is a non-adjusting event of such materiality that its non-disclosure would affect the ability of the users of financial statements to reach a proper understanding of the financial position; or

(ii) it is the reversal or maturity after the year end of a transaction entered into before the year end, the substance of which was primarily to alter the appearance of the company's balance sheet (window dressing).

In respect of each post balance sheet event which is required to be disclosed as above, the following information should be stated by way of notes in financial statements:

(i)   the nature of the event; and

(ii) an estimate of the financial effect, or a statement that it is not practicable to make such an estimate.

The estimate of the financial effect should be disclosed before taking account of taxation, and the taxation implications should be explained where necessary for a proper understanding of the financial position.

The date on which the financial statements are approved by the board of directors should be disclosed in the financial statements.

Question 2: Jurien Limited

MEMORANDUM

To: The Directors of Jurien Limited

From: Financial Adviser

Reference: Accounting treatment of items in current financial statements

Here is my advice on the three matters on which you have raised queries.

(a) In accordance with FRS 12 'Provisions, Contingent Liabilities and Contingent Assets' we must provide for the best estimate of the amount needed to settle the obligation, because there is a probable present obligation arising from a past event.

(b) In accordance with SSAP 17 'Accounting for Post Balance Sheet Events', this will be an adjusting event if it provides evidence of conditions existing at the balance sheet date. In other words, if we think the customer's difficulties existed at the balance sheet date, then the value of his debt should be written down in the accounts, i.e. we should make a provision. Unless there is clear evidence that the difficulties have only arisen after the balance sheet date, a provision should be made.

(c) SSAP 9 'Stocks and Long-term Contracts' contains reasonably clear rules on the allocation of overheads to stocks of finished goods:

 (i)   Only overheads relating to production may be included.

 (ii) The allocation of fixed production overheads must be based on the normal level of activity in the period.

 Two examples of overheads to be excluded:

 (i)   selling costs

 (ii) administrative overheads not contributing to bringing stocks to their present condition and location.

Financial Adviser

MULTIPLE CHOICE QUESTIONS

Question 1

A   Credit sales can be calculated as a balancing figure on the debtors control account.

Debtors control account

	£		£
Balance b/f	29,100	Bank takings	381,600
Bank – refunds	2,100	Expenses	6,800
Credit sales (balance)	412,400	Bad debts	7,200
		Discounts allowed	9,400
		Balance c/d	38,600
	443,600		443,600

Credit sales = £412,400, cash sales = £112,900, total sales = £525,300.

Question 2

D

	£
Opening stock	17,000
Purchases	91,000
Closing stock	(24,000)
Cost of sales	84,000

Sales = £84,000 × 100/60 = £140,000

Question 3

A   The rent expense for the year should be:

$$\frac{5}{12} \times £24,000 + \frac{7}{12} \times £30,000 = £27,500$$

Question 4

B   Cost of sales = 70% × £64,800 = £45,360

	£
Opening stock	28,400
Purchases	49,600
Cost of sales	(45,360)
Loss of stock	32,640

CHAPTER **17**   PRACTICE QUESTIONS

Question 1: B Letitslide

Trading and profit and loss account for year ended 31 December 20X5

	£	£
Credit sales (W2)		1,560
Cash sales (W2)		4,317
		5,877
Opening stock	1,310	
Add: Purchases (W3)	3,133	
	4,443	
Less: Closing stock	1,623	
		2,820
Gross profit		3,057
Expenses (W4)	1,090	
Bad debts (W6)	49	
Depreciation (W7)	60	
		1,199
Net profit		1,858

Balance sheet as at 31 December 20X5

	£	£	£
Fixed asset:			
Delivery van, at cost			900
Less: Depreciation (W7)			60
			840
Current assets:			
Stock		1,623	
Debtors (412–30)	382		
Less: Provision for doubtful debts (W6)	19		
		363	
Cash at bank		572	
Cash in hand		29	
		2,587	
Less:Current liabilities:			
Trade creditors	914		
Accruals	103		
		1,017	
			1,570
			2,410
Capital account:			
At 1 Jan 20X5 (W1)			1,652
Profit for year		1,858	
Drawings (W5)		1,100	
Retained profit for year			758
At 31 December 20X5			2,410

Note: as the cash account and bank account have already been summarised it is only necessary to post the other side of the cash and bank entries to the relevant accounts. Some information may be inserted immediately into the final accounts, so leave a page for each of the final accounts. Information can then be inserted as soon as it is available. For example, opening and closing stock can be put straight to the final accounts.

Workings

(W1)   **Opening statement of affairs**

	£
Stock	1,310
Debtors	268
Cash	62
Bank	840
	2,480
Less: Creditors (£712 + 116)	828
Capital at 1 Jan 20X5	1,652

Note: there is no need to complete this working before proceeding to post the transactions for the year. It is better to add the items as and when you find them in the question.

(W2)   **Sales control**

	£		£
Debtors b/d	268	Cheques for sales	1,416
Sales for year (bal fig)	5,877	Bad debt written off	30
		Cash takings	4,317
		Debtors c/d	382
	6,145		6,145
Balance b/d	382		

Note: the sales control account has been used to find total sales. An alternative approach would be to post the 'shop takings' straight to the trading account as cash sales and the balancing figure in the sales control account would then be £1,560, i.e. the credit sales.

(W3)   **Purchases control**

	£		£
Cash	316	Creditors b/d	712
Bank	2,715	Drawings	100
Balance c/d	914	Purchases	3,133
	3,945		3,945
		Balance b/d	914

(W4)   **Expenses**

	£		£
Cash	584	Creditors b/d	116
Bank	519	Profit and loss account	1,090
Balance c/d	103		
			1,206
	1,206		
		Balance b/d	103

(W5)   **Drawings**

	£
Purchases	100
Cash account	600
Bank account	400
	1,100

(W6)   **Bad debts account**

	£		£
Bad debt	30	Profit and loss account	49
Sales control account:			
Provision for doubtful			
debts account 5% × 382	19		
			49
	49		

Note: as there is no opening provision for doubtful debts, there is no need to show that account. The £19 can be inserted into the balance sheet.

(W7)   **Depreciation**

$$20\% \times 900 \times \frac{4}{12} = £60$$

Question 2: Ben White

Note: where a gross profit or mark-up is used to compute information for accounting purposes, the trading account is an integral part of the workings (as well as the solution). The missing information may be any item within the trading account. Write up the trading account with the information immediately available – in this question opening and closing stock – and insert further information when it becomes available through writing up the sales and purchases control accounts. In the question the purchases figures become available. The trading account can then be used to compute sales.

(a) **Trading and profit and loss account for year ended 30 June 20X6**

	£	£	%
Sales $\frac{125}{100} \times £12,000$		15,000	125
Opening stock	3,825		
Add: Purchases (W5)	12,175		
	16,000		
Less: Closing stock	4,000		
Cost of sales		12,000	100
Gross profit 25% × £12,000		3,000	25
Depreciation (10% × £5,000)		500	
Net profit		2,500	

(b) **Balance sheet as at 30 June 20X6**

	Cost £	Dep'n £	£
Fixed assets			
Plant and machinery	5,000	500	4,500
Motor van	700	-	700
	5,700	500	5,200
Current assets			
Stock		4,000	
Debtors (W4)		7,000	
Cash		1,950	
		12,950	
Current liabilities			
Creditors		3,500	
			9,450
			14,650
Loan (W6)			1,500
			13,150

Capital account

Balance at 1 Jul 20X5 (W1)	13,200
Legacy introduced	300
Net profit for year	2,500
Drawings (W7)	(2,850)
	13,150

Workings

(W1)   **Opening statement of affairs**

	£	£
Assets:		
Plant and machinery		5,000
Stock		3,825
Debtors		7,175
Cash at bank		2,200
		18,200
Less: Liabilities:		
Creditors	3,000	
Loan	2,000	
		5,000
Capital at 1 July 20X5		13,200

(W2)   **Bank**

	£		£
Balance b/d	2,200	Purchase	11,675
Capital – legacy	300	Loan	500
Cash (bal fig (i))	13,885	Van	700
		Drawings (£80 × 12)	960
		Drawings – income tax	600
		Balance c/d	1,950
	16,385		16,385
Balance b/d	1,950		

(W3)   **Cash**

	£		£
Sales control	15,175	Bank	13,885
		Drawings (bal fig (iv))	1,290
	15,175		15,175

(W4)   **Sales control**

	£		£
Debtors b/d	7,175	Cash (bal fig (iii))	15,175
Trading account – sales		Debtors c/d	7,000
(calculated from T/A			
using GP percentage)	15,000		
	22,175		22,175
Balance b/d	7,000		

(W5)   **Purchases control**

	£		£
Cash	11,675	Creditors b/d	3,000
Creditors c/d	3,500	Trading account – purchases	12,175
	15,175		15,175
		Balance b/d	3,500

(W6)   **Z Loan**

Sum owing	2,000
Less paid in year	500
	1,500

(W7)   **Drawings**

	£
Bank account	960
Bank account – income tax	600
Cash account	1,290
	2,850

Note re sequence of entries:

(i) Cash paid into bank is calculated as a balancing figure in the bank account (£13,885).

(ii) Total sales for the year is calculated from the trading account (cost of goods sold can be converted to sales by addition of 25% onto cost).

(iii) Cash collected from sales is calculated as balancing figure in sales control account (£15,175).

(iv) Drawings of £1,290 is balancing figure in the cash account.

CHAPTER 18   MULTIPLE-CHOICE QUESTION

A

	D £000	E £000	F £000	Total £000
6 months to 30.6.X0				
Salary		12	12	24
Profit share (5:3:2)	108	64.8	43.2	216
6 months to 31.12.X0				
Salary		18	12	30
Profit share (3:1:1)	126	42	42	210
	234	136.8	109.2	480

| CHAPTER **18** | PRACTICE QUESTION |

Oliver and Twist

(a)   **Trial balance as at 31 December**

	Dr £	Cr £
Capital account:		
Oliver		9,000
Twist		10,000
10% loan account:		
Twist		5,000
Williams		6,000
Current account balance on 1 January:		
Oliver		1,000
Twist		2,000
Drawings:		
Oliver	6,500	
Twist	5,500	
Sales		113,100
Sales returns	3,000	
Closing stock	17,000	
Cost of goods sold	70,000	
Sales ledger control account	30,000	
Purchase ledger control account		25,000
Operating expenses	26,100	
Fixed assets at cost	37,000	
Provision for depreciation		18,000
Bank overdraft		3,000
Suspense (bal fig)		3,000
	———	———
	195,100	195,100
	———	———

Note: the question requires a trial balance to be drawn up before any adjustments are made. Many candidates attempted to make adjustments before the extraction of the trial balance but this was not what was required.

The information in the question refers to 'closing stock' and 'cost of goods sold'. Both of these imply that the year-end adjustments for stock have already been made.

(b) *Note:* there is no set format per part (b). The key thing to remember is that parts (b) and (c) of the question are the normal parts of an accounts preparation from a trial balance question.

Adjustments to trial balance

Ref to question			Dr £	Cr £
(a)	(i)	Sales returns	100	
		Sales ledger control		100
	(ii)	Purchase ledger control	200	
		Sales ledger control		200
	(iii)	Sales ledger control	1,800	
		Sales		1,800

(b)	Disposal	5,000	
	Fixed asset cost		5,000
	Accumulated depreciation	5,000	
	Disposal		5,000
	Suspense	1,000	
	Disposal		1,000

(*Note:* The last entry arises as the transaction was originally inserted into the books as a one-sided transaction (Dr Bank). The missing credit entry must therefore make up part of the £3,000 suspense account balance.)

(c)	Expenses	500	
	Drawings – Twist		500
	Drawings – Oliver	1,000	
	Cost of goods sold		1,000
(d)	Interest expense	1,100	
	Interest accrual		1,100

(c)   **Profit and loss account for the year**

	£	£
Sales (113,100 + 1,800)		114,900
Less: Returns (3,000 + 100)		3,100
		111,800
Cost of sales (70,000 – 1,000)		(69,000)
Gross profit		42,800
Operating expenses (26,100 – 1,000 + 500)	25,600	
Loan interest	1,100	
		(26,700)
Net profit for year		16,100
Appropriations:		
Interest		
Oliver	900	
Twist	1,000	
		(1,900)
Salary – Oliver		(5,000)
		9,200
Balance of profit:		
Oliver	4,600	
Twist	4,600	
		(9,200)

Balance sheet as at 31 December

	£	£	£
Fixed assets:			
Cost (37,000 – 5,000)		32,000	
Depreciation (18,000 – 5,000)		13,000	
			19,000

Current assets:		
Stock	17,000	
Debtors (30,000 − 100 − 200 + 1,800)	31,500	
	48,500	
Current liabilities:		
Creditors (25,000 − 200)	24,800	
Interest	1,100	
Bank overdraft	3,000	
Suspense account	2,000	
	30,900	
Net current assets		17,600
		36,600
Loans		(11,000)
		25,600

	Capital £	Current £	Total £
Oliver (see working)	9,000	4,000	13,000
Twist (see working)	10,000	2,600	12,600
	19,000	6,600	25,600

Working

Current accounts

	Oliver £	Twist £		Oliver £	Twist £
Drawings	6,500	5,500	Balance b/d	1,000	2,000
Adjustment to drawings	1,000		Adjustment to drawings		500
			Interest on capital	900	1,000
			Salary	5,000	
Balance c/d	4,000	2,600	Profit	4,600	4,600
	11,500	8,100		11,500	8,100

CHAPTER **19**   MULTIPLE CHOICE QUESTION

C

Share capital	£'000
Opening 1,000,000 shares of 50p	500
Issue of 200,000 shares of 50p	100
Bonus issue 1,200,000/4 = 300,000 shares of 50p	150
	750

Share premium	*£'000*
Opening share premium	300
Issue of 200,000 shares at premium of 80p	160
Charge for bonus issue	(150)
	———
	310
	———

CHAPTER **19**   PRACTICE QUESTIONS

Question 1: Floyd Ltd

Profit and loss account for year ended 31 March 20X5

	£	£
Sales		998,600
Cost of sales (W1)		830,740
		———
Gross profit		167,860
Administrative costs (W1)		100,741
Debenture interest (9% × 75,000)		6,750
		———
Profit before taxation		60,369
Corporation tax		31,200
		———
Profit after taxation		29,169
Dividends:		
Paid	2,500	
Proposed (W4)	12,000	
	———	
		14,500
		———
Retained profit for year		14,669
Profit and loss account b/f		45,910
		———
Profit and loss account c/f		60,579
		———

Balance sheet as at 31 March 20X5

	Cost £	*Dep'n* £	£
Fixed assets:			
Tangible assets – plant (W3)	307,400	115,340	192,060
	———	———	
Current assets:			
Stock		61,070	
Debtors	52,030		
Less: Provision	2,601		
	———		
		49,429	
Cash at bank		41,118	
Cash in hand		126	
		———	
		151,743	
		———	

Creditors: amounts falling due within one year:

Creditors		38,274
Current taxation		31,200
Dividend payable (W4)		12,000
Debenture interest accrued		6,750
		88,224

Net current assets	63,519
Total assets less current liabilities	255,579

Creditors: amounts falling due after more
than one year:

9% debentures 20X9	75,000
	180,579

Capital and reserves:

Called up share capital: 25p ordinary shares	100,000
Share premium account	20,000
Profit and loss account	60,579
	180,579

Workings

(W1)

	Cost of sales £	Administrative costs £
Per question	800,000	100,000
Bad debts (W2)		741
Depreciation (W3)	30,740	
	830,740	100,741

(W2)   **Provision for doubtful debts account**

	£		£
Profit and loss account:		Balance b/d	1,860
Balance c/d 5% × 52,030	2,601	Administrative costs	741
	2,601		2,601

(W3)   **Accumulated depreciation account**

	£		£
		Balance b/d	84,600
		Profit and loss account:	
Balance c/d	115,340	Cost of sales 10% × 307,400	30,740
	115,340		115,340

(W4)   **Final dividend**

Number of 25p shares = 400,000

Hence dividend of 3p per share amounts to

$\frac{3}{100} \times 400,000 = £12,000$

Question 2: Nimrod Co Ltd

Trading and profit and loss account for year ended 30 September 20X7

	£	£
Sales		240,000
Less: Returns		1,116
		238,884
Stock at 1 October 20X6	42,744	
Purchases	131,568	
	174,312	
Less: Closing stock at 30 September 20X7	46,638	
		127,674
Gross profit		111,210
Discount received		5,292
		116,502
Rates	6,372	
Wages and salaries (W2)	24,840	
Insurance (W1)	5,388	
General expenses	1,308	
Bad debts (W4)	1,476	
Depreciation: Buildings (W3)	11,400	
Fixtures and fittings (W3)	7,200	
Debenture interest (W5)	2,400	
		60,384
Profit before tax		56,118
Taxation		20,000
Profit after taxation		36,118
Dividends:		
Preference: Paid	1,800	
Proposed (W6)	1,800	
Ordinary: Proposed (W6)	3,000	
		6,600
Retained for the year		29,518
Transfer to general reserve		24,000
		5,518
Profit and loss account b/f		6,000
Profit and loss account c/f		11,518

Nimrod Ltd

Balance sheet as at 30 September 20X7

	Cost £	Dep'n £	£
Fixed assets:			
Intangible assets:			
Goodwill	49,200	-	49,200
Tangible assets:			
Land	54,000	-	54,000
Buildings	114,000	29,400	84,600
Furniture and fittings	66,000	37,200	28,800
	283,200	66,600	216,600
Current assets:			
Stock		46,638	
Debtors	37,920		
Less: Provision (W4)	1,896		
		36,024	
Prepayments (W1)		300	
Cash in hand		696	
		83,658	
Creditors: amounts falling due within one year:			
Bank overdraft		18,000	
Creditors		18,900	
Dividend payable (W6)		4,800	
Accruals (W7)		2,040	
Corporation tax		20,000	
		63,740	
Net current assets			19,918
Total assets less current liabilities			236,518
Creditors: amounts falling due after more than one year:			
5% debentures			48,000
			188,518
Capital and reserves:			
Called up share capital:			
60,000 £1 ordinary shares			60,000
60,000 6% £1 preference shares			60,000
Share premium account			3,000
General reserve (30,000 + 24,000)			54,000
Profit and loss account			11,518
			188,518

Workings

Note: there is a lot of information to be inserted into the final accounts, but some of the balances per the trial balance need adjustment. Work through the additional information, removing the relevant balances from the trial balance into the workings. Balances not requiring adjustment can then be inserted into the final accounts.

(W1)

Insurance account

	£		£
Balance per trial balance	5,688	Profit and loss account	5,388
		Balance c/d – prepayment	300
	5,688		5,688

(W2)

Wages account

	£		£
Balance per trial balance	24,000	Profit and loss account	24,840
Balance c/d – accrual	840		
	24,840		24,840

(W3)

Accumulated depreciation account

	Buildings £	Furniture £		Buildings £	Furniture £
Balance c/d	29,400	37,200	Balance per trial balance	18,000	30,000
			Profit and loss a/c		
			$10\% \times 114{,}000$	11,400	
			$20\% \times (66{,}000 - 30{,}000)$		7,200
	29,400	37,200		29,400	37,200

(W4)

Bad debts account

	£		£
Per trial balance	2,028	Provision for doubtful debts account	552
		Profit and loss account	1,476
	2,028		2,028

Provision for doubtful debts account

	£		£
Bad debts account	552	Per trial balance	2,448
Balance c/d $5\% \times 37{,}920$	1,896		
	2,448		2,448

(W5) Debenture interest account

	£		£
Per trial balance	1,200	Profit and loss account	2,400
Balance c/d – accrual	1,200		
	2,400		2,400

(W6) Dividends

	£
Ordinary 5% × £60,000	3,000
Preference 3% × £60,000	1,800
	4,800

(W7) Accruals

	£
Wages (W2)	840
Debenture interest (W5)	1,200
	2,040

CHAPTER 20

PRACTICE QUESTION

General Warehouses plc

General Warehouses plc

Balance sheet as at 31 December 20X3

	£m	£m	£m
Fixed assets			
Intangible assets			
Goodwill			50
Tangible assets			
Plant and machinery			22
			72
Current assets			
Stocks		50	
Debtors		165	
Cash at bank and in hand		30	
		245	
Creditors: amounts falling due within one year			
Trade creditors	30		
Other creditors including taxation	55	85	
Net current assets			160
Total assets less current liabilities			232

Capital and reserves

Called up share capital	150
Share premium account	10
General reserve	10
Profit and loss account	62
	——
	232
	——

General Warehouses plc

Profit and loss account for the year ended 31 December 20X3

	£m	£m
Turnover (500 – 14)		486
Increase in stock of goods for resale		20
		——
		506
Purchases of goods for resale		257
		——
		249
Staff costs	90	
Depreciation	16	
Other operating charges (working)	59	165
	——	——
Profit from trading activities		84
Income from other fixed asset investments		8
		——
Profit on ordinary activities before taxation		92
Tax on profit on ordinary activities		25
		——
Profit on ordinary activities after taxation		67
Proposed dividend on ordinary shares		30
		——
Retained profit for year		37
		——

Reserves

	Share premium £000	General reserve £000	Profit and loss account £000	Total £000
At 1 January 20X3	10	10	25	45
Retained profit for the year			37	37
	——	——	——	——
At 31 December 20X3	10	10	62	82
	——	——	——	——

Working

The figure for other operating charges is as follows:

	£m
Carriage outwards	14
General distribution expenses	5
Vehicle hire	10
General administrative expenses	15
Directors' salaries	15
	——
	59
	——

EXAM-TYPE QUESTIONS

Question 1: Board of Directors

General Warehouses plc

Profit and loss account for the year ended 31 December 20X3

	£m	£m
Turnover (500 – 14)		486
Cost of sales		237
Gross profit		249
Distribution costs	115	
Administrative expenses	50	165
Profit from trading activities		84
Income from other fixed asset investments		8
Profit on ordinary activities before taxation		92
Tax on profit on ordinary activities		25
Profit on ordinary activities after taxation		67
Proposed dividend		30
Retained profit		37

Working

	Cost of sales £m	Distribution costs £m	Administrative expenses £m
Opening stock	30		
Purchases	270		
Purchases returns	(13)		
Carriage outwards		14	
Warehouse wages		40	
Salespersons' salaries		30	
Administrative wages			20
Delivery vehicle hire		10	
Distribution expenses		5	
Administrative expenses			15
Directors' salaries			15
Closing stock	(50)		
Depreciation		16	
	237	115	50

Tutorial note: This three column working will be needed in almost all questions requiring Format 1. It is a very fast way of getting the three totals in which all the expenses except interest have to be included. Note that all you need to do is list the items from the trial balance, then add any end of year adjustments. Negatives go in brackets, and you have the three totals you need.

Question 2: Ople plc

Profit and loss account for year to 31 March 20X2

	£'000	£'000
Turnover		8,500
Cost of sales (working)		(5,270)
Gross profit		3,230
Distribution costs (working)		(1,490)
Administration expenses (working)		(630)
Operating profit		1,110
Income from fixed asset investments – Dividends		240
Profit on ordinary activities before taxation		1,350
Tax on profit on ordinary activities		
Corporation tax based on profit for year	380	
Over-provision of last year's corporation tax charge	(30)	
		(350)
Profit after taxation		1,000
Dividends		
Preference – Paid 10p per share	100	
Ordinary		
Interim paid 2.5p per share	200	
Final proposed 2.5p per share	200	
		(500)
Retained profit for year		£500

Working

Analysis of costs

	Cost of sales £000	Distribution £000	Administration £000
Purchases (500 + 4,400 − 700)	4,200		
Audit			50
Depreciation	85	40	20
Salaries			95
Distribution		425	
Factory expenses	970		
Hire	15		
Office expenses			190
Legal expenses			35
Warehouse rent		65	
Wages 0 : 80 : 20		960	240
	5,270	1,490	630

Question 3: Small plc

Balance sheet as at 31 March 20X5

	£	£
Fixed assets		
Tangible assets:		
Land and buildings (W3)	120,000	
Plant and machinery (W3)	37,760	
		157,760
Current assets		
Stock	160,000	
Debtors	100,000	
Prepayments	80,000	
Cash at bank and in hand	90,000	
	430,000	
Creditors: amounts falling due within one year		
Debenture loan	10,000	
Trade creditors	170,000	
Proposed dividend	40,000	
	220,000	
Net current assets		210,000
		367,760
Creditors: amounts falling due after more than one year		
6% debenture stock		50,000
		317,760
Capital and reserves		
Called up share capital		200,000
Profit and loss account		117,760
		317,760

The accounts were approved by the directors on ....

Signed A. Director

(*Note:* as part of the debenture stock is payable within one year of the balance sheet date, that part of the liability must be shown under current liabilities.)

Workings

(W1) Depreciation

	£	£
Leasehold factory 2% of £200,000		4,000
Plant and machinery		
NBV b/f	50,000	
Additions	10,000	
Disposals at NBV	(12,800)	
Depreciation 20% ×	47,200	= 9,440
		13,440

(W2) Disposal of plant

	£	£
Proceeds		12,000
Cost	16,000	
Less: Depreciation	3,200	
		12,800
Loss on sale		800

(W3) Tangible assets

	Long leasehold property £	Plant and machinery £
Cost:		
At 1 April 20X4	200,000	80,000
Additions	-	10,000
Disposals	-	(16,000)
	200,000	74,000
Aggregate depreciation:		
At 1 April 20X4	76,000	30,000
Eliminated on disposals		(3,200)
Amount provided	4,000	9,440
At 31 March 20X5	80,000	36,240
Net book value at 31 March 20X5	120,000	37,760

(W4) Profit for year per TB

		£	£
			111,000
Less: Depreciation	(4,000 + 9,440)	13,440	
Loss on sale	(W2)	800	
Proposed dividend	(20% × 200,000)	40,000	
			54,240
			56,760

(W5) Profit and loss account

Retained profit as at 1 April 20X4	61,000
Add: Retained profit for the year (W3)	56,760
Retained profit as at 31 March 20X5	117,760

Question 4: Pride Ltd

Balance sheet as at 31 March 20X7

	Cost	Accumulated depreciation	Net book value
	£000	£000	£000
Fixed assets			
Land	210		210
Buildings	200	124	76
Plant and equipment (working)	300	136	164
	710	260	450
Current assets			
Stock		180	
Debtors (146 – 12)		134	
Prepayments		8	
Cash		50	
Total assets		372	
Less: Creditors, amounts falling due within 12 months			
Creditors	(94)		
Accruals	(4)	(98)	
Net current assets			274
			724
Less 10% debentures			(100)
			624
Issued share capital			
700,000 ordinary shares of 50p each			350
Share premium account			240
Profit and loss account			34
			624

Working

Plant and equipment

	Cost £000	Accumulated depreciation £000
At 1 April 20X6	318	88
Less: disposal	18	12
	300	76
Depreciation for the year		60
		136

CHAPTER 21 — **MULTIPLE-CHOICE QUESTION**

B As per FRS 3.

CHAPTER 21 — **EXAM-TYPE QUESTION**

Reporting financial performance

S Limited

Profit and loss account for the year ended 31 March 20X1

	Continuing operations £m	Discontinued operations £m	Total £m
Sales	1,646	200	1,846
Operating expenses	(860)	(182)	(1,042)
Operating profit	786	18	804
Loss on disposal of discontinued operations		(210)	(210)
Loss on disposal of fixed assets	(26)		(26)
Reorganisation costs	(84)		(84)
Profit/(loss) on ordinary activities before interest	676	(192)	484
Interest payable			(80)
Profit on ordinary activities before taxation			404
Taxation			(124)
Profit on ordinary activities after taxation			280
Proposed dividend			(120)
Retained profit			160

CHAPTER 22	MULTIPLE-CHOICE QUESTIONS

Question 1

B

	£
Net assets acquired: 80% of £140,000	112,000
Purchase price	160,000
Difference = goodwill on acquisition	48,000
Less amortisation (three years): $\frac{3}{5} \times$ £48,000	28,800
At 31 December 20X3	19,200

Question 2

D

	£
S's net assets at 31 December 20X3	
Share capital (200,000 × 50p)	100,000
Reserves	180,000
	280,000
Minority share = 40%	112,000

Question 3

C

		£
Reserves of S at 31 December 20X7		180,000
Reserves of S at 1 January 20X1: pre-acquisition		120,000
∴ Post-acquisition retained reserves of S		60,000
Group share = 75%		45,000
Add reserves of H		480,000
		525,000
Less goodwill:		
Cost of shares in S	280,000	
Net assets acquired (75% × £320,000)	240,000	
		40,000
		485,000

    EXAM-TYPE QUESTIONS

Question 1: Park Ltd and Gate Ltd

Calculation of goodwill

	£	£
Cost of investment in G		72,000
Less: Share of net assets acquired:		
Share capital	80,000	
Profit and loss account	37,500	
	117,500	
Park's interest	60%	70,500
Goodwill		1,500
Amortisation		300
Balance of goodwill		1,200

Calculation of minority interest

	£	£
Net assets of G		
Share capital	80,000	
Profit and loss account	66,000	
	146,000	
Minority interest 40%		58,400

Calculation of post-acquisition profit

	£
Park Ltd	62,700
Gate Ltd 60% × £28,500	17,100
	79,800
Less: Goodwill amortised	300
	79,500

Park Group

Consolidated balance sheet as at 31 December 20X4

	£	£
Fixed Assets		
Intangible assets		
Goodwill		1,200
Tangible assets		
Freehold property		99,000
Other fixed assets		217,300
		317,500
Current assets	130,100	
Less: Current liabilities	79,700	50,400
		367,900
Unsecured loan		(30,000)
		337,900
Share capital		200,000
Profit and loss account		79,500
		279,500
Minority interest		58,400
		337,900

Question 2: Redan Ltd and Pyrton Ltd

Calculation of goodwill

	£	£
Cost of investment in P		140,000
Less: Share of net assets acquired:		
Share capital	130,000	
Profit and loss account	50,000	
	180,000	
Redan's interest	70%	126,000
Goodwill		14,000
Amortisation (4 years)		11,200
Balance of goodwill		2,800

Calculation of minority interest

Net assets of P	219,000	
Minority interest	30%	65,700

Calculation of post-acquisition profit

	£
Redan Limited	175,000
Pyrton Limited 70% × (89,000 − 50,000)	27,300
	202,300
Less: Goodwill amortised	11,200
	191,100

Redan Group

Consolidated balance sheet as at 30 June 20X8

	£	£
Fixed assets		
Intangible assets		
Goodwill		2,800
Tangible assets		360,000
		362,800
Current assets	456,000	
Creditors: amounts falling due within one year	362,000	94,000
		456,800
Capital and reserves		
Called up share capital		200,000
Profit and loss account		191,100
		391,100
Minority interest		65,700
		456,800

CHAPTER **23**

MULTIPLE-CHOICE QUESTION

B The other lists contain items that would appear elsewhere in the cash flow statement: interest paid, equity dividends paid.

CHAPTER **23**	PRACTICE QUESTIONS

Question 1: Bogdanovitch plc

Cash flow statement for the year ended 31 December 20X9

Reconciliation of operating profit to net cash inflow from operating activities

	£
Operating profit	1,381
Depreciation charges (W3)	448
Increase in stocks	(660)
Increase in debtors	(323)
Increase in creditors	4
	850

Cash flow statement

	£	£
Net cash inflow from operating activities		850
Taxation (W4)		(255)
Capital expenditure		
Payments to acquire tangible fixed assets (312 + 366 (W2))	(678)	
Receipts from sales of tangible fixed assets (203 + 95)	298	(380)
		215
Equity dividends paid (W5)		(300)
		(85)
Financing		
Issue of shares	400	
		400
Increase in cash		315

Workings

(W1)	**Plant and machinery (NBV)**			
	£			£
Balance b/d	2,086	P + M – disposal		184
Bank – purchase	312	Depreciation (bal fig)		111
		Balance c/d		2,103
	2,398			2,398

Plant and machinery – disposal

	£		£
P + M (NBV)	184	Bank – proceeds	203
Depreciation – gain on disposal	19		
	203		203

(W2)   Fixtures and fittings (NBV)

	£		£
Balance b/d	1,381	F & F – disposal	100
Bank – purchase (bal fig)	366	Depreciation	351
		Balance c/d	1,296
	1,747		1,747

Fixtures and fittings – disposal

	£		£
F + F – NBV	100	Bank – proceeds	95
		Depreciation – loss on disposal	5
	100		100

(W3)   Depreciation (profit and loss)

	£		£
P + M – NBV	111	P + M – disposal	19
F + F – disposal	5	Profit and loss account	448
F + F – NBV	351		
	467		467

(W4)   Taxation

	£		£
Bank – tax paid (bal fig)	255	Balance b/d	257
Balance c/d	312	Profit and loss account	310
	567		567

(W5)   Dividends

	£		£
Bank – dividends paid (bal fig)	300	Balance b/d	132
Balance c/d	154	Profit and loss account	322
	454		454

Question 2: Algernon Ltd

(a) **Cash flow statement for the year 20X7**

	£	£
Cash received from customers (W1)		190,000
Cash paid to suppliers and employees (W2)		155,000
		———
Net cash inflow from operating activities		35,000
Returns on investments and servicing of finance		
Interest paid		(13,000)
Capital expenditure		
Payments to acquire tangible fixed assets		
(1,000 + 40,000)	(41,000)	
Payments to acquire investments	(30,000)	(71,000)
	———	———
		(49,000)
Equity dividend paid		(20,000)
		———
Net cash outflow before financing		(69,000)
Financing		
Issue of shares (10,000 + 2,000)	12,000	
Issue of debentures	50,000	
	———	
		62,000
		———
Decrease in cash (4,000 + 3,000)		(7,000)
		———

Note to the cash flow statement

Reconciliation of operating profit to net cash inflow from operating activities

	£
Operating profit before interest	33,000
Depreciation charges (1,000 + 1,000)	2,000
Increase in stocks	(10,000)
Increase in debtors	(10,000)
Increase in creditors	20,000
	———
Net cash inflow from operating activities	35,000
	———

Workings

(W1) **Receipts from sales**

Sales control

	£		£
Balance b/d	40,000	Cash receipts (bal fig)	190,000
Sales	200,000	Balance c/d	50,000
	———		———
	240,000		240,000
	———		———

(W2)   **Payments**

Purchases and wages control

	£		£
Cash paid (bal fig)	155,000	Balance b/d	40,000
Depreciation	2,000	Purchases re cost of sales (W3)	130,000
Balance c/d	60,000	Expenses	47,000
	217,000		217,000

(W3)   **Cost of sales**

	£		£
Opening stock	55,000	Cost of sales	120,000
Purchases and wages	130,000	Closing stock	65,000
	185,000		185,000

(*Note:* Little information has been given as to the nature of the costs of the company; for example, no information is supplied on wages and salaries. The payments figure thus includes all cash outflows relating to trading activities. Depreciation would have been charged in either cost of sales or expenses and this needs to be adjusted for. It does not matter whether the adjustment is shown in the purchases control or the cost of sales accounts.)

(b) Algernon Ltd has invested substantially in buildings, investments, stock and debtors in the year. The finance has come from new share capital in part but mainly from debentures. The gearing of the company has thus increased. The working capital has been financed by an equal increase in trade creditors.

The profits have been fully distributed as dividends despite the halving of profits from last year. It might have been wiser to cut back on dividends in the period of expansion until the benefits of the expansion are seen in the form of higher profits.

CHAPTER **23**   EXAM-TYPE QUESTION

Crash Limited

Crash Limited

Cash flow statement for the year ended 31 March 20X6

	£000	£000
Net cash inflows from operating activities		1,995
Returns on investments and servicing of finance		
Interest paid		(150)
Capital expenditure		
Purchase of fixed assets (see working)	(2,700)	
Proceeds of sale of fixed assets	375	
		(2,325)
		(480)

Financing
    Repayment of debentures   (750)
    Proceeds of issue of shares   1,200

450

Decrease in cash (165 – 135)   (30)

Note

Reconciliation of operating profit to net cash inflow from operating activities.

	£'000
Operating profit	555
Depreciation	1,500
Profit on sale of fixed assets	(75)
Increase in stocks	(135)
Decrease in debtors	60
Increase in creditors	90
Net cash inflow from operating activities	1,995

Working – Movement in fixed assets

Fixed assets – cost

	£000		£000
Opening balance	9,000	Transfer disposal	1,500
Revaluation	750		
Net assets purchased	2,700	Closing balance	10,950
	12,450		12,450

Fixed assets – depreciation

	£000		£000
Transfer disposal	1,200	Opening balance	3,300
Closing balance	3,600	Profit and loss account	1,500
	4,800		4,800

Fixed assets – depreciation

	£000		£000
Transfer cost	1,500	Transfer depreciation	1,200
Profit and loss account – profit	75	Proceeds of sale	375
	1,575		1,575

CHAPTER **24**	MULTIPLE-CHOICE QUESTIONS

Question 1

D

Question 2

B

CHAPTER **24**	PRACTICE QUESTIONS

Question 1: Calculating ratios

Tutorial note: Ensure calculations are shown clearly and note that return on owners' equity (ROOE) is based only on capital and reserves, while ROCE includes long-term creditors.

For part (b) comment on the liquidity position of the company, the declining profitability and effect of gearing and interest payable.

		20X1	*20X0*
(a)	Current ratio	$30{,}500 : 24{,}000 = 1.3{:}1$	$28{,}500 : 20{,}000 = 1.4{:}1$
	Quick ratio	$16{,}500 : 24{,}000 = 0.7{:}1$	$15{,}500 : 20{,}000 = 0.8{:}1$
	Stock turnover in days	$\dfrac{14{,}000}{42{,}000} \times 365 = 122 \text{ days}$	$\dfrac{13{,}000}{34{,}000} \times 365 = 140 \text{ days}$
	Debts turnover in days	$\dfrac{16{,}000}{60{,}000} \times 365 \text{ days} = 97 \text{ days}$	$\dfrac{15{,}000}{50{,}000} \times 365 = 110 \text{ days}$
	Creditors turnover in days	$\dfrac{24{,}000}{42{,}000 + 15{,}500}$	$\dfrac{20{,}000}{34{,}000 + 13{,}000}$
	(assume operating expenses incurred on credit terms)	$\times 365 = 152 \text{ days}$	$\times 365 = 155 \text{ days}$
	Gross profit %	$\dfrac{18{,}000}{60{,}000} \times 100 = 30\%$	$\dfrac{16{,}000}{50{,}000} \times 100 = 32\%$
	Net profit % (before tax)	$\dfrac{300}{60{,}000} \times 100 = 0.5\%$	$\dfrac{1{,}700}{50{,}000} \times 100 = 3.4\%$
	Interest cover	$\dfrac{2{,}500}{2{,}200} = 1.1 \text{ times}$	$\dfrac{3{,}000}{1{,}300} = 2.3 \text{ times}$
	Dividend cover	$\dfrac{(50)}{600} = (0.1) \text{ times}$ (No cover)	$\dfrac{1{,}100}{600} = 1.8 \text{ times}$
	ROOE (before taxation)	$\dfrac{300}{13{,}000} \times 100 = 2.3\%$	$\dfrac{1{,}700}{14{,}000} \times 100 = 12.1\%$
	ROCE	$\dfrac{2{,}500}{13{,}000 + 6{,}000} \times 100 = 13.2\%$	$\dfrac{3{,}000}{14{,}000 + 5{,}500} \times 100 = 15.4\%$
	Gearing	$\dfrac{6{,}000}{13{,}000 + 6{,}000} \times 100 = 31.6\%$	$\dfrac{5{,}500}{14{,}000 + 5{,}500} = 28.2\%$

(b) There has been a decline in the liquidity position of the business. The 'weak' position in 20X0 where quick assets (debtors and bank) do not cover the immediate liabilities has deteriorated even further in 20X1. If this trend were to continue, the going concern ability of the business would probably be in question. In addition, the cover provided by profits over interest payable has more than halved; this would be considered a poor indicator by the interest bearing creditors. Such creditors may question the decision to declare the same level of dividend for 20X1 as for 20X0, even though the business made an after tax loss.

The business's profitability shows only a small 2% drop at the gross profit level but because of the significant levels of operating expenses and interest payable the net profit percentage in 20X1 is only one seventh of its 20X0 level. Clearly improvements are required if the business is to continue to report positive profit after tax figures.

Finally, management has increased the level of fixed assets; with such poor trading results they should be asked if such expansion was necessary, and when the benefits from the use of such resources can be expected to accrue.

Question 2: B Ltd

(a) (i) Ratios of particular significance to shareholders:

	20X6	20X7
Earnings per share	$\frac{9,520}{39,680} \times 100$	$\frac{11,660}{39,680} \times 100$
	$= 23.99p$	$= 29.39p$
Dividend cover	$\frac{9,520}{2,240}$	$\frac{11,660}{2,400}$
	$= 4.25$ times	$= 4.86$ times

Note:

Earnings per share $\dfrac{\text{Net profit for year after tax}}{\text{No. of equity shares in issue}}$

Dividend cover $= \dfrac{\text{Profit for the financial year}}{\text{Ordinary dividend}}$

(ii) Ratios of particular significance for trade creditors:

	20X6	20X7
Current ratio	$\frac{92,447}{36,862}$	$\frac{99,615}{42,475}$
	$= 2.51$	$= 2.34$
Quick ratio	$\frac{92,447 - 40,145}{36,862}$	$\frac{99,615 - 50,455}{42,475}$
	$= 1.42$	$= 1.16$

Note::

Current ratio $= \dfrac{\text{Current assets}}{\text{Current liabilities}}$

Quick ratio $= \dfrac{\text{Current assets excluding stock}}{\text{Current liabilities}}$

(iii) Ratios of particular significance for internal management:

	20X6	20X7
Return on capital employed	$\dfrac{15,254}{40,740} \times 100\%$	$\dfrac{18,686}{50,000} \times 100\%$
	$= 37.4\%$	$= 37.4\%$

Turnover/Fixed assets

$$\frac{486,300}{4,995} = 97.36 \text{ times} \qquad \frac{583,900}{12,700} = 45.97 \text{ times}$$

(Tutorial note:

$$\text{Return on capital employed} = \frac{\text{Profit before taxation}}{\text{Share capital and reserves}}$$

It can also be calculated as:

$$\frac{\text{Profit before interest and taxation}}{\text{Share capital and reserves and long term liabilities}}$$

$$\text{Turnover/Fixed assets} = \frac{\text{Turnover}}{\text{Tangible fixed assets (NBV)}}$$

Other management ratios include Operating profit/Sales and Debtors/Sales.)

(b) Earnings per share has increased by 22.5% due to improved profits. There has been no change in share capital. The dividend cover (the number of times the ordinary dividend is covered by the available profits) has increased because the percentage of profits paid out as a dividend has decreased. The dividend itself has gone up 7% which is clearly not as much as the earnings improvement. The company is adopting a cautious policy but the dividend looks secure.

The current ratio is decreasing but it is still at an acceptable level. The quick ratio (measure of the company's liquidity) is also decreasing and at a faster rate due to the increasing investment in stock (current ratio is down approximately 7% and the quick ratio about 18%). The quick ratio is above the generally desired level of 1, but the company should watch this area carefully.

Return on capital employed has remained constant. The ratio of turnover to fixed assets has reduced dramatically due to the high investment in fixed assets. These should help increase turnover and profitability in future years.

CHAPTER **24**   EXAM-TYPE QUESTION

Brood Limited

(a)

				30 April	
				20X0	20X1
(i)	Return on capital employed				
	5,000 / 48,600	6,500 / 72,300		10.3%	9.0%
(ii)	Return on owners' equity				
	3,600 / 28,600	3,700 / 32,300		12.6%	11.5%
(iii)	Current ratio				
	38,600 /28,500	43,000 /17,400		1.35:1	2.47:1
(iv)	Quick ratio				
	22,200 / 28,500	24,600 /17,400		0.78:1	1.41:1
(v)	Gearing				
	20,000 / 48,600	40,000 /72,300		41.1%	55.3%

The return on capital employed and the return on owners' equity both show a decline of nearly 10%. Gross profit has remained steady and the expenses have not risen in line with increased sales revenue, so the cause is probably that the new capital raised by the debenture issue has not yet been deployed to increase profit.

The current ratio and the quick ratio were somewhat low at 30 April 20X0, because of the high bank overdraft. About half of the funds raised by the debenture issue has been used to raise the overdraft, resulting in a movement to unnecessarily high ratios by 30 April 20X1.

Expansion of the business as funds are deployed in the future development of the business should mean that these ratios return to a lower level.

The gearing ratio has risen from a fairly high level as a result of the debenture issue. This means that the business is vulnerable to a downturn in profits as almost half the current operating profit is absorbed by interest.

Index

FTC Foulks Lynch
A **Kaplan Professional** Company

STUDY TEXT REVIEW FORM
ACCA Paper 1.1 (UK)

Thank you for choosing the official text for your ACCA professional qualification. As we are constantly striving to improve our products, we would be grateful if you could provide us with feedback about how useful you found this publication.

Name: ....

Address: ....

....

Email: ....

Why did you decide to purchase this Study Text?

Have used them in the past	☐
Recommended by lecturer	☐
Recommended by friend	☐
Saw advertising	☐
Other (please specify)...	

How do you study?

At a college	☐
On a distance learning course	☐
Home study	☐
Other (please specify)...	

Within our ACCA range we also offer Exam Kits and Pocket Notes. Is there any other type of service/publication that you would like to see as part of the range?

CD Rom with additional questions and answers	☐
A booklet that would help you master exam skills and techniques	☐
Space on our website that would answer your technical questions and queries	☐
Other (please specify)...	

During the past six month do you recall seeing/receiving any of the following?

Our advertisement in *Student Accountant* magazine?	☐
Our advertisement in any other magazine? (please specify)	☐
....	
Our leaflet/brochure or a letter through the post?	☐
Other (please specify)...	

Overall opinion of this Study Text

	Excellent	Adequate	Poor
Introductory pages	☐	☐	☐
Syllabus coverage	☐	☐	☐
Clarity of explanations	☐	☐	☐
Clarity of definitions and key terms	☐	☐	☐
Diagrams	☐	☐	☐
Activities	☐	☐	☐
Self-test questions	☐	☐	☐
Practice questions	☐	☐	☐
Answers to practice questions	☐	☐	☐
Layout	☐	☐	☐
Index	☐	☐	☐

If you have further comments/suggestions or have spotted any errors, please write them on the next page.

Please return this form to: Veronica Wastell, Publisher, FTC Foulks Lynch, FREEPOST NAT 17540, Wokingham RG40 1BR

Other comments/suggestions and errors

....
....
....
....
....
....
....
....
....
....
....
....
....
....
....
....
....
....
....
....
....
....
....
....
....
....
....
....
....
....
....
....
....

Other comments/suggestions and errors

....
....
....
....

FTC Foulks Lynch
A **Kaplan Professional** Company

ACCA Order Form

Swift House, Market Place, Wokingham, Berkshire RG40 1AP, UK
Tel: +44 (0) 118 989 0629   Fax: +44 (0) 118 979 7455

Order online: www.financial-training.com
Email: publishing@financial-training.com

Examination Date:	**Study Text** £23.00	**Exam Kit** £13.00	**Pocket Notes** £7.00
Dec 04 ☐ **Jun 05** ☐			
(please tick the exam you intend to take)			
Part 1			
1.1 Preparing Financial Statements (UK)	☐	☐	☐
1.1 Preparing Financial Statements (International)	☐	☐	☐
1.2 Financial Information for Management	☐	☐	☐
1.3 Managing People	☐	☐	☐
Part 2			
2.1 Information Systems	☐	☐	☐
2.2 Corporate & Business Law	☐	☐	☐
2.2 Corporate & Business Law (Global)	☐	☐	☐
2.2 Corporate & Business Law (Scottish)	☐		
2.3 Business Taxation – FA 2004	☐	☐	☐
2.4 Financial Management & Control	☐	☐	☐
2.5 Financial Reporting (UK)	☐	☐	☐
2.5 Financial Reporting (International)	☐	☐	☐
2.6 Audit & Internal Review (UK)	☐	☐	☐
2.6 Audit & Internal Review (International)	☐	☐	☐
Part 3			
3.1 Audit & Assurance Services (UK)	☐	☐	☐
3.1 Audit & Assurance Services (International)	☐	☐	☐
3.2 Advanced Taxation – FA 2004	☐	☐	☐
3.3 Performance Management	☐	☐	☐
3.4 Business Information Management	☐	☐	☐
3.5 Strategic Business Planning & Development	☐	☐	☐
3.6 Advanced Corporate Reporting (UK)	☐	☐	☐
3.6 Advanced Corporate Reporting (International)	☐	☐	☐
3.7 Strategic Financial Management	☐	☐	☐
Research and Analysis Project Guide (supporting Oxford Brookes University BSc (Hons) in Applied Accounting)	£20 ☐		

Postage, Packaging and Delivery (per item):   Note: Maximum postage charged for UK orders is £15   **TOTAL**

Study Texts and Exam Kits	First	Each Extra	Pocket Notes	First	Each Extra
UK	£5.00	£2.00	UK	£2.00	£1.00
Europe (incl Republic of Ireland and Channel Isles)	£7.00	£4.00	Europe (incl Republic of Ireland and Channel Isles)	£3.00	£2.00
Rest of World	£22.00	£8.00	Rest of World	£8.00	£5.00

Product Sub Total £.................   **Postage & Packaging £**.................   **Order Total £**.................   **(Payments in UK £ Sterling)**

Customer Details

☐ Mr   ☐ Mrs   ☐ Ms   ☐ Miss   Other ....

Initials:........................... Surname: ....

Address: ....

....

....

....

Postcode: ....

Delivery Address – if different from above

Address: ....

....

Postcode: ....

Telephone: ....

Email: ....

Fax: ....

Delivery please allow:	United Kingdom	– 5 working days
	Europe	– 8 working days
	Rest of World	– 10 working days

Payment

1 I enclose Cheque/Postal Order/Bankers Draft for £.......................................
   Please make cheques payable to '**The Financial Training Company Ltd**'.

2 Charge MasterCard/Visa/Switch/Delta no:

⬚⬚⬚⬚ ⬚⬚⬚⬚ ⬚⬚⬚⬚ ⬚⬚⬚⬚

Valid from: ⬚⬚⬚   Expiry date: ⬚⬚⬚

Issue no:

(Switch only) ⬚⬚

Signature: .... Date: ....

Declaration

I agree to pay as indicated on this form and understand that The Financial Training Company's Terms and Conditions apply (available on request).

Signature: .... Date: ....

Notes: All orders over 1kg will be fully tracked & insured. Signature required on receipt of order. Delivery times subject to stock availability. A telephone number or email address is required for orders that are to be delivered to a PO Box number.

ACCA
Official Publisher